Septem'

 Beyond Texas Through Time

Gift from ....
during meeting in
San Antonio re
"Alamo" research
via .... GLO ...

Beyond Texas Through Time

Breaking Away from Past Interpretations

EDITED BY
Walter L. Buenger and Arnoldo De León

TEXAS A&M UNIVERSITY PRESS   *College Station*

Copyright © 2011
by Texas A&M University Press
Manufactured in the United States of America
All rights reserved
First edition

This paper meets the requirements
of ANSI/NISO Z39.48-1992 (Permanence of Paper).
Binding materials have been chosen for durability.

LIBRARY OF CONGRESS CATALOGING-IN-PUBLICATION DATA

    Beyond Texas through time : breaking away from past interpretations / edited by Walter L. Buenger and Arnoldo De León. — 1st ed.
        p. cm.
    Includes index.
    ISBN-13: 978-1-60344-234-3 (cloth : alk. paper)
    ISBN-10: 1-60344-234-0 (cloth : alk. paper)
    ISBN-13: 978-1-60344-235-0 (pbk. : alk. paper)
    ISBN-10: 1-60344-235-9 (pbk. : alk. paper)
    [etc.]
    1. Texas—Historiography.   2. Cultural pluralism—Texas.   I. Buenger, Walter L. (Walter Louis), 1951–   II. De León, Arnoldo, 1945–
F385.2.B49   2011
976.40072'2—dc22
2010029263

*With affection and gratitude
we dedicate this volume to
our friend and colleague*
Robert A. Calvert,
*whose legacy continues
in the essays
contained in this collection.*

Contents

Acknowledgments	ix
Editors' Introduction	xi
Three Truths in Texas	1
Walter L. Buenger	
Into the Mainstream:	50
The Emergence of a New Texas Indian History	
Pekka Hämäläinen	
Strange Brew:	85
Recent Texas Political, Economic, and Military History	
Keith J. Volanto	
Why Is Big Tex Still a White Cowboy?	125
Race, Gender, and the "Other Texans"	
Michael Phillips	
Deconstructing Texas:	179
The Diversity of People, Place, and Historical Imagination in Recent Texas History	
Carlos Kevin Blanton	
Beyond Parochialism:	221
Modernization and Texas Historiography	
Nancy Beck Young	
About the Contributors	271
Index	273

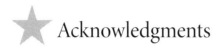# Acknowledgments

We immediately recognize our debt to those whose writings from 1988 to 2010 provided the works critically analyzed in *Beyond Texas Through Time*. Similarly, we acknowledge the support we received from Mary Lenn Dixon, editor-in-chief of Texas A&M University Press, who enthusiastically embraced the proposal for an update to the original *Texas Through Time*. We thank Roberto R. Treviño of the University of Texas at Arlington, Gregg Cantrell of Texas Christian University, and David Vaught of Texas A&M University who gave of their time to read and appraise select sections of the manuscript. We would be remiss if we did not also thank the six contributors to the volume, all of whom immersed themselves for months reading widely on the history of Texas historical writings.

Walter L. Buenger
Texas A&M University

Arnoldo De León
Angelo State University

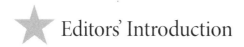# Editors' Introduction

Over the past twenty years the study of Texas history has taken paths little noted by either the general public or historians. This collection of essays assesses and summarizes recent scholarly work. The title, *Beyond Texas Through Time: Breaking Away from Past Interpretations,* communicates that much new literature has appeared, some of it of a completely different type. The title also consciously recalls an earlier work: *Texas Through Time: Evolving Interpretations* (1991).

That previous volume serves as a starting point for the essays that follow and also serves as a basis for comparison. In the last twenty years or so, scholars have interrogated Texas history using imaginative new approaches. They have engaged different audiences, including national ones. They have rejected traditionalism and offered a version of the Texas story that challenges exceptionalism. Some have also contested the revisionism of the late twentieth century, providing alternative views that often stress the importance of culture and identity. The meaning of the word "Texan" has been amplified to incorporate diversity. Significantly, historians today situate Texas history in a national context, thereby supplanting the old construct that isolated the state from outside currents. While skeptics would argue that much remains the same, amid that continuity new conversations have emerged about how best to comprehend the Texas historical legacy. These stimulating dialogues not only stress the importance of tying Texas to the nation, they also illustrate how work on the state could prompt new avenues of interpretations for all historians. In the end, then, the study of Texas history offers hope for moving beyond the old parochialism and past the tendency of those working outside of Texas to ignore the region.

In contrast, *Texas Through Time,* written between 1988 and 1990, grew out of a sense of mission and frustration. The editors, Walter L. Buenger and Robert A. Calvert, were committed to changing Texans' perceptions of their state. For too long, they lamented, Texans had viewed their state's past romantically, heroically, and in the end, inaccurately. This ethnocentric and gender-skewed version of Texas history, which they rendered as the "Texas myth," posited the Texas chronicle to encapsulate epic events of white males, who from the 1820s through around the 1870s and 1880s, led the conquest of the wild frontier, tamed lawless lands, and pacified savage Indians. After almost a century of studying and writing Texas history, Buenger and Calvert fretted, scholars had made hardly a dent on this long-standing interpretation. In the face of almost a century that separated a bygone age that appeared incompatible with the more current trends of the late twentieth century, Texans needed to reassess the manner in which they remembered their state.

Buenger and Calvert identified two camps then dominating Texas scholarship: the traditionalists (the keepers of tradition) and revisionists (those who called for overturning old-school interpretations). The former strove to preserve the historical heritage that had its roots in the frontier milieu. Traditionalists, on the one hand, stood fast in approaching Texas history, as had a long line of scholars since the late nineteenth century, thereby perpetuating the Texas myth. They wrote from a consensus mind-set that saw Texas history shaped by white sacrifice, Anglo moxie, and American resourcefulness. Building on national trends beginning in the 1960s, revisionists, on the other hand, had finally offered a counterapproach to traditionalism. At the forefront of this surge was the New Social History, the then popular research concept that privileged ordinary people in history, asserting that they influenced historical events as meaningfully as elites.

But despite the promise of this approach, Buenger and Calvert warned that revisionists needed to pursue newer orientations and more creative lines of inquiry. Should they fail to do so, they feared, the Texas myth would remain intact, ready to repel any assault upon it. No valid synthesis of Texas history existed as of the late 1980s, they noted, except the old one. Given such a condition, Texas scholarship still seemed parochial, very much in the periphery of the national literature and in urgent need of catching up.

A last purpose, then, behind the publication of *Texas Through Time* was to encourage more innovative, imaginative, and insightful ways of thinking about Texas history. Alerted to the deficiencies that plagued Texas historical writings (as indicated by the several essays that comprised the book), Buenger and Calvert hoped scholars would be stirred to abandon old staid topics that even engaged the revisionists. Scholars would excitedly enter into fresh dialogues and thereby propel Texas history into the mainstream of national historiography. Students of the Texas chronicle would refocus, taking up such questions as proper periodization for a history that spanned numerous centuries instead of just the nineteenth. They would analyze the pivotal time when the state became less Southern and more American. They would give equal coverage to twentieth-century modernization as they did to other well-defined epochs. Having redefined their history, students of Texas topics would silence the criticisms leveled at their work by historians in other parts of the country or, better yet, end the habit of those historians simply ignoring Texas history.

Editors' Introduction

Without a doubt, at least some historians of Texas achieved many of these goals and others not even imagined two decades ago. *Beyond Texas Through Time* provides a snapshot of twenty years of innovation, change, and, yes, even some continuity. To cite but a few examples, since the late 1980s Texas scholars have rigorously investigated subjects current in the national scholarship, among them whiteness; gender; collective or historical memory; racial, group, and national identity; political culture; and place. During the period, Texas historians caused an impressive rethinking of minority history, depicting Indians, Tejanos, and African Americans as human actors (instead of stock caricatures) who shaped the state's history in conjunction with white Texans. Historians offered erudite and illuminating discussions of military, environment, immigration, economic, and art/literary history, and in so doing integrating Texas history into the larger literature. In some areas, Texas scholarship even led the profession, a giant leap from the lowly regard it mustered some twenty years before.

Still, much in modern-day historical writings appears redolent of the pre-1991 scholarship. Given that state of affairs, *Beyond Texas Through Time* encourages scholars to draw back and cogitate on the history of history with a wider lens. They should revisit what forces caused change or prevented change from occurring.

Beyond Texas Through Time, as did *Texas Through Time,* suggests areas for possible new pursuits and encourages the start of a new debate about how best to approach the past. In the essays that follow contributors recognize many new prospects for discovery, but most of all they encourage readers and writers of Texas history to think anew about the past. A pluralistic approach, referenced by several of the contributors in the collection, allows a place for all groups (including women) in the Texas experience. An interdisciplinary perspective forces historians to use alternative foci to study problems that cannot be fully fleshed out using conventional historical analyses. The world-systems paradigm compels scholars to place Texas beyond a narrow context—indeed, positions it in an international structure. A modernization framework can help identify the importance of more contemporary times and free historians from overemphasizing the worth of the frontier era. Such are some of the grand possibilities that can readily lead Texas history away from the exceptionalist model that continues to find appeal in present-day historical scholarship.

Beyond Texas Through Time in some respects validates the anticipation that contributors to *Texas Through Time* had about the future of Texas history writing. Even though traditionalism remains a potent force, the scholarship during the last two decades has fulfilled the expectation that long-standing interpretations of Texas history would be revised. Further, nuance has increasingly come to characterize historical explanations. Lastly, the larger profession today grants Texas history deserved respect.

The historiographic essays found in this collection, therefore, serve a range of functions. Most obviously, they keep new and established practitioners of history abreast of knowledge being introduced by recently published books and articles. They identify topics currently in favor and those that have lost appeal. They explain changing views toward historic occurrences and offer reasons as to why historians, influenced by the times during which they conduct their investigations, reexamine conclusions advanced by earlier generations. Historiographic essays in and of themselves inform students how trained historians set about practicing their trade as they utilize time-tested (or original) investigative methods, apply their own analytical strategies, or introduce new research visions. In the end, however, such essays, like any good history, center on what changed and why it changed or did not change over time. Even more they focus on the very nature of history.

The salient march of Texas historiography for the period beginning in the late 1980s owed much to unfolding currents at the national and state levels as well as to new directions underway in the mainstream literature. Transforming American life was the long end to the Cold War, freeing the post-1960s generation from the distress that dogged their predecessors. The prosperous years that began during the Bill Clinton administration (1993–2001) further enabled young folks basking in the era's material bountifulness to make a choice between the liberalism of the 1960s and the conservatism that lingered following the Reagan-Bush era (1981–93). Nationwide, the computer revolution modified cultural (and research) habits forever, transforming patterns by which people lived and conducted affairs both privately and publicly. The World Wide Web came into being in 1991 (coincidentally, in the same year as the publication of *Texas Through Time*). It was followed by other life-morphing electronic creations such as the Internet and the proliferation of search engines such as Google that facilitated interaction with all corners of the earth. (Incidentally, the Internet made research easier, as the new information technology allowed researchers to tap into lesser known depositories or to exploit documents held in distant archives, doing so from the convenience of their office.)

Still other forces of national magnitude produced new writings deliberating the past and asking new questions of it. The national economy not only experienced greater diversification (expansion occurred in the electronics, service, and telecommunications fields, among other sectors) but also achieved heightened connections to the world economy. Globalization wrought deep changes

Editors' Introduction

to American society due to the interrelatedness of international markets. The impact of such global alignment was unanticipated in some fronts, as in the matter of cheap foreign labor: increasingly, immigrants (mainly from Mexico and Latin America) flooded the nation to fill low-paying jobs in construction, agriculture, and the service component of the economy. The increased visibility of third-world immigrant communities in the United States unquestionably influenced the way historians interpreted the past.

There occurred also during this time period a weakening of American liberalism and an ascendancy of conservatism. In this post–civil rights America, new sociopolitical discord surfaced surrounding proper approaches and adequate solutions to issues that divided the country, among the most disruptive social development being the increased "browning of America." As a result, the new "culture wars" of the 1990s and beyond erupted over immigration, gender, sexual preference, ethnicity, and many other concerns that came to be debated by those on the left and the right not solely in the open arena but in the academy and scholarly outlets as well.

Texas kept stride with the many advances sweeping the nation. To diversify its economy it enticed the software industry, biotechnology enterprises, telemarketing firms, advertising companies, and health care corporations to the state. It lured computer manufacturers so that as of 2001 the two most successful producers of personal computers—Dell and Compaq—had established their headquarters in Texas. A growing population aligned Texas with national demographic trends, and by 2000, the state had surpassed New York as hosting the second highest number of residents within its borders.[1] Demography rearranged the structure of the old society as the aforementioned immigration from Mexico and other Latin American countries put a new face on the city, the schools, and the labor force. By the year 2003, according to census figures, Anglo-Americans no longer made up the majority of Texans; a combination of Tejanos, African Americans, Asians, and other peoples of color constituted slightly more than 50 percent of the population. For the most part, Texans accepted the changing times, even displaying quiet tolerance toward minorities and women. True that Texans put up stubborn resistance to sensitive matters like gay marriages, free choice, and ethnic studies programs, and even evolution, but in so doing, they exhibited attitudes that showed their ideological stands harmonizing with national sentiments. Increasingly, Texas appeared more and more like the rest of the country—highly urbanized, high-tech oriented, and culturally diversified.

Still, many Texans recoiled in fright or anger as the old Texas slipped away. Part of Texas historical writings thus found appeal in the Texas myth and celebratory history continued to have a following. Such recalcitrance presented obstructions to historians wishing to see balance in Texas historiography and wanting to stay apace with the less parochial national literature.

While the old Texas seemed at odds with the modern day, both in its reality and in its publicly consumed history, Texas historians sought out more nuanced ways to interpret a mythic past. According to the essays included in this collection, various interpretive currents directed the course of Texas historical writings after the late 1980s. Paramount were developments in the national literature, such as the New Indian History. In this historiographic school, historians positioned themselves in indigenous space and from that observation post attempted to ascertain how Native Americans grasped events around them and acted to control them; this perspective is discussed fully in one of the enclosed essays. Philosophical concepts (such as postmodern theory) proposed in the graduate school classroom questioning pre-1990s paradigms also accounted for new historiographic treks. The inquiries of minority and women scholars through the lens of race and gender also swayed reassessments of long-standing propositions, such as those extending to subaltern peoples. Scholars from companion disciplines (among them archaeologists, anthropologists, and geographers) applied their insights to the study of Texas history and in the process submitting findings that would have been improbable to an earlier generation of writers. Cultural studies, whiteness studies, new borderlands histories, transnational history, world system theory, modernization theory, intergenerational models, an understanding of ethnogenesis, and sundry other conceptualizations that contested entrenched beliefs inevitably generated new historiographic results. All of the above factors prompted the departures that characterized Texas historical writings since *Texas Through Time* saw print.

Indeed, recently published works on Texas embraced a multitude of analytical frameworks. To be sure, no one investigative tool dominated scholarly study; researchers turned both to old methods and devised newer ones in an attempt to document the Texas epic. Narrative elite history, on the one hand, retained its appeal, as did the New Social History. On the other hand, scholars followed more imaginative fact-finding avenues including theoretical throughways, sophisticated computer considerations, postmodern modes of interrogation, and other insights.

The contributors to *Beyond Texas Through Time* belong to a cast of Texas historians whose insights rest on the groundwork laid before them by revisionists of the 1970s and 1980s and on developments that have gained credence in the larger literature as of late.[2] In tracking the historiographic trajectory of the last twenty years, they had license to structure the content of their essays for

Editors' Introduction

this collection as they saw fit. Although some included articles and dissertations in their discussions, most limited their study to books (by one count, some 1,600 books were published on Texas history between the late 1980s and 2010). Necessarily, writers could only sample what had been written on their particular subject(s): all judiciously selected monographs that more clearly added to historiographic discourses or represented major patterns or trends.

Structurally, *Beyond Texas Through Time* contains one major overview article explicating the broader historiography of the last twenty years and five thematic essays. Three of these latter five works examine writings on major topics that have earnestly attracted scholars since the 1990s. Two of the six articles, those by Pekka Hämäläinen on Indians and by Nancy Beck Young on modern Texas and the process of modernization, reflect on fields that researchers came to regard as compellingly significant during the last decade; scholarly outpourings on these two academic areas grew to a degree that they demanded special historiographic treatment.

According to Walter L. Buenger in the lead essay in this collection, three discernible groups worked concurrently to interpret the Texas past. They included updated traditionalists, persistent revisionists, and cultural constructionists. The first school embraced those interpreters still faithful to a traditional methodology, though they adjusted to new developments in the scholarship by applying revisionists themes. Persistent revisionists unceasingly sniped at the consensus generation in a gallant effort to dismantle the Texas myth. Cultural constructionists looked for the roots of political, social, and economic events in culture as it changed or persevered. The three camps subtly influenced one another and offered a hint of convergence, but in the end remained distinct. This did not prevent historians from arguing that what happened in Texas mattered to the rest of the nation and from demonstrating they could write about Texas and lead the profession in new paths.

It is now maintained (and treated thusly), that Native Americans—and not one particular European power—commanded the Far North. In the New Indian History, Hämäläinen observes in his essay in this volume, Indians gained center stage in the master narrative. Practitioners of the New Indian History now saw Indian peoples shaping events about them through adaptability, resilience, and heroic struggle. Indians negotiated with whites on Indian terms, not on those dictated by viceroys, kings, or presidents.

Expectedly, interpretations of Texas history became markedly nuanced. As Keith J. Volanto explains in his essay for this book, biographies written during the last two decades sketched more humanized subjects. New studies unearthed social determinants in unlikely places, as in the economic circumstances of the

EDITORS' INTRODUCTION

pre–World War II era that produced a recategorization of poor white tenant farmers: as nonwhite! He explains how new studies no longer focused on one cause as inducing change, but that an interconnection among politics, economics, culture, and even military engagements engineered historical motion.

Uninhibited by a consensus mind-set, or by a 1960s culture for that matter, historians after the late 1980s broached subjects previously spurned by those before them as too discordant or too delicate. As a result, explains Michael Phillips in his contribution to this collection, they created a body of scholarship based on postmodern theory. These historians eschewed the Texas myth as a creation of nineteenth-century patricians and submitted their own version of events by scrutinizing the Texas past by asking more fitting questions: about whiteness, racial identity, prejudice, collective memory, sexuality, and gender. In light of demographic changes occurring, they wondered if the Texas myth could remain germane when the majority of students in the public schools found it almost inapplicable to their experience. In short, historians after the late 1980s connected their scholarship to a society ebbing forth.

Between the late 1980s and about 2010, historians made unquestionable progress toward deconstructing pre-1980s views of Texas peoples and places, according to Carlos Kevin Blanton in his contribution to this book. Now historians directed their attention toward diversity and the agency of neglected peoples, among them the marginalized segments of the community. The idea of "place," for years designating location, became a concept that encompassed borders, multicultural regions, diverse landscapes, metropolitan environments, as well as settings that fostered differences in cultural orientation.

The new historiography illuminated some pivotal eras in the Texas chronicle, among them those that pinpointed the historical moment when Texas forged a closer nexus with the nation. In her contribution to this collection, Nancy Beck Young argues that New Deal programs loosened the bond that allied Texas with the South as Texans during this period overcame their long-standing suspicion of federal intervention into state matters and acquiesced at cooperating with New Deal farm policies. After World War II, Young writes, Texas drew even closer to national life, promoting the general welfare as a leading oil producer, as a supporter of the common defense (it became the site of numerous military bases), and as a training camp for political leaders (it sent three presidents to the White House). These eras coincided with modernization in Texas. For Young, the earliest phase in the drift toward modernity harked back to the 1930s, but the transition accelerated during the decades of the 1940s when Texas took leave of its rural moorings, stabilized its economic system (counting on oil revenues), entered a political era featuring distinct

Editors' Introduction

divisions between Democratic liberals and conservatives, and made progress on race relations.

Notwithstanding these headways, aspects of the Texas myth persevered, as evident in the preoccupation with recounting the Battle of the Alamo and the lingering influence of the Dunning school of Reconstruction. As had been the case before the late 1980s, historians still did not extend deserved coverage to topics such as slavery and the agrarian revolt, as well as to twentieth-century events, especially those that occurred after the 1960s. African-Texas history fell behind aggregations to Tejano history and women's history. Too few works appeared on Euro-American groups such as German, Czech, Irish, and Jewish Americans, as well as on the many other "ethnics" (Asians come to mind) who over the years clearly contributed to the making of Texas. Historians overlooked the theme of religion (and spirituality) at a time when the subject emerged as one of the most productive fields in U.S. history and claimed by the 1990s a strong presence in the national historiography. The few publications treating the visual arts, literature, and even historical writings tended to be descriptive narratives sans theoretical foundation. The histories of gays and lesbians, as well as the subject of sexism, went well nigh ignored. Evaluated in this manner, Texas historiography between the late 1980s and 2010 appeared still somewhat of a work in progress.

Nonetheless, it is apparent from the contents of the following essays that scholars succeeded during the last twenty or so years in reevaluating earlier knowledge, in enhancing the study of Texas history to mirror developments in the national literature, and in highlighting previously neglected issues and providing a nuanced explanation of the Texas past. Such progress appeared necessary at a time when even the long-standing narrative of a homogenous U.S. society faced a challenge with no substitute for it yet to gain credence. That transformation of America in the last decades of the twentieth century (mentioned above) made more visible different religious loyalties, diverse cultural traditions, and the "browning" of the nation. It sparked the rise of a younger set of historians who pondered the past through an alternative lens. This latter assemblage of intellectuals (collectively consisting of Chicanos/Latinos/blacks/Asians/women/gays), whose voices older interpreters of the country's history had ignored (and even silenced), introduced new themes into the master narrative, ones seldom contemplated by a previous generation.

Works written during the recent past, therefore, propose some suggestions for "reconceptualizing" Texas history. The new synthesis would encompass those themes that scholars explored during the last twenty years (as a result of societal—as well historiographic—changes at both the national and state levels), among them population heterogeneity, culture, gender, violence, identity, and immigration. Such a history would reflect the growing ethno-racial reality of the state. Underscored would be the similarities between Texas and the nation and de-emphasized would be episodes that purportedly made Texas an exception to the national experience. Historians should not have to wrestle with the exasperating question of whether the state is southern or western, but should consider the state as a component of a larger enterprise, a component that fits into the nation and into the world in different ways at different times. An updated rendition of Texas history would stress the relevancy of recent times, certainly the twentieth century, which has a closer association with the fast-paced world of the electronic revolution than does the nineteenth century. Such a version of the Texas story suits a complex, globalized society.[3]

Notes

1. Robert A. Calvert, Arnoldo De León, and Gregg Cantrell, *The History of Texas,* 4th ed. (Wheeling, Ill.: Harlan Davidson, 2007), 421–22, 416.

2. This corps of writers, who came of age during the 1990s and in the last few years, is at times referred to as *postrevisionists,* though no particular name applies correctly to them.

3. For an elaboration of similar themes—that a region or state need not be distinctive but actually representative of a national experience, that there can exist a connection between region and state history and national as well as international history, and that regional or state scholarship can impact a national historiography—see Laura F. Edwards, "Southern History and U.S. History," *Journal of Southern History* 75 (August 2009): 533–64.

Beyond Texas Through Time

# Three Truths in Texas

Walter L. Buenger

Texas history still moves in a multilinear fashion. Indeed, over the twenty years since the writing and publishing of the essays in *Texas Through Time: Evolving Interpretations* (1991), the two interpretive streams so obvious then have grown to three truths about Texas, three evolving, sustained, and only partially connected ways of seeing the past, operating at the same time.[1] Like planets in close orbit, updated traditionalists, persistent revisionists, and cultural constructionists exerted gravitational pulls on one another, and there have been some hints of convergence. Yet at least in the near term the three truths seem destined to continue on their largely independent paths, and in that sense Texas history remains nonlinear as well as multilinear. Despite that, or perhaps because of that, over the past twenty years historians writing at least in part on Texas have moved onto the center stage of American history both demonstrating the importance of events within Texas and pioneering new ways of looking at the past.

Within their respective realms each of these distinct approaches to the Texas past changed over the past two decades, but their basic nature, derived from their different origins, development, focus, evidence, and audience, remained intact. Updated traditionalists continued to mix two strands whose origins date back to before 1960: the impulse to preserve and commemorate the revered past, and the top-down perspective common to many earlier historians but made famous by consensus historians in which elite male political, military, and business leaders stood for the entire community. From the 1960s through the 1980s, practitioners of a traditional approach, not surprisingly, focused on the mid-nineteenth century, drew upon standard written sources in English, and wrote for a public long nourished on stories from that golden age of Texas. Those who leaned heavily to the commemorative side continued to stress the moral and ethical lessons illuminated by the past and conveyed a sense that Texas, though still special, had declined since its golden age. Those who leaned toward the consensus side or who modeled their work after professional historians from even earlier eras were usually less celebratory, but still typically emphasized the importance of Protestant Anglo males. Yet after the late 1980s, for updated traditionalists that golden age expanded to include the World War II years as well as the mid-nineteenth century, and the heroes of the past included a sprinkling of noteworthy Latinos and prominent women. Military history, the Alamo, westward expansion, ranching, and the Texas rangers remained favored topics. Elites still represented the whole.

Persistent revisionists continued the pattern begun in the 1960s with the rise of New Social History of broadening the definition of a Texan to include rich and poor, all ethnic and racial groups, and men and women. With almost missionary zeal, into the early 1990s, revisionists focused on refuting the traditionalist approach and of necessity plowed the ground of the mid-nineteenth century, but they often highlighted the state's southern as opposed to western roots and emphasized class and the influence of economic change. They used a broad array of written evidence in several languages, incorporated quantitative and oral evidence, and often drew upon methods pioneered in other disciplines. While they hoped to reach the broader history profession they often wrote to persuade traditional historians and advance revisionist history with the Texas public. In the past twenty years, the energetic study of Indians, the pre-1821 period, and Tejanos in the twentieth century, in particular, has continued the long revisionist tradition of borrowing from other disciplines and often has incorporated a more transnational approach. Moving in these new directions certainly expanded revisionism, but it also demonstrated its limitations. Still, at the heart of revisionism, whatever its new shading or nuance, has remained a struggle to balance depicting the many obstacles to be overcome by poor whites, Tejanos, blacks, Indians, women, and other subsets of society with a sturdy assertion that these groups were in many respects agents of their own fate.

While the presence of a third truth, a third distinct approach to Texas history, seemed obvious, naming it proved difficult in large part because it has not yet become as philosophically coherent a school of thought as traditionalism or revisionism. Simply calling it the third way offered some promise because it suggested that the approach occupied a different and distinct space from traditionalism and revisionism. It underscored that Texas history has been nonlinear as well as multilinear. One approach has not evolved out of the other and replaced it. Still the term seemed too vague on the one hand and suggested more cohesiveness on the other than probably existed. Postrevisionism kept coming to mind as a possible descriptive phrase, but that too was vague. Besides, it connoted too strong a link with other posts such as postmodernism or poststructuralism, and it presented the problem of what comes next, the post-

post-revisionist school. Perhaps the most troubling feature of postrevisionism, however, was that it implied evolution from revisionism to postrevisionism, and that may simply not have been true. Words such as *transcend* conveyed that this third truth extended beyond the old borders of Texas history and of Texas itself, but every iteration of the word required too extensive an explanation to be helpful. Finally and somewhat reluctantly cultural constructionism emerged as the logical choice because it best conveyed the probable origins, focus, evidence base, and audience of this third truth, and it captured its gradual development and enduring characteristics.

Cultural constructionism first emerged during the mid-1990s and sprang from a variety of intellectual sources. Early practitioners shared the revisionist and traditionalist conviction that the structure of the past could be discerned and conveyed, and thus they were part of the modern attempt to know and analyze the past through the use of empirical evidence. Yet cultural constructionists also in part drew upon or at least were cognizant of the concepts sometimes described as postmodernism or poststructuralism that emphasized the fluidity, mutability, and constructed nature of the past and our knowledge of the past, and they utilized theories and approaches from anthropology or other disciplines that fostered a similar sense of the past.[2] Thus practitioners of the third truth focused on a nuanced, interconnected past, and the human creation and influence of cultural characteristics including gender, group identity, regional and national citizenship, and memory. While they shared the evidence base used by persistent revisionists, in interpreting it and expanding beyond it they often relied on new theories and models developed in the broader history profession. This allowed them to write in a more relevant way for a national audience of other historians and to cross the spatial and intellectual borders of Texas and Texas history.[3]

Once across these borders, cultural constructionists increasingly moved beyond debates about Texas exceptionalism and avoided being drawn into the long-running arguments between traditionalists or revisionists. Indeed, they soon operated on a different plane from older approaches, a plane distinguished by more than anything else a reliance on the explanatory power of culture. Unlike persistent revisionists who often saw the economy or technology as the driver of all significant change, as this strand of truth developed its proponents increasingly privileged cultural continuity or change when explaining the past. Drawn to the violent points of conflict in the past, cultural constructionists saw the origins of that cultural change or continuity in the interaction between disparate groups in specific places and times. Instead of looking at groups in isolation they looked at groups' connections to one another and to the larger whole, and they found unity and coherence in the past from those interconnections.

By the start of the new century, four enduring traits, present to a varying degree, characterized cultural constructionists. Compared to updated traditionalists and persistent revisionists they relied more heavily on theory and more readily accepted the validity of using theory. They focused on connections between groups instead of on one group at a time. By employing new arguments and new approaches different from updated traditionalists and persistent revisionists, they avoided being drawn into the debate between the two older camps and in the process transcended the borders of Texas, making their work applicable to a much broader field. They transcended the old and connected the distinct groups in Texas by emphasizing the importance of culture and by theorizing that culture has often been constructed by human actions and interactions over time.

In the end, better than any other term, cultural constructionism encapsulated where the third approach came from, how it developed, and what endured. The term implied reliance on theory, underscored the primacy of culture, and suggested that change or continuity was bound up in the interconnections between groups. It symbolized a distinct approach that crossed entrenched spatial and intellectual borders, cutting loose its practitioners from older and often debilitating debates. Cultural constructionists were seldom consistent in every feature, but taken collectively they offered a third way of understanding the Texas past.

While all three truths had their own specific reasons for continuity and change, they also evolved because of broader societal factors and their relationship with one another. In the past twenty years Texas history sprang from new public remembrances; the social and psychological stresses of the times; demographic and cultural change within Texas; emerging business models, new technology, and market forces in publishing; and stronger connections between Texas and the outside world. Revisionists and traditionalists, in particular, also influenced one another. Revisionists, for example, pushed traditionalists to update and oftentimes revived facets of traditional work when writing a synthesis. While one group did not replace the other and the three groups did not converge on one path, they were in part defined by their relationship to one another. This was in many ways a fruitful tension leading to the publication of some 1,600 books on Texas history over the last two decades, and while basic continuities with twenty years ago remain, there is now far less reason to worry about the study of Texas being on the edge of the broader profession.

1988–91: A Bipolar World

This tripartite and nonlinear nature of truth differed from what Robert A. Calvert and I hoped for twenty years ago, and those hopes offer a convenient starting point for understanding the relationship of each truth to the other and more broadly for examining change over time in the study of Texas. In our essay "The Shelf Life of Truth in Texas," written between 1988 and 1990 and appearing in *Texas Through Time*, we posited that ideally one way of viewing the past, one perceived truth, succeeded and largely supplanted older models, older truths. Following C. Vann Woodward we argued that all truth in history should have a limited shelf life and then be discarded. We, of course, realized that was not happening in Texas where traditionalism, focused then almost exclusively on the Texas Revolution, the Civil War, Reconstruction, and the "conquest" of the western frontier, still held firm. For many historians, the mid-nineteenth century explained the present, and for the general public, history underscored uniqueness, justified racism or other prejudices, and confirmed political ideology. Society's needs dictated history's narrative. Some professional historians of Texas, who as late as the 1980s were often only grudgingly accepted into the larger fraternity of American historians, also proved slow to adopt the techniques and approaches developed in that larger profession; they instead stuck to tried-and-true Texas topics and the interpretations of earlier generations of Texas historians. We argued that this contributed—along with societal needs—to a much slower rate of change in Texas studies, to a longer "shelf life of truth." Instead of experiencing the generational revisions common to the larger profession, in Texas old verities remained.[4]

Yet through the 1980s conscientious revisionist historians, such as the contributors to *Texas Through Time*, worked zealously to overthrow this old imperium and raise up unrepresented groups and peoples—African Americans, Mexican Americans, the common folk, and women in particular. Perhaps because few histories had been published on Native Americans in the 1980s, little attention was paid to that significant group in *Texas Through Time*, but inability to deal adequately with Indians has long been and remains characteristic of revisionism. Still, historians who focused on the unrepresented and moved beyond the repetitive study of the mythic nineteenth century received glowing evaluations of their scholarship in all the essays in *Texas Through Time*. All the contributors not only openly championed revisionism, they also optimistically anticipated that with the passage of time and the industrious production of more books and articles a counternarrative to the traditionalists would emerge triumphant, and Texas history would proceed along one path.[5]

At about the same time as *Texas Through Time* came out, Robert A. Calvert and Arnoldo De León first published their groundbreaking text, *The History of Texas* (1990), providing another classically revisionist vantage point on the state of the field some twenty years ago.[6] This text avowedly drew heavily on the perspectives of New Social History that had swept the larger profession in the two decades prior to its publication. New Social History depended upon the expansion of the evidence consulted and the asking of fresh questions. It often rested on evidence that could be quantified, such as the census, tax records, birth and death records, wills and probates, and immigration records. It depended on close studies of communities instead of sweeping panoramas of larger vistas. Like all texts, *History of Texas* represented the particular creation of the authors, but as those authors declared, their book had "the stamp of contemporary historical writing." When it came time in the text to look at antebellum society, the authors consciously drew on such heavily quantitative work as Randolph B. Campbell and Richard G. Lowe, *Wealth and Power in the Antebellum South* (1977). Yet for lack of an alternative, they also drew on older, more traditional, and often less critical studies for essential information, such as Robert C. Cotner, *James Stephen Hogg: A Biography* (1959). Thus while Calvert and De León reflected the clear influence of revisionism, their text also demonstrated the continued hold of some older works.[7]

This continued influence of older works was nowhere more evident than in the treatment of Texas Indians found in *History of Texas,* a treatment limited by lack of information and the blinders of an older age. For example, all the Indians of South Texas were lumped into two groups, Coahuiltecan and Karankawan. More recent research has emphasized that the Indians of South Texas fell into dozens of linguistic groups and had a more formally organized society than Calvert and De León realized. Calvert and De León's textbook also lacked a sense of change over time in the Indian community. The Comanches seemed always in Texas instead of moving into the region after the Spanish arrived and steadily expanding their power and influence. There is little sense of the transformation of the Wichita from a largely agrarian people to mounted hunters and trading partners of the Comanches and Caddos. This flat and undifferentiated rendition of Texas Indians sprang in part from the lack of comprehensive studies of Indians among "contemporary historical writing," but while some revisionists recognized this problem, as a group Indians simply did not seem that central to the narrative.[8] This mind-set sprang from the failure to adequately consider the complexity of Indian culture and history, to ask what changed over time and what did not. It sprang from the failure to see the Spanish and Indians as intimately connected, connected in ways determined by Indians as much as by Spaniards. It sprang from a Eurocentric point of view that saw Indians as either victims or enemies. The first two chapters, for example, focused on Texas before 1821, a time when Indians remained the dominant force in most of Texas. Of the forty-six pages in those two chapters approximately seven focused on Indians. This marginalization and characterization of Indians as either victims or wily enemies has remained a difficult hurdle for revisionist historians of Texas, limiting their ability to include Indians as fellow Texans.[9] Unable to appreciate all aspects of Indian culture and committed to building a synthesis drawn from both traditional and revisionist sources, the tool kit and mind-set of revisionists failed when it came to Indians, and this was true of even such model works as *History of Texas*.

In the end, however, both for its faults and its strengths *History of Texas* was, like *Texas Through Time,* a classically revisionist creation, and as such it demonstrated New Social History's essential differences from consensus history: people at the bottom of the social pyramid mattered as much as those at the top, and society was divided into cohesive groups determined by class, race, ethnicity, and sex. Those influenced by new social history looked at varied groups instead of assuming that one group stood as representative of the whole. In the case of *History of Texas* the authors explicitly examined "unsung subjects who contribute to the Texas saga, among them plain white folks, women, and minorities."[10] This fostered a disjointed history: a dab of this about African Americans, a dab of that about Tejanos, a quick mention of women, and then on to plain white folk. Connecting the history of the groups, especially those that, like Indians, lay largely outside the Eurocentric world, proved difficult if not impossible for revisionists. Not just textbooks fell victim to this, but so did most work in the new social history vein that attempted to move beyond the local and particular. This led to calls for the creation of a new synthesis with "unifying themes and interesting narrative."[11]

This new synthesis was intended to replace traditional views expounded by many writers, but especially by T. R. Fehrenbach, whose *Lone Star: A History of Texas and the Texans* first appeared in 1968 and was reprinted numerous times, including as late as 2000. In the eyes of revisionists, Fehrenbach served as a revealing caricature of the problems with traditional history. He dismissed all other groups besides Anglos as inferior and undeserving of control of Texas while paying scant attention to women and to the common folk. His 2000 edition, unchanged from 1968 except for the inclusion of a six-page chapter on the post-1960s decades, still contained this sentence: "Votes for Negroes, desegregation, welfare, and various forms of so-called civil rights for the non-peer group were forced down the Texan throat from outside." Thus he ignored the considerable effort that many Texans of varied classes, races, and ethnicities made to end discrimination and encourage equal opportunity. Instead, the only true Texans remained Anglos motivated by the "frontier ethic." He insisted in his preface to the 2000 edition that little had changed since the 1960s in the basic nature of Texas or of Texas history because "the Texan mystique was created by the chemistry of the frontier in the crucible of history and forged into an enduring state of heart and mind."[12]

Fehrenbach mixed a Progressive-era historian's unadulterated march of the frontier westward with a generous portion of Texas chauvinism and romanticism. As he wrote, "the great difference between Texas and every other American state in the twentieth century was that Texas had a history." For Fehrenbach, Texas had a usable past distinct from the rest of the United States. That frontier past taught manliness, honor, and the special place of Texas and Texans in the historical pantheon.[13]

When Fehrenbach and other traditionalists of the 1980s and before drew on the work of professional historians, as indicated previously, they drew on those who came of age before 1960, such as Charles Ramsdell, Rupert Richardson, Eugene C. Barker, Walter P. Webb, and H. Bailey Carroll. While some of these placed Texas in a larger national and international picture, and while none were as chauvinistic as Fehrenbach, they did little to encourage looking at the past from the point of view of women, African Americans, Tejanos, and Indians. They did much to glorify the great white men of the past, be they Texas Rangers or the Anglo colonizers of Texas. To the chagrin of revisionists, the ideas and approaches of the pre-1960 professional historians of Texas allowed popular historians in the traditionalist vein to fill the need for a usable past that reassured modern Texans that they sprang from a special place where sun-drenched white men strode nobly into the frontier.[14]

That was the state of the bipolar world of Texas history in the late 1980s and early 1990s. On one side of the divide stood Calvert, De León, and the revisionists; on the other, Fehrenbach and the traditionalists. The limits of revisionism and the manner in which it renewed and replenished traditional approaches lay hidden. Instead, revisionists anticipated that sooner or later through more exhaustive research and better writing, the traditionalists would vanish, a new synthesis would emerge, and one smooth stream of Texas history would flow to the sea. It did not happen. Instead, traditionalists updated the time periods and types of people they wrote about and survived with their essential essence secure. Revisionists persisted in their efforts to write better case studies and a better synthesis. Meanwhile, a third truth, cultural constructionists, emerged.

An Aerial View of Change

All three groups proved amazingly productive. Not only were over 1,600 first-edition books on Texas history published between 1988, when the drafting of the essays in *Texas Through Time* began, and 2009, when this essay was completed, but those books also covered every imaginable topic and time period in ways unanticipated by those calling for change two decades ago. A few descriptive statistics give an aerial view of the extent of change from previous decades. Thanks in part to an explosion of new titles from smaller for-profit presses, some 32 percent of those books focused on the years after 1932, a sign that perhaps the revisionist argument was winning out and the pull of the nineteenth century was waning. It turned out that was only partially true, and that many of those books approached the twentieth century in very traditional ways. They celebrated the exploits of the World War II generation, recorded the trials and triumphs of modern ranching, and narrated the twists and turns in the public lives of prominent male (and sometimes female) politicians. In addition, over 31 percent of all books still focused on the classic time period, 1821 to 1886. The Texas Revolution, the Civil War, and the western frontier still drew much attention. Yet other signs indicated the extension and continuity of revisionism. Over 5 percent of the books focused on the years before 1821, a slight upturn from previous years. Tejanos in the twentieth century and women and gender in all time periods received substantially more attention. Revisionist studies of these topics often used an interdisciplinary approach that had long characterized New Social History, but interestingly many of the works on women were more traditional than they were revisionist. In a further departure from the pattern of the late 1980s, over 3 percent of the books focused on Indians. Still, the most impressive feature of the list was the diversity of topics covered by authors over the past two decades. As the table below demonstrates, despite the persistence of traditional topics such as ranching and the Texas Rangers no one area of study dominated the list.[15]

Within each of those categories were books that defy easy characterization as either traditional or revisionist. Not all books on the Alamo were traditional. Not all books on women were revisionist. Indeed, not all books fit into either of those two categories, and after the mid-1990s books that fit the cultural constructionist model increasingly appeared. Reviews of books, descriptions on the press Web sites, and reading a selected number confirmed the tri-part nature of the list. Some 45 percent were updated traditionalist, 46 percent persistent revisionist, and 9 percent cultural constructionist.[16] Considering that the cultural constructionists' work only began appearing in the mid-1990s their 9 percent is

Topic of study, 1988–2009

Texas Rangers and ranching	8.2%
Women and gender	8.2%
Tejanos in the twentieth century	5.9%
Civil War	5.1%
Alamo and Texas Revolution	4.6%
Indians	3.2%
Petroleum industry	1.9%
World War II	1.0%
Other	61.9%

a respectable share and seems to be growing. Among books published in 2008 and 2009 the cultural constructionists made up about 15 percent, with most of the growth coming at the expense of the revisionists. Still, despite the general perception among professional historians that historical approaches come and go, the Texas traditionalists and revisionists are not near extinction. Especially if you look beyond professional historians publishing at major university presses, continuity as much as change characterized Texas history.[17]

Updated Traditionalists

It bears repeating, however, that in most cases, even traditionalists evolved from earlier patterns. They showed more concern for the ordinary person, undoubtedly at least in part a reaction to the revisionists' bottom-up approach. They were slightly less given to Texas chauvinism perhaps because by the 1990s Texans had less need of a celebratory past. The moral lessons to be gleaned from the past became a bit less clear-cut in a world in which right and wrong seemed muddled. Not surprisingly, these changes led traditionalists to new topics. For example, in *Damming the Colorado: The Rise of the Lower Colorado River Authority, 1933–1939* (1990), John A. Adams Jr. took a laudatory and top-down, but thorough and empirical, look at the rise of one of the key economic and environmental institutions of twentieth-century Texas. Engineers and bureaucrats replaced politicians, military men, and business elites as the creators of a new age. In a similar vein, Robert D. Auerbach's *Deception and Abuse at the Fed: Henry B. Gonzalez Battles Alan Greenspan's Bank* (2008) chronicled the life of one of the political heroes of post–World War II liberals and Tejanos. Susan E. Cayleff, in *Babe: The Life and Legend of Babe Didrikson Zaharias* (1995), memorialized the life of one of the leading women athletes of the past century, and while the author struck a celebratory tone she focused on the role of women and the impact they made on modern life. All these books demonstrated that while the impulse to celebrate the past and draw lessons from it as well as the tendency to focus on representative elites remained, the range of examples for appropriate behavior and lives to be remembered broadened significantly.[18] That said, as a detailed look at the following examples of traditional works demonstrated, such authors and their books remained in a distinct class with more similarity to consensus historians and T. R. Fehrenbach than Robert Calvert and Arnoldo De León. These examples, while not necessarily the best of traditional books and certainly not all of them, clearly illuminated the characteristics of this updated genre, delineated change and continuity over time, and offered interesting points of contrast with books supporting the other two truths.

Bruce L. Brager, in *The Texas 36th Division: A History* (2002), demonstrated both how updated traditionalists changed and how they remained the same. Brager focused primarily on the division's famous exploits in World War II and offered a balanced account claiming that "The men of the 36th, and their bosses, usually performed with the steady competence and professionalism expected of American soldiers." Markedly he devoted as much attention to the common soldiers as to the officers and leaders. Brager, though, remained uninterested in any significant analysis of changes in the ways of war, in the action of the other side, or in any detailed description of the impact of war on the common soldier. Instead, he accurately preserved the record and commemorated the memory of a storied military unit. He also took the division's origins back to the legendary past, to the Alamo and to Hood's Texas Brigade in the Civil War, whose reputation he described as "one of the best brigades, if not the best, in the Confederate Army."[19] Even in celebrating the achievements of the World War II generation, updated traditionalists hearkened back to the golden era of Texas history.

Anne J. Bailey, in *Texans in the Confederate Cavalry* (1998), offered another example of the updated characteristics of traditional writing on Texas. Bailey's book, meant for a more popular audience, provided a blend of a top-down focus on elites complete with photographs and sidebars and an insistence that "the great majority of the Texans who served in the Confederate cavalry were ordinary men whose names never made it into the history books." Bailey demonstrated some change over time and the wearing away of the bravado that young Texans exhibited at the start of war. Yet she, like Brager, linked the Texas cavalry back to the 1836 revolution. Despite admitting that most Texans had never fought Indians and most of the ones mentioned by name were born outside the state, she insisted that "Texas' military heritage, born in a revolution against Mexico in the 1830s and maturing in the Mexican-American War of the 1840s, touched all who lived there." Comments on how the war forced changes in tactics and arms and the observation that day-to-day life was anything but glamorous balanced out this insistence on Texas "singularity."[20] Still no effort was made to compare Texas cavalrymen with those from other states or to make distinctions within the group. One model soldier stood for all soldiers, and that remained a sure mark of the traditional approach. This soldier often amounted to an archetypical Texan—brave, undisciplined, combative, and naturally skilled on horseback. Thus as the war drew to a close in 1865 the Texans did not just leave the 8th Texas Cavalry to go home; they left to go fight for Texas west of the Mississippi.[21]

No description of the work of updated traditionalists would be complete without mention of studies of the Texas Rangers and ranching, pillars of pre-1960 writing on Texas, and as it turned out, pillars of post-1988 writing as well. Chuck Parsons, author of *John B. Armstrong: Texas Ranger and Pioneer Ranchman* (2007), dug deep in the archival records and tried for a balanced portrait of the treatment of Tejanos in South Texas. He described some denizens of the region in 1875 as "nothing more than organized mobs of Anglo citizens who in all likelihood suspected any Mexican, no matter on which side of the river he resided, to be a cattle thief and summarily executed any they caught." Yet he insisted that the Rangers had to step in and restore order and stop the killing of innocent Tejanos. A few pages later it passed without comment when Armstrong and other Rangers rode into a ranch in Mexico with orders to "shoot everyone except old men, women, and children." It turned out to be the wrong ranch, but that did not bring back to life the seven Mexican citizens killed by Armstrong and the other rangers.[22] Following in the steps of Walter Prescott Webb, Parsons implied that Rangers could do no wrong even if other Anglos could, and that Rangers were the prototypical Texans—big, strong, silent men of action who gave women their proper respect and who tamed the West, moving Texas toward civilization and prosperity.[23]

Parsons also retold familiar southern myths about Reconstruction and had Armstrong leaving Tennessee in the early 1870s to escape carpetbaggers and the rigors of Reconstruction, even though Tennessee was specifically excluded from the Reconstruction acts, readmitted to the Union in 1866, and under control of white conservatives by 1869. Despite attempts to respond to modern criticism, old prejudices and attitudes remained in even updated traditionalist works published at respected presses. It was little wonder that exasperated revisionists remained focused on countering the traditional narrative.[24]

Persistent Revisionists

Revisionists certainly attacked the myth of Reconstruction, provided alternatives to stereotypical depictions of Texans in the Civil War, and countered biased depictions of Tejanos and the Rangers. As in the case of traditional works, the following examples of revisionist work from the past two decades were not necessarily the best of the genre and were certainly not all of the hundreds of books produced. Instead, they illustrated the strengths and weaknesses of persistent revisionists and offered a telling contrast to traditionalists. They suggested why Texas history remained multilinear.

Carl H. Moneyhon, in *Texas after the Civil War: The Struggle of Reconstruction* (2004), provided the most up-to-date summary of the numerous archival-based studies of Reconstruction, and he added to our understanding of the economy's role in the outcome of events. Moneyhon concluded that Reconstruction was a "tangled reality" with much violence and voter fraud and no clear heroes. It was a time of great opportunity that in the end resulted in limited changes for blacks and for the state as a whole. What Moneyhon lacked, as do most studies of Reconstruction and its aftermath, was any detailed, archival-based study of ordinary whites and the lingering impact of Reconstruction on their lives. Perhaps because of the ongoing influence of the work of Eric Foner, who focused so forcefully on the role on African Americans in Reconstruction, the entire field struggled to capture the experience of white southern yeoman who remembered and interpreted the Civil War and Reconstruction in profoundly different ways from their black counterparts. Connecting the black experience and the white experience remained difficult for revisionists in Texas and outside of Texas.[25]

Richard Lowe, in *Walker's Texas Division, C.S.A.: Greyhounds of the Trans-Mississippi* (2004), came closer than most in recovering the history of ordinary whites, at least in wartime. His statistical analysis of the men who formed the only division in the Confederate army composed entirely of Texans indicated that after controlling for their age, their wealth and status fit the norm for Texas. Rich and poor alike formed the division. On the battlefield the division achieved considerable success, but instead of glorifying the troops as "noble warriors" Lowe insisted they mimicked the full range of behavior of the larger population. Lowe also offered a far more realistic assessment of the breakup of the division at the conclusion of the war. Aware that the war was lost by mid-May 1865 and unwilling to risk their lives for a lost cause, they ignored the pleas of their officers and simply left for home. These were "citizen soldiers," and "when their officers asked them to remain soldiers after all hope for victory had vanished, they turned almost overnight into civilians again." Because of its strong empirical base and Lowe's insistent focus on the common soldier, this work came as close to history of the war from the bottom up as we will likely see, and it moved a healthy step beyond the tendency to view Civil War units in isolation from what happened in the rest of the war and at home. Lowe skillfully corrected past misconceptions, added new information about everyday soldiers and their families, but advanced few themes that transformed the field or spoke to a larger literature focused on why soldiers fought and how the war transformed them.[26]

This lack of a grand overarching theme that addressed the larger literature was even more true of Charles H. Harris III and Louis R. Sadler in *The Texas Rangers and the Mexican Revolution: The Bloodiest Decade, 1910–1920* (2004). The authors stated their purpose to be "neither to justify nor condemn but rather to paint as accurately as possible a portrait of the Rangers, warts and all." Although like other revisionists they struggled to move beyond the point of view of their target groups, Anglos and Rangers, they sought to reverse both the flattering portrait of the Rangers found in Webb's work and the work of those in the traditionalist school, and to counter some of the more extreme criticism by Chicano scholars of the 1970s and 1980s. In great detail and after more than two decades of research, the authors demonstrated that the Rangers' organization was "understrength, underpaid, and living on its reputation." The authors clearly stated that the Ranger force was neither the grossly racist and blood-crazed collection of Anglos of its harshest critics or the valiant heroes of its staunchest defenders. Still, after so many pages spent recounting every event of the decade and charting every member of the force, Harris and Sadler never defined the Rangers and never related them to the larger history of Texas, let alone North America.[27]

Clearly, persistent revisionists struggled mightily over the past twenty years to change approaches to Reconstruction, the Civil War, and the Rangers. While they swept the graduate school seminars clean they failed to unify the production of history.[28] Instead, traditionalists nodded toward the modern age and budged a bit in their Anglo-centric focus on the glories of the nineteenth century, but change was surprisingly limited. Indeed, Texas A&M University Press published Moneyhon, *Texas after the Civil War* and also published Parsons, *John B. Armstrong,* indicating that the multipart nature of the study of Texas history extended to the halls of the state's leading scholarly presses. This continued lack of convergence also suggested that the innate nature of persistent revisionism limited its impact and that writing more detailed archival-based works on timeworn topics would little change Texas history as a whole. Some persistent revisionists wondered the same thing as they looked at the avalanche of detail in works like Harris and Sadler, *The Texas Rangers and the Mexican Revolution*. Heading in new directions, they focused on different topics—Indians, Texas before 1821, and Tejanos in the twentieth century, but despite this new initiative, this evolution in approach, revisionists kept their tunnel vision on one group at a time.[29]

Over the past two decades, revisionist work on Texas Indians has been truly stunning in both its quantity and its quality. Take, for example, F. Todd Smith, *From Dominance to Disappearance: The Indians of Texas and the Near Southwest, 1786–1859* (2005). Smith saw his study as a sequel to earlier revisionist work on a previous time period and set out to examine "the relations between the Indian tribes and the various Euroamerican groups in Texas and the Near Southwest." Smith argued that into the 1830s the Indians dominated Texas, but the increasing tide of Americans with little interest in coexisting with Indians and the ravages of disease and war pushed Indians out of Texas. As he put it: "Within a quarter century of gaining independence from Mexico, the citizens of Texas had caused almost all of the Indians to disappear from the region entirely. Although Indians had been at the center of most events in Texas prior to 1860, they would have less than a minimal impact upon the state following the outbreak of the Civil War."[30] Smith's work thus fit within the standard boundaries of persistent revisionism. It built on earlier works, adding another link in our chain of understanding. Smith challenged other revisionists to understand Indian influence on diplomacy, war, and the economy, but in the end viewed Indians as victims of the expansion of white Americans into their region. Most revisionists could easily understand the end result as the outgrowth of white American action, because it fit their Euro-American point of view. Some had greater difficulty placing Indians at center stage and seeing even eighteenth-century events as the result of Indian agency.

Studies of the eighteenth century and of Texas before 1821 further stretched revisionism, but they also confirmed its limitations. For decades scholars usually focused on the development of Spanish institutions in the northern frontier of New Spain. Jesús F. de la Teja, in *San Antonio de Béxar: A Community on New Spain's Northern Frontier* (1995), argued instead that "economic and political forces" shaped the Mexican and Canary Islander settlers into a "single community" by the close of the eighteenth century. De la Teja acknowledged that without the presidio there would have been no reason for San Antonio to exist, and certainly it would not have thrived. Yet de la Teja focused on the social structure, population makeup, economy, and local institutions of which that presidio was a part. He viewed Spanish institutions as being either cast aside for substantially new and different practices or adapted to the frontier and evolving over time instead of simply being transplanted. Community was built from "a shared struggle for survival among people who originally had little in common." Community came from the blending of families of settlers from other regions of northern New Spain, Canary Islanders, and mission Indians who came to have a similar sense of belonging.[31]

De la Teja moved beyond the revisionist pattern of the late 1980s and early 1990s by providing an essential portrait of how a community came into being and changed over time, and in some ways he even anticipated some of the approaches used by those who stressed the construction of culture. It was in that sense a model revisionist work, and a work that some might use to counter my point that Texas history was essentially divided into three disconnected, nonsequential units. Yet the treatment of Indians and blacks in the book argued for the persistence of revisionist habits and the lack of convergence in Texas history. Indians were the "other," whose impact kept the garrison at San Antonio and limited the growth of a ranching economy, but who had no distinct culture and aspirations of their own. Even in the case of mission Indians, de la Teja seldom focused on what they brought to the mix, yet he documented a large number of *coyotes,* a blend of Indian and Mestizo people. Indeed, the offspring of Indian and Spanish unions seemed to dominate the population of San Antonio. There also appeared to have been a relatively small number of black slaves and some mulattos, although the term was used rather loosely according to de la Teja. In the end, de la Teja, like Calvert and De León, remained essentially focused on Euro-Americans and seemingly assumed that the Indian and black part of the mix conformed to the dominant European model instead of examining the intersection of distinct cultures. In the mid-1990s, revisionists, even the most persistent and dedicated, still struggled to include all groups equally and simultaneously.[32]

By that time, however, crosscurrents were at work among some revisionists that expanded long-standing concepts and more fully anticipated some of the techniques and approaches of cultural constructionists. For example, in *Rise of the Mexican American Middle Class: San Antonio, 1929–1941* (1991), Richard A. Garcia pondered what it meant to be a Mexican American, and he concluded that in San Antonio by 1941 a middle class had emerged—"Mexican in culture but American in politics and philosophy." As with earlier revisionist works, Garcia borrowed heavily from the social sciences and was preoccupied with class. He divided the 1930s Tejano community in San Antonio into three classes: *ricos,* elite Mexicans who had fled their country in the 1910s and wanted to retain an undefiled Mexican culture; a middle class, who using the League of United Latin American Citizens (LULAC) sought to be both Mexican and American; and a poor working class. Garcia depicted what he called a "hegemonic struggle" between the *ricos* and the middle class for control of the "search for identity."[33]

Garcia thus illustrated how revisionists' concern for class formation, class conflict, ethnicity, assimilation, and pluralism persisted. Garcia's work, however, both reached back toward the consensus school and anticipated post-1991 patterns. Drawing on the older school of immigration history, he viewed all immigrants as essentially the same and motivated by similar concerns. He insisted that "Mexicans flocked to the Southwest for the same reasons immigrants from Europe had come to the United States; the differences were only in degree, not in kind." This approach precluded any meaningful comparison with other immigrant groups. Unlike Emilio Zamora in *World of the Mexican Worker in Texas* (1993), Garcia downplayed the agency and viability of the working class, declaring that "the laboring sector of the Mexican community was poor, not only economically but also culturally." Like other revisionists Garcia had difficulty seeing through the eyes of those outside his target group. Yet he was able to focus, at least in an inchoate manner, on the construction of a new middle-class ethos that allowed the surge of Americanism associated with World War II to spread more broadly through the Tejano community. In *Rise of the Mexican American Middle Class,* Garcia demonstrated the continued resilience of traditional views of immigration and the limits of revisionists' ability to connect disparate classes, but he also suggested a way out of this trap—looking at a struggle for identity as a source of change.[34]

Thus, even when writing on the history of Indians, the eighteenth century, and twentieth-century Tejanos, all fields that by their very nature pushed revisionism beyond where it stood twenty years ago, adherents of that school of thought remained largely within fixed boundaries. They could not always adequately balance the ability of a group to influence its own destiny with a clear-eyed depiction of the obstacles placed in front of that group by the larger society of which they were a part. Bits and pieces of more traditional approaches repeatedly cropped up. Given the obsession with building a counternarrative to the traditionalists, comparing Texas with other parts of the United States or with Mexico and fully addressing current literature in the broader profession remained difficult. Revisionists' efforts still focused on correcting traditionalism's excesses and omissions, and in that sense those efforts remained part of an intra-Texas dialogue. Ironically, in struggling mightily against the traditionalists they came to resemble them in crucial ways. Both could not hold the entire range of

Texans in view at once, and both wound up undergirding Texas exceptionalism. The path lay open for a new approach to Texas history that more fully connected to the outside world and presented the history of all groups of Texans.

Cultural Constructionists

Benjamin Heber Johnson shared Garcia's fascination with LULAC, but not as the beginning point of change. Instead, he viewed it as evidence that a new identity emerged from the conflict in South Texas in the 1910s. Comparing Johnson, *Revolution in Texas: How a Forgotten Rebellion and Its Bloody Suppression Turned Mexicans into Americans* (2003), with Garcia, *Rise of the Mexican American Middle Class,* and with Harris and Sadler, *The Texas Rangers and the Mexican Revolution,* offered an entry point to understanding the third approach to Texas history. Johnson's work and the other illustrative examples that follow, in varying degrees drew on theoretical approaches first used in other fields of history, examined the often-violent interaction of diverse groups, and focused on cultural and intellectual transformation. In so doing they avoided the revisionist tendency to resurrect traditionalist viewpoints and moved beyond the compulsion to view everything done before as a building block for a new history. They also dealt coherently and evenhandedly with distinct groups. In the process they shunned the top-down and celebratory nature of the traditionalists. Perhaps of greatest importance they avoided being drawn into the back-and-forth dialogue between revisionists and traditionalists. As a result they more completely engaged the broader profession and opened up the possibility of comparing and connecting Texas with other parts of the world.

Johnson, for example, focused on the impact of violence in the 1910s, a time of rapid and tumultuous political, economic, and demographic transition for South Texas and Mexico with new jobs created in Texas and a growing incentive to leave Mexico. Within this state of flux, Johnson found three groups competing for control of the future identity of Tejanos and newly arrived Mexican immigrants. Tejanos with deep roots in the Rio Grande Valley and whose elite families were often closely interwoven with long-standing Anglo political bosses worked to maintain their traditional power and resisted the racist impulses of newly arrived Anglos. Tejano Progressives hoped to use the boom times to modernize and revitalize their compatriots by fusing "Mexican and American traditions." A third group, inspired by the goals of the Mexican Revolution, hoped for land redistribution, the elevation of the poor, and perhaps even a rejoining of the region with Mexico. According to Johnson these three groups struggled in the aftermath of the violent encounters at mid-decade between Anglos and ethnic Mexicans to control the creation of a new identity for Mexicans in Texas.[35]

At mid-decade, rumors of Mexican conspiracies to retake South Texas and cross-border incursions led to massive retaliation by the Texas Rangers, local law enforcement, vigilante groups, and the U.S. Army. Harris and Sadler pointedly criticized Johnson for accepting the most extreme casualty figures: dozens of Anglo farmers and up to 5,000 ethnic Mexicans killed. This criticism of Johnson should be taken with a grain of salt since Harris and Sadler, despite claims to be impartial, went out of their way to disparage J. T. Canales, the main Tejano critic of the Rangers. They often resorted to saying, in effect, that while there were cases of abuse and brutal killings of Mexicans by the Rangers, things could have been worse. In any event, while Johnson may have gotten the details wrong, as revisionists often accuse those who lean heavily on theory of doing, his main argument did not concern the number of deaths, but instead the impact of violence that Johnson insisted led to the ascendancy of the Tejano Progressives and the eventual creation of a Mexican American identity and culture. Violence led to changing habits of mind.[36]

Unlike Richard Garcia, Johnson argued that the urge to create LULAC and use it to seek American rights for Tejanos sprang from this earlier transformation in identity and culture. Class, ideology, or even the economy had little to do with this basic change in mind-set. Instead, reaction to the violent encounter between Anglos and ethnic Mexicans, the competition between the factions in the ethnic Mexican community, and the events connected to World War I stimulated change and a new emphasis on American citizenship. Johnson seemed to ignore class in particular, something no persistent revisionist was likely to do, but instead focused on the creation of new attachments, new ideas, and the emergence of a new consciousness that not only accepted but also celebrated the ideal of being an American citizen and worried about the "risk of becoming a people belonging to no nation at all."[37]

While unclear whether this cultural change extended to the working class, or to ethnic Mexicans not born in Texas, Johnson offered a different way of conceiving of the region of Texas south of the Nueces River, a region he argued that was drawn into closer contact with the rest of the state of Texas and the entire United States after 1910. That brought Tejanos both the promise of the ideals of being an American and the reality of increased segregation and racially motivated violence. In what has become a classic explanatory device for cultural constructionists and a key point to look for when distinguishing them from revisionists and traditionalists, change grew from the rubbing together of disparate parts of the transborder society.[38]

Not all works in the cultural constructionist category struggled to analyze class. Neil Foley, in *The White Scourge: Mexicans, Blacks, and Poor Whites in Texas Cotton Culture* (1997), brought class front and center by employing whiteness theory. Foley argued that the movement of Mexicans north into the midsection of Texas from 1900 to 1940 together with the introduction of new technology, new business methods, and especially New Deal policy, helped usher in a new tripartite world with Mexicans/poor whites in between black and white. Poor whites became less white and Tejanos became semiwhite.[39]

Foley selected as his area of study a diamond-shaped region bounded by Corpus Christi in the south, Dallas in the north, Houston in the east, and San Antonio in the west. He called this region Central Texas, a designation that the citizens of Dallas, Houston, and Corpus Christi would have considered odd. Somewhat hesitantly, he lumped the region's Germans and Czechs, who in some counties formed the largest demographic group, into the category of Anglo. Having battled southern whites over prohibition in the 1910s and the Ku Klux Klan in the 1920s, and having made common cause with blacks and Tejanos in those fights, Germans and Czechs might have found that a bit odd as well. Czechs, who arrived in Texas slightly later than Germans, may still have been subject to some of the same prejudice that Foley asserted caused Anglos to question the whiteness of Mexicans. Catholics among these ethnic groups had an additional reason to distance themselves from southern white Baptists and find common ground with Mexican immigrant co-religionists. Thus, Foley's study lacked nuance and a clear understanding of significant details of the region's ethnic history.[40]

Still, Foley's point was that the region stood between the people, the economy, and the culture of areas to the north, south, east, and west. It was a border area where distinctive groups connected, and Foley's ability to hit upon a method to highlight the impact of these connections separated his study from previous work. His Central Texas also contained a large part of the Blackland Prairie and other especially fertile soil for cotton. The region, lacking transportation, lay largely outside the cotton-growing belt until the 1870s. At that point and lasting until the 1930s it became one of the most rapidly expanding and dynamic areas for the cultivation of cotton in the country. Most especially in the forty years Foley studied, it was an area where working side by side Mexican and black seasonal laborers and sharecroppers pushed out the more prosperous and higher-status Anglo male share tenants, undermining those tenants' conceptions of their manhood and altering women's perception of their place in the new order. In the process, the gulf between white landowners and all other classes, races, and ethnic groups increased. It would have been interesting to know if that was equally true of German and Czech Texan landowners. In this and in other instances whiteness seemed too clumsy a tool to explain everything. Yet in looking beyond the binary demographics of a typical southern or western place and in focusing on how new types of gender, class, and racial distinctions were constructed over time, Foley offered a way to consider Texas few had fully appreciated before.[41]

Foley's *White Scourge* and Johnson's *Revolution in Texas* were far from the only works of the last two decades to fit within the new rubric. Cultural constructionists often worked in such fields as the history of women and gender and asked how the particular experience of women grew from their interactions in a larger society. Here, Angela Boswell, in *Her Act and Deed: Women's Lives in a Rural Southern County, 1837–1873* (2001), and Judith N. McArthur, in *Creating the New Woman: The Rise of Southern Women's Progressive Culture in Texas, 1893–1918* (1998), offered excellent examples of this approach. Boswell focused on Colorado County, a place within Foley's target area that contained significant numbers of Germans, Anglos, and African Americans, and she asserted that while reality might force them into different modes of action they sought a gendered ideal in which women left much of the public life up to men. Thus, despite the interaction of three groups and the distinct legal system at work in Texas, women of all backgrounds moved when they could toward a southern ideal form. They constructed a common culture. McArthur highlighted the role of women's associations in building interest in progressive causes such as prohibition and suffrage, and how they took advantage of state politics and the expanded role of the federal government during World War I to create support for their cause among women and men. While McArthur focused mainly on middle-class and elite white women, she illustrated how they navigated the racial and ethnic shoals unique to turn-of-the-century Texas. In typical cultural constructionist fashion, the outcome of events was often shaped by the presence and interaction of disparate groups—Anglos, Germans, and blacks.[42]

Cultural constructionists also focused on memory, and in particular on the role of memories of the Alamo, in creating and changing Texas culture. Holly Beachley Brear, in *Inherit the Alamo: Myth and Ritual at an American Shrine* (1995), and Richard R. Flores, *Remembering the Alamo: Memory, Modernity, and Master Symbol* (2002), provided among the more revealing explanations of why and how the culture of Texas evolved. Brear focused on how the Alamo myth was used by elite Anglo women to enshrine the 1836 Battle of the Alamo as the formative event and the Anglo heroes as the primary creators of Texas. Once constructed this myth helped exclude Mexican Texans from power and influence. In a similar vein Flores highlighted how the development of the mythic Alamo between 1880 and 1920 helped ensure Anglo dominance of the political, economic, and social structure in San Antonio. Both Brear and Flores illustrated how memory became a frequent part of cultural constructionist work and advanced the argument that memory, both what was remembered and what was forgotten, brought power and privilege.[43]

Yet violence, more often than any other theme, tied together cultural constructionists, and lynching evoked all the nuances and gruesomeness of violence better than any other topic in the Texas past. William D. Carrigan, in *The Making of a Lynching Culture: Violence and Vigilantism in Central Texas, 1836–1916* (2004), drew together the different strands of the third truth about Texas, and examining his work in some detail more fully illuminates the characteristics of that approach and the transformative effect of violence. Like Foley and Boswell, Carrigan also focused on Central Texas and the construction of the region's particular culture. Like Johnson he emphasized the importance of ethnic and racial violence. Like Brear and Flores memory provided his main explanatory device. Carrigan asked why churchgoing whites could brutally torture and kill a young black man in Waco on May 15, 1916. Viewed by some fifteen thousand cheering and jeering whites, this event seared the conscience of much of the nation and fueled the growth of the National Association for the Advancement of Colored People, which publicized that lynching in widespread attempts to stop that all-too-common practice. Instead of the impact of the lynching of Jesse Washington or even its details, however, Carrigan concentrated on its cause and the reason it was widely condoned in the white community of Central Texas. As he put it: "What draws a historian to Jesse Washington are the throngs who attended and then celebrated his death." What produced this celebration of violence?[44]

Carrigan's book differed from most studies of lynching in that it covered a longer time span in an area greater than one specific lynching site. Starting in 1836, Carrigan highlighted events in seven counties immediately around Waco, and he focused on "the roles of the frontier and local and state officials, economic tension, political conflict, and black resistance—but also acts of violence that many studies of lynching ignore, particularly citizen violence against Native Americans and vigilante executions of Anglo-Americans." Instead of borrowing whiteness theory, Carrigan selected another strand current in the profession, and he insisted that historical memory of eight decades of "vigilantism, lynching, and murder" gave the mob all the justification it needed to lynch Jesse Washington. While admitting that lynching had many causes, memory sanctified a culture of violence.[45]

Looking at not only the past, but also how a people came to remember the past and what impact that had on day-to-day actions, Carrigan deeply explored the source of violence and the reason for its persistence and acceptance by the larger white community. Indeed, he so focused on the white community that he could be accused of the same tunnel vision as revisionists. Yet he shared cultural constructionists' concern with the violent contact among groups and their conviction that the interaction between groups molded their culture. Some of this violence in the early days of Anglo settlement was directed against Tejanos, but few remained in the region by the late 1840s. Instead, the target of Anglo violence shifted first to Indians, then to black slaves, especially those thought to be resisting slavery, to whites allegedly guilty of crimes or who opposed the political will of the majority, and then during Reconstruction to blacks whom whites wanted to keep in their place. According to Carrigan these violent deeds lived on in white collective memory in ways that celebrated their effectiveness in bringing civilization and justice to society. Indian killers, whites in Ku Klux Klan–like organizations during Reconstruction, and lynch mob leaders, all men of action, achieved fame, and the next generation emulated them.

Carrigan's use of memory also shared with Foley's and Johnson's work the typical weaknesses of the cultural constructionist approach. Theory obscured nuance and complexity. Memory alone failed to explain the explosion in the number of lynchings in Texas and in the South after the mid-1880s. Not all areas of Texas shared the same memories, and certainly they were not shared by other regions of the South where lynching was more common. Carrigan ignored the vast upsurge in population after Reconstruction. Many whites and blacks were new to the region and would not have grown up hearing the myths and legends of earlier heroes. In addition, memory did not adequately explain the huge size and festive demeanor of the crowds drawn to lynching or the sadism of the white lynch mobs.[46] Still, Carrigan expanded on typical notions of the construction of culture to include not only an acceptance of violence, but also the commemoration of violent heroes whose actions saved society from a legal system that moved too slowly or from threats that demanded vigilante action. Culture meant habits and it meant memories. It also meant that memories changed over time like other facets of culture.[47]

Not all authors in the cultural constructionist camp who drew heavily on theory lacked nuance and complexity. Juliana Barr in *Peace Came in the Form of a Woman: Indians and Spaniards in the Texas Borderlands* (2007) argued that at least in the eighteenth century, "cross-cultural relations in Texas appear far different from those in other regions." One key difference was that as Todd Smith and others had pointed out, the Indians were the dominant partner in their relations with the Spanish. What Barr added to this earlier work was not only a comparative perspective with other portions of the Americas but also an insistence that because of this dominance, Indian notions of gender were more significant than European notions of race in Texas. As she put it: "It is not that race was not there—of course it was; it had become a central component of Spanish worldviews well before the eighteenth century—but gender prevailed over it, because native controls prevailed over those of Spaniards." Because Indians held the upper hand militarily and economically in Texas, European success in dealing with Indians depended on their culture changing enough to employ gender and kinship, either real or fictive. European culture had to evolve toward Indian culture to survive.[48]

Like others who focused on culture and its construction and who employed theoretical concepts common in the broader profession, Barr adeptly examined the connections and interactions among cultural groups. She also added complexity and nuance by taking great pains to explain the differences between Comanches, Apaches, Wichitas, Caddos, Cantonas, Payayas, and others. Each had slightly different kinship and gender patterns. Each had different economies, diplomatic alliances, and military power; and that often led to a different interface with the Spanish and one another. In every instance, however, Barr argued that Indians ultimately called the shots. She also insisted that given the language barriers between the Spanish and Indians, symbols and gestures that usually involved women served as a form of communication. When the Spaniards sought peace with the Indians they achieved the best results when they understood and acted upon the Indian concepts of the connection between peaceful intent and gender. Thus when Spaniards included women among their settlements and trade missions, returned captive Indian women and children, and understood the function of women as part of the negotiation process, they successfully signaled peaceful intent. Men had gender roles as well, and again the Spanish established peace when they at least dimly understood and acted upon Indian concepts of maleness. As Barr put it, "the prevalence of gendered codes of rank, status, and identity forcefully demonstrated natives' power to make Spaniards accede to the concepts and rules governing native polities."[49]

While most who have examined the role of culture emphasized change, Barr insisted that in some ways nothing basic changed in Indians' relationship to the Spanish from 1690 to 1820. Disease and war certainly caused Indian tribes to make and remake themselves. The movement of Comanches into Texas in a major way altered everything. Yet gender and kinship shaped the actions of all Indians. Because Indians remained dominant, their culture changed less than in other areas where they encountered Europeans in large numbers. Thus she further moved beyond an "Anglo-centered narrative of conquest, colonization, and expansion" to argue for the relative stability of Indian life in Texas. In the end, Barr's work offered to those primarily interested in Texas an insistence on Indian dominance and the importance of gender. To those focused on the colonial period in the Americas she offered the question of whether Texas was unique. Did other colonial areas where Indian power remained also experience relative continuity in their culture? In asking these comparative questions Barr differed from Johnson, Foley, and Carrigan and increased the efficacy of the third way to understand Texas history.[50]

While the jury is yet out on whether colonialists will listen to Barr's arguments, if the past offers any guide Texas historians of the traditionalist and revisionist schools will likely nod politely, argue with some of her points, and largely ignore her work. A knee-jerk reaction to the use of gender, her subordination of race, and the habit of viewing all theoretical works as lacking in nuance and knowledge of the particular details of Texas history will limit acceptance and incorporation of her argument. Other cultural constructionists will likely share the same fate, and Texas history, at least in the immediate future, will remain divided into three truths that subtly evolve within their boundaries but diverge from one another.

Why Three Histories?

In a sense then, the foremost reason Texas history remained divided had to do with the essential characteristics of persistent revisionism and updated traditionalism rather than the merits and possibilities of works by cultural constructionists. This has been particularly true of revisionists who have sought a new synthesis. Ironically, those who took on the task of providing one new plotline for Texas history have instead done the most to preserve a tripartite past. Revisionist synthesis, which on the surface should have been the point where all sides met and moved forward together, instead preserved the distinctiveness of the traditional approach and encouraged cultural constructionists to move in completely new directions.

Two recent synthetic works, Jesús F. de la Teja, Paula Marks, and Ron Tyler, *Texas: Crossroads of North America* (2004) and Randolph B. Campbell, *Gone to Texas: A History of the Lone Star State* (2003), demonstrated the limits of revisionists' ability to revise old truths, incorporate new ones, and establish a dominant new view of Texas history. They display many of the limitations of Calvert and De León, *History of Texas,* and a few new problems as well. Despite considerable effort, the application of a full range of skills, and the production of well-written and stimulating books, bits and pieces of past interpretations and past points of view still lingered and resurfaced in these two works. At the same time they incorporated few of the organizational techniques that allowed cultural constructionists to focus on more than one group at a time.[51]

Campbell's *Gone to Texas* provided a beautifully composed and cogent narrative line from prehistoric times to the present. The author drew on recent scholarship to focus on such noncelebratory events as the brutal and stunningly gruesome lynching of hundreds of blacks by whites in the late nineteenth and early twentieth century. While hewing to his well-established argument that Texas was essentially a southern state, Campbell took a slightly more nuanced view than in previous works of what it meant to be southern in the early twentieth century. Texans, he pointed out, grew more diverse and used different historical symbols and memories to establish identity. In many ways the content and character of *Gone to Texas* surpassed the most optimistic expectations of twenty years ago for a new synthesis.[52] Yet critics have pointed to two problems: his treatment of Indians and the top-down approach Campbell used when writing of the twentieth century. The problems of revisionism persisted along with the goals of revisionism.

Problems in incorporating Indians in such revisionist work as *Texas Through Time* and the first edition of *History of Texas* hint at something endemic in the nature of revisionism that limits the ability to conceptualize Indians and others largely outside the culture and worldview of Europeans and Euro-Americans. Ironically, the same group that struggled mightily to understand the full range of the differences and similarities between white Americans and black Americans failed to capture Indian agency. Thus, in *History of Texas* and in Randolph B. Campbell, *An Empire for Slavery: The Peculiar Institution in Texas, 1821–1865* (1989), the authors stressed the flexibility and variability of the slave system and the ability of slaves to develop a distinctive culture that allowed survival.[53] When it came to Indians, however, the task proved more difficult. Gary Clayton Anderson made this point in *The Conquest of Texas: Ethnic Cleansing in the Promised Land, 1820–1875* (2005). Although criticized for annoying factual errors and too frequent hyperbole, Anderson's work should not be completely dismissed, for he evocatively argued that southern whites never intended to share Texas with Indians. He also made the important point that the editors of *Texas Through Time* left out an essay about Indians, and he argued that in *Gone to Texas,* despite good intentions, when it came to Indians, "Campbell utilizes the same rhetoric as many authors who have preceded him."[54]

In arguing that Campbell echoed Fehrenbach, Anderson distorted Campbell's purpose. The actual point about Campbell and Indians was far more subtle. Campbell attempted to present both sides of the argument—traditional and revisionist. Witness this quote from his conclusion to a section on the Indian and South Texas frontiers that Anderson roundly criticized: "Some historians have seen the stories of these frontiers as the triumphant march of white civilization; others view them as matters of raw exploitation by Anglos, and the decimation of earlier arrivals. Certainly elements of both views were present, allowing every reader to place his or her interpretation on the meaning of these frontiers." In this respect Campbell's approach resembled that of Harris and Sadler in their book on the Rangers in the 1910s. He walked the middle between extremes and in the process displayed an occasional and unintentional lack of understanding or empathy with Indians.[55] In addition, like most revisionists he had difficulty in focusing on more than one target group at a time, his synthesis derived in part from very traditional sources, and Indians emerged as victims or villains with little room for their own contribution to their success and demise. For example, post–Civil War Indian raiders were described as striking the frontier with "murderous effect," and there was little attempt to see the strategy of warfare and raiding from the Indian point of view, as does recent cultural constructionist work. Likewise, the eventual expulsion of Indians was seen as "sadly ironic" in the classic sense that Indians were the victims of white aggression. This traditional view was compounded by the lack of a clear overarching theme when it came to the interaction of Indians and Euro-Americans in Texas.[56]

Creating a revisionist synthesis seemed fraught with the danger of dredging up some relic from the past while collecting information, particularly when the topic fell outside the special competence and research interests of the author. Despite earlier efforts at a balanced approach, when Campbell's synthesis reached the 1890s the number of pages devoted to politics and gubernatorial elections and administrations increased. When he reached the 1930s, subheadings became "The 'Pappy' Lee O'Daniel Era," and often the broader and more nuanced story of Texas was subsumed under the plotline of the great men who dominated Texas politics. While Campbell's narrative sometimes reflected the limitations of the literature produced over the past few decades, more existed on the twentieth century than appeared in this work. Civil rights for African Americans and Mexican Americans, for example, received some coverage but as essentially political and legal events, not broader cultural, social, demographic, and economic transformations, and here, at least, a voluminous recent literature existed.[57] Ironically, this admirable new synthesis, at least when it came to the twentieth century, restored, as one reviewer put it, the "top down," political leader as exemplar of all, approach of the old consensus school and thus contributed to the persistence of traditional concepts and attitudes toward Texas history.⁵⁸

Despite their best attempts, by the very nature of their methods, approaches and mind-set, revisionists were caught in a loop in which they reintroduced and perpetuated traditional interpretations, as demonstrated in *Texas: Crossroads of North America*. Like the authors of *The History of Texas* in 1990, de la Teja, Marks, and Tyler declared that their book "is a distinctly modern history of Texas." They went to particular pains to emphasize Spanish Texas, calling it "the formative period of the state's history." They often discussed such contemporary topics as identity formation and public memory. The authors made a laudable attempt to avoid allowing the recent past to "descend into a general recitation of diverse events and developments." Thus they provided a glimpse of some of the best of revisionist scholarship in the 1990s and even some of the promising new effort by cultural constructionists. In the process, however, they also demonstrated the remarkable staying power of traditional history in Texas.⁵⁹

This juxtaposition of new and old made for an occasional jarring moment while reading *Texas: Crossroads of North America*, including, not surprisingly, the discussion of the role of Indians in Spanish Texas during the first two decades of the nineteenth century. De la Teja, Marks, and Tyler acknowledged that Texas was "still a country of Indians," and that the wealth and military might of the Comanches and Wichitas "required Spanish officials to deal with them as equals."⁶⁰ A paragraph or two in the text detailed the now well documented transformation and regeneration or decline of particular Indian groups, and in general the text conveyed a clear sense of change over time in the Indian world. These observations differed from Calvert and De León's 1990 version of Texas history and reflected the remarkable outpouring of scholarship on Texas Indians in the intervening years.

For the most part, however, Indians in *Texas: Crossroads of North America* appeared primarily through a European lens. Indians challenged or presented problems for Tejanos of European or mixed European and Indian descent who sought to control Texas. Thus the text moved only a step beyond depicting Indians as barbarous enemies in need of control or removal and did not differ that markedly from the depiction of Indians that drew Anderson's scorn in *The Conquest of Texas*. Indians remained the "other" and not a people in their own right with aspirations, goals, and aims for Texas. They were not Texans, although Anderson himself occasionally had trouble seeing Indians as Texans.⁶¹ Texts and synthetic works that appeal to a wider readership often suffer from this type of tunnel vision. Viewing a particular time as "formative," in this case arguing for a formative Spanish presence and persistent influence in Texas, caused people or events running counter to that master narrative to either emerge as the villains of the story or become marginalized.[62]

Nonetheless, the treatment of Indians improved from 1990 to 2004, seemingly indicating that Texas history moved toward convergence into one truth that included modern insights on the past. Despite detours, the occasional backward step, and the detritus of past interpretations and points of view, new scholarship changed the presentation of the past. The depiction of Reconstruction in *Texas: Crossroads of North America* told a different tale in that it did not reflect the recent scholarship on the period and instead retreated toward a more traditional view. Reflecting the best scholarship of its time, *History of Texas* offered a stunningly clear vision of pervasive white on black violence, black economic trials and occasional triumphs, and black success in building stable churches and family units. Readers found none of this in *Texas: Crossroads of North America*. What the authors offered often came across as uncomfortably close to the interpretation of Reconstruction entrenched in Texas history via Charles W. Ramsdell's *Reconstruction in Texas* (1910). Focus on ordinary blacks shrank, and in its place the authors of *Texas: Crossroads of North America* presented a romanticized view of whites like Samuel Maverick who suffered severe challenges and economic losses during Reconstruction. While lacking the racism and paternalism that made every white action seem justified by the trying conditions and every black action the result of being unschooled in freedom, the authors of *Texas: Crossroads of North America* failed to clearly convey that the status of African Americans lay at the heart of every facet of Reconstruction. Instead, the heart of Reconstruction often seemed the "blatant use of military power" by the North. In addition, Reconstruction seemed very much a top-down affair with much attention to prominent politicians and little mention of what went on at the grass-roots level or among everyday whites and blacks. While well written and compelling in many ways, *Texas: Crossroads of North America*'s depiction of Reconstruction once again illustrated that some interpretations never die.[63] In reaching back to build a synthesis based on all the work that has gone before, revisionists dredged up facets of the traditional school, be they interpretations of the Rangers, approaches to Indians, or generalizations about Reconstruction. In doing so they legitimized updated traditionalists and estranged cultural constructionists.

By repelling opponents and attracting adherents many basic characteristics of all three genres served to keep the three histories intact. As has been demonstrated, cultural constructionists on the one hand often employed a nomenclature that seemed artificial to those in the other camps. They often seemed to force the story to fit the theory instead of building from the facts toward a theory. Revisionists, on the other hand, had their own characteristics that inhibited them from accepting the work of cultural constructionists. They often viewed the use of theory skeptically, with Harris and Sadler being an extreme example of this skepticism. As any number of revisionists demonstrated, indeed as almost all of them demonstrated, perhaps because of that skepticism about theory they had difficulty dealing with more than one target group at once. Traditionalists, meanwhile, still accepted timeworn interpretations of such events as Reconstruction, leading revisionists to focus all the more on refuting these interpretations.

What needs additional emphasis, however, is that often the process of attraction and repulsion did not matter because proponents of the three truths spoke to and with different audiences. Revisionists and traditionalists, in comparison with cultural constructionists, exhibited an intra-Texas focus—writing for an audience of historians and general readers interested in Texas. Cultural constructionists, in contrast, often wrote more for a subfield like colonial history in Barr's case or race and ethnicity in Foley's case. At the same time, traditionalists were often removed from the dialogue taking place in the larger historical profession, seldom attending the meetings of the American Historical Association or the Organization of American Historians. Instead, they attended, if they attended a professional meeting at all, the meetings of the Texas State Historical Association. This group, as Richard B. McCaslin made clear in his well-researched history, had long nurtured a strain that turned the study of Texas inward and separated it from the larger profession. It provided a meeting ground for traditional and revisionist historians, but often seemed alien to cultural constructionists interested in building a national reputation.[64]

Each genre's typical choice of venues for publication also mattered in explaining the entrenched distinctiveness of the three approaches to Texas history. Some 40 percent of the books published between 1988 and 2009 in the cultural constructionist category were published at out-of-state university presses such as Johns Hopkins University Press, Yale University Press, and Duke University Press.[65] This compared to only 14 percent published at out-of-state university presses for the entire list of over 1,600 books. Of the remaining cultural constructionist books, almost all were published at the University of Texas Press and Texas A&M University Press. Again this was a much higher figure than for the list of all books published on Texas history between 1988 and 2009, as demonstrated by the following table.

Prominent out-of-state university presses and the presses of the two flagship public universities in Texas probably published almost all the books in

Publication venues for Texas history, 1988–2009

Non-Texas university presses	14%
UT/A&M presses	28%
Other Texas not-for-profit presses	25%
Trade presses	33%

the cultural constructionist category for fairly straightforward reasons. These presses and their manuscript reviewers were the most attuned to the national history audience, the group most likely to hear the message conveyed by cultural constructionists. They were also the logical choices for young historians eager to make a name in the profession who were told by deans and department chairs that publishing at conspicuous presses helped secure tenure and promotion. All presses wanted to sell books, and to do so they published books that fit their lists of previously published works and that appealed to their established markets. Authors in turn looked at publishers' lists and the markets they would reach through that particular venue. As a result of these factors, segregation of the types of history emerged, a structural division that influenced who published, who read, and who purchased different types of new books on Texas history. Out-of-state university presses almost never published updated traditional histories. Indeed, their list split about evenly between books by persistent revisionists and cultural constructionists. Trade presses and the other not-for-profit Texas presses, besides the University of Texas Press and Texas A&M University Press, published the bulk of the updated traditionalist work and some revisionist work. Only the University of Texas Press and Texas A&M University Press published extensively in all three categories. Those who produced updated traditionalist work were unlikely to even see the efforts of cultural constructionists unless through the efforts of the University of Texas Press and Texas A&M University Press, and as we have seen these presses often reinforced the traditionalist approach instead of wholeheartedly encouraging a new approach.[66]

Choices of presses were not only segregated, there was also a certain democratization of presses and publishing in that authors had more choices about where to publish and how to market their books as the twenty-year span progressed. Indeed, more books emerged on Texas history with each passing year. A look at the books published on Texas history between 1988 and 2007 revealed that after dividing the era into five-year blocks, at some point in the mid-1990s the rate of publication began to accelerate, with a higher percentage of the books on the list published in the second decade than in the first.[67]

Even if they had wanted to, the editors and outside manuscript readers for

Rate of publication, 1988–2007

1988–92	20%
1993–97	24%
1998–2002	28%
2003–2007	28%

the University of Texas Press and Texas A&M University Press could not have shut traditionalists out of the market or even encouraged them to adopt a more revisionist point of view. The demand was there and the presses were available. When it came to Texas history, book publishing increased instead of declined.

Again the causes and consequences of this increased rate of publication were fairly obvious. The Texas population grew and society changed even more completely from rural to urban and suburban, making for more readers about Texas and more nostalgia for a simpler past with obvious moral lessons. The Internet allowed greater direct marketing of books, and presses made a concerted effort to control costs by finding inexpensive foreign production facilities and better managing other costs and inventories. Perhaps the period of 1995–2007 was simply a boom cycle to be followed by an inevitable bust in the number of presses and number of books about Texas, but predictions of calamity in the book publishing trade seemed overdrawn.[68] Instead, the book trade experienced a democratization that allowed almost anyone with a story to tell a chance to tell it. No structural limits kept updated traditionalists from celebrating the past and highlighting the contribution of great men and women. Persistent revisionists could sell enough copies of almost any attempt to broaden who should be considered a Texan and what should be considered Texas history. If they survived rigorous peer review, cultural constructionists could find an outlet for their work. That peer review was made somewhat less problematic by their choice of topics and approaches popular in the broader profession. Strikingly, compared to twenty years ago, Texas topics, if done in new ways, enjoyed greater acceptance on a national level, and as books that focused at least in part on Texas won increasing praise, major presses grew even more receptive. Nothing in the industry's structure prevented authors from finding markets for reasonably well written books on Texas. In the end, just as the nature of each genre encouraged the continuation of three distinct, slowly evolving truths about Texas history, so too did the book publishing industry.

The exact twists and turns of those three evolving truths grew in large measure from the time of their production. Changes in the approach and topics of study of updated traditionalists, especially, undoubtedly owed much to the events and particular circumstances of the last twenty years. World War II's fifty-year anniversary in the early 1990s, for example, sparked public attention and adoration for the generation that fought the war. At the same time, it was hard to ignore that Texas had a woman governor, a woman U.S. senator, and numerous other prominent female politicians. The role of women in sports and other facets of public life also increased exponentially. Tejanos rose to political prominence as well, both as mayors and as members of the U.S. House of Representatives. It was natural, then, for traditionalists to update their approach by focusing on World War II and allowing into their narrative an occasional prominent woman or Tejano. African Americans proved slower to move into this type of history, perhaps because it was easier to accept Tejanos as closer to white. The huge upsurge in the Mexican American population in Texas likewise encouraged revisionist historians to look back at such key events as the Tejano civil rights movement and to make sure that Tejanos were included as one of the groups that made up the Texas population in earlier days. Interest in Tejanos led naturally to the expansion of revisionist interest in such topics as the Texas Rangers and ranching. At a time in the late 1990s when gay marriage, gay rights, women's rights, the role of men in family life, and other such issues drew public attention it was natural enough for cultural constructionists to move from a focus on ethnic and racial identity to gender. The times, as much as some larger dialogue in the historical community, explained the shift within the boundaries of each of the three truths.

Along with their innate characteristics and the nature of the publishing business, the times also explained the relative isolation of the three parts of Texas history. Yes, updated traditionalists, persistent revisionists, and cultural constructionists influenced one another, but all kept a degree of isolation from the others. Updated traditionalists with their own presses, their own access to history associations, and their own audiences for their work moved a bit toward a more revisionist approach, but it was not surprising that they remained separate, remained focused on a celebratory history and on elites. Just as they did two decades ago, traditionalists still offered to an audience made nervous by modernity the reassurance that virtue could be found in the past. As some authors have pointed out, as urban centers in Texas sprawled out into once rural counties, it was natural enough to lament the passing of an age and seek solace in past glories.[69] More surprising was the sustained distinctiveness of revisionism from those focused on more recent innovations in the study of Texas history.

Persistent revisionists and cultural constructionists should have rubbed shoulders often enough for cross-fertilization of ideas to bring them closer together, but such cross-fertilization did not usually occur. They did not always attend the same historical meetings, and they often read books from different presses. The tendency of revisionists to begrudgingly use theory furthered the distance between them. Graduate school training cemented that difference with a large number of those who wrote on cultural constructionist themes being trained out of state or at the University of Texas. With some notable exceptions, other graduate schools tended to train those who wrote in the revisionist mode. After graduate school, where historians worked made some difference. If they were out of state or at large, diverse, PhD-granting departments, there was a higher probability that they wrote in the cultural constructionist vein or at least were willing to engage the arguments presented in books that drew heavily on theory. In an earlier time, revisionists had trouble moving into positions of influence in Texas universities and colleges, but they eventually did. Perhaps we are at the beginning of that process and cultural constructionists will either merge with or replace revisionists. For the moment, however, that has not happened.

2011: Convergence?

Interestingly, fusion occurred on a national level, particularly in such areas as the study of the Atlantic World or anything else intrinsically transnational, international, and comparative. Perspectives that lifted readers and authors outside of an ingrained mind-set often led to a creative borrowing of ideas and approaches, and perhaps in time this will lead to a merger between persistent revisionists and cultural constructionists. Juliana Barr, for example, drew comparisons between Texas and elsewhere, but others interested in the construction of culture, such as Foley, Johnson, and Carrigan, have not been overtly comparative in their writing. Encouragingly, however, some revisionists, especially those who focus on ethnic Mexicans in Texas, naturally took a transnational and international approach, offering a potential bridge between the two camps. Emilio Zamora's *Claiming Rights and Righting Wrongs in Texas: Mexican Workers and Job Politics during World War II* (2009) exemplified this type of work.[70]

Pekka Hämäläinen's *The Comanche Empire* (2008) suggested even more strongly the possibility of convergence between revisionists and cultural constructionists. In this engaging and stimulating book, Hämäläinen blended the revisionists' insistence on Indian agency and their eighteenth-century ascendancy with the cultural constructionists' capacity to view more than one group at a time. His work also displayed a keen understanding of the study of empires

and their political, social, and military dimensions current in the larg
sion, and this invited a degree of comparison with a Comanche empi
together, as Hämäläinen insisted, with different sinews than eightee
early nineteenth-century Euro-American empires. While some have pointed out that in essence Hämäläinen repeated the essential point that Comanches controlled much of Texas and New Mexico, this use of theory allowed him to do it in a much more sophisticated manner and from the point of view of the Indians. Comanches were not barriers to white expansion; they were actors in their own right, responsible for both their successes and failures. Taken as a whole the book offered a model for the merging of revisionist and cultural constructionist approaches.[71]

Andrés Reséndez provided another example of possible convergence between revisionists and cultural constructionists in *Changing National Identities at the Frontier: Texas and New Mexico, 1800–1850* (2004). Reséndez focused on the creation of new identities both in Texas and in New Mexico, thus adding a very useful wider lens to the typical study of Texas. Indeed, this broader, comparative, and transborder lens was a characteristic of some of the most compelling books in the cultural constructionist approach to Texas history. Reséndez, however, paid very close attention to the role of the state and to the economic influences on cultural formation, classic revisionist tropes. This marriage of approaches allowed Reséndez to highlight the fluid role and nature of borders—local, regional, and national. Borders contributed to change and to the multiple and diverse nature of identities. This blending of economic and cultural causation and outcomes offered other historians much to contemplate, including the possibility of bridging some of the bedrock differences between approaches to the Texas past.[72]

Limited convergence sometimes seemed possible even between traditional, revisionist, and cultural constructionist approaches. Gregg Cantrell, for example, in *Stephen F. Austin: Empresario of Texas* (1999), ably demonstrated that you could take a new look at a very traditional topic, an icon of early Anglo Texas, and employ the study of gender, ethnicity, and race. Like Zamora and Reséndez, Cantrell successfully used Mexican sources and tried to present the Mexican point of view. Indeed, Cantrell moved beyond a simple look at one border to explore three by looking at Austin's connections between the South and slavery, the West and exploitation of resources, and Mexico whose language and culture Austin eagerly adapted. Cantrell explored the inner person using concepts of gender and sexuality current in the profession, and he highlighted both the doubts and motivation buried within Austin. His portrait of Austin's relationships with other members of his family revealed a man who wanted to fulfill his father's mission to settle Texas, pay off the family debt, and move beyond his father's shadow. This nuanced work might be about one of the Anglo elite of the Texas past, but it revised an heroic portrait, reflected recent scholarly efforts in such areas as the role of the family and sexuality, and spoke to an audience both within and outside of Texas. In that sense, it was an early example of the possibility of convergence of the streams of Texas history.[73]

Despite the promise of convergence in the works of Zamora, Barr, Hämäläinen, Reséndez, and Cantrell, Texas history remains, and in the near future is likely to remain, largely unchanged in its essential essence and tripartite nature. The reasons for this began with the inherent characteristics of the three groups, characteristics that both repelled adherents of other approaches and sustained their distinctiveness. Revisionists, especially those producing synthetic works, tended to undergird traditionalism as much as they countered it. Certain structural barriers also accounted for, and probably will continue to account for, distinctiveness. These included segregation by presses and historical associations, the role of graduate school training, and the varied influence of the larger profession. Easy access, a type of democratization of publishing, also played a role. Then, while the times encouraged some convergence, the inclusion of a limited number of women in traditional works for example, the times also encouraged proponents of each truth to follow their own path. Given the entrenched nature of these trends, especially the tendency of revisionists to attract and repel the other camps, eminent convergence of the three groups seems unlikely.

Indeed, if convergence of all three groups occurs and one truth about Texas history emerges, the process will probably come through revisionism, the pivot point between traditionalists and cultural constructionists. Increasingly shut out of a national audience and labeled "Texas Historians," revisionists wrote for a Texas audience and often carried forward bits and pieces of traditional interpretations. Their focus on correcting the errors of commission and omission of the traditionalists turned them inward instead of toward a national audience. De-emphasizing theory, they found it difficult to deal with many cultural groups at once. There seems little hope that the majority of revisionists will see, and perhaps because of the nature of their approach they cannot see, Texas as fluidly connected to a world beyond, other than to engage in the tiresome and often ahistorical argument of whether Texas should be called part of the South or the West. Revisionists' work remained valuable because of their careful attention to detail and ability to move beyond elites and beyond celebration. Ironically, however, they may now be preventing that natural cycle of a new brand of truth emerging every twenty years. Then again history, even on the national and international stage, may have never worked that way.

Perhaps it was a mistake to ever assume that one truth neatly succeeded another even on the larger stage of American and world history. Histories of dead white males have made a remarkable comeback on the national stage and coexist with tightly focused studies arguing for the construction over time of gender, ethnicity, and race. Obviously these varied approaches apparent on the national stage did not operate in isolation from one another. A multiplicity of methods and interpretations coexist outside of Texas history, and they sometimes seem to at least in part cross-pollinate one another.[74] In the main, however, Texas history remains an unhealthy distortion of the national model, or even the southern or western models, and the failure of all three sides in the struggle over truth to seriously engage the others on core issues limits understanding. As it did twenty years ago, the relative strength of the updated traditionalists in Texas places an additional burden on the entire field, making it easy for professional historians in other areas of study or other places to label all studies of Texas as parochial and old fashioned. Revisionists' reluctance or inability to seriously engage cultural constructionists and their focus on a Texas audience adds to the burden of studying Texas.[75] To a lesser degree than they once did, these limits on the ability of Texas history to change and the biases of the larger profession still discourage the next generation of professional historians from studying Texas.

Two other types of convergence, however, gave promise that focus on Texas would no longer be considered peripheral and provincial: highlighting Texas as a trendsetter for the nation and writing books on Texas that set the history profession on new paths. William R. Childs, in *The Texas Railroad Commission: Understanding Regulation in America to the Mid-Twentieth Century* (2005), exemplified this first type of convergence when he argued that the blend of state and national regulation of the petroleum industry that emerged in Texas in the early twentieth century not only set the pattern for other states, it also marked an example of how circumstances in Texas influenced what happened on the national stage. Regulatory patterns did not just flow from the national level down, they moved from the state level up.[76] Zamora's *Claiming Rights and Righting Wrongs in Texas* provided a similar example of how events in Texas set a regional and perhaps national pattern. For the twentieth century, at least, scholars increasingly looked to Texas for explanation and examples of what happened in a wider region and in the country as a whole.[77] Similarly, works about Texas now often serve as trendsetters for the larger profession. Foley was among the first to seriously consider what it meant for Mexican Americans, African Americans, and Anglos to move into increased contact. Hämäläinen's argument about the distinctive nature of the Comanche empire, an empire that functioned in a non-European manner but still exerted considerable power and influence, likewise signaled that books focused at least in part on Texas had advanced ahead of the profession.[78]

To end, then, on a more hopeful and more realistic note than twenty years ago—Texas history remains multilinear and now has divided into three distinct camps instead of two. These three camps have not sprung directly one from the other, and have demonstrated only limited potential for convergence. That disjunctive nature will not soon change, but thanks in large part to those who work in or on the border of cultural constructionism, that may no longer limit its promise and potential as much as it once did. Within Texas, convergence of the three truths about the past will not soon occur. Within the larger history profession accepting the importance of what happened in Texas, especially in the twentieth century, and recognizing pathbreaking work that focuses on Texas has already occurred.

Notes

1. Walter L. Buenger and Robert A. Calvert, eds., *Texas Through Time: Evolving Interpretations* (College Station: Texas A&M University Press, 1991).

2. The influence of postmodernism or poststructuralism is much debated. Some claim descent, but others resent being included in this group. My point is that postmodernism and poststructuralism highlighted trends and patterns of thought that may have been part of a "modern" approach to history but were little used. Using these patterns and trends became easier in the wake of discussion of postmodernism and poststructuralism. On the various intellectual trends that influenced the 1990s, see Ernst Breisach, *Historiography: Ancient, Medieval, and Modern,* 3rd ed. (Chicago: University of Chicago Press, 2007), 417–30; Ernst Breisach, *On the Future of History: The Postmodernist Challenge and Its Aftermath* (Chicago: University of Chicago Press, 2003); Keith Jenkins, *Rethinking History,* 2nd ed. (London and New York: Routledge, 2003). For an early example of the use of anthropology to explain Texas history and its impact, see Holly Beachley Brear, *Inherit the Alamo: Myth and Ritual at an American Shrine* (Austin: University of Texas Press, 1995).

3. On the influence of culture and its supplanting of class and other economic-based explanations of the past, see Jonathan Daniel Wells, "The Southern Middle Class," *Journal of Southern History* (JSH) 75 (August 2009): 651–62; Victoria E. Bonnell and Lynn Hunt, eds., *Beyond the Cultural Turn: New Directions in the Study of Society and Culture* (Berkeley: University of California Press, 1999). On memory and culture, see Kerwin Lee Klein, "On the Emergence of Memory in Historical Discourse," *Representations* 69 (Winter 2000): 127–50; W. Fitzhugh Brundage, "Contentious and Collected: Memory's Future in Southern History," *JSH* 75 (August 2009): 751–66.

4. Walter L. Buenger and Robert A. Calvert, "The Shelf Life of Truth in Texas," in *Texas Through Time*, ed. Buenger and Calvert, ix–xxv. For reflections on a field where the call to revise and move on from traditional interpretations has been particularly intense and has yet to completely change public perceptions, see Jon M. Giggie, "Rethinking Reconstruction," *Reviews in American History* (*RAH*) 35 (December 2007): 545–55.

5. Looking back, the most glaring omission in *Texas Through Time* was the absence of a separate essay on Indians, but that field was just beginning to blossom, as some of the contributors realized. See Donald E. Chipman, "Spanish Texas," in *Texas Through Time*, ed. Buenger and Calvert, 127–28; Gary C. Anderson, *The Conquest of Texas: Ethnic Cleansing in the Promised Land, 1820–1875* (Norman: University of Oklahoma Press, 2005), 13–14.

6. Robert A. Calvert and Arnoldo De León, *The History of Texas* (Arlington Heights, Ill.: Harlan Davidson, 1990). I have only referenced texts in this essay whose first editions appeared after 1988, and I have only discussed those first editions. Another useful way of sketching historiographic change is to compare the various editions of the long-running text *Texas: The Lone Star State*, which first appeared in 1943. Compare, for example, Rupert N. Richardson, Adrian Anderson, and Ernest Wallace, *Texas: The Lone Star State*, 4th ed. (Englewood Cliffs, N.J.: Prentice Hall, 1988) with Rupert N. Richardson, Adrian Anderson, Cary D. Wintz, and Ernest Wallace, *Texas: The Lone Star State*, 10th ed. (Upper Saddle River, N.J.: Prentice Hall, 2010). It would also be revealing to look at successive editions of *The History of Texas*. See, for example, Robert A. Calvert, Arnoldo De León, and Gregg Cantrell, *The History of Texas*, 4th ed. (Wheeling, Ill.: Harlan Davidson, 2007).

7. Calvert and De León, *History of Texas*, viii. Also see Randolph B. Campbell and Richard G. Lowe, *Wealth and Power in the Antebellum South* (College Station: Texas A&M University Press, 1977); Robert C. Cotner, *James Stephen Hogg, a Biography* (Austin: University of Texas Press, 1959); Robert A. Calvert, "Agrarian Texas," in *Texas Through Time*, ed. Buenger and Calvert, 212–13; Calvert and De León, *History of Texas*, 125, 213.

8. Calvert and De León did have access to the pathbreaking work, Elizabeth A. H. John, *Storms Brewed in Other Men's Worlds: The Confrontation of Indians, Spanish, and French in the Southwest, 1540–1795* (Norman: University of Oklahoma Press, 1975). This work offered a detailed and reasonably accurate view of Texas Indians as well as a sense of change over time while stressing that the Indians were the equals of the Spanish and French in determining the outcome of events. Most of the innovative work on individual tribes and work on the years after the 1790s, however, was not published before the drafting of History of Texas.

9. Calvert and De León, *History of Texas*, 3–6, 26–27, 39. For a sampling of the impressive studies of Texas Indians, see Juliana Barr, *Peace Came in the Form of a Woman: Indians and Spaniards in the Texas Borderlands* (Chapel Hill: University of North Carolina Press, 2007); Pekka Hämäläinen, *The Comanche Empire* (New Haven,

Conn.: Yale University Press, 2008); David La Vere, *The Texas Indians* (College Station: Texas A&M University Press, 2004); Gary Clayton Anderson, *The Indian Southwest, 1580–1830: Ethnogenesis and Reinvention* (Norman: University of Oklahoma Press, 1999); F. Todd Smith, *From Dominance to Disappearance: The Indians of Texas and the Near Southwest, 1786–1859* (Lincoln: University of Nebraska Press, 2005); Anderson, *Conquest of Texas*.

10. Calvert and De León, *History of Texas*, vii.

11. Buenger and Calvert, "Shelf Life," xxxiv–xxxv. For another call for synthesis, see Randolph B. Campbell, "Statehood, Civil War, and Reconstruction," in *Texas Through Time*, ed. Buenger and Calvert, 196. He answered his own call in Randolph B. Campbell, *Gone to Texas: a History of the Lone Star State* (New York: Oxford University Press, 2003).

12. T. R. Fehrenbach, *Lone Star: A History of Texas and the Texans* (New York: Da Capo Press, 2000), 713, 714, xiii. Compare this treatment of the modern era with Calvert and De León, *History of Texas*, 325–444.

13. T. R. Fehrenbach, *Lone Star: A History of Texas and the Texans* (New York: Macmillan, 1968), 711. Also see T. R. Fehrenbach, *Seven Keys to Texas* (El Paso: Texas Western Press, 1983).

14. Buenger and Calvert, "Shelf Life," xiv–xxxv. For how these traditionalists depicted Indians, see Anderson, *Conquest of Texas*, 3–17. For perspective on the professional historians who led the Texas State Historical Association and influenced the depiction of Texas history, see Richard B. McCaslin, *At the Heart of Texas: One Hundred Years of the Texas State Historical Association, 1897–1997* (Austin: Texas State Historical Association, 2007), 53–216. For his debt to Webb, see Fehrenbach, *Lone Star* (1968), xii.

15. This list of over 1,600 titles from 1988 to 2009 grew from looking at bibliographies in recent texts, by examining reviews in the Southwestern Historical Quarterly, from the list of Texas books on the Web page of each major university press in Texas, from the many books I have reviewed and read over the past twenty years, and from the contributions of other authors in this volume. Katherine Walters reviewed the list, adding to it and correcting it. She has my thanks. Second and third editions, articles, dissertations, and reprints were not included. All types of histories were included, but works that were simply lists of books or were primarily literary or artistic criticism were excluded. Books were assigned to categories according to the Library of Congress subject headings and a review of their introductions when possible. The list is no doubt incomplete and there may be some errors in assigning books to categories, but the statistics offered would probably be little changed by the addition or subtraction of a few titles.

16. The dividing line between an updated traditionalist approach and persistent revisionism was usually fairly obvious, since traditionalists focused on elites and took a celebratory tone. They also usually failed to offer much analysis of gender, race, or ethnicity even when looking at women, blacks, or Latinos, and often had embedded

in them pre-1960 interpretations of such topics as Reconstruction. See, for example, Chuck Parsons, *John B. Armstrong: Texas Ranger and Pioneer Ranchman* (College Station: Texas A&M University Press, 2007), 2. The dividing line between persistent revisionists and cultural constructionists was less clear, particularly for early works in the cultural constructionist genre. Still focusing on new topics such as gender, memory, identity, and how they were created and drawing heavily on theory usually indicated that a work was cultural constructionist. This was especially straightforward when works looked at the connections between groups. This seemed to become more common as one moved toward the present. Compare Brear, *Inherit the Alamo* with Barr, *Peace Came in the Form of a Woman*.

17. For an example of the frequently mentioned idea that historical approaches come and go and change with the times, see Brendan McConville, "Sam Adams: Forgotten Founder?" *RAH* 37 (December 2009): 497–500.

18. John A. Adams Jr., *Damming the Colorado: The Rise of the Lower Colorado River Authority, 1933–1939* (College Station: Texas A&M University Press, 1990); Robert D. Auerbach, *Deception and Abuse at the Fed: Henry B. Gonzalez Battles Alan Greenspan's Bank* (Austin: University of Texas Press, 2008); Susan E. Cayleff, Babe: *The Life and Legend of Babe Didrikson Zaharias* (Urbana: University of Illinois Press, 1995).

19. Bruce L. Brager, *The Texas 36th Division: A History* (Austin: Eakin Press, 2002), 268, 8. For other more traditional looks at the World War II era, see Thomas E. Alexander, *The Stars Were Big and Bright: The United States Army Air Forces and Texas during World War II* (Austin: Eakin Press, 2000); Thomas E. Alexander, *The Wings of Change: The Army Air Force Experience in Texas during World War II* (Abilene, Tex.: McWhiney Foundation Press, 2003); Thomas E. Alexander, *Rattlesnake Bomber Base: Pyote Army Airfield in World War II* (Abilene, Tex.: State House Press, 2005); Dede Weldon Casad, *Texans of Valor: Military Heroes of the Twentieth Century* (Austin: Eakin Press, 1998); Tom Killebrew, *The Royal Air Force in Texas: Training British Pilots in Terrell during World War II* (Denton: University of North Texas Press, 2003).

20. Anne J. Bailey, *Texans in the Confederate Cavalry* (Abilene, Tex.: McWhiney Foundation Press, 1998), 83, 21, 14.

21. Bailey, *Texans in the Confederate Cavalry*, 79–82. For other more traditional looks at the Civil War, see Evault Boswell, *Texas Boys in Gray* (Plano: Republic of Texas Press, 2000); Stephen Chicoine, *Confederates of Chappell Hill, Texas: Prosperity, Civil War, and Decline* (Jefferson, N.C.: McFarland, 2005); Edward T. Cotham Jr., *Battle on the Bay: The Civil War Struggle for Galveston* (Austin: University of Texas Press, 1998); Edward T. Cotham Jr., *Sabine Pass: The Confederacy's Thermopylae* (Austin: University of Texas Press, 2004); Donald S. Frazier, *Blood and Treasure: Confederate Empire in the Southwest* (College Station: Texas A&M University Press, 1995); Donald S. Frazier, *Cottonclads! The Battle of Galveston and the Defense of the Texas Coast* (Fort Worth: Ryan Place Publishers, 1996); Donald S. Frazier, *Fire in the Cane Field:*

The Federal Invasion of Louisiana and Texas, January 1861–January 1863 (Abilene, Tex.: State House Press, 2008); Jeffrey Wm. Hunt, *The Last Battle of the Civil War: Palmetto Ranch* (Austin: University of Texas Press, 2002); Clayton E. Jewett, *Texas in the Confederacy: An Experiment in Nation Building* (Columbia: University of Missouri Press, 2002); Thomas Reid, *Spartan Band: Burnett's 13th Texas Cavalry in the Civil War* (Denton: University of North Texas Press, 2005).

    22. Parsons, *Armstrong*, 12, 20. Studies of ranching tend to stress the same values and emphasize the same role models as studies of rangers. As in this case, they also often involve the same individuals. For other examples of studies of rangers and ranching in a more traditional mode, see Charlena Chandler, *On Independence Creek: The Story of a Texas Ranch* (Lubbock: Texas Tech University Press, 2004); Lawrence Clayton, *Historic Ranches of Texas* (Austin: University of Texas Press, 1993); Lawrence Clayton, *Longhorn Legacy: Graves Peeler and the Texas Cattle Trade* (Abilene, Tex.: Cowboy Press, 1994); Lawrence Clayton, *Watkins Reynolds Matthews: A Biography* (Austin: Eakin Press, 1994); Lawrence Clayton, *Contemporary Ranches in Texas* (Austin: University of Texas Press, 2001); Lawrence Clayton, *Cowboys: Ranch Life along the Clear Fork of the Brazos River* (Austin: Eakin Press, 1997); Lawrence Clayton, Jim Hoy, and Jerald Underwood, *Vaqueros, Cowboys, and Buckaroos* (Austin: University of Texas Press, 2001); David Dary, *Cowboy Culture: A Saga of Five Centuries* (Lawrence: University Press of Kansas, 1989); Lester Galbreath, *Campfire Tales: True Stories from the Western Frontier* (Albany, Tex.: Bright Sky Press, 2005); Ed Gooding and Robert Nieman, *Ed Gooding: Soldier, Texas Ranger* (Longview: Ranger Publishing, 2001); James Kimmins Greer, *Texas Ranger: Jack Hays in the Frontier Southwest* (College Station: Texas A&M University Press, 1993); Allen G. Hatley, *Bringing the Law to Texas: Crime and Violence in Nineteenth-Century Texas* (LaGrange: Centex Press, 2002); Thomas W. Knowles, *They Rode for the Lone Star: The Saga of the Texas Rangers* (Dallas: Taylor, 1999); Stephen L. Moore, *Savage Frontier: Rangers, Riflemen, and Indian Wars in Texas*, 3 vols. (Denton: University of North Texas Press, 2006); Stephen L. Moore, *Taming Texas: Captain William T. Sadler's Lone Star Service* (Abilene, Tex.: State House Press, 2000); Chuck Parsons and Gary P. Fitterer, *Captain C. B. McKinney: The Law in South Texas* (Wolfe City, Tex.: Henington, 1993); Chuck Parsons and Marianne E. Hall Little, *Captain L. H. McNelly, Texas Ranger: The Life and Times of a Fighting Man* (Austin: State House Press, 2001).

    23. Walter Prescott Webb, *The Texas Rangers* (New York: Houghton Mifflin, 1935).

    24. Parsons, *Armstrong*, 1–2. On Reconstruction, see Eric Foner, *Reconstruction: America's Unfinished Revolution, 1863–1877* (New York: Harper and Row, 1988). For the specific dates of Tennessee's readmission to the Union and reestablishment of white conservative control, see William J. Cooper Jr. and Thomas E. Terrill, *The American South: A History* (New York: McGraw-Hill, 1991), 404.

    25. Carl H. Moneyhon, *Texas after the Civil War: The Struggle of Reconstruction* (College Station: Texas A&M University Press, 2004), 205. Moneyhon, as in all more synthetic works, drew heavily on the efforts of others, and he recognized that

not enough had been done on whites and the post-Reconstruction years. See pages 188–205, 227–28. For an exception to this pattern, see Randalph B. Campbell, *Grass-Roots Reconstruction in Texas 1865–1880* (Baton Rouge: Louisiana State University Press, 1997). For perspective on connecting blacks and whites in the South by focusing on labor, see Jacqueline Jones, "Labor and the Idea of Race in the American South," *JSH* 75 (August 2009): 613–26; Nicole Etcheson, "Reconstruction and the Making of a Free-Labor South," *RAH* 37 (June 2009): 236–42. For a thought-provoking summary of approaches to Reconstruction and a comparison with other such efforts, see Edward L. Ayers, *What Caused the Civil War? Reflections on the South and Southern History* (New York: Norton, 2005), 145–66. On the role of memory in shaping attitudes toward Reconstruction, see David W. Bright, *Race and Reunion: The Civil War in American Memory* (Cambridge, Mass.: Harvard University Press, 2001).

26. Richard Lowe, *Walker's Texas Division, C.S.A.: Greyhounds of the Trans-Mississippi* (Baton Rouge: Louisiana State University Press, 2004), 259, 253. For a brief review of recent literature, see Marc Egnal, "Why They Kept Fighting," *RAH* 37 (June 2009): 220–25.

27. Charles H. Harris III and Louis R. Sadler, *The Texas Rangers and the Mexican Revolution: The Bloodiest Decade, 1910–1920* (Albuquerque: University of New Mexico Press, 2004), 8, 502. By the late 1980s students of the Texas Mexican experience had moved beyond simple ethnic nationalism and a lack of differentiation in their definition of Tejanos, but Harris and Sadler do not incorporate this more recent literature. See Arnoldo De León, "Texas Mexicans: Twentieth-Century Interpretations," in *Texas Through Time,* ed. Buenger and Calvert, 41–49. Their work also lacks the comparative focus present in Andrew R. Graybill, *Policing the Great Plains: Rangers, Mounties, and the North American Frontier, 1875–1910* (Lincoln: University of Nebraska Press, 2007). Also see Elliot Young, review of Charles H. Harris III and Louis R. Sadler, *The Texas Rangers and the Mexican Revolution: The Bloodiest Decade, 1910–1920* in *American Historical Review* (*AHR*) 110 (October 2005): 1197.

28. For a sampling of recent revisionist work on Reconstruction, see Dale Baum, *The Shattering of Texas Unionism: Politics in the Lone Star State during the Civil War Era* (Baton Rouge: Louisiana State University Press, 1998); Dale Baum, *Counterfeit Justice: The Judicial Odyssey of Texas Freedwoman Azeline Hearne* (Baton Rouge: Louisiana State University Press, 2009); Barry A. Crouch, *The Freedman's Bureau and Black Texans* (Austin: University of Texas Press, 1992); Barry A. Crouch and Donaly E. Brice, *Cullen Montgomery Baker, Reconstruction Desperado* (Baton Rouge: Louisiana State University Press, 1997); Barry A. Crouch, *The Dance of Freedom: Texas African Americans during Reconstruction,* edited by Larry Madaras (Austin: University of Texas Press, 2007); William L. Richter, *Overreached on All Sides: The Freedmen's Bureau Administrators in Texas, 1865–1868* (College Station: Texas A&M University Press, 1991); James M. Smallwood, Barry A. Crouch, and Larry Peacock, *Murder and Mayhem: The War of Reconstruction in Texas* (College Station:

Texas A&M University Press, 2003); James M. Smallwood, *The Feud That Wasn't: The Taylor Ring, Bill Sutton, John Wesley Hardin, and Violence in Texas* (College Station: Texas A&M University Press, 2008); Patrick G. Williams, *Beyond Redemption: Texas Democrats after Reconstruction* (College Station: Texas A&M University Press, 2007). Revisionist work on the Civil War has been more limited, but see Ralph A. Wooster, *Lone Star Regiments in Gray* (Austin: Eakin Press, 2002); Ralph A. Wooster, *Texas and Texans in the Civil War* (Austin: Eakin Press, 1996). Some of the work on the Rangers actually moves beyond revisionism and will be cited below, but for a well-crafted comparative study, see Graybill, *Policing the Great Plains.* Also see Paul Cool, *Salt Warriors: Insurgency on the Rio Grande* (College Station: Texas A&M University Press, 2008).

29. For historians' views of some recent works, see Young, "Review of Charles H. Harris III and Louis R. Sadler, *The Texas Rangers and the Mexican Revolution: The Bloodiest Decade, 1910–1920,*" 1197; Jahue Anderson, "Review of David La Vere, *The Texas Indians* and Gary Clayton Anderson, *The Conquest of Texas: Ethnic Cleansing in the Promised Land, 1820–1875,*" H-AmIndian, H-Net Reviews, December 2006, at http://www.h-net.msu.edu/reviews/showrev.cgi?path=249441170438296.

30. Smith, *From Dominance to Disappearance,* xiii–xiv, 246.

31. Jesús F. de la Teja, *San Antonio de Béxar: A Community on New Spain's Northern Frontier* (Albuquerque: University of New Mexico Press, 1995), xi, 160.

32. De la Teja, *San Antonio de Béxar,* 24. This was also characteristic of some of the other fine work on Texas before 1821. See, for example, Donald Chipman, *Spanish Texas, 1519–1821* (Austin: University of Texas Press, 1992); Gerald E. Poyo and Gilberto M. Hinojosa, eds., *Tejano Origins in Eighteenth-Century San Antonio* (Austin: University of Texas Press, 1991). For a contrasting approach, see Ramón A. Gutiérrez, *When Jesus Came the Corn Mothers Went Away: Marriage, Sexuality, and Power in New Mexico, 1500–1846* (Stanford, Calif.: Stanford University Press, 1991).

33. Richard A. Garcia, *Rise of the Mexican American Middle Class: San Antonio, 1929–1941* (College Station: Texas A&M University Press, 1991), 11.

34. Garcia, *Rise of the Mexican American Middle Class,* 30, 54. For a more revisionist approach to immigration history that stressed the differences between immigrant groups and the tendency for some traits to persist over the generations, see John Bodnar, *The Transplanted: A History of Immigrants in Urban America* (Bloomington: Indiana University Press, 1985). Also see Emilio Zamora, *World of the Mexican Worker in Texas* (College Station: Texas A&M University Press, 1993); Emilio Zamora, *Claiming Rights and Righting Wrongs in Texas: Mexican Workers and Job Politics during World War II* (College Station: Texas A&M University Press, 2009).

35. Benjamin Heber Johnson, *Revolution in Texas: How a Forgotten Rebellion and Its Bloody Suppression Turned Mexicans into Americans* (New Haven, Conn.: Yale University Press, 2003), 39. For another very interesting examination of the development of Mexican American identity, see Anthony Quiroz, *Claiming Citizenship: Mexican Americans in Victoria, Texas* (College Station: Texas A&M University Press, 2005).

36. See, especially, Harris and Sadler, *The Texas Rangers and the Mexican Revolu-*

tion, 296–97. But also compare Harris and Sadler, *The Texas Rangers and the Mexican Revolution*, 210–318; 427–506, with Johnson, *Revolution in Texas*, 71–175.

37. Johnson, *Revolution in Texas*, 189. For another insightful look at the transformation of the region, see Elliott Young, *Catarino Garza's Revolution on the Texas-Mexico Border* (Durham, N.C.: Duke University Press, 2004).

38. Compare Johnson, *Revolution in Texas*, 176–211 with Garcia, *Rise of the Mexican American Middle Class*, 221–322.

39. Neil Foley, *The White Scourge: Mexicans, Blacks, and Poor Whites in Texas Cotton Culture* (Berkeley: University of California Press, 1997). For penetrating critiques of Foley's work, see Carlos Kevin Blanton, "George I. Sánchez, Ideology, and Whiteness in the Making of the Mexican American Civil Rights Movement, 1930–1960," *JSH* 72 (August 2006): 569–604; Zamora, *Claiming Rights and Righting Wrongs in Texas*, 9–11, 247–48.

40. For a map of what he calls Central Texas, see Foley, *White Scourge*, 16. For a recent study of Germans in a region on the border of what Foley called Central Texas, see Walter D. Kamphoefner, "The Handwriting on the Wall: The Klan, Language Issues, and Prohibition in the German Settlements of Eastern Texas," *Southwestern Historical Quarterly* 112 (July 2008): 53–66. Also see Walter L. Buenger, *The Path to a Modern South: Northeast Texas between Reconstruction and the Great Depression* (Austin: University of Texas Press, 2001), 75–103, 195–252; Walter L. Buenger, "Memory and the 1920s Ku Klux Klan in Texas," in *Lone Star Pasts: Memory and History in Texas*, ed. Gregg Cantrell and Elizabeth Hayes Turner (College Station: Texas A&M University Press, 2007), 119–142.

41. On the Blackland Prairie and the people of the midsection of Texas, see Rebecca Sharpless, *Fertile Ground, Narrow Choices: Women on Texas Cotton Farms, 1900–1940* (Chapel Hill: University of North Carolina Press, 1999); Rebecca Sharpless and Joe C. Yelderman Jr., eds., *The Texas Blackland Prairie: Land, History and Culture* (Waco, Tex.: Baylor University Press, 1993); Thad Sitton and Dan K. Utley, *From Can See to Can't: Texas Cotton Farmers on the Southern Prairies* (Austin: University of Texas Press, 1997). For another whiteness study that deals with some of the ethnic groups Foley mentioned, see Cynthia Skove Nevels, *Lynching to Belong: Claiming Whiteness through Racial Violence* (College Station: Texas A&M University Press, 2007). For one of the most nuanced looks at the white-black binary in Texas, see Gregg Cantrell, *Kenneth and John B. Rayner and the Limits of Southern Dissent* (Urbana: University of Illinois Press, 1993). This study of a white father and a black son shows the impact of race on a slightly earlier time period than Foley examines.

42. Angela Boswell, *Her Act and Deed: Women's Lives in a Rural Southern County, 1837–1873* (College Station: Texas A&M University Press, 2001); Judith N. McArthur, *Creating the New Woman: The Rise of Southern Women's Progressive Culture in Texas, 1893–1918* (Urbana: University of Illinois Press, 1998).

43. Brear, *Inherit the Alamo*; Richard R. Flores, *Remembering the Alamo: Memory, Modernity, and Master Symbol* (Austin: University of Texas Press, 2002). Other recent

books on the Alamo and San Antonio that emphasize memory and identity include Laura Hernández-Ehrisman, *Inventing the Fiesta City: Heritage and Carnival in San Antonio* (Albuquerque: University of New Mexico Press, 2008); Randy Roberts and James S. Olson, *A Line in the Sand: The Alamo in Blood and Memory* (New York: Free Press, 2001); Raúl A. Ramos, *Beyond the Alamo: Forging Mexican Ethnicity in San Antonio, 1821–1861* (Chapel Hill: University of North Carolina Press, 2008).

44. William D. Carrigan, *The Making of a Lynching Culture: Violence and Vigilantism in Central Texas, 1836–1916* (Urbana: University of Illinois Press, 2004), 2. Also see Patricia Bernstein, *The First Waco Horror: The Lynching of Jesse Washington and the Rise of the NAACP* (College Station: Texas A&M University Press, 2005). On another nearby lynching, see Monte Akers, *Flames after Midnight: Murder, Vengeance, and the Desolation of a Texas Community* (Austin: University of Texas Press, 1999).

45. Carrigan, *Lynching Culture,* 3.

46. For a more in-depth discussion of the causes of lynching, see Buenger, *Path to a Modern South,* 19–26, 165–73.

47. For a thoughtful comment on memory and Texas and an introduction to some of the growing literature, see Gregg Cantrell and Elizabeth Hayes Turner, "A Study of History, Memory, and Collective Memory in Texas," in *Lone Star Pasts,* ed. Cantrell and Turner, 1–14. Also see Flores, *Remembering the Alamo;* Brear, *Inherit the Alamo.*

48. Barr, *Peace Came in the Form of a Woman,* 287, 289. In addition to Smith, *From Dominance to Disappearance,* for discussions of Indians' impact on the Southwest, see Hämäläinen, *Comanche Empire;* Brian DeLay, *War of a Thousand Deserts: Indian Raids and the U.S.-Mexican War* (New Haven, Conn.: Yale University Press, 2008).

49. Barr, *Peace Came in the Form of a Woman,* 15.

50. Ibid., 287, 288.

51. Besides Campbell, *Gone to Texas,* and Jesús F. de la Teja, Paula Marks, and Ron Tyler, *Texas: Crossroads of North America* (Boston: Houghton Mifflin, 2004), other recent textbooks include Kenneth Wayne Howell, Keith J. Volanto, James M. Smallwood, Charles D. Grear, and Jennifer S. Lawrence, *Beyond Myth and Legend: A History of Texas* (Wheaton, Ill.: Abigail Press, 2008).

52. See, in particular, Campbell, *Gone to Texas,* 324–29.

53. See, for example, the brief discussion of slave religion in Calvert and De León, *History of Texas,* 107. Also see Randolph B. Campbell, *An Empire for Slavery: The Peculiar Institution in Texas, 1821–1865* (Baton Rouge: Louisiana State University Press, 1989); Buenger and Calvert, "Shelf Life," xxii–xxv.

54. Anderson, *Conquest of Texas,* 13; also see pages 359–61. On factual errors, see Randolph B. Campbell, "Review of Gary Clayton Anderson, *The Conquest of Texas: Ethnic Cleaning in the Promised Land, 1820–1875,*" *East Texas Historical Journal* 44, no. 2 (2006): 70–71. Also see Barr, *Peace Came in the Form of a Woman,* 1–15; Campbell, *Gone to Texas,* 194–206.

55. Campbell, *Gone to Texas,* 206. Also see page 83 for his similar statement about the role of missions in Indian life.

56. Ibid., 291, 296. On motivation behind Indian raids and warfare, compare Campbell, *Gone to Texas* with DeLay, *War of a Thousand Deserts.*

57. Campbell, *Gone to Texas,* 392. For a sampling of the voluminous literature available before the publication of *Gone to Texas* in 2003 on the broad movement for Mexican American and African American rights, see Francisco E. Balderrama and Raymond Rodríguez, *Decade of Betrayal: Mexican Repatriation in the 1930s* (Albuquerque: University of New Mexico Press, 1995); Garcia, *Rise of the Mexican American Middle Class;* Leticia Magda Garza-Falcón, *Gente Decente: A Borderlands Response to the Rhetoric of Dominance* (Austin: University of Texas Press, 1998); Richard Griswold del Castillo and Richard A. Garcia, *César Chávez: A Triumph of Spirit* (Norman: University of Oklahoma Press, 1995); Ignacio M. García, *United We Win: The Rise and Fall of La Raza Unida Party* (Tucson: University of Arizona Press, 1989); Ignacio M. García, *Viva Kennedy: Mexican Americans in Search of Camelot* (College Station: Texas A&M University Press, 2000); Benjamin Márquez, *LULAC: The Evolution of a Mexican American Political Organization* (Austin: University of Texas Press, 1993); Rodolfo Rosales, *The Illusion of Inclusion: The Untold Political Story of San Antonio* (Austin: University of Texas Press, 2000); Guadalupe San Miguel Jr., *Brown, Not White: School Integration and the Chicano Movement in Houston* (College Station: Texas A&M University Press, 2001); Zamora, *World of the Mexican Worker in Texas;* Thomas H. Kreneck, *Mexican American Odyssey: Felix Tijerina, Entrepreneur and Civic Leader, 1905–1965* (College Station: Texas A&M University Press, 2001); Ernest Obadele-Starks, *Black Unionism in the Industrial South* (College Station: Texas A&M University Press, 2000); John Downing Weaver, *The Senator and the Sharecropper's Son: Exoneration of the Brownsville Soldiers* (College Station: Texas A&M University Press, 1997).

58. Mary L. Kelley, "Review of Randolph B. Campbell, *Gone to Texas: A History of the Lone Star State,*" H-Texas, H-Net Reviews, January 2004, at http://www.h-net.org/reviews/showrec.cgi?path=282501078820056.

59. De la Teja, Marks, and Tyler, *Texas: Crossroads of North America,* xiii, xiv, xvi.

60. Ibid., 129, 131.

61. See Anderson, *Conquest of Texas,* 359–61, for an example of Anderson falling into the language trap of referring to Texans versus Indians, the insiders versus the outsiders.

62. Compare de la Teja, Marks, and Tyler, *Texas: Crossroads,* 129–32 with Calvert and De León, *History of Texas,* 26–28. Also see Anderson, *Conquest of Texas,* 3–17; Barr, *Peace Came in the Form of a Woman,* 1–15.

63. De la Teja, Marks, and Tyler, *Texas: Crossroads,* 275. Compare de la Teja, Marks, and Tyler, *Texas: Crossroads of North America,* 272–86, with the more detailed and nuanced treatment of Reconstruction in Calvert and De León, *History of Texas,* 127–52. For works available in the late 1980s, see Alwyn Barr, "African Americans in Texas: From Stereotypes to Diverse Roles," in *Texas Through Time,* ed. Buenger and

Calvert, 50–80. De la Teja, Marks, and Tyler could have made better use of such informative works as Campbell, *Grass-Roots Reconstruction in Texas;* Crouch, *The Freedman's Bureau and Black Texans;* Richter, *Overreached on All Sides;* Smallwood, Crouch, and Peacock, *Murder and Mayhem;* Baum, *The Shattering of Texas Unionism.* De la Teja, Marks, and Tyler also had the advantage of time to read and consider fully the monumental work, Foner, *Reconstruction.*

64. McCaslin, *At the Heart of Texas,* 125–259.

65. See, for example, Susan Wiley Hardwick, *Mythic Galveston: Reinventing America's Third Coast* (Baltimore: Johns Hopkins University Press, 2002); David J. Weber, *Bárbaros: Spaniards and Their Savages in the Age of Enlightenment* (New Haven, Conn.: Yale University Press, 2005); Young, *Catarino Garza's Revolution on the Texas-Mexico Border.*

66. This type of breakdown may be unique to Texas, but it might be interesting to compare the publications produced by the University of Texas Press and Texas A&M University Press with other flagship state presses such as the University of California Press or the University of North Carolina Press.

67. While a few books may have been inadvertently left off the list, given the large number of books on the list I doubt that enough were left out to change the upward trend line.

68. The number of books found for 2008 and 2009 was down slightly from 2007, but that may have been simply because reviews had not yet appeared and they did not make it on the other lists consulted to prepare the list of over 1,600 books published between 1988 and 2009.

69. For an interesting description of the transformation of once-rural Texas over the past forty years, see Linda Scarbrough, *Road, River, and Ol' Boy Politics: A Texas County's Path from Farm to Supersuburb* (Austin: Texas State Historical Association, 2005).

70. For a thoughtful description of the work on the Atlantic World see Alison Games, "Atlantic History: Definitions, Challenges, and Opportunities," *AHR* 111 (June 2006): 741–57. For examples of recent cross-border work, see Zamora, *Claiming Rights and Righting Wrongs in Texas;* Young, *Catarino Garza's Revolution on the Texas-Mexico Border.*

71. Hämäläinen, *Comanche Empire.* For a review of this work that points out the similarities with some very traditional and some revisionist books, see Dan Flores, "Review of Pekka Hämäläinen, *Comanche Empire,*" *Montana: The Magazine of Western History* 59 (Winter 2009): 74–76.

72. Andrés Reséndez, *Changing National Identities at the Frontier: Texas and New Mexico, 1800–1850* (Cambridge: Cambridge University Press, 2004).

73. Gregg Cantrell, *Stephen F. Austin: Empresario of Texas* (New Haven, Conn.: Yale University Press, 1999). For a work that focused even more squarely on sex and the family, see Mark M. Carroll, *Homesteads Ungovernable: Families, Sex, Race, and the Law in Frontier Texas, 1826–1860* (Austin: University of Texas Press, 2001). For an

example of an author who took a traditional topic and a popular approach, but still made a significant revisionist point, see James M. Smallwood, *The Feud That Wasn't: The Taylor Ring, Bill Sutton, John Wesley Hardin, and Violence in Texas* (College Station: Texas A&M University Press, 2008).

74. On trends in the United States, see Jill Lepore, "Historians Who Love Too Much: Reflections on Microhistory and Biography," *Journal of American History* 88 (2001): 129–44; Richard D. Brown, "Microhistory and the Post-Modern Challenge," *Journal of the Early Republic* 23 (2003): 1–20; Robert E. Shalhope, "Resurrecting Dead White Males," *RAH* 33 (June 2005): 162–68; Peter C. Messer, "The Romance of an Enlightened Founding," *RAH* 34 (September 2006): 307–14.

75. For an example of one historian whose work lies between the revisionist and cultural constructionist camp and seriously engaged the scholarship of Neil Foley, see Blanton, "George I. Sánchez, Ideology and Whiteness in the Making of the Mexican American Civil Rights Movement, 1930–1960." Also see Zamora, *Claiming Rights and Righting Wrongs in Texas,* 1–22.

76. William R. Childs, *The Texas Railroad Commission: Understanding Regulation in America to the Mid-Twentieth Century* (College Station: Texas A&M University Press, 2005). For a similar argument about government policy, see Keith J. Volanto, *Texas, Cotton, and the New Deal* (College Station: Texas A&M University Press, 2005).

77. In Randall B. Woods, *LBJ: Architect of American Ambition* (New York: Free Press, 2006), for example, Texas assumes a major role in shaping and renewing Lyndon Johnson and his policies. Also see Kent B. Germany, "Historians and the Many Lyndon Johnsons: A Review Essay," *JSH* 75 (November 2009): 1001–28.

78. For evidence of the impact of works that focus at least in part on Texas, see Jared Farmer, "Borderlands of Brutality," *RAH* 37 (December 2009): 544–52.

Into the Mainstream

The Emergence of a New Texas Indian History

Pekka Hämäläinen

At the turn of the 1980s, Native American history had entered a new era. Awakened by the Red Power movement of the 1960s and 1970s, inspired by the concurrent rise of social and subaltern histories, disillusioned by U.S. imperialism in Southeast Asia, and galvanized by the runaway success of Dee Brown's *Bury My Heart at Wounded Knee* (1970), the historians of indigenous North America found new purpose and new relevance.[1] They questioned old sensibilities and formulated new questions—How to write about Native past without imposing Western concepts on it? What are the parallels between the Vietnam War and the conquest of the Native American West? Shouldn't the approaching Columbus Quincentenary be a cause of criticism rather than celebration?—and in doing so transformed Native American history. They changed how we see America's first peoples and brought them to the center of historical inquiry. If earlier Native peoples had appeared in most historical works as blurry sketches on the frontier, posing a savage obstacle to Euro-American settlement or signifying a tragic victim of it, they now came in sharper focus as fully fledged historical actors. The movement was well off the ground by the 1970s, and by the 1980s it had a name: the New Indian History.[2] Yet a decade after its launch, the New Indian History had barely reached Texas. This changed dramatically over the years that followed the publication of *Texas Through Time* (1991), and after the 1990s those who wrote about Texas Indians often led rather than followed national trends.

The New Indian History has reconfigured not only Native American history but also American history in general. At the heart of the New Indian History was—and is—a simple shift in perspective with immense implications. Instead of observing things from colonial frontiers outward, the traditional default position of historical inquiry, the revisionist scholars placed themselves in Indian country to look how Native peoples saw and shaped historical developments. Often operating from the methodological middle ground where history and anthropology blend into ethnohistory, during the last two decades they have reconfigured the meaning of the events—first encounters, cross-cultural exchanges, colonial expansion, geopolitical shifts, environmental change—that gave rise to modern America. By underscoring indigenous agency, they have dismantled the persistent stereotype of Indians as passive victims of Euro-American conquest and recast them as co-creators of a complex world that was new for all.

The New Indian History features hundreds of works, among which a handful help define its content and contours: its emphasis on Native agency and insistence that Indians played a formative role in the making of colonial America; its insistence on the diversity, sophistication, and resilience of North America's indigenous societies and cultures; its linkages to the New Social History and subaltern studies; and its commitment to both historical and anthropological methods. Francis Jennings's prodigious body of work made it clear that the idea of a savage, infantile indigenous North America was nothing but a European fabrication, and that white settlers came to settle not a virgin but a "widowed land," a human landscape wrecked by imported Old World diseases. Focusing on eastern North America, Neal Salisbury and James Axtell have drawn attention to the long struggles for cultural hegemony in early America, and Colin G. Calloway has revealed the formative role that Native societies played in the making and unmaking of Anglo-America—including the American War of Independence. James H. Merrell has illustrated how Indians, Europeans, and Africans, while retaining distinct ethnic and cultural forms, blended together to forge a new world in which Native peoples held an ever-smaller foothold. Shifting the focus westward to the Great Lakes, Richard White has unveiled a resilient multiethnic contact zone where French and Indian peoples clashed and, failing to coerce one another, created a mutual world—a middle ground—on a series of cross-cultural practices that were neither entirely Indian nor European in nature. In a similar vein, Daniel H. Usner Jr. has shown how in the lower Mississippi valley Natives and newcomers created a flexible frontier exchange economy that followed its own distinct cultural logic and largely existed outside the grip of the expanding Atlantic economy. James F. Brooks and Alan Gallay have revealed how a defining North American institution—slavery—involved and transformed not only Europeans and Africans but Native Americans as well. In 2000, Alan Taylor placed Native societies at the center of his reexamination of early America and produced a stunning synthesis that effectively rendered the traditional Eurocentric narratives obsolete.[3]

The New Indian History forms the backdrop for this essay, which examines the major trends in the historiography on Native peoples in Texas during the last two decades. It shows how the New Indian History of Texas mirrors the genesis of its national counterpart and yet has a flavor that is distinctly Texan. Many of the works I review below challenge, at least implicitly, enduring popular stereotypes about the first peoples of Texas: that they were by rule nomadic, militaristic, and unsophisticated; that Texas Indian history is, for all practical purposes, synonymous with Comanche history; and that Euro-American colonialism ignited an asymmetrical struggle for survival with clear ethnic demarcation lines and inevitable outcomes. The essay will also trace how the history of Texas Indians has reflected the broader concerns of American Indian scholarship and, equally important, how the historians of indigenous Texas have contributed to the continuing florescence of the New Indian History. During the past twenty years, in fact, Texas Indian history has percolated—along with its immediate context, the study of indigenous Southwest—from the margins into the mainstream of Native American history.

There are several reasons for this, a couple of them obvious. Since the 1990s, many historians who write about Texas Indians have made a conscious effort to write for a national rather than a "Texas History" audience, and their work draws from the broadest historiographical currents; their studies are grounded in Texas, but their concerns and ambitions are national, hemispheric, and global. With that broadening of visions, new interpretive approaches have come to inform Texas Indian history, opening up entirely new lines of inquiry from gender relations and cross-cultural violence to identity formation and comparative transnational histories. Then there is the creative thrust emanating from the blurring of academic boundaries: many current writers of Texas Indian history appear to be Indian historians only secondarily. Like their counterparts elsewhere, they have embraced more complex narrative modes in which Native American history intertwines with, and partly blends into, colonial, borderlands, transatlantic, and environmental histories, producing works that speak to scholars in several fields. And finally, maybe Texas history itself has something to do with the rise of Texas Indian history. For well over a century, Texas was a remarkably fluid borderland world where numerous Native societies, Spaniards, French, Mexicans, and Anglo-Americans vied for power and jockeyed for position. It was a world of open outcomes where many cultural formations, social arrangements, and systems of power could come into existence—a veritable laboratory for the study of cross-cultural relations. For many scholars who came of age with the many "new" histories, Texas suddenly seemed irresistible.

The vigor of Texas Indian history is visible throughout the field, but two strands stand out: tribal histories and histories of Indian-white relations.

Rethinking the Tribal History

An anachronism cuts through this essay: it reviews the histories of the Native peoples who lived within the boundaries of the modern state of Texas, but Texas as a distinct political or cultural entity did not start to take shape until the mid-nineteenth century—by which time most "Texas Indians" had already disappeared from the historical record or were in deep decline, verging toward collapse. The rise of Anglo-Texas and its relentless drive to impose its claimed boundaries would eventually become a massive fact for the region's Indians—virtually all Native groups were expulsed from the state by 1880. Yet "Texas Indians" never really existed. Most Native nations living in what would become Texas also lived in other states that did not yet exist: New Mexico, Oklahoma, Kansas, Colorado, and, south of the Rio Grande, Tamaulipas, Nuevo León, Coahuila, and Chihuahua. Their territories and historical influence extended far beyond the boundaries of Texas, which makes them a rather problematic subject for our purposes: focusing only on the Texas aspects of their past would diminish them as historical actors, while granting detailed coverage to, say, Comanche activities in Zacatecas or New Mexico would undermine the very agenda of this volume. My solution to this dilemma is a slightly tilted balance: I have covered the works that examine such wide-ranging nations as the Apaches, Jumanos, Wichitas, Caddos, Comanches, and Kiowas in full but will pay relatively greater attention to the segments that focus on Texas.

Although only a piece in more expansive Native histories, Texas nevertheless formed a broad canvas on which Indians forged a remarkably diverse array of cultures and ways of life. Scholars have traditionally divided Texas Indians into three broad groups that reflect the state's distinctive bioregions: there are the hunter-gatherers on the Gulf Coast, the nomadic bison hunters on the western high plains, and the semisedentary hunter-farmers of the eastern prairies and forests. This basic division has continued to inform the recent scholarship, which has produced several innovative tribal histories within each subregion. In the 1990s, in fact, these tribal histories formed the cutting edge of Texas Indian history, paving the way for the broadly conceived synthetical and interpretive works of the new millennium.

One of the most impressive of the new tribal histories is Nancy Parrott Hickerson's study of the Jumanos, an enigmatic group of hunters and farmers of the far southern plains. It has been an old debate in southern plains ethnology whether "Jumanos" referred to a specific ethnic group or was applied more generally to disparate groups sharing a broad territorial base. Hickerson, in her *The Jumanos* (1994),[4] says that both views are correct—an insight that allows her to rescue the Jumanos from obscurity and bring a vast slice of early American history into sharper focus.

The recorded history of the Jumanos is short—they first appear in the accounts of the sixteenth-century Spanish explorers and fade from the historical record soon after 1700—but during that brief window they left a deep historical imprint on the southern plains. The Jumanos, Hickerson argues, were a multiethnic yet distinct group of Tanoan speakers who occupied a wide range between New Mexico in the west and the plains-prairie ecotone in the east and employed a range of economic strategies: some lived as bison hunters on the open plains of the Llano Estacado and the Edwards Plateau, others farmed small plots along the Rio Grande, and still others occupied frontier villages near Salinas, partly blending into the Puebloan world.

Although widely scattered, Hickerson argues that the Jumanos shared several cultural and linguistic traits and were connected through a sophisticated commercial network that mantled the southern plains. Indeed, it was as middleman traders that the Jumanos would come to play their most lasting historical role. Perusing through the meager archaeological, historical, and linguistic evidence with a fine comb, Hickerson shows how the Jumanos controlled an interregional trade system linking the Puebloan and Caddoan worlds through the plains—an intermediary role that continued into the colonial period when Spanish settlers in New Mexico and Nueva Vizcaya attached themselves to the Jumano trade network. Thanks to their far-reaching connections, the Jumanos obtained horses early, possibly from Nueva Vizcaya, and may have introduced equestrianism among the Caddos, Tonkawas, and other Texas nations. But the dynamism and diversity that defined the Jumanos, Hickerson suggests, also contributed to their downfall. Their wealth and commerce drew competitors from the north, and they were powerless against the expanding Apaches who committed to equestrian life and warfare more fully than the Jumano generalists. Hickerson's argument that many Jumanos were gradually absorbed into Apache bands, rendering a strong multiethnic touch to the new masters of the southern plains, is fresh and intriguing. Her hypothesis that some Jumanos survived in central Texas to become the nucleus of the Kiowa Indians is bound to remain more controversial.

If Hickerson has filled a large gap in the sixteenth- and seventeenth-century southern plains (and Texas) history, Robert A. Ricklis has lifted the Karankawas from the depths of historical neglect and misrepresentation. His *The Karankawa Indians of Texas* (1996)[5] dismantles a number of stereotypes about the Karankawas, perhaps the most slandered of Texas Indians. Rather than the giant-size cannibal primitives of older histories, Ricklis's ethnohistory casts them as an adaptive society of hunter-gatherer-fishers struggling to maintain their way of life in their rapidly changing coastal homelands. Instead of accepting the traditional view of the Karankawas as sixteenth-century immigrants to Texas, Ricklis, through a careful examination of archaeological evidence, extends their presence on the coastal plains back some two millennia. The Karankawas disappeared as an ethnic group in the mid-nineteenth century, but Ricklis refuses to read back their decline under Euro-American colonialism to exhaust their story: after decades of mutual violence with Spanish newcomers, the Karankawas incorporated the Franciscan mission of Refugio into their seasonal subsistence pattern as a supplementary source of meat and grain. Although the arrangement eventually led to the Hispanization of the Karankawas, it did for a while buttress their survival. This is a significant contribution to the wave of new mission studies that examine colonial religious institutions from the indigenous perspective and question the assumption that cross-cultural accommodation automatically erodes indigenous traditions.[6]

Kelly F. Himmel has further deepened our understanding of the Karankawa survival and decline with *The Conquest of the Karankawas and the Tonkawas* (1999), which draws on the world systems theory, historical sociology, structure/agency theory, and postcolonial theories of racial "othering"—all approaches that figured little in the pre-1988 Texas Indian scholarship. Where Ricklis emphasizes indigenous adaptability, Himmel stresses geography and human agency: the Karankawas offered Spanish Texas a buffer against the imperial ambitions of the Louisiana-based French, English, and Anglo-Americans, and therefore could draw concessions from the Spaniards—only to lose those privileges with the rapid Anglo-Americanization of Texas after the 1830s. Himmel accentuates his point with a contrast to the Tonkawas who were useful to the Spanish, Mexican, and even Anglo-Texans as a barrier against Apache and Comanche raids but lost their political leverage when Texas statehood made border control the responsibility of the U.S. Army. Himmel concentrates on geopolitics, but he also incorporates cultural analysis to show how Anglo-Texans reinvented the Karankawas and Tonkawas as uncivilizable savages to justify their dispossession. That the Tonkawas had been staunch allies of Anglo-Texas meant little when cotton Texas began to boom: they were removed to a reservation in Indian Territory in 1859.

The books on the Jumanos, Karankawas, and Tonkawas are important in their own right, but together they have engendered a larger historiographical shift: they have rectified a long-standing imbalance in Texas Indian history, which tended to focus on the big nations—above all the Comanches—at the expense of the smaller groups. Still, in terms of sheer output—three biographies and four tribal histories—the Comanches have continued to dominate the recent Texas Indian scholarship.[7]

The four Comanche histories of the 1990s and 2000s are an eclectic lot. The novelist-poet Stanley Noyes's *Los Comanches* is a sprawling, at once impressionistic and narrative-driven account of the Comanches and their relations with Euro-Americans before the U.S. annexation of Texas. Noyes focuses on Comanche relations with Spain, Mexico, and the Republic of Texas and stops his history in 1845 because, he states, the story of the Anglo-Comanche clash on the Texas frontier is so well known. The book sheds slivers of light on warfare and captivity in Comanchería and the shifting, multiangled geopolitical struggles on its borders, but its insights rarely rise above the anecdotal with Noyes's "cinematic" technique of flashbacks and vignettes of Comanche society and culture; *Los Comanches* is heavy on action but short of analysis.

Like T. R. Fehrenbach's popularized and still popular *Comanches* (1974), the book it most resembles, *Los Comanches* depicts the Comanches, even if unintentionally, as enigmatic, warlike people, the perennial other who can be marveled at rather than understood. It lodges firmly on the traditional side of the crevasse that has opened during the past two decades in Texas historiography between the conventional histories and the new revisionist studies, but it stands there rather alone. The revisionist scholars have all but taken over Texas Indian history in terms of the number of books published, and their sometimes aggressive criticism has punched several holes in the intellectual and theoretical foundations of the older scholarship. And yet, the revisionists' hold over the broader readership remains tenuous at best. Although often widely respected in academia, they are not necessarily widely read outside of it. Whether the revisionists will succeed in drawing in the popular audience is difficult to predict, but there are some clues: Fehrenbach's *Comanches* is still, after more than three decades after its initial publication, being reprinted.[8]

If *Los Comanches* represents the conventional drama-centered approach to Indian history, Gerald Betty's *Comanche Society* (2002) exemplifies the opposite approach. *Comanche Society* is a theory-driven attempt to understand Comanche actions and institutions—migrations, wars, nomadism, horse pastoralism, social organization—through the interpretive lens of kinship. More an exercise in sociobiology or evolutionary psychology than history, the book makes an unflinchingly determined—and deterministic—bid to explain the totality of Comanche history as a function of kinship. Where *Los Comanches* belongs to a historiographical line that extends Fehrenbach's *Comanches* and, ultimately, Rupert Norval Richardson's *The Comanche Barrier to South Plains Settlement* (1933), *Comanche Society* marks a solitary resurgence of the mid-twentieth-century anthropological practice of dissecting indigenous societies into their composite parts and debating which one of those parts defined the whole.[9]

Paramount among the new Comanche histories are Morris W. Foster's *Being Comanche* (1991) and Thomas W. Kavanagh's *Comanche Political History* (1996), two works that exist in a fruitful dialogue with each other. Foster's innovative ethnohistory opened a new chapter in Comanche studies—and in Texas Indian history in general—by focusing not only on the Comanches' relations with Euro-Americans but also on their intracommunity organization, which both structured and was restructured by their foreign political maneuvering. Much of *Being Comanche* deals with the Comanches' social organization after their final defeat and 1875 confinement in Indian Territory and thus falls outside the scope of this volume, but Foster's first chapter on the nomadic phase alone redirected Comanche scholarship on new paths. In contrast to E. Adamson Hoebel and Ernest Wallace's 1954 classic *The Comanches,* which for decades remained the yardstick for Comanche ethnology, Foster argues that the Comanches' flexibly informal social organization was a source of strength rather than weakness. Comanches, he shows, were more than the sum of their relations with Euro-colonial powers. They survived and even expanded in the midst of Euro-American settlements for nearly two centuries by constantly readjusting their social and economic arrangements to meet new challenges. That flexibility carried over from the nomadic life in Texas to reservation existence in Oklahoma. The social gatherings and face-to-face relations that had sustained the Comanche community on the open plains continued to do so, even if in mutating forms, in the confines of the reservation. The Comanche history in Oklahoma, in other words, marks less a break than continuation of the Comanche history in Texas.[10]

Kavanagh's *Comanche Political History* builds upon Foster's insights while also challenging them. Kavanagh shares Foster's view of the adaptability of the Comanches, again contesting the old idea of the Comanches as a robust yet rigid obstacle to Euro-American expansion, but he sees that flexibility manifesting itself more on the macroscale, in the ethnogenesis of the Comanche community. The Comanches, Kavanagh insists, were less a "tribe," a fixed political entity, than an ever-changing constellation of political groups—family clusters, local bands, and regional divisions—that rose and fell in line with the availability of such economic and political resources as bison, commerce, and Euro-American gifts. He traces every major historical source of Comanche–Euro-American relations in a roughly chronological order, detailing Comanche interactions with New Mexico and Texas through the Spanish, Mexican, and American periods. The effect may be encyclopedic and mechanistic—the changes in Comanche political organization are reduced to shifts in colonial realms and seem to take place in a cultural and social vacuum—but *Comanche Political History* renders an invaluable historiographical service. This is particularly true for Texas history. By offering a thorough chronology of Comanche-Spanish, Comanche-Mexican, and Comanche-Anglo interactions in war, trade, and diplomacy in Texas, Kavanagh puts to rest the enduring notion that Comanche-Texas relations were defined by violence and distrust.

One of the iconic horse-mounted buffalo tribes of the plains and the last of the Texas Indians to leave the state, the Comanches immediately captured the Anglo-Texan imagination. The popular fascination translated into scholarly interest in the early twentieth century, and Comanche studies have dominated Texas Indian historiography ever since. The Comanche-centric tradition did not start to break until recently, and the first to experience a historiographical restoration were the Caddos. Indeed, the 1990s witnessed a virtual burst of Caddoan studies. Timothy K. Perttula's 1992 *"The Caddo Nation"* launched the line and was followed, in a rapid succession, by F. Todd Smith's *The Caddo Indians* (1995), Cecilia Carter's *Caddo Indians* (1995), and David La Vere's *Caddo Chiefdoms* (1998).[11]

These four studies complement rather than compete with one another, providing a broad and multiangled view into Caddo history. Drawing mainly on archaeological evidence, Perttula reconstructs a sequence of precipitous population decline among the three Caddoan confederacies—the Kadohadachos, Hasinais, and Natchitoches—caused by droughts and disease and culminating in around 1650, a finding that makes the Caddos' postcontact flexibility analyzed by Carter and Smith all the more remarkable. Smith focuses on the strategic importance of the Caddos on the Texas-Louisiana borderlands and at the convergence of competing Euro-American powers—first Spain and France, then Spain and the United States, then Mexico and the United States, and, finally, the Texas Republic and the United States—that allowed them to engage in effective play-off politics. Carter, an enrolled member of the Caddo Tribe of Oklahoma, traces a similar sequence of geopolitical balancing but links the Caddos' resilience to the strength of their cultural traditions.

La Vere, in contrast to Smith's and Carter's chronological analysis, takes a thematic and emphatically multidisciplinary approach to Caddo history, but he also draws on their insights. Like Carter, La Vere stresses the importance of cultural traditions and shows how the Caddos' conviction in their ideals of kinship, reciprocity, and chiefly power allowed them to bend European needs to their advantage. They assumed an active role in the postcontact gun and horse trade by becoming middlemen between the Puebloan and Mississippian peoples, and they maintained their commercial and diplomatic power into the eighteenth century in face of Apache, Osage, and Choctaw raids. What gives La Vere's version particular resonance is his grasp of the complex, interlaced trajectories of external and internal change. To cope with the mounting pressures of Euro-American colonialism, he argues, the Caddos became more unified even as one group, the Kadohadachos, exploited its geopolitical centrality to gain prominence over other Caddo chiefdoms. Over time, the Kadohadachos came to symbolize to the wider Caddoan community its link to the splendor of their Mississippian past—a belief that was shattered with the death of the last great Kadohadacho chief, Dehahuit, in 1833.

The prolific Smith has also written the first scholarly history of the Wichita Indians, whose experiences in Texas had close parallels with those of the Caddos. Indeed, Smith's *The Wichita Indians* (2000) is in many ways a companion volume to his *The Caddo Indians:* both display extensive use of underutilized French and Spanish sources, both provide a chronology-driven and policy-centered analysis of their subject, both emphasize external relations over internal dynamics and cultural analysis, and both structure the indigenous past around shifts in Euro-American colonial fortunes. As in his Caddo history, geography is destiny, although with somewhat different outcomes: while the Caddos benefited, at least initially, from their location in between Euro-American empires, the Wichitas were squeezed between the rock of Spanish Texas and the hard place of the expansionist Comanches, Osages, and Anglo-Americans. The interpretation, then, is distinctly declinist: caught in the middle, the Wichitas struggled to adapt to the rapidly shifting colonial world that gradually subsumed theirs. Smith ends his narrative in the U.S. annexation of Texas in 1845, when the Wichitas' power was all but broken, but his earlier book, *The Caddos, the Wichitas, and the United States* (1996) picks up the story from there, tracing the horror and suffering of Caddos and Wichitas under the belatedly adopted and soon abandoned reservation system of Texas. Like Foster's *Being Comanche,* Smith's *The Caddos, the Wichitas, and the United States* also shows how the relocated Caddos and Wichitas adapted but never abandoned their traditions in the alienating conditions of Indian Territory, where they were forced to share a reservation with their former Comanche and Kiowa enemies.[12]

Like the Caddos and Wichitas, the Lipan Apaches are finally emerging behind the long Comanche shadow. Although they played a formative role in Texas history for nearly four centuries, the Lipan Apaches had never been the subject of a comprehensive history until Thomas A. Britten's *The Lipan Apaches: People of the Wind and Lightning* (2009).[13] Drawing on archaeology, ethnographic studies, Lipan oral histories, and archival sources, Britten provides a sweeping view into the history of the Lipans from their emergence in the Texas High Plains in the sixteenth century through their successive dispossessions in the hands of the Comanches, Spaniards, Mexicans, the Texas Republic, and the United States. Britten traces how the Lipans adopted horses—one of the first Native groups in North America to do so—and how their equestrian mobility fixed them as a perennial threat in the minds of Euro-American newcomers. Britten paints a bleak picture of Lipan past that is not unlike Smith's rendering of Wichita history. Pushed from the north by the expanding Comanches and curbed in the south by Spanish Texas, the Lipans shifted from one coping strategy to another: they abandoned the plains homelands for the desert lands of southern Texas and Coahuila by the mid-eighteenth century; they sought protection at Texas missions in the 1750s and 1760s only to become targets of a systematic war of extermination by Spaniards who aligned themselves with the Comanches; and, as the rise of Anglo-Texas made tribal dissolution imminent, they forged an alliance with the more populous Mescaleros, Tonkawas, and Kiowa Apaches, vanishing from historical record by 1884. What elevates Britten's history above the many passionate but simplistic studies of Native American dispossession is its meticulous attention to the Lipans' creative adaptability in the face of overwhelming odds. Britten shows how the Lipans managed to maintain a foothold in Texas by repeatedly reinventing their economy, by residing on both sides of the U.S.-Mexico border to elude colonial control, by accepting veritable vagrancy as a survival mechanism, and, finally, by seeking a kind of alliance that promised biological survival through ethnic termination.

Innovative tribal histories have given the Indian history of Texas a vibrant new look. Old stereotypes of stagnant, inherently warlike indigenous societies have been taken apart, and the Native nations of Texas now appear as politically creative, socially complex, and culturally dynamic entities capable of constantly reinventing themselves to survive in rapidly changing conditions. The old classification of Texas Indians into coastal hunter-gatherers, plains hunters, and prairie agriculturalists continues to frame the field but now appears less a rigid division than a continuum that featured such economically and culturally diverse groups as the Jumanos. And while Texas Indian history will always be defined by the expulsion of all Native societies from the state in the late nineteenth century—the twentieth-century Texas Indian history is a history of a few minority fragments—some scholars have begun to look beyond the removal into the cultural and historical continuities that link such Oklahoma peoples as Comanches and Wichitas to their Texas pasts.

But there are still gaps to be filled. Many of the new tribal histories are rather narrowly conceived political studies that focus on such male activities as diplomacy, trading, and raiding. In contrast with the most ambitious and challenging tribal histories from the broader national scene—Loretta Fowler's *Arapahoe Politics* (1982), John H. Moore's *The Cheyenne Nation* (1987), Daniel K. Richter's *The Ordeal of the Longhouse* (1992), Frederick E. Hoxie's *Parading through History* (1995), Claudio Saunt's *A New Order of Things* (1999), and Susan Miller's *Coacoochee's Bones* (2003)—Texas scholars are yet to fully incorporate ecological interpretations, cultural analysis, decolonization theories, and current theoretical approaches to ethnicity, class, and gender in the study of individual Native nations and societies.[14]

Moreover, while intensive, the coverage has not been exhaustive. The Kiowas, major players in Texas history, and many smaller tribes await up-to-date histories.[15] Just how big historiographical holes such selective coverage leaves is suggested by Maria F. Wade's painstaking *The Native Americans of the Texas Edwards Plateau* (2003), which identifies no less than twenty-one different Native groups living on the seventeenth-century Edwards Plateau. The histories of the removed southeastern Indians in Texas form another underexplored topic. David La Vere's *Contrary Neighbors* (2001) examines the (mostly) violent clash between removed and resident Indians across the southern plains and prairies—a clash that he sees somewhat simplistically as one over modes of production between southeastern agriculturists and plains hunters—but the relations between the removed tribes and Anglo-Texas need more concerted examination; the only recent study to have done so is Dianna Everett's *The Texas Cherokees* (1990), which emphasizes the Cherokees' desperate efforts for accommodation and their deepening factionalism in the geopolitical vortex of Texas borderlands. And most important: Texas historiography still features only one tribal history written by a tribal member.[16]

Where People and Fields Meet: Texas and the Histories of American Encounters

Out of tribal histories has grown another flourishing subfield of Texas Indian history, the study of Native American–Euro-American relations. Most of the tribal histories discussed above double as studies of Indian-white relations as they examine how internal dynamics and external relations became intertwined to shape tribal experiences. But the new works on Indian–Euro-American relations in Texas have another source: the rising field of borderlands studies, which during the past two decades has revolutionized American history by drawing attention to cross-cultural encounters in places that fall in between the traditional units of historical analysis—empires, nation states, civilizations, and ethnic cores. Where earlier scholarship sought the makeup of American history—especially early American history—from metropolitan designs, dividing frontiers, rising national power, and hardening borders, borderland histories have emphasized indigenous agency, cultural hybridity, and enduring local arrangements.[17]

I will start the discussion on the historiography of Indian–Euro-American relations in Texas with studies that examine Indian-white relations primarily from a Euro-American perspective and will then move to studies that shift the angle of vision to the Native side. I will conclude by reviewing works that focus on the final defeat and dispossession of Texas Indians in the mid- and late nineteenth century.

The Columbus Quincentenary in 1992 saw the publication of two major syntheses, Donald E. Chipman's *Spanish Texas* and David J. Weber's *The Spanish Frontier in North America,* which represent two contrasting approaches to Texas and Texas Indian history.[18] Chipman's masterful narrative history focuses on Spanish exploration, settlement, and institutions in Texas, and while it does not ignore indigenous Texas, Indians mostly appear as raiders, diplomatic prospects, or targets for missionizing; they are a foil on which Spanish dreams of colonization and fears of failure are reflected. Chipman should not be criticized for delving into all things Spanish, but his narrative shortchanges the significance the Native Americans had in shaping the Spanish colonial experience in Texas. Chipman's Indians are a perennial yet marginal threat to Spanish Texas, an ambiguous frontier concern eclipsed by the far-graver dangers posed by French and Anglo-American imperialism. The opening chapter of *Spanish Texas,* which emphasizes the diversity of the region's indigenous peoples, anticipates a narrative in which Indians would be central actors, but then the Indians fade out of focus.[19]

Weber's *The Spanish Frontier,* in contrast, makes it clear that coming to terms with indigenous societies—both conquered and subjugated ones—was critical for Spain's colonial experience in North America in general and in Texas in particular. *The Spanish Frontier* is a broadly conceived work that outlines the Spanish colonial experience in North America, but its principal goal is to explore the three centuries of change along the frontier that spanned the continent. Weber defines frontiers not as dividing boundaries but as fluid meeting places of different cultures, a nonreductionist approach that opens an illuminating window into Spanish-Indian relations: Indians emerge as major protagonists, the Spanish frontier is recast as a contact zone of contestation and accommodation, and Spanish colonialism emerges as an inherently negotiated process. One of Weber's great themes is to dispel the myth of the reactionary and unimaginative Spanish colonists by elucidating the creativity and flexibility with which Spanish officials approached the Indian question, and the isolated and often neglected Texas is his case in point. Texas, precisely because of its demographic weakness and strategic vulnerability, was often among the first in Spain's American colonies to implement new frontier policies, including the late eighteenth-century shift from war and missions to diplomacy and commerce as tools of frontier pacification. Such a dynamic Indian policy allowed Texas, a small colonial island in a vast indigenous sea, to survive and, to a degree, even prosper.

Weber's choice to frame his study of New Spain's North American extension around the concept of the frontier rather than that of the borderlands, the time-honored interpretive device since Herbert Eugene Bolton's classic 1921 study that coined the term,[20] captures the extent to which Native American history had come to inform larger colonial histories. Unlike his predecessors, Weber does not cast Spain's North American colonies as an obstacle—or a historiographical foil—for the westward expanding Anglo-Americans; for him, the relationship with Native powers was the critical factor shaping Spanish colonial experience in the far north. The importance of indigenous presence and purposes for the understanding of Spanish imperialism also informs Weber's recent synthesis *Bárbaros* (2005), which narrows the time frame of *The Spanish Frontier* to the late Bourbon era but expands its geographic scope to both Americas, providing a unique comparative view of cross-cultural encounters at the edges of the empire. *Bárbaros* focuses on the late eighteenth-century Bourbon efforts to secure the empire's strategic frontiers where the empire faced expansionist Euro-American rivals, an effort that hinged on Spain's ability to control and co-opt the independent Indians caught in the middle. Weber's comparative lens is particularly revealing for Texas. Placed in a hemispheric context, Spanish Texas and the Texas Indians find their closest parallels not in the bordering New Mexico or Louisiana but in Chile and in the La Plata provinces of today's Uruguay.

Spanish settlers in both Texas and La Plata felt threatened by other Euro-American powers—the former by France and then Britain, the latter by Portugal—which allowed the regions' Native groups to deal alternatively with various colonial powers and play them against one another. The agricultural Caddos of the Texas-Louisiana borderlands find their historical counterpart in the nomadic Charrúas of La Plata: although their lifeways diverged, both groups capitalized on their location on strategic frontiers to amass power that belied their numbers. The Comanches, too, find in *Bárbaros* an illuminating parallel in the far south—the Araucanians of south-central Chile. While again different in their economic strategies—the Araucanians were initially part-time farmers—the two groups had strikingly similar historical trajectories at the edges of the Spanish Empire. Both incorporated Spanish horses and metal weaponry to counter Spanish colonialism, both built extensive trading networks on stolen Spanish livestock, both used their equestrian power to conquer vast grassland territories, both spread their language and culture among surrounding Native societies, both developed more centralized and hierarchical sociopolitical systems to better deal with the demands of colonial officials, and both came to dominate vast regions in the midst of Spanish colonial outposts. Like no other work, *Bárbaros* examines Spanish and Native Texas as part of the larger hemispheric history, shedding much-needed comparative light on Texas and, through it, on other American places and societies.[21]

The Mexican period and the Indian policies of the Mexican Republic have not received as intensive coverage as the Spanish period in recent Texas historiography. Nearly three decades after its publication, Weber's 1982 *The Mexican Frontier* remains the definite work. *The Mexican Frontier* focuses on Anglo-American infiltration and expansion into the Southwest, a threat that loomed across Mexico's North American frontier through its brief existence, but it also incorporates Indians as major historical protagonists. The Mexican Republic, Weber argues, lost its hold on the Southwest largely because it failed to contain the regions' independent Indians, whose raids engulfed the borderlands and extended deep into Mexico. The failure to pacify the Indians alienated the beleaguered northern citizens from Mexico City and kept the borderlands sparsely populated—a fatal weakness the westward-moving Anglo-Americans were able to exploit, especially in Texas.[22]

While Weber's grand narrative of Mexican-Indian relations in Texas still holds, recent works have added important nuances to it. The most significant of the new studies is Andrés Reséndez's *Changing National Identities at the Frontier* (2005), which directs attention to the shifting and partially overlapping ethnic identities among the many peoples of Texas, including the Native Americans. Like Mexicans and Anglo-Americans, Native peoples adopted (or at least projected) situational identities to cope with the often-ambiguous political and economic circumstances on the borderland that was being simultaneously pulled toward two nation-states, Mexico and the United States. Groups like the Comanches and Kiowas, Reséndez shows, could be loyal Mexican subjects, steadfast friends of the Americans, or fiercely independent nations depending on the situation. Like Euro-Americans, Native Americans could manipulate national labels and symbols to further their own interests. Although the rise of nation-states would eventually circumscribe their lives, Native peoples were not passive victims in the sweeping historical sequence whereby Southwest borderlands became bordered lands.[23]

Major works like Weber's *The Spanish Frontier* and Reséndez's *Changing National Identities* feature key elements of the New Indian History—they look at both sides of frontiers, emphasize Native agency, and incorporate indigenous voices—but, in the end, they are Native American histories only secondarily. Their task is to explain such Euro-American-centered historical problems as the Spanish experience in North America or the shift from Spanish to Mexican to American rule in the Southwest, and, appropriately, they include Native Americans only to the extent that they are relevant to their master narratives. But the past two decades have witnessed the rise of revisionist studies that have located Indians at the very center of colonial and early national histories. By looking at developments from the Indian side and by foregrounding indigenous agency, they have questioned the validity of the entrenched colonist-colonized dichotomy and have suggested alternative ways to think about the Indians, European imperialism, and the directions of change. Such scholarship reached an early fruition in Richard White's 1992 *The Middle Ground,* and the first major work in Texas history was Gary Clayton Anderson's *The Indian Southwest* (1999).[24]

The Indian Southwest examines Indian–Euro-American and Indian-Indian relations across the so-called near Southwest (Texas, eastern New Mexico, and the southern Great Plains) from the sixteenth to the early nineteenth century. The book is in some ways a companion volume to two previous theoretically oriented *longue durée* overviews of cross-cultural relations in the Southwest—Edward H. Spicer's *Cycles of Conquest* (1962) and Thomas D. Hall's *Social Change in the Southwest* (1989)—which it both engages and challenges. While Spicer and Hall framed their monumental histories around acculturation and world systems theory, respectively, Anderson's overarching theme is ethnogenesis, the emergence, disappearance, and reinvention of human societies. Mirroring Spicer, Anderson emphasizes the dynamic (if not indeed cyclical) nature of southwestern history, and like Hall, he embeds his interpretation in economic forces, but his conclusions differ significantly from those of his predecessors. Both Spicer and Hall saw an uneven but in time overwhelming expansion of Euro-American imperialism as the defining theme of southwestern history, whereas Anderson finds the governing feature in a recurring process of indigenous ethnogenesis that thwarted Euro-American hegemonic ambitions in the Southwest into the 1830s. One of Hall's key insights was that the great historical turning point in the Southwest was not so much the U.S. incorporation between 1821 and 1848, but the late eighteenth-century Bourbon Reforms, which laid the foundation for daily life in the region through Indian pacification and economic development. Such views hold little interest for Anderson, who portrays the old Southwest as a vibrant ethnic stew in which the constantly transforming Native societies—the Jumanos, Apaches, Comanches, Wichitas, and Caddos—managed to control their economies and destinies through the Spanish colonial era.[25]

Anderson's self-proclaimed ambition is to challenge a "Bolton school" of borderlands history as represented by Spicer and David Weber among others and the formalist school of historical thinking as reflected by Hall and Richard White—the former for what he sees as its disregard for Native peoples and agency, the latter for its anachronistic reliance on concepts like supply and demand, rational choice, and profit motive in analyzing the economic behavior of precapitalist indigenous societies. The critique is misguided; if anything, *The Indian Southwest* builds upon the insights forwarded by the historians Anderson criticizes. His argument of the centrality of Native notions of kinship, exchange, and reciprocity in Indian–Euro-American transactions is conceptually a near replica of White's *The Middle Ground,* and his portrayal of the Southwest echoes Weber's vision of the beleaguered Spanish colonists whose attempts to exert control over Native societies failed more often than succeeded.

Where *The Indian Southwest* does break new ground is in its analysis of Indian-Indian relations in the Southwest and particularly in Texas. The ability of Native societies to resist Euro-American incorporation, Anderson shows, stemmed from their success in subjugating and absorbing other Native societies. Behind the failure of Spanish colonialism on the southern plains was a repeating cycle of indigenous expansion, dispossession, and amalgamation. By uncovering that cycle, Anderson bestows Texas Indian history with a dynamic chronology, which, in an abridged form, runs as follows. The multiethnic Jumanos, whose seventeenth-century ascendancy sprang from their ability to control long-distance commerce in colonial products, were replaced in the early eighteenth century by the horse-mounted Apaches, who occupied the Jumanos' trading niche, absorbed some of their members into their ranks, and adopted a policy of alternate raiding and trading toward Spanish Texas and New Mexico. Wichita and Caddo traders eclipsed the Apaches by the mid-eighteenth century, and thus empowered, blocked the expansion of Spanish mercantilism to the interior, but they, too, failed to maintain their power: their allies the Comanches, "the masters of ethnogenesis," extended their influence across the southern plains by the late eighteenth century, dispossessing some of their Native rivals, absorbing others, and eventually dominating all. The broad outlines of this indigenous history were known before, but *The Indian Southwest* makes the first systematic effort to explain its mechanics: in the shifting world of the southern plains, where Euro-American interventions, new technologies, erratic climate, and fluctuating animal populations kept things in a flux, those with the greatest capacity for reinvention prevailed. Only after the 1830s, Anderson argues, when the expansion of the United States realigned Indian-centered regional economies, turned existing alliances obsolete, and triggered devastating disease epidemics, did the era of indigenous power in Texas come to an end.

Like Anderson, Martha McCollough examines, in her *Three Nations, One Place* (2004),[26] the political and economic maneuverings Native societies employed to preserve their autonomy in the face of Spanish colonialism. But where Anderson takes a sprawling panoramic view of the Southwest, McCollough provides a focused comparative analysis of the adaptive strategies of two contrasting Native societies, the nomadic Comanches and the agricultural Hasinais (the third nation of her title is New Spain). The canvas is smaller than Anderson's but the narrower lens provides a more penetrating look. McCollough frames her analysis around world systems theory, regional analysis, and social history, a multifaceted approach that yields a layered picture of the governing conditions that determined the limitations of Native autonomy and power in colonial Texas. The world systems approach shows how the Comanches and Hasinais became entangled in an expanding web of global markets and how each group struggled to identify new economic and political opportunities among the myriad of influences that were rapidly changing the world. The key opportunity, the regional analysis shows, was trade in colonial products, although the two groups were differently positioned to exploit the colonial commercial geography. The more mobile Comanches became interregional actors, stealing horses in Spanish New Mexico and Texas and selling them to French Louisiana, while the Hasinais enhanced their economic and political clout by playing off Spanish and French interests on the Texas-Louisiana borderlands. But McCollough's look into Comanche and Hasinai social histories illustrates that power came with cost. Both groups decentralized their political structures in order to better exploit economic openings on colonial frontiers, although differences were again at least as significant as the similarities. Comanches, McCollough argues, retained their power throughout the Spanish era because their mobile and dispersed settlement patterns allowed them to avoid disease epidemics and adapt to changing geopolitics, whereas the more sedentary Hasinais grew increasingly weaker. The withdrawal of the French from Louisiana in 1763 undermined their borderland tactics, Comanches' growing commercial reach left them economically marginalized, disease epidemics decimated their numbers, and Osage raids from the north turned their homelands into war zones.

Here, in the reconstruction of these contrasting indigenous trajectories, is McCollough's main contribution to Texas history. Her dual history of the Comanches and Hasinais sheds new light on both groups in ways in which traditional tribal histories cannot. The similar yet distinct histories of the two societies highlight the cultural variability of Texas Indians and the complexity of Texas colonial history. The Comanches and Hasinais fared differently at the edges of European imperialism because they were unequally situated to exploit its offerings and escape its threats and because their distinctive cultural backgrounds guided their adaptive strategies on particular paths. As in many works reviewed here, geography conditions change, but in *Three Nations* its stranglehold on history is diluted by culture.

Juliana Barr's *Peace Came in the Form of a Woman* (2007) narrows Anderson's and McCollough's temporal and geographical sweep to eighteenth-century Texas, but the tighter focus is offset by Barr's conceptual and theoretical ambition. Cutting-edge Native American and borderlands history, *Peace Came in the Form of a Woman* engages the recent studies that have shown how indigenous cultural forms persisted on colonial frontiers, providing a Texas version of Richard White's Great Lakes middle ground, Jane T. Merritt's culturally porous mid-Atlantic frontier, and Kathleen DuVal's lower Arkansas valley Native ground. More than a full-blown middle ground, Barr's Texas resembles DuVal's Native ground, a contested contact zone where colonists had to accept and adapt to indigenous cultural forms. Barr also builds on the broad foundation laid by James Brooks's *Captives and Cousins* (2002), which brought Indian slavery, gendered notions about masculine honor and interethnic violence, and nondominant frontiers in the borderlands to the core of early American history. Indeed, *Peace Came in the Form of a Woman* introduces to Texas historiography many of the themes of *Captives and Cousins,* which focuses on New Mexico and its borderlands and discusses colonial Texas only fleetingly.[27]

Like Brooks, Barr makes an efficient use of gender as an analytical lens into larger cross-cultural dynamics on colonial borderlands. Adopting a thematic approach, she traces how Native notions of kinship, masculinity, femininity, and honor shaped and structured Indian-Spanish relations in such arenas as diplomacy, marriage, religion, exchange, violence, and captivity. Spanish colonial Texas emerges here as a demographically and politically feeble outpost, an isolated ethnic enclave whose attempts to extend Spanish influence into Native domains were doomed to fail. That failure, according to Barr, was most visible in Spanish designs to use gender as a rhetoric device to denigrate, disfranchise, and eventually reconfigure Native societies. Texas, she argues, became a unique borderland setting where indigenous ideas of gender remained the standard for more than a century after the first wave of colonization.

Examples abound. Caddos, alienated by Spanish refusals to marry into their families, gravitated toward French Louisiana rather than Spanish Texas. The beleaguered Coahuiltecans, Tonkawas, and Karankawas sought protection from Apache expansion in Franciscan missions, but instead of becoming docile mission Indians, they clung to their cultural values and traditional annual round and left the Franciscans every spring. In Spanish-Apache interactions in Texas—just as in New Mexico—the capturing and redemption of Native women and children became both the central cause for declaring war and the central conduit for making peace. And when Spaniards moved to forge a broad alliance with the powerful *norteños* (the allied Comanches, Wichitas, and Caddos) in the 1770s, they soon discovered that the only way to have peace was to accept Native women as political mediators, welcome Native men as brothers, and use language that bespoke to indigenous sensibilities about masculine honor. Peace, in short, could only be had in Native terms. A major work not only in Texas Indian history but in the New Indian History in general, *Peace Came in the Form of a Woman* provides a model for North American borderlands and frontier studies in which gender as an analytical tool has often figured prominently but never quite as powerfully.

My *The Comanche Empire* (2008) again adopts a wide angle to reexamine cross-cultural power relations across the Southwest, the Great Plains, and northern Mexico. It challenges the long-standing idea of the Comanches as an obstacle to Euro-American expansion, arguing that the barrier metaphor leaves out half of the story.[28] The Comanches not only resisted Euro-American imperialism, I argue, but overturned the conventional colonial dynamic. They reduced Euro-American imperial regimes to building blocks of their own imperial organization that dominated the Southwest for over a century. That imperial structure was not a mirror image of the classic Western empires with central metropolises and demarcated frontiers—the nomadic Comanches relied on more informal arrangements—and yet it eclipsed its various Euro-American and Native rivals in military prowess, political prestige, economic power, commercial reach, and cultural influence. The Comanche empire was powered by violence—its economic foundation rested on coerced extraction of resources and labor through raiding, slaving, and tribute payments—but it was, above all, an economic construction that allowed the Comanches to control trade on colonial frontiers and across the Great Plains. Hard military and economic power translated into softer forms of power, and Comanches spread their language and culture across the mid-continent and incorporated foreign ethnicities as adopted kinspeople, dependents, and vassals. Their standards of war, peace, exchange, and atonement largely determined how things were done on what historians have labeled as the *Spanish* or *Mexican* borderlands. Comanches' foreign political ascendancy sprang from their cultural flexibility, their willingness to constantly reinvent themselves. As their external ambitions reached imperial heights, Comanches developed a centralized political system, a dynamic market-oriented dual economy of hunting and pastoralism, and a hierarchical social organization with room for a complex division of labor and vast gradations in possession and privilege.

The Comanche Empire reevaluates the dimensions of indigenous agency and proposes a new model for the history of Native–Euro-American relations in North America, one that embraces the contingency of historical change, challenges the assumption that the fate of Native societies was an irreversible slide toward dispossession, and does not automatically prioritize Euro-American initiatives over indigenous ones. Comanche imperialism, it argues, helps explain why Mexico's far north is today the American Southwest: it is the forgotten component in the sprawling colonial drama that saw Spain failing to colonize the interior of North America and Mexico losing its northern half to the United States in a mere generation. Comanche ascendancy devastated and marginalized New Mexico, accelerating its gravitation toward U.S. wealth and protection during the Mexican era, but its most tangible legacy was in Texas. Comanche power politics reduced Texas to a tributary captive state and raiding hinterland, profoundly altering its historical trajectory.

The Comanche Empire discusses the impact of Comanche policies in Texas through the revolutionary and early statehood eras, a theme that is fully developed in Brian Delay's *War of a Thousand Deserts: Indian Raids and the U.S.-Mexican War* (2008), a brilliantly detailed study of the causes and consequences of indigenous violence in Texas and northern Mexico in the 1830s and 1840s.[29] Together, the two books show how Texas' split from Mexico and its tenure as the Lone Star State both had a Comanche dimension: Mexico's decision to open the state to Anglo immigration was motivated by the need to protect it against Comanche raids—raids that soon engulfed much of northern Mexico, rendering Mexican efforts to recapture Texas impossible. The linkages between American and Comanche expansions culminated in the U.S.-Mexican War, in which Mexico faced not one but two invading powers at once. The ensuing U.S.

takeover of the Southwest cannot be fully understood without an indigenous framework: by 1846, Comanches had turned much of northern Mexico into a shattered raiding domain that was militarily and psychologically susceptible for the U.S. occupation.

New Questions and Larger Contexts: Texas Indians and Anglo-American Takeover

The Comanche empire disintegrated under spiraling ecological degradation and the defeat of the Comanche nation at the hands of Texas militia and the U.S. Army, but the Comanches' history is only one among the many stories of Texas Indian dispossession.[30] A topic long skirted by professional historians, the Anglo-American takeover of the Native Texans has come under intensive scrutiny in recent years, and among the new studies three stand out: F. Todd Smith's *From Dominance to Disappearance* (2005), Gary Clayton Anderson's *The Conquest of Texas* (2006), and Andrew Graybill's *Policing the Great Plains* (2007). Although different in their analytical and narrative modes, these three books together provide a comprehensive up-to-date narrative of the long decline of Native power in Texas from the early nineteenth century to the dawn of the twentieth century.[31]

From Dominance to Disappearance is Smith's explicit sequel to Elizabeth A. H. John's magisterial *Storms Brewed in Other Men's Worlds* (1975), which chronicled Spanish-Indian relations in and around New Mexico and Texas from first encounters to the closing years of the eighteenth century, when Anglo-American influences slowly began to penetrate the region.[32] John ended her narrative in the period of tenuous accommodation between the Spaniards and Indians, and Smith, leaving out New Mexico, picks up the story from there and follows it through the short-lived Texas reservation experiment in the 1850s. As in his trilogy on Wichita and Caddo histories, Smith focuses on geopolitics and economic trends and, based on shifts in indigenous fortunes in those arenas, divides Texas Indian history into two distinct parts. The first, extending from the mid-1780s to the Texas Revolution, is marked by Indian dominance. It was a chaotic period in Texas, witnessing intensifying Spanish-U.S. rivalries on and over the Texas-Louisiana border, bitter civil disputes during the prolonged Mexican War of Independence, and a growing presence of Anglo filibusters and removed southeastern Indians; yet the powerful resident Native nations, the Comanches, Wichitas, and Caddos, retained control over their homelands, livelihoods, and the regional economy. The Spanish and then the Mexican Texas could not seriously challenge indigenous autonomy. But the balance of power shifted abruptly against the Indians in the late 1830s, when Texas won its independence and was flooded by American settlers. For the first time, Texas Indians lost their demographic advantage over Euro-Americans, and the result was their swift defeat and dispossession. Native power in Texas, Smith argues, was broken in the 1840s, and by the end of the next decade it was gone.

That rise-and-fall scheme structures Smith's book, providing a useful chronological baseline for Texas Indian history, but Smith also adds significant nuance to the picture. His analysis advances on two levels, gauging the overall balance of power between Native and European Americans while also tracing the distinct trajectories of individual indigenous communities. The result is the most comprehensive account of Texas Indian dispossession to date, one that dismantles a number of long-standing stereotypes about the Indian-white clash in Texas. Smith shows, for instance, how some Native groups sought accommodation rather than confrontation with the Anglo newcomers in their efforts to preserve their homelands, and how the Republic of Texas exploited those efforts to enforce asymmetrical treaties that engendered Anglo dominance and Native dependence. The Anglo-American conquest of Texas that Smith uncovers was not only a bloody military affair but a subtle diplomatic project as well.

Another key insight is that there was more than just one dispossession narrative: some Native communities all but disappeared well before the onset of large-scale Anglo intrusion in the 1830s, while others expanded their domains, often at the expense of other Indian groups, through the first half of the nineteenth century. The dispossession of Texas Indians thus appears something much more complicated than a simple Indian-white conflict. But eventually—and perhaps inevitably—a less ambiguous story emerges. The rapidly procreating land-hungry Anglo-Texans betray their treaty obligations, invade Native homes, and wreck indigenous ecosystems; the Anglo voices promoting coexistence with Indians drown in a rising tide of racially driven expansionist fervor; and the federal government, its authority circumscribed by the unique conditions of Texas' entrance into the Union, fails to preserve a Native foothold in Texas. *From Dominance to Disappearance* traces each of the many Native roads out of the increasingly Anglo-dominated Texas—the Comanche, Kiowa, Wichita, and Caddo exoduses to Indian Territory; the Tonkawa and Lipan Apache migrations to Mexico; the Karankawas' collapse into extinction—in a measured, dispassionate manner that has a crushing emotional effect. In a narrative packed with numerical data, a single figure can speak volumes. On the eve of the Civil War, 213 Coushattas and Alabamas remained the only reservation Indians living in Texas.

Anderson's *The Conquest of Texas* focuses on the Anglo-Americanization of Texas between 1820 and 1875 and partly overlaps with *From Dominance to Disappearance,* but the two books could hardly be more different in tone. Where Smith is neutral and scholarly, Anderson is all fury and admonition. For him, the Anglo takeover of Texas is a story of greed, brutality, and anarchy undergirded by a culture of violence that arose from a transplanted Southern code of honor, toxic racial hatred, and the lack of restraining political institutions. Anderson's historiographical target is the Texas creation myth, which demonized Indians as savage raiders and rapists, celebrated white settlers as harbingers of civilization, and canonized the Texas Rangers as the protectors of order. His counternarrative casts the making of Anglo-Texas as a spontaneous and haphazard but eventually systematic policy of ethnic cleansing. Its agents were white Texans across the social strata—settlers, ranchers, businessmen, land speculators, politicians, journalists, desperados, Rangers—who conducted vigilante raids into Indian villages, authorized wanton massacres of Native women and children, and vilified Indians to justify their eradication in the name of progress and freedom.

This story of Indian declension is a disturbing read. Anderson chronicles in detail how the Anglo immigrants to Texas clashed immediately and violently with the host Indians; how the removal of thousands of southeastern Indians wrecked the delicate Native-Tejano political economy in Texas; how Anglo land lust and Indian hating turned Comanche, Kiowa, Wichita, and Caddo homelands into war zones; how a combination of racist rhetoric and mob violence forced the dismantling of the newly established Texas reservations; and how the paramilitary Texas Rangers indiscriminately killed Indians along the chaotic frontier for five decades. The picture that emerges from Anderson's account is Anglo-Texans harassing and slaughtering peaceful Indians with nearly pathological zeal, an interpretation that will—and has—struck many as biased, a kind of latter-day Texas Black Legend.[33] *The Conquest of Texas* is passionate work with a maximized argument that rests on a reversal of the Texas myth: here Indians are the heroic freedom fighters and whites the savages. The book delivers a necessary corrective to Texas hagiography, but its portrayal of Texas Indians is sanitized and simplistic, glossing over issues like indigenous militarism and Indian-Indian violence. If earlier histories of the rise of Anglo-Texas—books like Richardson's *The Comanche Barrier to South Plains Settlement* and T. R. Fehrenbach's *Lone Star* (1968)—often depicted Indians as predatory raiders without order, *The Conquest of Texas* tends to reduce them to victims without agency. But in the end *The Conquest of Texas* is an Indian history only secondarily. Its real subjects are Anglo-Texan politics and their agonizing, harrowing legacy in the Southwest.[34]

Thesis-driven and doggedly revisionist, *The Conquest of Texas* promotes a new brand of Texas exceptionalism: the history of the state between 1845 and 1875, Anderson argues, was "unique and more violent than any of the other states that Texas joined in 1845, or that joined later."[35] Graybill's *Policing the Plains,* in contrast, places the consolidation of Anglo rule in Texas in an international context by comparing the parallel roles of the Texas Rangers and Canada's North-West Mounted Police in rendering their respective sections of the North American frontier safe for Euro-American settlement, capitalism, and big business. Although the book is only concerned with Anglo-Native relations after the Texas legislature institutionalized the Rangers as a police constabulary in 1874, the picture it yields is illuminating. The Rangers and the Mounties played nearly identical roles in Indian–Euro-American relations— both became powerful instruments of industrial incorporation and indigenous dispossession—but their tactics were a study in contrast: the Rangers relied on lethal force to keep the Comanches, Kiowas, and Apaches out of Texas and in Indian Territory and New Mexico, where they became the responsibility of the federal government, while the Mounties relied mostly on nonviolent means to keep the Indians peaceful in their ancestral lands.

Why the difference? Where Anderson sees Ranger brutality as a direct expression of an Anglo-Texan mentality and its distinct combination of land lust and genocidal racism, Graybill's comparative approach provides a complex model that incorporates historical, cultural, economic, and social explanations. The two constabularies, he emphasizes, derived from distinct martial traditions and were differently organized. One was modeled after the centrally run and strictly disciplined Royal Irish Constabulary; the other drew from a long tradition of local volunteer militias. One was led by well-educated career officials and took pride in its professionalism; the other paraded its individualism and informal structure. It also mattered that the Mounties were a federal body and the Rangers a state-controlled one: the Mounties served as the face of the Dominion throughout the North-West territories, drawing on its deep resources and moderated by its laws, whereas the Rangers were a tool to meet the narrowly self-interested needs of a state that often openly flouted federal imperatives. Such juxtapositions allow Graybill to provide a fresh interpretation of the final dispossession of Texas Indians, one that makes the process seem at once contingent and inescapable—contingent because Texas shared many of its governing conditions with the North-West Territories where Native subjugation was relatively nonviolent, inescapable because so many of the things that defined Anglo-Texas—its troubled history with nonwhite peoples, its culture of individuality, its informal frontier institutions, its staunch defiance of the federal government—primed it for ethnic violence.

Taking the Measure of the Field: Two Generations, Two Overviews

In 2004, David La Vere published *The Texas Indians,* the first comprehensive overview of Texas Indian history in two generations, supplanting W. W. Newcomb Jr.'s *The Indians of Texas* from 1961. La Vere is a historian and Newcomb was an anthropologist, but a comparison of the two works makes it possible to gauge how the field has changed since the 1960s and especially over the past two decades when historians became interested in Texas Indian history in large numbers.

The first thing that grabs attention is language. Reflecting the conventions of his era, Newcomb labeled the Coahuiltecans and Karankawas as "Savages of the Western Gulf Area" and the Jumanos, Wichitas, Caddos, and Atakapas as "Barbaric Gardeners." Adhering to the stereotype of single-minded war-driven plains nomads, his Comanches were "the Terror of the Southern Plains" and the Kiowas "Far-Ranging Raiders." La Vere abandons the dated, racially laced classifications and sets out to demystify the Indians by peeling off stereotypes. His discussions of Native cultural traditions, social arrangements, and political actions are sprinkled with adjectives like "dynamic," "complex," and "resilient"—staple epithets in the New Indian History.[36]

The second major difference is organization. Newcomb discussed each of the major Native nations separately, detailing their subsistence strategies, material culture, social organization, and religious practices, an approach that reflected the guiding boundaries of the field of Native American history well into the 1980s. Indians were considered more of ethnological than historical interest, and scholars saw them more as cultural artifacts than historical agents. La Vere, in contrast, adopts a chronological approach and traces the major epochs in Texas Indian history—the emergence of first civilizations, encounters with Europeans, the Apacheanization of the Jumano world, the brief Apache-Spanish dominance in west Texas in the early eighteenth century, the concurrent consolidation of Native-French relations in east Texas, the rise of Comanches and their allies in northwest Texas, the clash between the host and the removed Indians, and the Anglo-Indian wars and the expulsion of Native nations from Texas. Although change often comes to Native Texas from without—the introduction of the horse and foreign diseases, the arrival of the Spanish mission system, the withdrawal of France from North America, and the Anglo influx emerge as major turning points—Indian agency shapes events and outcomes. Indians occupy center stage in La Vere's narrative, which traces how Native societies variously retreated and expanded, warred and accommodated, splintered and merged, simplified and diversified their economies to survive and exploit the forces unleashed by European colonialism.

La Vere's survey also makes it possible to assess the progress in the various subfields within Texas Indian history. The structure and themes of *The Texas Indians* reflect the prodigious strides that historians have made in the study of individual tribes and Indian-colonial relations in Texas. Especially striking is the sophistication with which La Vere is able to trace the migrations, colonial encounters, survival strategies, and eventual dispossession of such smaller groups as the Akokisas, Bidais, Deadoses, Mayeyes, Yrvipiames, Yojuanes, Yguaces, and Tiguas. Drawing on the work of Nancy Parrott Hickerson and Gary Clayton Anderson in particular, La Vere puts to rest the old idea of Texas as a tribal graveyard, where numerous little Native societies were squeezed out of existence under the double pressure of indigenous expansions (first Jumano, then Apache, and finally Comanche) and Spanish colonialism. Native groups may have vanished from the historical record, but their members survived, sometimes in fragments under new names, more often melting into multiethnic Jumano, Apache, Comanche, and Spanish communities. Biological purity or national exclusiveness carried little significance in colonial and indigenous Texas.

Like much of the recent scholarship, *The Texas Indians* dwells on the eighteenth and nineteenth centuries, but it also looks deeply into the preceding centuries and ahead into the twentieth century. Scholars like Timothy K. Perttula and Donny L. Hamilton have expanded the long tradition of Texas Indian archaeology through numerous case studies, and La Vere provides an enlightening synthesis of the accumulated but often fragmented evidence.[37] The common cultural canvas of kinship, gender, and religion is never far from sight, but La Vere's main theme of early Texas Indian history is accelerating divergence, which culminated in the rise of distinct regional cultural spheres by the late first millennia. By 1000, he concludes, Texas had become a confluence of several contrasting cultural traditions: the Mississippian culture was spreading in from the east and the Puebloan culture from the west, producing numerous local variants of both in between. And by 1500, out of that divergence had emerged the familiar ethnic map of the Caddos, Wichitas, Atakapas, Tonkawas, Karankawas, Coahuiltecans, and Apaches that Spanish colonists would soon encounter.

The Texas Indians ends with an overview of twentieth-century Texas Indian history, still "an open field" in La Vere's words. La Vere reviews the experiences of the former Texas Indians in Oklahoma—the Comanches, Kiowas, Wichitas, Caddos, and others—but more pertinent for our purposes is what he has to say about the remaining resident Texas tribes, the Alabama-Coushattas, Tiguas, and the Kickapoo Traditional Tribe of Texas. The histories of these three tribes, La Vere notes, mirror the twentieth- and twenty-first-century experiences of many other Native peoples in the United States. They have endured government neglect, acculturation pressures, ecological exploitation, and the threat of termination, and they have sought economic openings in forestry, tourism, and gaming, often with mixed results. But the history of the Texas tribes, La Vere's survey suggests, is also distinct and in deeply ironic ways. The Alabama-Coushattas, Tiguas, and Kickapoos have found unexpected opportunities in Texas precisely because the state's record with Native Americans has been so dark. Many Texans have been pleasantly surprised to find that there are Indians still living among them, and the state has sometimes shown exceptional largesse toward the remaining tribes, whose very weakness ensures that the financial burden will remain small. The future—and future studies—will show whether there is a tipping point, after which Native potential and perseverance become once again too much for Texans to accept.

Pasts, Futures, Memories

During the past two decades, Texas Indian history has changed almost beyond recognition. Gone are the old stereotypes of Indians as primitives beyond the pale, as helpless victims of the Anglo-American expansion or exquisitely violent insurgents who resisted the conquest to the last heroic breath. Renounced, too, is the notion of Native American history as an exotic subcategory in Texas history and of Indians as bystanders of the more important story of the creation of an Anglo-American state out of a wilderness. Instead of such worn formulations we now have the new Texas Indian history, a robust, self-consciously revisionist movement that has all but displaced the older histories. For good or ill, its concerns and sensibilities are now the new orthodoxy.

The New Indian History has changed how we see Texas Indians as historical actors—creative, accommodating, forceful, and flawed all at once; they have finally emerged behind the cardboard caricatures as full-fledged human beings. But the new Texas Indian history has also reconfigured Texas history itself. Such seemingly self-evident concepts as "colonial Texas" or "the Spanish frontier" have been historicized and their validity as foundational concepts challenged. The linearly progressing Euro-American-centric master narrative has been realigned toward an indigenous axis, and a sense of contingency—and drama—has been restored to it. The old interpretations that lionized the lives and actions of the Texas frontiersmen who pacified the Natives have been replaced by more expansive narratives that capture the enormity of the human tragedy that flowed from the dispossession of the Texas Indians.

Historians of indigenous Texas have also entered nationwide debates, elevating colonial Texas from a regional curiosity to one of the focal points of North American historiography. Scholars of ethnogenesis, gender, violence, and slavery in early America now have to look to Texas to locate the cutting edge of their respective fields. By writing extensively on the nineteenth century, moreover, historians of Texas Indians have helped move the New Indian History beyond the confines of early American history, where its impact has been most pronounced.[38] And finally, the new Texas Indian history has challenged our understanding of what Indian agency means. Studies of other American places have underscored Indians' ability to bend others to their will and govern their own destinies even under the direst of conditions, but historians are yet to recover the full extent of Indian agency in American history. Indians, the consensus view goes, managed to postpone dispossession by forcing modifications in colonial policies, but not much more. They maneuvered, resisted, adapted, and survived, but the governing historical processes emanated from the designs and dynamics of colonial powers. It is at this historiographical juncture that Texas Indian history has perhaps made its most visible intervention. Recent scholarship has recast colonial Texas as a world of Indian dominance—dominance that ranged from sporadic frontier moments when Indians determined the terms of interaction to entire epochs of indigenous hegemony—an insight that raises challenging questions for historians of other places and periods. Was Texas unique or are there other examples of nearly complete Indian dominance over colonial regimes? What are the connections between local and regional developments—such as the Indian ascendancy over Spanish and Mexican Texas—and larger continental trends like the rise of the United States or the emergence of the modern geopolitical map? Is it possible to write the histories of other North American regions with Native peoples at their center, and what would such histories look like?

Yet the story of Texas Indians is not complete. The new Texas Indian history is in many ways only a framework that needs more detail and nuance to satisfy. Although there have been important recent openings, a comparative history of pre-1900 Texas and Texas Indians is still in its infancy, allowing lingering notions of Texas exceptionalism to creep into scholarship. We also need histories that ask some hard questions about the indigenous societies and their adaptive choices. For example, what role has class played in Texas Indian history? Have historians stressed the homogeneity of Native societies over their schisms and fault lines over wealth, rank, and race? What is the legacy of human bondage among societies like the Comanches who practiced large-scale slavery in the pre-reservation period? Have historians tended to infantilize Indians as economic actors? Was there, for example, such a thing as Native consumerism, and if so, what role did it play in colonial relations and may it have contributed to the decay of indigenous ecosystems? Have historians overemphasized tradition over calculation and the structural over the situational when explaining the behavior of Texas Indians, thereby reinforcing, even if unintentionally, the conventional view of Indians as inflexible reactionists incapable of modernization? And, finally, there are the big, largely unanswered questions about the historical memory of Texas and the Indians' place in it. How are Texas Indians remembered outside academia—in museums, monuments, and schools—and how much have the revisionist views penetrated those venues? If Texans insist on depicting Indians in certain ways—menacing, nomadic, unchanging—is it simply to justify their dispossession, or is there something else, something distinctly Texan, behind it? Or am I just promoting yet another brand of Texas exceptionalism by asking that?

Notes

1. Dee Brown, *Bury My Heart at Wounded Knee: An Indian History of the American West* (New York: Bantam Books, 1970). No one did more than Vine Deloria Jr. to bring the concerns of the Red Power movement into academic debates. See, for example, Vine Deloria Jr., *Custer Died for Your Sins: An Indian Manifesto* (New York: Macmillan, 1969); and Vine Deloria Jr., *We Talk, You Listen: New Tribes, New Turf* (New York: Macmillan, 1970).

2. For historiographical overviews of the New Indian History, see R. David Edmunds, "New Visions, Old Stories: The Emergence of a New Indian History," *OAH Magazine of History* 9 (Summer 1995): 3–9; William T. Hagan, "The New Indian History," in *Rethinking American Indian History,* ed. Donald L. Fixico (Albuquerque: University of New Mexico Press, 1997), 29–42; and Ned Blackhawk, "Look How Far We've Come: How American Indian History Changed the Study of American History in the 1990s," *OAH Magazine of History* 19 (November 2005): 13–17.

3. Francis Jennings, *The Invasion of America: Indians, Colonialism, and the Cant of Conquest* (Chapel Hill: University of North Carolina Press for the Institute of Early American History and Culture at Williamsburg, 1975); Francis Jennings, *Founders of America: How Indians Discovered the Land, Pioneered in It, and Created Great Classical Civilizations; How They Were Plunged into a Dark Age by Invasion and Conquest, and How They Are Reviving* (New York: W. W. Norton, 1993); Neil Salisbury, *Manitou and Providence: Indians, Europeans, and the Making of New England, 1500–1643* (New York: Oxford University Press, 1982); James Axtell, *The Invasion Within: The Contest*

of Cultures in Colonial North America (New York: Oxford University Press, 1985); James Axtell, *Natives and Newcomers: The Cultural Origins of North America* (New York: Oxford University Press, 2000); Colin G. Calloway, *The American Revolution in Indian Country: Crisis and Diversity in Native American Communities* (New York: Cambridge University Press, 1995); Colin G. Calloway, *New Worlds for All: Indians, Europeans, and the Remaking of Early America* (Baltimore: Johns Hopkins University Press, 1997); James H. Merrell, *The Indians' New World: Catawbas and Their Neighbors from European Contact to the Era of Removal* (Chapel Hill: University of North Carolina Press, 1989); Richard White, *The Middle Ground: Indians, Empires, and Republics in the Great Lakes Region, 1650–1815* (New York: Cambridge University Press, 1991); Daniel H. Usner Jr., *Indians, Settlers, and Slaves in a Frontier Exchange Economy: The Lower Mississippi Valley before 1783* (Chapel Hill: University of North Carolina Press, 1992); James F. Brooks, *Captives and Cousins: Slavery, Kinship, and Community in the Southwest Borderlands* (Chapel Hill: University of North Carolina Press for the Omohundro Institute of Early American History and Culture, 2002); Alan Gallay, *The Indian Slave Trade: The Rise of the English Empire in the American South, 1670–1717* (New Haven, Conn.: Yale University Press, 2002); and Alan Taylor, *American Colonies: The Settling of North America* (New York: Viking, 2001). Other major works in the New Indian History outside the Southwest include: Matthew Dennis, *Cultivating a Landscape of Peace: Iroquois-European Encounters in Seventeenth-Century America* (Ithaca, N.Y.: Cornell University Press, 1993); Eric Hinderaker, *Elusive Empires: Constructing Colonialism in the Ohio Valley, 1673–1800* (New York: Cambridge University Press, 1997); Andrew R. L. Cayton and Fredrika J. Teute, eds., *Contact Points: American Frontiers from the Mohawk Valley to the Mississippi, 1750–1830* (Chapel Hill: University of North Carolina Press for the Omohundro Institute of Early American History and Culture, 1998); Elliott West, *The Contested Plains: Indians, Goldseekers, and the Rush to Colorado* (Lawrence: University Press of Kansas, 1998); Jill Lepore, *The Name of War: King Philip's War and the Origins of American Identity* (New York: Vintage, 1998); Daniel K. Richter, *Facing East from Indian Country: A Native History of Early America* (Cambridge, Mass.: Harvard University Press, 2001); Alan Taylor, *The Divided Ground: Indians, Settlers, and the Northern Borderlands of the American Revolution* (New York: Vintage, 2006); and Ned Blackhawk, *Violence over the Land: Indians and Empires in the Early American West* (Cambridge, Mass.: Harvard University Press, 2006).

4. Nancy Parrott Hickerson, *The Jumanos: Hunters and Traders of the South Plains* (Austin: University of Texas Press, 1994).

5. Robert A. Ricklis, *The Karankawa Indians of Texas: An Ecological Study of Cultural Tradition and Change* (Austin: University of Texas Press, 1996).

6. Kelly F. Himmel, *The Conquest of the Karankawas and the Tonkawas, 1821–1859* (College Station: Texas A&M University Press, 1999). For examples of the new mission studies, see Kent G. Lightfoot, *Indians, Missionaries, and Merchants: The Legacy of Colonial Encounters on the California Frontiers* (Berkeley: University of California Press, 2004); James A. Sandos, *Converting California: Indians and Franciscans in the*

Missions, 1769–1836 (New Haven, Conn.: Yale University Press, 2004); Richard Steven Street, *Beasts of the Field: A Narrative of California Farmworkers, 1769–1913* (Stanford, Calif.: Stanford University Press, 2004); and Steven W. Hackel, *Children of Coyote, Missionaries of St. Francis: Indian-Spanish Relations in Colonial California, 1769–1850* (Chapel Hill: University of North Carolina Press for the Omohundro Institute of Early American History and Culture, 2005).

7. The biographies are Jodye Lynn Dickson Schilz and Thomas F. Schilz, *Buffalo Hump and the Penateka Comanches* (El Paso: Texas Western Press, 1989); William T. Hagan, *Quanah Parker, Comanche Chief* (Norman: University of Oklahoma Press, 1993); and Bill Neeley, *The Last Comanche Chief: The Life and Times of Quanah Parker (New York: John Wiley, 1995)*. Quanah Parker is also one of the five main characters examined in Jo Ella Powell Exley's *Frontier Blood: The Saga of the Parker Family* (College Station: Texas A&M University Press, 2001), which the author describes as a biography of the Parker clan.

8. Stanley Noyes, *Los Comanches: The Horse People, 1751–1845* (Albuquerque: University of New Mexico Press, 1993); and T. R. Fehrenbach, *Comanches: The Destruction of a People* (New York: Da Capo Press, 1974).

9. Gerald Betty, *Comanche Society: Before the Reservation* (College Station: Texas A&M University Press, 2002); and Rupert Norval Richardson, *The Comanche Barrier to South Plains Settlement: A Century and a Half of Savage Resistance to the Advancing Frontier* (Glendale: Arthur H. Clark, 1933).

10. Morris W. Foster, *Being Comanche: The Social History of an American Indian Community* (Tucson: University of Arizona Press, 1991); Thomas W. Kavanagh, *Comanche Political History: An Ethnohistorical Perspective* (Lincoln: University of Nebraska Press, 1996); and Ernest Wallace and E. Adamson Hoebel, *The Comanches: Lords of the South Plains* (Norman: University of Oklahoma Press, 1954).

11. Timothy K. Perttula, *"The Caddo Nation": Archaeological and Ethnohistorical Perspectives* (Austin: University of Texas Press, 1992); F. Todd Smith, *The Caddo Indians: Tribes at the Convergence of Empires, 1542–1854* (College Station: Texas A&M University Press, 1995); Cecilia Carter, *Caddo Indians: Where We Came From* (Norman: University of Oklahoma Press, 1995); and David La Vere, *Caddo Chiefdoms: Caddo Economics and Politics, 700–1835* (Lincoln: University of Nebraska Press, 1998).

12. F. Todd Smith, *The Wichita Indians: Traders of Texas and the Southern Plains, 1540–1845* (College Station: Texas A&M University Press, 2000); and F. Todd Smith, *The Caddos, the Wichitas, and the United States, 1846–1901* (College Station: Texas A&M University Press, 2000).

13. Before Britten's *The Lipan Apaches: People of the Wind and Lightning* (Albuquerque: University of New Mexico Press, 2009), the principal monographs on the Lipan Apaches are John Upton Terrell's overview of all plains Apache groups and Thomas F. Schilz's seventy-page overview of Lipan Apache history. See John Upton Terrell, *The Plains Apache* (New York: Crowell, 1975); and Thomas F. Schilz, *Lipan Apaches in Texas* (El Paso: Texas Western Press, 1987).

14. Loretta Fowler, *Arapahoe Politics, 1851–1978: Symbols in Crises of Authority* (Lincoln: University of Nebraska Press, 1982); John H. Moore, *The Cheyenne Nation: A Social and Demographic History* (Lincoln: University of Nebraska Press, 1987); Daniel K. Richter, *The Ordeal of the Longhouse: The Peoples of the Iroquois League in the Era of European Colonization* (Chapel Hill: University of North Carolina Press for the Omohundro Institute of Early American History and Culture, 1992); Frederick E. Hoxie, *Parading through History: The Making of the Crow Nation in America, 1805–1930* (New York: Cambridge University Press, 1995); Claudio Saunt, *A New Order of Things: Property, Power, and the Transformation of the Creek Indians, 1733–1816* (New York: Cambridge University Press, 1999); and Susan Miller, *Coacoochee's Bones: A Seminole Saga* (Lawrence: University Press of Kansas, 2003).

15. The period under review here has witnessed three studies on the Kiowas: John R. Wunder's tribal history in Chelsea House's series, which provides short tribal portraits for general readers; Charles M. Robinson III's conventional life-and-times biography of Satanta, a prominent late nineteenth-century Kiowa leader who fiercely resisted the United States' assimilation policies; and Stan Hoig's survey of the Kiowas' late nineteenth-century military and political history through the life and actions of Kicking Bird, a prominent peace leader who opposed Satanta's confrontational policy. See John R. Wunder, *The Kiowa* (New York: Chelsea House, 1989); Charles M. Robinson III, *Satanta: The Life and Death of a War Chief* (Austin: State House Press, 1998); and Stan Hoig, *The Kiowas and the Legend of Kicking Bird, with Three Kiowa Tales by Col. W. S. Nye* (Niwot: University Press of Colorado, 2000). Ironically, new ethnohistorical interpretations of the Kiowas have tended to appear in works that focus on other Native nations of Texas. See, for example, Hickerson, *The Jumanos;* Kavanagh, *Comanche Political History,* and Pekka Hämäläinen, *The Comanche Empire* (New Haven, Conn.: Yale University Press, 2008).

16. Maria F. Wade, *The Native Americans of the Texas Edwards Plateau, 1582–1799* (Austin: University of Texas Press, 2003); David La Vere, *Contrary Neighbors: Southern Plains and Removed Indians in Indian Territory* (Norman: University of Oklahoma Press, 2001); and Dianna Everett, *The Texas Cherokees: A People between Two Fires, 1819–1840* (Norman: University of Oklahoma Press, 1990).

17. For recent historiographical discussions of North American borderlands, see Jeremy Adelman and Stephen Aron, "From Borderlands to Borders: Empires, Nation-States, and the Peoples in between in North American History," *American Historical Review* 104 (June 1999): 814–41; John R. Wunder and Pekka Hämäläinen, "Of Lethal Places and Lethal Essays," *American Historical Review* 104 (October 1999): 1229–34; Samuel Truett and Elliott Young, "Making Transnational History: Nations, Regions, and Borderlands," in *Continental Crossroads: Remapping U.S.-Mexico Borderlands History,* ed. Samuel Truett and Elliott Young (Durham, NC: Duke University Press, 2004), 1–32; David J. Weber, "The Spanish Borderlands, Historiography Redux," *The History Teacher* 39 (November 2005): 43–56; and Benjamin Heber Johnson, "Problems and Prospects in North American Borderlands History," *History Compass* 4 (2006): 1–7.

18. Donald E. Chipman, *Spanish Texas, 1519–1821* (Austin: University of Texas Press, 1992); and David J. Weber, *The Spanish Frontier in North America* (New Haven, Conn.: Yale University Press, 1992).

19. A similar fading out of indigenous peoples and perspectives also blemishes Randolph B. Campbell's recent Texas history textbook, *Gone to Texas: A History of the Lone Star State* (New York: Oxford University Press, 2003).

20. Herbert E. Bolton, *The Spanish Borderlands: A Chronicle of Old Florida and the Southwest* (New Haven, Conn.: Yale University Press, 1921).

21. David J. Weber, *Bárbaros: Spaniards and Their Savages in the Age of Enlightenment* (New Haven, Conn.: Yale University Press, 2005).

22. David J. Weber, *The Mexican Frontier, 1821–1846: The American Southwest under Mexico* (Albuquerque: University of New Mexico Press, 1982).

23. Andrés Reséndez, *Changing National Identities at the Frontier: Texas and New Mexico, 1800–1850* (New York: Cambridge University Press, 2005). Other notable recent contributions include Brian Delay, "Independent Indians and the U.S.-Mexican War," *American Historical Review* 112 (February 2007): 35–68, which traces how Comanche, Kiowa, and Apache raids into Mexico influenced how Americans and Mexicans viewed and rhetorically denigrated each other in the years leading up the U.S.-Mexican War; and Raúl A. Ramos, *Beyond the Alamo: Forging Mexican Identify in San Antonio, 1821–1861* (Chapel Hill: University of North Carolina Press, 2008), which explores how interactions with indigenous societies helped shape the ethnic identity of the Tejano population in San Antonio.

24. Gary Clayton Anderson, *The Indian Southwest: Ethnogenesis and Reinvention* (Norman: University of Oklahoma Press, 1999).

25. Edward H. Spicer, *Cycles of Conquest: The Impact of Spain, Mexico, and the United States on the Indians of the Southwest* (Tucson: University of Arizona Press, 1962); and Thomas D. Hall, *Social Change in the Southwest, 1350–1880* (Lawrence: University Press of Kansas, 1989).

26. Martha McCollough, *Three Nations, One Place: A Comparative Ethnohistory of Social Change among the Comanches and Hasinais during Spain's Colonial Era, 1689–1821* (New York: Routledge, 2004).

27. Juliana Barr, *Peace Came in the Form of a Woman: Indians and Spaniards in the Texas Borderlands* (Chapel Hill: University of North Carolina Press, 2007); Jane T. Merritt, *At the Crossroads: Indians and Empires on a Mid-Atlantic Frontier, 1700–1763* (Chapel Hill: University of North Carolina Press for the Omohundro Institute of Early American History and Culture, 2003); and Kathleen DuVal, *The Native Ground: Indians and Colonists in the Heart of the Continent* (Philadelphia: University of Pennsylvania Press, 2006).

28. For the genesis and persistence of the barrier paradigm, see Richardson, *The Comanche Barrier to South Plains Settlement;* Wallace and Hoebel, *Comanches;* Fehrenbach, *Comanches;* and McCollough, *Three Nations, One Place.*

29. Brian Delay, *War of a Thousand Deserts: Indian Raids and the U.S.-Mexican War* (New Haven, Conn.: Yale University Press, 2008).

30. I emphasize in *The Comanche Empire* the Comanches' own role in the decline of the bison herds, the foundation of their economy, an argument that draws from Dan Flores's classic 1991 article on the southern plains bison ecology. See Dan Flores, "Bison Ecology and Bison Diplomacy: The Southern Plains from 1800 to 1850," *Journal of American History* 78 (September 1991): 465–85.

31. F. Todd Smith, *From Dominance to Disappearance: The Indians of Texas and the Near Southwest, 1786–1859* (Lincoln: University of Nebraska Press, 2005); Gary Clayton Anderson, *The Conquest of Texas: Ethnic Cleansing in the Promised Land* (Norman: University of Oklahoma Press, 2006); and Andrew Graybill, *Policing the Great Plains: Rangers, Mounties, and the North American Frontier, 1875–1910* (Lincoln: University of Nebraska Press, 2007).

32. Elizabeth A. H. John, *Storms Brewed in Other Men's Worlds: The Confrontation of Indians, Spanish, and French in the Southwest, 1540–1795* (Norman: University of Oklahoma Press, 1975).

33. See, for example, Benjamin Heber Johnson's review in *The Western Historical Quarterly* (Spring 2007): 69–70; and Larry McMurtry, "Texas: The Death of the Natives," *New York Review of Books,* September 21, 2006, 63–65.

34. T. R. Fehrenbach, *Lone Star: A History of Texas and Texans* (New York: Macmillan, 1968).

35. Anderson, *The Conquest of Texas,* 359.

36. David La Vere, *The Texas Indians* (College Station: Texas A&M University Press, 2004); and W. W. Newcomb Jr., *The Indians of Texas: From Prehistoric to Modern Times* (Austin: University of Texas Press, 1961).

37. Outstanding recent contributions to Texas Indian archaeology include Susan C. Vehik and Timothy G. Baugh, "Cultural Continuity and Discontinuity in the Southern Prairies and Cross Timbers," in *Plains Indians, A.D. 150–1500: The Archaeological Past of Historic Groups,* ed. Karl H. Schlesier (Norman: University of Oklahoma Press, 1994), 239–63; Vance T. Holliday, *Paleoindian Geoarchaeology of the Southern High Plains* (Austin: University of Texas Press, 1997); Donny L. Hamilton, *Prehistory of the Hustler Hills: Granado Cave* (Austin: University of Texas Press, 2001); and Timothy K. Perttula, *The Prehistory of Texas* (College Station: Texas A&M University Press, 2004).

38. For an assessment critiquing the New Indian History for neglecting the post-1800 North American history, see Nicolas G. Rosenthal, "Beyond the New Indian History: Recent Trends in the Historiography on the Native Peoples of North America," *History Compass* 4 (July 2006): 963–65.

Strange Brew

Recent Texas Political, Economic, and Military History

Keith J. Volanto

An interesting blend of older and newer styles of scholarship epitomizes recent Texas political, economic, and military historiography. Early writers within these oldest subfields of Texas history typically employed a top-down approach, producing monographs depicting the lives and actions of elite white males while retelling episodes of party politics, the rise of business enterprises, and the exploits of famed military units and individuals. With the arrival of the New Social History in the 1960s, many Texas historians began to fundamentally change the manner in which they approached their craft. Strongly influenced by the social movements of the times, revisionists began to undertake concerted efforts to rewrite history from "the bottom up" in order to replace traditional storylines with correctives that championed the accomplishments of "average Texans" (especially previously excluded groups), gave them agency, and studied their everyday lives. This new emphasis led to the study of such topics as voter behavior, the lives and struggles of working-class people, and the wartime experiences of the common soldier.

During the past two decades, authors continued to publish books influenced by these older styles, but alongside them has appeared a body of historical works utilizing innovative methods of research and writing. Largely avoiding previous historiographical battles concerning "proper" history as either the celebration of exceptional people and institutions or solely the study of the common person, advocates of this new methodology, which I label *postrevisionist*, do not follow a single model or doctrinaire mind-set. Instead, they share the concepts of balance and inclusion as their unifying principles. Postrevisionist historians seek to broaden knowledge of the Texas past by promoting balanced interpretations through acceptance of diverse perspectives while demonstrating tolerance for, if not complete acceptance of, inventive approaches, original methods, and fresh avenues of inquiry.

Four salient strands of postrevisionist history emerge from the current crop of scholarship. One type combines aspects of older and newer methodologies to advance an eclectic approach. Previously, traditionalists concentrated solely on political, economic, and military institutions or explored the lives of elite politicians, entrepreneurs, or military officers. Later, the revisionists eschewed the elite perspective, focusing instead on the average voter, worker, or soldier. Often trained well after the historiographical battles of the 1960s and 1970s, some postrevisionists feel comfortable borrowing from both approaches, arguing that they can form a more complete picture by combining elite and common perspectives. Similar in some ways to the manner in which certain psychologists borrow from multiple approaches to treat patients, or musicians might borrow freely from multiple styles and forms to produce a unique sound, these historians adopt an eclectic approach to produce a synthetic and more balanced style of history.

Another variety of postrevisionism openly welcomes the use of interdisciplinary methods for historical inquiry. Although some political historians as early as the 1960s pioneered the use of statistical analysis to predict and explain voter behavior, a branch of postrevisionist historians has since borrowed from a much wider range of nonquantitative disciplines often ignored by historians to integrate elements of sociology, psychology, anthropology, archaeology, and other fields into their works. (Also included in this group should be scholars from these other disciplines who use the methods of their profession to investigate historical topics.) These changes not only reflect broader disciplinary interests and training on the part of the authors but also the wider acceptance of these methods by the historical community. Attesting to this fact is the growing popularity of journals that promote interdisciplinary historical applications, such as *The Journal of Interdisciplinary History* and *Social Science History.*

A third major strand consists of works that encourage the placement of Texas history into regional, national, or international contexts. Those embracing this outlook argue that certain Texas historical topics cannot be viewed solely within an insular framework. What happens in Texas does not always stay in Texas, but rather, sometimes has national and even global implications. Conversely, regional, national, and foreign political issues; economic developments; and military affairs can sometimes influence Texas in ways that are best understood if historians survey a broader landscape than just the boundaries of the Lone Star State. A cadre of Tejano historians, in particular, has shown a new path by elaborating on aspects of political, economic, and military topics within the context of the situation in Mexico at various moments in time.

One final form of postrevisionist history combines two or more subfields in an effort to broaden the range of inquiry. Works that analyze the interaction of politics, economics, and culture, for example, represent a new way of viewing the history of the Lone Star State. Authors who have begun to analyze the connection between war and society or the economic ramifications of the military, for example, mark a prominent break from previous research and writing, showing that there can be more to Texas military history than a biography of a famous general or the description of a foot soldier's experiences during a campaign.

In this essay, I will provide numerous examples to demonstrate how recent works displaying the influence of older and newer methods have been creating an intriguing mixture of historical scholarship over the past two decades. For better clarity, I have divided the essay by subfield, discussing many works displaying older and newer approaches and themes as well as highlighting some new interpretive trends appearing within them. I will conclude with an attempt to explain why this jumble of historical forms exists in the recent literature, and I will speculate on how long this mixed bag of scholarship might endure.

Recent Texas Political History

Throughout much of the twentieth century, traditional works of Texas political history often consisted of laudatory biographies of white male politicians, narrative tomes covering pivotal elections, and studies focusing on party politics and political movements. Eventually, as the New Social History began to impact the study of Texas politics, many historians sought to present nonelite viewpoints and give agency to previously excluded groups, especially women and minorities. The past two decades have witnessed a continuation of these older conventions but also the emergence of new postrevisionist concerns for presenting more realistic and balanced portrayals of people and events, often incorporating fresh methodologies and wider perspectives than previously utilized.

Approaches

Texas historians continue to produce countless biographies of the state's elite Anglo political leaders. From the Texas Revolution through the twentieth century, the lives of famous politicians continue to receive copious amounts of attention. Whether providing abridged versions of their political lives in essay collections, such as *Profiles in Power* (1993, 2004) or book-length treatments, authors have long enjoyed exploring the political lives of influential establishment politicians. Although numerous works can be cited as examples, Carolyn Barta's *Bill Clements: Texian to His Toenails* (1996) in many ways typifies the continuation of this standard, top-down approach. Beginning with family background information and the young man's upbringing in Highland Park, the author enthusiastically charts Clements's rise from oil field-worker to founder of SEDCO (eventually the world's leading offshore oil drilling equipment supplier) to his successful run as Texas' first Republican governor since Reconstruction, followed by an elaboration of his gubernatorial policies and a favorable assessment of his character and political legacy. Similar storylines continue to appear in numerous recent works covering Texas governors, congressmen, state legislators, and even influential political advisers.[1]

Writers in the past two decades have also produced a number of fine biographies of important Texas leaders who were not from the political establishment. Although departing from the study of Anglo male elites, the approach remains the same, with authors depicting their African American, Tejano, and female subjects as influential leaders who had a tangible impact on the politics of the state. Gregg Cantrell trod new ground, for example, with his dual biography *Kenneth and John B. Rayner and the Limits of Southern Dissent* (1993), which chronicled the lives of a southern planter-politician and his mulatto son who later moved to East Texas and became a firebrand Populist leader. This work, followed by a revised version concentrating solely on John Rayner (2001), marked the first time that a black populist leader received book-length treatment. Historians have now also given attention to the lives of prominent Tejano political figures, including El Paso mayor Raymond Telles, civic leader Felix Tijerina, and American GI Forum founder Hector P. García. Many biographies of politically active white females, such as liberal *Texas Observer* publisher Frankie Carter Randolph, feminist judge Sarah T. Hughes, and the series of profiles on female Texas state legislators appearing in *Capitol Women* (2000), all commemorate the active roles that these influential women played within the political system in Texas. The past two decades also witnessed the beginning of scholarly research delving into the seriously neglected field of minority women in Texas politics. The careers of Mexican American political women have received attention in the form of biographical essays appearing in *Chicanas in Charge* (2006) and *Políticas* (2008). Recent biographies of black Texas females involved in politics include Mary Beth Rogers's *Barbara Jordan* (1998) and Merline Pitre's *In Struggle against Jim Crow* (1999), covering the life of Houston NAACP leader Lulu B. White.[2]

Narratives detailing institutional political battles mark another traditional approach enduring to the present day. Whether reciting the details of political campaigns or describing the inner workings of partisan politics, work in this genre continues unabated. Joel Silbey's recent book on Texas annexation, titled *Storm over Texas* (2005), provides one convenient example. A renowned national political historian, Silbey focused on the political fight over annexation in Washington, D.C., arguing that the struggle transformed the slavery issue into the major political issue of the time, eventually leading the country to civil war. By doing so, however, this approach overemphasizes the role of national leaders and their political parties. The concentration on the positions taken by politicians, their speeches, and their artful maneuvers, in fact, is so narrow that major Texas political leaders, most noteworthy, Sam Houston, are left almost entirely out of the narrative.[3]

Beginning in the 1960s, social historians began to use numerous methods to delve into the lives of nonelites. The use of oral history interviews has been one means of recapturing aspects of their lives. Another technique that historians employ to explore nonelites' thinking is to cite letters written to leaders and institutions. By the 1990s, historians provided a wealth of new information through these approaches, but many topics still needed to be examined. The role of women within the Populist movement in Texas has been largely ignored, for example, but Marion Barthelme recently provided an important contribution to the history of the movement by editing a series of almost two hundred letters written by women to the *Southern Mercury,* the main Populist newspaper in Texas. Collectively, the letters not only reveal the attitudes and concerns of many Texas farm women, they also demonstrate the point that despite being denied the right to vote, many of them were hardly passive and apolitical. They depict women intimately involved in the movement, relating their extensive knowledge of the important political issues affecting their lives and revealing how they exerted a strong influence on their husbands and fellow rural men alike.[4]

Quantitative analysis emerged as another important element of the New Social History. The methodology sought to apply scientific rigor to the study of history while opening up the search for truth to fresh modes of inquiry. Elections, voter behavior, and a host of other phenomena could be explored, researchers argued, through the application of advanced statistical analysis. While some scholars began to incorporate more basic statistical information (often in the form of percentages and rates) into their books and articles, many others became bewildered by the deluge of works packed with tables containing intricate explanations using such alien terms as *cross-tabulation, correlation, multivariate regression,* and *logarithmic transformation.* Nevertheless, the increased availability of computers and software conducive to statistical analysis, such as SPSS (originally, Statistical Package for the Social Sciences), promoted further use of complex techniques in historical studies while graduate programs began to teach courses on the theory and application of quantitative methods.

Texas political historians have not applied the approach as extensively as others, yet the use of advanced statistical techniques to study Texas elections persists, as evidenced by the publication of Dale Baum's *The Shattering of Texas Unionism* (1998) which provides an extensive quantitative look at Texas Civil War and Reconstruction-era elections. A tour de force of statistical analysis, Baum's work investigates every major statewide vote from 1859 to 1869, showing the potential explanatory power of these methods while drawing new conclusions about many of the period's key electoral battles. Among his findings: Houston won in 1859 not by winning over many supporters of Gov. Hardin Runnels as previously supposed, but by attracting new voters while his opponent failed to mobilize about one-third of his former supporters from the 1857 election; the strongest opponents of secession were wheat farmers and Disciples of Christ adherents in North Texas plus German Lutherans in Central Texas, while counties with high levels of cotton and hog production and large concentrations of Methodists, Baptists, and Presbyterians strongly favored disunion; and Governor Davis did not steal the 1869 gubernatorial election from Andrew Jackson Hamilton as many have alleged.[5]

While these older approaches endure, the past two decades have seen the arrival of postrevisionist works applying new methods to the study of Texas political history. Although not completely rejecting older lines of inquiry, postrevisionists have now broadened the acceptability of subjects for investigation as well as the means of researching and presenting historical knowledge.

One innovative approach involves the study of social networks within reform movements. Two standout examples involve the study of the Populist and Progressive movements in Texas. With the publication of *American Populism* (1993), Robert C. McMath followed a current trend within Populist historiography, moving away from straight political concerns toward the study of the social and cultural bases of the movement. Tapping into the latest social studies of rural America, McMath adds greatly to our knowledge of Populism by describing how the Farmers' Alliance and the Populist Party took advantage of existing social networks within rural America to spread rapidly across the South. By targeting individuals, churches, and social clubs in areas already familiar to them, Alliance publicists maximized their effectiveness and garnered converts who shared mutual anxieties about their worsening economic situation.

In *Creating the New Woman* (1998), Judith N. McArthur shows how conservative, white, urban, middle-class Texas females used their reform clubs to create a public culture whereby disfranchised women could exert themselves in the public arena. Through their discovery that "the personal was political," these women assumed the role of "municipal housekeepers" to overcome gender expectations by using arguments that reinforced the traditional ideals of domesticity and maternalism. In this manner, Texas Progressive women justified their activism by emphasizing the need to participate within the political process to strengthen families through campaigning for such reforms as compulsory education, restriction of child labor, wage-and-hour legislation, and factory safety measures.[6]

The use of nonquantitative interdisciplinary methods to analyze Texas politics represents another important recent approach gaining wider acceptance. One noteworthy example is Chandler Davidson's *Race and Class in Texas Politics* (1993). Viewing Texas politics through the lens of a political sociologist, Davidson uses the state's post–World War II political history as a case study to challenge political scientist V. O. Key's 1949 prediction of a coming two-party system in the South characterized by class-based politics. Through his examination of various social groups, he characterizes as mythical the idea that most Texans are conservative. Instead, he concludes that massive conservative campaign funding, intentionally biased electoral devices, and deliberately fanned racial fears have created the necessary wedge issues to lure enough working-class whites to the Republican Party in order to disrupt potential progressive coalitions based on class that Key predicted would arrive.[7]

In the concluding chapter of *Felix Longoria's Wake* (2003), Patrick J. Carroll creatively uses another interdisciplinary approach in an effort to explain the internal dynamics of the Longoria affair. Specifically, Carroll demonstrates how the episode could be viewed through disparate theoretical frameworks and eventually synthesizes many of them. Classical Marxists, for example, would highlight inherent class conflicts existing in Texas at the time while de-emphasizing issues of honor, patriotism, racism, and ethnicity as social constructs of secondary consideration. Modernization theorists, however, would argue that the positive economic growth taking place in post–World War II Texas translated into positive social development, including higher forms of social justice. Adherents to Immanuel Wallerstein's world systems theory would posit that the restrictions placed on Mexican Americans in South Texas reflected realities derived from the area's subordinate ("peripheral") economic status in relation to the predominant section above the Nueces Strip (a "core area") controlled by Anglos. Thus, "the zone's racially, ethnically, and nationalistically validated limits on labor rewards created an inequitable socioeconomic climate that bred conflicts like the one that swirled around Felix Longoria's wake." Carroll also cites the work of many humanist scholars who stress the role of human emotions and different ways in which individuals and groups respond to situations as insightful in helping to understand the Longoria incident. Ultimately, he concludes that a complex combination of structural and emotive forces led to the event: postwar economic expansion in a region with a historically near-feudal agricultural economy stimulated the Tejano desire for enhanced social status. These developments, coupled with genuine individual and communal bereavement for the fallen soldier, help to explain the experience. Overall, Carroll shows that through the inclusion of an interdisciplinary approach, researchers can reveal broader dimensions of understanding to such incidents of prejudice in the Texas past.[8]

Texas political historians often study aspects of the state's political history within a "vacuum," that is, within the state's borders, but postrevisionists have recently expanded the field of inquiry to present Texas politics within a broader framework by placing political events within national and international contexts. Some Tejano political historians, for example, have employed these techniques to illuminate certain aspects of the struggle for Mexican American civil rights that have hitherto been ignored or underemphasized. In *LULAC, Mexican Americans, and National Policy* (2005), Craig A. Kaplowitz analyzes the relationship between LULAC and national policy making. By looking beyond Texas borders and examining the organization in a national policy-making context, he shows that the organization had a far stronger impact during the latter half of the twentieth century than previously described. Although the group experienced significant decline at the grassroots level due to the rising activism of Chicano militants, the group maintained its role as the primary voice of Mexican Americans among government leaders.[9]

One last new approach employed by some postrevisionist historians involves synthesizing many of the aforementioned older and newer approaches. In my *Texas, Cotton, and the New Deal* (2005), for example, I combine multiple approaches to move beyond standard administrative histories to describe the Agricultural Adjustment Administration's (AAA) efforts to aid Texas cotton farmers during the Great Depression. Borrowing from political science bureaucratic studies, I employ a model that analyzes policy creation and implementation, followed by feedback and policy modification. In the policy-creation phase, I expound on the roles of various elite participants in Washington, D.C. in the traditional manner of many institutional histories. However, in detailing aspects of the implementation and feedback stages, I give agency to average farmers by documenting their roles in carrying out the government's plans and noting their impact on the AAA's ever-evolving policies. Letters sent by growers to government officials reveal that the farmers were not simply passive recipients of government largesse. Their level of enthusiasm and degree of participation directly determined the degree of success or failure for the programs.[10]

Themes

Similar to the variety of approaches adopted, a mélange of old and new themes also characterize recent Texas political historiography. The continued outpouring of biographies alone demonstrates the persistent popularity of the notion that Texas' state and national political elites are important historical actors worthy of continued study. Many of these life histories are less celebratory than biographies from decades ago (plus writers are now studying female and minority leaders), yet the impulse to focus on the lives of elites and their actions remains strong.

Another enduring theme is the continued emphasis on conflict when describing the African American civil rights movement. For many writers, conflict characterized the battle for civil rights in Texas, and their work emphasizes the strong degree of resistance often encountered during the desegregation and voting-rights struggles in the courts, on school campuses, and in the streets. Victories were achieved through the unrelenting efforts of activists pressuring the system for change. In these works, actions undertaken by white establishment figures to collaborate with change are often de-emphasized or ignored.[11]

Similarly, Chicano historians continue to produce work on the Mexican American civil rights efforts of the 1960s and 1970s through a framework emphasizing conflict. Armando Navarro's *The Cristal Experiment* (1998) provides an insider's perspective (as a contemporary political organizer and activist) on the rise and fall of the Chicano movement in Crystal City, Texas. The author stresses the power struggle between the Anglo elites and the Hispanic majority in the South Texas town, describing the efforts that produced the activists' success in the form of more community control of schools and governing institutions as well as examining the reasons for the movement's failures.[12]

While these older concepts have continued into the twenty-first century, the last two decades have seen historians emphasize several new themes. One noteworthy change involves the humanizing of Texas political figures. Thankfully, most serious Texas writers no longer depict the leaders of the Texas Revolution, for example, as demigods chiseled out of marble. Recent biographers, in fact, have shed much new light on important Texas founders. Utilizing modern scholarship, these writers have humanized personalities and placed them in proper context, portraying them as complicated figures passing through different life stages, experiencing self doubts, yet still committed to particular political ends. This is Gregg Cantrell's method in *Stephen F. Austin* (1999), the most significant treatment of Austin since Eugene C. Barker's 1925 biography. Cantrell portrays Austin as a man possessing a host of energy despite frequent bouts of ill health and as an ambivalent pursuer of policies that promoted the spread of slavery despite occasionally questioning the institution. Likewise, in his reevaluation of the life of Sam Houston published in 2002, James L. Haley acknowledged the well-traveled ground regarding "the Raven" but instead focused on explaining Houston's complex personality and character at various times during his lengthy political career.[13]

Another emergent theme stresses the political discord that existed among Texans during the mid-nineteenth century. While earlier depictions de-emphasized or ignored inner conflict within Texas in favor of promoting the idea of consensus, this conception no longer holds weight within the academy. Paul D. Lack's *The Texas Revolutionary Experience* (1992) began the effort to correct the view of a unified resistance movement during the Texas Revolution by emphasizing the internal conflicts, personal animosities, and plague of individualism that characterized much of the separatist effort. At many points during the rebellion, squabbling among autonomous communities, competing interest groups, rival leaders, and insubordinate militants threatened to endanger the Texans' ability to respond to Santa Anna's challenge. Rather than describing a heroic movement led by selfless individuals whose political and martial success was never really in doubt, Lack provides much material and analysis to posit that the revolutionaries may have indeed won in spite of themselves.[14]

Other historians have recently carried the theme of political discord to their analysis of the Civil War and Reconstruction periods. In *Texas Divided* (1990), James Marten analyzes numerous groups within Texas—conditional Unionists, unconditional Unionists, German immigrants, Tejanos, African Americans, wartime draft dodgers, and assorted lawbreakers—that did not accept the prevailing political orthodoxy. He also studies the concerted efforts of the controlling authorities and their minions to stamp out dissent and impose conformity within the state during the late antebellum, Civil War, and Reconstruction years. Marten finds that Confederate authorities and citizens struggled throughout the war years to maintain internal order, and these divisive feelings endured well into the postwar era. His emphasis on dissension is in line with a growing literature that centers Unionists and their experiences, rather than the Confederate state, as the focus of inquiry.[15]

While a flight from consensus marks recent mid-nineteenth-century political historiography, a number of works stressing the practice of consensual politics during the civil rights movement is gradually appearing. As previously noted, there is no shortage of works viewing the civil rights era in Texas as a time of intense legal and sometimes physical conflict, nor accounts depicting the radical goals of militant activists. Some recent works, however, have sought to reexamine the period differently. While certainly not ignoring the struggle to change the system, these historians highlight instances of Mexican American and African American leaders working within the system, reveal the role of minority leaders covertly working behind the scenes with white business elites to quietly foment change, and remind readers that the ultimate goal of most activists was acceptance of equality by Anglos rather than a radical overturning of Texas society. In *Viva Kennedy* (2000), for example, Ignacio M. García examines the efforts of middle-class Mexican Americans to help elect John Kennedy in the 1960 presidential election through the Viva Kennedy clubs. Motivated by their faith in the American dream, these activists worked within the American political system to support a candidate who they believed would improve their standing within society.[16]

With respect to African American civil rights efforts, William Henry Kellar provides a thorough discussion of Houston's desegregation struggle, noting the role of white businessmen who reluctantly supported a peaceful, albeit slow, transition. "Houston's business and political leaders acquiesced in limited school desegregation," he notes in the penultimate chapter of *Make Haste Slowly* (1999), "because the alternative—a city disrupted by racial violence—seemed more distasteful. Houstonians had learned the lessons of Little Rock and desegregated the country's largest segregated school district peacefully." Kellar also agrees with the notion that these same elites worked with black community leaders quietly to desegregate public facilities in the city, though they were largely driven to such actions by African American protesters performing sit-ins and other forms of nonviolent protest.[17]

New Interpretive Trends

Using familiar and innovative methods, many historians in recent years, especially postrevisionists, have developed new interpretive trends for some key political topics. In certain cases, such as Reconstruction studies, this translates to a greater understanding of the era's complexity than previously appreciated. In other instances, such as the study of the New Deal in Texas, this means bringing the first true scholarly attention to key facets of the topic beyond the study of elite political figures. In yet other circumstances, such as the evaluation of Lyndon Johnson, the passage of time and the availability of more source material have led to the beginning of a truly balanced interpretation of the man and his works.

As is well known, for the first three quarters of the twentieth century, the Dunning school of interpretation cast a long shadow over the study of Reconstruction politics in Texas. Not possessing the pro-Confederate bias of previous Reconstruction-era historians (who were usually conservative southerners), revisionists provided a decidedly sharper critique of the available primary sources and also approached the subject of blacks without the racially biased perspective of prior scholars, resulting in the massive overturning of the traditional narrative. Recently, postrevisionist historians have moved beyond the concerns of the revisionists to investigate other aspects of the period. Randolph B. Campbell, for example, employed a comparative study of Texas counties in *Grass-Roots Reconstruction in Texas, 1865–1880* (1997) to examine Reconstruction at the local level, demonstrating that Texas subregions encountered distinct experiences due to varying degrees of economic upheaval, political chicanery, and racial violence. James M. Smallwood and others are also reinterpreting the manner in which historians depict the era's violence, arguing that many episodes that historians once viewed as merely family feuds or isolated violent acts perpetuated by infamous bandits can best be understood within the backdrop of continued hard feelings and grudges carried over from the Civil War years. They reveal, for example, that the notorious desperado Cullen Montgomery Baker used the "Lost Cause" as a justification for his attacks against ex-slaves and white Unionists, while the famous "Lee-Peacock Feud" was actually a settling of old scores from the war perpetrated by disgruntled ex-Confederates (the Lee Gang) against wartime Unionists (the Peacock faction).[18]

Another emergent trend is the appearance of works touting the success of many New Deal programs operating in Texas. With the possible exception of World War II, no twentieth-century event contributed more to the development of modern Texas than the Great Depression. Yet until recently historians wrote relatively little on the New Deal era in Texas. What explains the fact that a potentially rich scholarly area like New Deal studies has received relatively little attention from Texas historians? One reason might be the fact that, despite numerous examples one could cite to show clearly that a majority of Texans approved of most Roosevelt administration efforts and willingly accepted various forms of government aid, modern Texas does have a strong antigovernment reputation. Writing about federal government action to solve an economic crisis simply does not have much appeal for many homegrown historians raised on a tradition that complains about long lines at post offices (while ignoring longer waits at a doctor's office) and celebrates free enterprise (but berates high gas prices). Another possibility may simply be that the Great Depression is not compelling for them when compared to other topics. Despite its great importance to the state's history, researching and writing about the New Deal might not seem as exciting as recounting exploits of revolutionaries campaigning against Santa Anna, Texas Rangers fighting off Comanche warriors, or the excitement generated by the initial blast of a massive oil gusher. Perhaps the recent economic downturn that Texas and the nation began to experience at the end of the George W. Bush administration will compel more historians to revisit the Great Depression.

Despite the paucity of work on the New Deal in Texas relative to the vast potential for scholarship on this period, there are historians who are tapping into this rich field. Most of the recent research has consisted of local- and state-level examinations of the impact of New Deal policies and programs, reflecting a trend begun in the late-1960s that sought to deviate from previous studies that emphasized national-level personalities, Washington politics, and bureaucratic infighting. Starting with James T. Patterson's *The New Deal and the States* (1969), in which the author argued that the most important aspects of the New Deal involved how the government's policies actually functioned in the field rather than as inside-the-beltway politics, many New Deal scholars shifted their focus to examine how Roosevelt's programs operated at the grassroots level, highlighting the role of common people as active participants, elaborating on problems encountered, and evaluating the benefits (or harm) that the programs delivered to constituents. Within the past twenty years, Texas historians have investigated the Lower Colorado River Authority, the National Youth Administration, the Civilian Conservation Corps, the Post Office Murals initiative, and the Agricultural Adjustment Administration's programs to aid the state's cotton farmers. Overall, these works reveal a picture of government officials working with citizens to overcome problems of inexperience, local resistance, and unanticipated circumstances to aid Texans during the Depression. While navigating through uncharted waters, New Dealers were generally successful in terms of stabilizing the state's overall economy, even while failing to generate complete economic recovery by the end of the 1930s.[19]

One final example of a new interpretive trend concerns recent efforts to explain Lyndon Johnson in more complex terms, though authors have yet to come to any definite consensus on the president. The most recognized LBJ biographies that have appeared during the past twenty years have resulted in radically different conclusions about the man, his motivations, and his legacy. Journalist Robert Caro began his intended four-volume look at the life of Lyndon Johnson in 1982 with the publication of *The Years of Lyndon Johnson: The Path to Power.* Since then, he has followed up with volumes two and three, subtitled *Means of Ascent* (1990) and *Master of the Senate* (for which Caro won the 2003 Pulitzer Prize for biography). Employing doses of psychobiography, his works tend to portray Johnson as a selfish, attention-craving egomaniac obsessed with attaining and holding power for its own sake. Many critics, however, have pointed out that while much in Johnson's rise to the presidency merits censure, Caro's description of LBJ and his motivations appear to be a one-dimensional caricature—the genuine desire for Johnson to help people, even paternalistically, often fails to enter the author's analysis.[20]

Of all the Johnson biographies, Robert Dallek's two-volume *Lyndon Johnson and His Times* (1991, 1998) has been the most widely praised for its balance. A presidential historian rather than a journalist, Dallek's accounts exude complexity and historical context as he navigates through the density of Johnson's life story. Although far from uncritical, the author succeeds in providing depth to LBJ. While definitely a man who burned with ambition, Johnson also cared about people and sought to aid them through government intervention, just as he helped the folks in his congressional district by supporting numerous New Deal programs during the Depression.[21]

Recent Texas Economic History

For much of the twentieth century, the type of scholarship produced by American economic historians remained consistent: a focus on the history of a company, a particular industry, or a biography of a successful entrepreneur. Prior to the 1960s, Texas economic historians wrote in a similar vein, with a strong emphasis on the operations of the state's plantations, ranches, and petroleum companies along with celebratory biographies of big planters, large cattlemen, and oil barons. As Walter Buenger has noted, many of these earlier works retained a wistful reverence for the past as a presumably better time when compared to the present. Revisionists then sought to correct this impression and its top-down approach by focusing on the lives of Texas laborers. These historiographical tendencies endure among many current writers, but the last two decades have also witnessed a rise in works bent on presenting a more complex depiction of the past Texas economy and its major players by utilizing new approaches and methods of inquiry.[22]

Approaches

As in the case with political history, an assortment of conventional and innovative approaches to the examination of Texas economic history has appeared over the last twenty years. Standard entrepreneurial biographies continue to abound in the current literature. Robert McDaniel's laudatory tome to his great-uncle—*Pattillo Higgins and the Search for Texas Oil* (1989)—contains several characteristics of the older style still prevalent in many life histories of Texas business figures. The author clearly admires his subject, chronologically details aspects of Higgins's personal life and work (though often failing to provide proper context within the greater scope of economic history), excuses him for many personal transgressions (such as marrying his adopted daughter), and tends to exaggerate the man's overall importance, at one point describing him as the "father of the liquid fuel age."[23]

Histories of large ranches and corporate entities continue to receive ample attention. Most of these books cover familiar ground designed to heighten the importance of the founders and the institution they created. Works in this genre tend to follow similar general patterns. Steve Kelton's work on the Renderbrook Ranch, for example, devotes space to the genesis of the enterprise, elaborates on driving elite personalities, details notable business developments, and proposes reasons for the ranch's survival in the modern world. Among the better corporate histories, Christopher J. Castaneda and Joseph A. Pratt's *From Texas to the East* (1993) benefits from complete access to the company archives of the Texas Eastern Corporation. The focus of the scholars, however, is the traditional business historian's top-down focus on the natural gas company's founding after World War II, important managerial decisions such as the acquisition of the "Big Inch" and "Little Big Inch" pipelines, expansion and diversification efforts, and the company's ultimate demise after a 1989 corporate takeover.[24]

Social historians continue to produce an impressive volume of work on Texas laborers: concerned with preserving knowledge of their everyday lives, documenting their toil, and giving them proper dignity. Some recent books recreating the economic and social lives of small cotton farmers via oral histories represent significant achievements. Among these monographs, Thad Sitton and Dan Utley's *From Can See to Can't* (1997) bears special attention for the authors' extensive use of interviews to illustrate a year in the lives of southern Blackland Prairie growers. The authors expertly detail many field tasks and domestic chores that farm men and women performed, along with opportunities for leisure and visiting with relatives and neighbors during the season's "laying by" time and following the fall harvest.[25]

While historians continue to use these older means to study aspects of the

Texas economy, others are applying a host of fresh approaches to offer new insights and to address previously ignored subjects. One method moves beyond coverage of the customary topics that appear in biographies of Texas businessmen, such as background information, personality traits, and business pursuits, to provide greater depth to the individual by delving into their involvement in important non-business-related activities. Don E. Carleton adopts this style in portions of *A Breed So Rare* (1999), his extensive biography of independent oilman J. R. Parten. While the author dedicates much space to many facets of his subject's personal and business life, Carleton also gives much attention to Parten's fierce defense of academic freedom while a member of the University of Texas Board of Regents. Victoria and Walter Buenger take a similar approach in their biography of venerable Fort Worth merchant Marvin Leonard. Extending their treatment further than personal and family details and descriptions of company growth and innovation, the authors also discuss Leonard's efforts to bring social change to Fort Worth by breaking down employment barriers for Jews, blacks, and Mexican Americans as well as working quietly with African American leaders to peacefully end segregation in the city.[26]

In recent decades, historians have employed numerous interdisciplinary techniques to recover features of past economic life in Texas. In some instances, the nature of the problem necessitates the use of new methods, such as efforts to recreate the lives of Tejano workers on South Texas ranches during the 1800s. In *Tejano Empire* (1998), Andrés Tijerina attempts to overcome the potential hindrance created by the dearth of traditional printed primary sources by showing that one can glean a large amount of information from folkloric sources. He argues that historians can analyze songs, ballads, art, and the oral tradition to help understand various aspects of nineteenth-century ranch life.[27]

Some postrevisionist historians have recently used interdisciplinary methods, not because of a lack of primary sources, but rather, as a means of employing a fresh new concept to the economic arena. One such scholar, Neil Foley, has received extensive critical acclaim for his application of the concept of whiteness to the study of early twentieth-century Central Texas cotton culture. Whiteness studies focus on the social construction of the idea of whiteness and the social, political, and cultural advantages given to those determined to be white by American society. Among his many findings in *The White Scourge* (1997), Foley demonstrates that class was the primary factor regarding relations among Anglo landowners and laboring blacks, Mexicans, and poor whites. While race automatically stigmatized African Americans as inferior in the minds of white landlords and credit merchants who also accepted stereotypical notions of Mexican inadequacy, impoverished white tenants and sharecroppers also found themselves perceived as inferior. Embarrassed by the poverty, lifestyle, and cultural traits exhibited by these nontenured growers, the Anglo rural elite no longer considered them fully white and treated them accordingly.[28]

The eclectic mixture of older approaches, another hallmark of postrevisionism, certainly has its adherents in Texas economic history. The authors of *Giant under the Hill* (2002), for example, combine elite and common perspectives in their lively telling of the Spindletop oil discovery. Much of the first half of the book follows standard top-down history methods, giving much attention to the familiar story of how Pattillo Higgins and his associates hit pay dirt on Spindletop Hill. After the description of the find, however, when the authors' attention shifts to the changes coming to Beaumont and the surrounding area, the main subject of the book changes. The elites are placed on the back burner as the focus turns to the lives of the oil field workers and the boomtown's residents. This approach results in a balanced presentation of the discovery, the subsequent transformation of Beaumont, and the event's long-term ramifications.[29]

One last approach with much potential as a clean break from previous explorations of Texas economic topics involves the integration of formerly distinct subfields. A strong need exists for authors to widen their coverage of economic topics by stressing the interconnections between economics and other aspects of society, including politics and culture. Past works have occasionally touched upon links between economics and politics, but not to the extent that Walter Buenger explores this interaction in *The Path to a Modern South* (2001). Rather than delivering a straightforward description of Northeast Texas' economic transformation from the 1880s through the 1920s, Buenger instead presents a complex portrait of the interrelations among regional economics, politics, society, and culture. He demonstrates that the area's move from a cotton-dominated economy to a more diversified economy greatly impacted aspects of the area's politics and culture, and vice versa. Rapid population growth, for example, spawned by the arrival of railroads, expanded agricultural acreage, and large numbers of lumber-industry jobs initially resulted in increased lynchings, as many locals sought brutal means to control the rise of unknown African American individuals in their midst. Over time, however, moderating forces began to prevail as leaders sought to check an outflow of black laborers (the same railroads bringing black laborers in, could also take them out) and the number of lynchings declined. Another illustration of the assimilation of economics and politics discussed involves the competitive multifactional nature of the local Democratic Party. Without a predominant conservative elite such as existed elsewhere in the South, local reformers were able to encourage gradual acceptance of increased government involvement in many economic matters, leading the way to the election of a strong supporter of government activism, Wright Patman, who began representing Northeast Texas in the U.S. House of Representatives even before the New Deal delivered large amounts of federal aid. These are just two examples of the numerous symbiotic relationships that Buenger identifies and develops within his detailed narrative to provide complexity, yet greater understanding, to this story of regional transformation.[30]

Themes

In surveying the recent literature on Texas economic history, one readily notes the concurrent presence of works displaying old and new themes. Celebratory biographies of big ranch families, corporate businessmen, and risk-taking entrepreneurs continue to appear, not seeming to suffer the decline in popularity that befell admiring works on politicians following the Vietnam War and Watergate years. The subjects of these compositions often exude the qualities of rugged individualism, ingenuity, strong faith, and a certain gambling streak. By transference, the virtues of these elite actors were supposedly the driving forces behind much of Texas' past economic growth. The protagonist in Riley Froh's *Edgar B. Davis and Sequences in Business Capitalism* (1993), for example, exudes these qualities. A late-comer to the Texas oil business, Davis was already an established businessman, having succeeded as a New England shoe manufacturer and Sumatra rubber plantation director before turning to wildcatting. According to Froh, Davis's strong inner faith was his inspiration and motivation, underpinning his work ethic, daring, and determination whenever situations looked bleak, such as when his financial resources dwindled in the months just prior to striking it big in 1922 at Luling, Texas. In this telling, his finding of significant oil deposits occurred partially because of luck, but primarily because of Davis's belief that his hard work would be ultimately rewarded.[31]

In addition to works touting the individualism of entrepreneurs, other authors continue to cite the historic importance of government involvement in Texas economic matters, especially the petroleum industry. William R. Childs's *The Texas Railroad Commission* (2005) advances this theme while discussing the rise of the state agency that has played the most vital role in fostering economic development in twentieth-century Texas. Childs skillfully describes the inner dynamics of the regulatory process, revealing the noneconomic factors that often impact regulatory decisions, such as state politics, legal issues, and the personalities of various commission members. By the late 1940s, he argues, the Railroad Commission was able to secure its authority in Texas to such an extent that its decisions directly impacted international oil prices, though never to the extent of actually controlling global prices as its forceful chairman Ernest Thompson claimed.[32]

While these and other traditional themes received ongoing attention in recent decades, several postrevisionist scholars began to show that the study of Texas economic history has reached a certain level of maturity by producing more complex inquiries, publishing works that examine the multifaceted nature of the state's economic past and producing new monographs placing the Texas economy within national and international contexts.

Several recent works have appeared portraying a much more diverse Texas economy than was previously represented. Authors have increased their output on a wide range of new agricultural and industrial topics to show that there is much more to the story of Texas' economy than cotton plantations, cattle ranches, and oil wells. C. Allan Jones strongly develops this theme in *Texas Roots* (2005), his survey of antebellum Texas agriculture and rural life. The author divides his overview into two main sections—the first examines Tejano ranching and farming while the second focuses on the arrival of the Anglos and their agricultural and cattle-raising practices. Although Jones discusses cotton plantations, he treats the subject in a noncelebratory manner and, literally, includes the topic as only one chapter in the story of pre–Civil War agrarian Texas. In separate chapters, Jones devotes equal space to the rural life of small-scale farmers, hunting and stock raising, and the raising of other crops such as corn, sugarcane, and wheat, which he argues was more relevant to the lives of a majority of Texans living at the time.[33]

New attention given to twentieth-century industrial topics is another means by which Texas historians have promoted the theme of a more diverse Texas economy. In the process, these writers have demonstrated how Texas has come to more closely resemble the national economy. In fact, in recent years there has been a proliferation of non-petroleum-related business histories focusing on companies founded during the twentieth century. The aforementioned work of Castaneda and Pratt contributed to explaining the role of the natural gas industry to the Texas economy. Other volumes have elaborated on such widely varied industries as electronics, airlines, construction, the medical profession, broadcasting, and food service.[34]

A growing number of postrevisionist historians are giving increased significance to shifting regional economies. As previously mentioned, Walter Buenger brought attention to the changes transpiring in Northeast Texas at the turn of the twentieth century and their relationship to the region's politics, society, and culture. Kyle G. Wilkison also documents the arrival of commercial cotton culture to East and Central Texas during the late nineteenth century and its subsequent impact on the region's economy, society, and politics. In *Yeoman, Sharecroppers, and Socialists* (2008), Wilkison demonstrates how the advent of railroad transportation led to a horde of settlers and land speculators who drove up land values to such an extent that yeoman farm children coming of age could no longer afford to own land as their parents had before them. Increasingly, they gave up aspirations of owning semisubsistence farms and settled for tenancy relationships, which, in turn, led not only to a breakdown in their traditional way of life, but also drove many plain folk to support radical political protest movements such as the Greenbackers, the Populists, and the Socialists.[35]

In the coming years, the impact of globalization on the Texas economy will receive extensive consideration from scholars as they assess the impact of NAFTA and other channels by which Texas entered the global marketplace in numerous new ways during the late twentieth and early twenty-first centuries. Sociologist Robert Lee Maril presents a foreshadowing of this future research with his study of the political economy of Texas bay shrimpers. Coupling his findings as a participant-observer aboard a shrimp boat with qualitative methods, Maril details the challenges faced by the fishermen to continue in their chosen occupation, concluding that the main factors determining their economic survival are largely beyond their control: the prices they receive at the dock for their catches (determined by the global market) and the rules governing how they can operate in Texas waters.[36]

New Interpretive Trends

Among the new trends of interpretation appearing in the recent literature, works that include new perspectives on Texas laborers are especially prominent. Whether attempting to incorporate the experiences of previously excluded groups of workers for the first time or seeking to explore new concepts such as worker cohesion in the workplace, historians are creating fresh avenues to expand the investigation of Texas' economic matters.

One new important movement involves highlighting the significant roles played by Tejanos, African Americans, and women on Texas farms and in the cattle business. Even after the rise of the New Social History, not much has been written until recently on black cowboys, for example, let alone on ranching women or females on the cattle trails of Texas. Further, while well known that farm women performed numerous arduous tasks, few historians examined the details of their lives and contributions to their families and the overall Texas economy. Writers are beginning to address this profound void in the scholarship. Regarding the contributions of women to the Texas cattle industry, for example, sociologist Elizabeth Maret alludes to the past during her study of women's roles in the modern Texas beef cattle industry, arguing the case for continuity between women's historic involvement in the industry and today's rising number of visible responsibilities for females within the industry. This theme is developed more fully in Sara Massey's edited volume *Texas Women on the Cattle Trails* (2006). In a series of sixteen essays, professional and amateur historians tell the story of women who took part in the great Texas cattle drives of the late nineteenth century. Whether fulfilling conventional gender roles (such as tending children or acting as cooks and servants) or pushing accepted social boundaries by working as a wrangler or herd driver, the book completely disputes the long-standing belief that women played no part in cattle drives except to serve as barmaids and prostitutes in Kansas boomtowns at trail's end.[37]

Another growing trend in Texas economic history involves studies emphasizing worker solidarity under rough labor conditions. In particular, recent scholarship focusing on Texas company towns is not only shedding light on details of workers' everyday lives, but is also showing how laborers interacted, organized, and held together to protect themselves. According to Marilyn D. Rhinehart in *A Way of Work and a Way of Life* (1992), worker cohesion characterized life in the West Texas coal mining company town of Thurber. Although the Texas Pacific Coal and Oil Company, which established Thurber, tried in various ways to maintain control over their Italian, Anglo, African American, and Hispanic workers, the nature of their dangerous work underground forged a strong bond among them that endured. Despite ethnic differences, the long hours spent digging coal while kneeling or lying on their sides, threatened by a series of common dangers, and emerging from the ground resembling one another as they stood covered in coal dust and smelling of soot and sweat galvanized the laborers. This unity provided the workers with some leverage as they dealt with numerous restrictions placed on them by management. In the end, their solidarity not only allowed them to set their own work pace with minimal supervision, but ultimately also enabled them to agitate successfully, without violence, for more enlightened company policies and union recognition.[38]

Recent Texas Military History

No state celebrates its military heritage like Texas. For as long as there has been Texas history, amateur and professional historians have given tremendous attention to martial topics, especially nineteenth-century subjects. Similar to the political and economic history of Texas, standard coverage typically entailed admiring retellings of the exploits of Texas' fighting heroes through such means as traditional biographies, combat memoirs, and narrative campaign histories. By the 1980s, the study of Texas military history broadened to reflect the impact of the New Social History. Advocates for a New Military History sought to investigate the experiences of the common soldier in wartime. Each older style still retains their supporters today, but Texas military history now also has its postrevisionists. Similar to the political and economic postrevisionists, they have moved beyond the celebration of elite personalities and institutions or focusing exclusively on the experiences of the common soldier. Instead, they endorse the use of eclectic approaches, multiple perspectives, interdisciplinary techniques, and the placement of certain Texas military topics within broader national or international contexts.

Approaches

As in past decades, Texas military historians continue to produce traditional biographies of notable leaders. Long a favorite of readers and writers alike, there is no shortage of sympathetic life histories detailing the exploits of famous officers fighting within Texas or beyond its borders. Paul H. Carlson's biography of General William R. Shafter, *Pecos Bill* (1989), contains many of this genre's key elements. After dispensing with his background and Civil War activities, the author concentrates on the details of Shafter's experiences in Texas as a frontier commander of black troops. While informative regarding Shafter's military performance in West Texas, as often occurs with elite biographies, most of the narrative centers upon the main subject (and the assorted patrols, scouting missions, and border incursions that he directed). Other key elements of the story that might have been explored are left out, including the interaction between Shafter and the African American troops that he led.[39]

Battle and campaign narratives, often favorites of traditionalists, remain as standard types of military publication. Whether attempting to draw attention to a forgotten battle or long-ignored military maneuvers, or reexamining the details of familiar operations and debating their overall importance, battle and campaign narratives remain popular devices to chronicle aspects of military conflicts involving Texans. The customary formula for these works involves setting the scene before a battle or campaign by describing the strategic setting, introducing the principal actors (especially prominent officers), describing the details of the subsequent actions, explaining why successes were achieved or not, and assessing the significance of what occurred. Among the better battle narratives to come out recently is Edward T. Cotham Jr.'s *Sabine Pass* (2004), in which the author clearly demonstrates the strategic importance of Texas and the Trans-Mississippi theater to the Confederate war effort, reminds readers of the value of Texas cotton to the Confederacy and Sabine Pass's connection to that phase of the war by acting as a hub for blockade running, provides a thorough examination of the battle, and concludes with reasons for the Union's overwhelming defeat.[40]

By the early 1990s, social history began to make a strong impact on the study of Texas military subjects. A great wave of popular interest in the Civil War, driven by Ken Burns's wildly received 1990 PBS documentary series, fueled a massive publishing boom on topics dealing with the conflict, especially the experiences of ordinary soldiers. Responding to the public's desire for first-hand accounts of the war spurred by the wide acclaim given to the film director's skillful use of common soldiers' letters and memoirs, some scholars and popular writers scurried to publish diaries and selected correspondence of enlisted men to present views of the war from the "bottom up"—a hallmark of the New Military History. While some collections have been more revealing about the everyday life of average soldiers than others, the editors' approach has generally been the same—to compile these primary sources and present explanatory notes with the text in order to place the documents in proper context.[41]

Another example of social history's impact on the study of Texas military history topics is the use of oral history interviews and memoirs in order to recreate common soldiers' wartime experiences. Among the most interesting in this genre are World War II prisoner of war narratives based on these types of primary sources. Over the past two decades, Texas historians have devoted much coverage to members of the Texas National Guard's 36th Division's "Lost Battalion" who were captured in Java soon after the outbreak of hostilities and shipped to Burma to work on the infamous Burma-Thailand Railway depicted in the 1957 film *Bridge on the River Kwai*. In 1993, Robert S. La Forte and Ronald E. Marcello published *Building the Death Railway,* an account of the prisoners' experiences based on oral interviews with twenty-two soldier and sailor survivors. Kelly E. Crager recently combined personal memoirs and oral histories with official army documentary sources in *Hell under the Rising Sun* (2008) to present a comprehensive treatment of the prisoners' story from their initial enlistment to their liberation. Finally, Frank Fujita relates another interesting facet of the Lost Battalion's tale in *Foo: A Japanese-American Prisoner of the Rising Sun* (1993). Separated from his comrades because of his ethnicity (he was only one of two Japanese Americans to be captured by Japan during the war), Fujita tells his story based on a secret diary that he kept as a prisoner, describing daily life, the harsh treatment he often received, and how Japanese officials forced him to deliver propaganda broadcasts.[42]

Another concern of 1960s revisionists, the inclusion of perspectives from previously excluded groups, continues to have its adherents. Objective biographies of Native American leaders provide one means of balancing the historical record of conflict on the Texas frontier. Two recent works lead the way in this genre. In 1993, William T. Hagan published *Quanah Parker,* on the life of the Comanche warrior. Limited by the lack of written documentation to recount Quanah's formative years, however, Hagan focuses primarily on the leader's role in fostering accommodation between his people and the U.S. government after moving to an Oklahoma reservation. Likewise, for his biography of Satanta, Charles M. Robinson III relies on oral tradition to supply information concerning the Kiowa chief.[43]

Historians are also beginning to investigate the Tejano experience during twentieth-century American military conflicts. Of particular note, José A. Ramírez has recently produced *To the Line of Fire!* (2009), the first book to focus exclusively on the Tejano community during World War I. In concise, informative chapters, Ramírez describes how the war impacted Mexican Americans in Texas, determining that, in many ways, their experiences paralleled other groups. They generally responded patriotically to the call to arms while some resisted. New Tejano recruits became exposed to life beyond the barrios and ranches of Texas, first in training camp, then overseas, broadening their worldview. They also endured the horrors of trench warfare while distinguishing themselves in battle. On the home front, Ramírez relates how, despite the isolated actions of some dissidents and despite becoming the targets of constant surveillance by government authorities, most Tejanos continued to sustain the war effort through such activities as participation in bond drives and aiding the Red Cross. The Spanish-language press in Texas also supported the war and did its part to promote patriotism. Ultimately, Ramírez concludes, the events of World War I helped to transform the Tejano community, leading veterans and civic leaders to more openly oppose prejudice and discrimination. As a result, they founded several civil rights groups, eventually merging them into the League of United Latin American Citizens.[44]

More publications now exist that investigate the experiences of African American troops based in Texas during the late nineteenth and early twentieth century. Popular interest in black frontier "Buffalo Soldiers" boomed beginning in the 1960s. William A. Dobak and Thomas D. Phillips, however, reject this label in *The Black Regulars, 1866–1898* (2001), arguing that many of the African American soldiers found the term offensive. Rather than portraying these men as victims of discrimination or as the U.S. Army's "secret weapon" against the Indians, the authors argue instead that their experiences were no better or worse than the white regulars. Garna L. Christian provides evidence to the contrary when looking at the post–Spanish-American War period. In *Black Soldiers in Jim Crow Texas, 1899–1917* (1995), the author studied African American soldiers stationed in Texas at the turn of the twentieth century, focusing on eight different violent racial incidents between the soldiers and Texas communities who did not want them stationed nearby. In every occurrence, including the well-known events in Brownsville and Houston, Christian shows that local white treatment of the black soldiers as second-class citizens and the racial pride of the African American soldiers who resented their treatment provided the combustible elements for the ensuing conflagrations.[45]

Postrevisionist approaches are now influencing the writing of Texas military history. Many recent Texas Confederate regimental and divisional histories are now utilizing one postrevisionist method—the eclectic mix of top-down and bottom-up approaches in order to paint a broader picture of the military units' sagas. While giving due attention to standard institutional subjects of inquiry, such as the group's formation, leader profiles, campaign maneuvers, and combat descriptions, most unit histories currently include soldiers' diaries and correspondence plus information about the social, economic, and educational background of the officers and men. The best narratives, such as Richard G. Lowe's volume on Walker's Texas Division, extensively integrate soldier correspondence and recollections in order to capture the common soldiers' perspectives in the midst of the general actions being described.[46]

In recent years, some postrevisionist scholars have also sought to provide balanced perspectives on certain Texas military events by incorporating Mexican sources. The scholarly community received Stephen L. Hardin's *Texian Iliad* (1994) with much acclaim, hailing the work as an objective recreation that not only devotes much attention to the common soldiers serving in both armies, but also strives for balance by using available Texan and Mexican sources to describe each side's military organization, training, and weaponry along with judicious evaluations of Texan and Mexican leaders and their important decisions. In 2007, Gregg Dimmick sought to convey aspects of the Mexican perspective to the Texas Revolution by publishing the first edited English version of General Vicente Filisola's stern public critique of General José Urrea's 1838 published diary account of the conflict. Although obviously biased, Filisola's account provides Texas readers with a wealth of information on the revolution from his viewpoint.[47]

The strand of postrevisionism employing interdisciplinary techniques to describe historical events has begun to impact Texas military history. A classic example of this technique is Gregg Dimmick's use of archaeological methods in *Sea of Mud* (2004) to analyze the maneuvers of the main Mexican army in the

Texas Revolution after Santa Anna's defeat at San Jacinto. After poring through extensive published and unpublished Mexican sources to retrace general movements and then working with an archaeological team of investigators to unearth an impressive array of artifacts that substantiated his thesis, the author explains why there was no Mexican military counterattack despite the existence of substantial residual forces. In a word: mud. Dimmick demonstrates that Mexican forces attempted to employ a tactical withdrawal in order to reconstitute, but became bogged down after a tumultuous rainstorm. The muddy terrain became so difficult to navigate that it sapped remaining resources and morale, leading to an eventual retreat from the province.[48]

Further interdisciplinary methods used by some postrevisionists involve the use and interpretation of historical memory. Of the Texas military topics in which historians study the interaction between memory and history, the most numerous concern the story of the Alamo, though scholars have scrutinized the topic differently. In *A Line in the Sand* (2001), for example, Randy Roberts and James S. Olson examine the Alamo story and image in mainstream popular memory. After presenting an overview of the Texas Revolution and the Alamo's place within it, the authors focus on the efforts in later years to preserve the site, revive the mission as a revered site, and, most importantly, how the Alamo image has been depicted, interpreted, and used by individuals and interest groups over the years. Tejano historians, however, demonstrate a keen interest in investigating the Alamo phenomenon from the Mexican American perspective. In *The Alamo Remembered* (1995), Timothy Matovina culls through an extensive array of mostly unknown documents to provide an informative collection of Tejano accounts and reflections on the Alamo battle. Through such sources as military reports, interviews, diaries, memoirs, correspondence, petitions and depositions, and newspaper stories, he shows that much of the Tejano community responded to the battle with ambiguity, often sympathizing with the defeated Anglos, but clearly understanding the Mexican viewpoint. In *Remembering the Alamo* (2002), Richard R. Flores traces the origin of the Alamo's symbol of Anglo-Texan pride to the 1880–1920 era and attempts to connect it to the simultaneous capitalist transformation of South Texas, which resulted in widespread land displacement and exploitation of local Mexican workers.[49]

Themes

Along with producing a body of work that utilizes both older and innovative approaches, recent purveyors of Texas military history have also published a combination of monographs that not only echo traditional themes but also espouse new arguments and give attention to fresh subjects of inquiry. Among the standard storylines, the idea of the Alamo as the cradle of Texas liberty because of the heroic sacrifice of its defenders continues to maintain the longest shelf life. Revisionists of many different stripes enjoy poking holes in the thought of the Alamo's defenders as true bravery and virtue personified, but many traditionalists continue to cling to this laudatory impression as one can clearly perceive by observing the ongoing argument about the manner of Davy Crockett's death. While James E. Crisp, in *Sleuthing the Alamo* (2005), and others have accepted the credibility of the Mexican sources describing the execution of a wounded and captured Crockett, traditionalists such as Bill Groneman, in *Defense of a Legend* (1999), vehemently deny the notion. Regardless of what actually happened, the point is that many will never accept an alternate reality to the creation myth on which they were raised.[50]

Another standard theme that persists in many works is the depiction of fighters from the Lone Star State as exceptional fighting men with a unique sense of heroism and gallantry, especially in defense of their homeland. This view frequently appears in many regimental histories of the Civil War. The major reason Texans fought for the Confederacy is often depicted as simply a consequence of their southern sense of honor and duty plus their staunch determination to protect their families and their land. This theme is carried through some works so extensively that one searches vainly for references to slavery as a major cause of the war. As one historian concluded about a Texas cavalry regiment he studied: "The veterans of the 13th Texas could look back on their service to the struggling Confederacy in terms of the fulfillment of duty and a deep sense of personal honor not dependent on the military outcome of the war.... The driving purpose of the soldiers of this regiment was the protection of their homes and families from invasion and occupation. Judged by that standard, they were successful."[51]

Amid the continuation of these and other traditional themes, other scholars are presenting new themes allowing for a broader view of Texas military events. In recent decades, for example, some historians have begun to forcefully argue for acceptance of the Texas navy's importance to the Texas Revolution. In the past, authors have documented the flotilla's exploits, but have often treated their actions in a vacuum by failing to integrate their efforts into the larger story of the revolt. Beginning with chapters in Richard V. Francaviglia's *From Sail to Steam* (1998), scholars have begun to place the Texas navy within the larger context of the conflict. While Jonathan W. Jordan claims too much credit for the Texas fleet by equating its service with the rebel army's triumph at San Jacinto in *Lone Star Navy* (2005), his work and John Powers's *The First Texas Navy* (2006) both provide a welcome addition to the standard "landlocked" studies

111

of the Texas Revolution. By showing the value of Texas naval patrols and the interception of Mexican supply ships in the Gulf of Mexico, they make a strong case for the Texas navy as an important contributor to victory.[52]

Another emergent theme to appear in the recent literature is the importance of the Second World War to the military experience of the Lone Star State. Texas military history has long suffered from a bias against the twentieth century. Although the unfortunate dearth of studies covering aspects of Texas involvement in the First World War, the Korean War, and the Vietnam War persists, attention to World War II has expanded since the fiftieth anniversary of the bombing of Pearl Harbor as numerous new volumes began to examine the conflict's connection to the state. Among the commemorative works produced in 1991, the best proved to be *1941: Texas Goes to War,* a collection of essays dealing with various aspects of the war from the Texas viewpoint. Because so little primary-source research had been completed by the early 1990s, many of the articles relied heavily on statistical and anecdotal evidence, but the work did establish guidelines for subsequent serious scholars of Texas and World War II to follow. The book references the military service of Texans, the state's role as a vital military training ground, aspects of life at POW camps located in Texas, the impact of the war on local communities, and the valuable contributions of women and minorities—all subjects that have since begun to be investigated by a growing number of Texas historians.[53]

New Interpretive Trends

For the first half of the twentieth century, military historians wrote about the frontier army with a celebratory flair, typically describing the soldiers and their officers as brave men doing no wrong. After the Vietnam War, many revisionists began to counter this portrayal as unfounded, often replacing the traditional depiction with characterizations of frontier soldiers as brutal subjugators of the Native Americans. In the past two decades, many postrevisionist historians of the frontier military are moving beyond these extremes. Some still focus on frontier military campaigns but produce more balanced portrayals of the conflicts than previously written. Among the more interesting postrevisionist works, however, are those that concentrate on noncombat-related topics.

Some historians recently have given renewed attention to the multiple roles played by the U.S. Army on the Texas frontier, noting the myriad of nonmilitary services that soldiers provided. In *The Frontier Army in the Settlement of the West* (1999), Michael L. Tate synthesizes a vast amount of primary and secondary source material to highlight the army's various multidimensional responsibilities in the West, giving attention to the Texas experience. The author shows the incredible potential for more detailed research for noncombat studies of the U.S. frontier military in Texas through discussion of such topics as the soldiers' roles as explorers, civilian escorts, law enforcement personnel, scientists, writers and artists, road builders, settler and surveyor protectors, and stimulators for local economies.[54]

Thomas T. Smith ably describes this latter function in *The U.S. Army and the Texas Frontier Economy, 1845–1900* (1999), wherein the author describes the economic impact of the frontier army on the development of West and South Texas. Through exhaustive research in government reports, he reveals how government spending and noncombat services provided by the U.S. military, such as soldier pay, military contracts with local residents, road construction and harbor improvement projects, and the protection of trade routes contributed significantly to the state's economy from 1845 to 1900.[55]

Robert Wooster acknowledged the army's wider roles in order to place Fort Davis within a larger socioeconomic context in *Frontier Crossroads* (2006), viewed by many as the future standard model for presenting frontier fort histories. In addition to describing pertinent military operations and recreating aspects of the daily lives of soldiers, dependents, and civilians living "within the walls" as most standard fort histories do, Wooster combines themes that Tate and Smith referenced by demonstrating the fort's importance to the local economy and explaining the multitude of tasks that the post's inhabitants performed to establish control of the region and to promote its settlement and development.[56]

Conclusions

This survey of the literature has shown recent Texas political, economic, and military history to be a strange brew of scholarship indeed, but why does this insoluble mixture of old and new developments typify work in these subfields today? Will this blend of disparate styles continue to coexist indefinitely? Older historiographical traditions persist to the present day due to a combination of internal and external factors working within and upon the profession. The nature of these forces, in all likelihood, guarantees that the existing cacophony of methods will continue to characterize political, economic, and military history for the foreseeable future.

One reason is that the type of training that a graduate student receives retains a powerful influence upon a scholar. Those mentored to view history primarily as either the story of elites and institutions or to totally reject such a notion will invariably produce works following their chosen approach and continue to espouse familiar themes. Although not true for all scholars, academic inertia may further set in as many choose to maintain their original research interests and immunize themselves from historiographical changes within the profession. Regarding popular authors, the lack of formal history training also influences the manner in which many nonacademic historians approach their topics, leading many to adopt strictly traditional or rigidly revisionist approaches. Unfinished agendas provide another impetus for traditionalists and revisionists to continue along their chosen paths. Many times, one reads on dust jackets that a traditional or revisionist work is to be commended for being "the first book to explore" a certain subject. Just as traditionalists have not written on the lives of every political figure or major political issue, every entrepreneur or company, and every general or military campaign, revisionists have not analyzed all topics related to the average Texas voter, laborer, or soldier.

The power of the marketplace remains the most important external force upon the profession, driving the persistent production of traditional and revisionist works. Because there remains a constant appetite among popular audiences for works reflecting both styles of scholarship, academic presses and trade publishing houses will continue to cater to this demand. General readers who were raised to believe that proper history is solely the study of powerful men and epic institutions flock to biographies of political titans, sagas of large ranches, and standard military campaign narratives while shunning competing styles of scholarship. Other readers who show disdain for elite history tend to gravitate toward stories of civil rights battles, descriptions of life on Texas farms or in the oil fields, or Civil War soldier diaries. As long as these desires among popular audiences remain, historians and popular writers alike will continue to satisfy this need.

Just as revisionists rose to challenge traditionalists, the postrevisionists are now becoming ascendant. While a lag time existed between the acceptance of postrevisionist styles by American history scholars and their later reception by Texas historians, such was also the case when revisionism first came on the scene. This inertia is now dissipating. As more Texas historians practice the newer approaches and develop innovative themes and interpretive trends, their scholarship increasingly resembles the larger profession that has already embraced numerous postrevisionist techniques. Although no longer alienated from the larger profession, it remains to be seen which strands of postrevisionism in Texas history will endure and which will fade. Certain interdisciplinary approaches that are currently in vogue among some postrevisionists, such as historical memory and whiteness studies, may become standard procedure. If these approaches do not fade, it will be a consequence of their proven explanatory power, acceptance by an increasing number of scholars, a growing number of graduate students trained to employ these methods, and the help provided by market pressures to publish more of such works.

Postrevisionist scholarship that melds subfields has a huge potential to transform the study of numerous time periods and historical subjects. Broadening the investigation of political, economic, and military subjects to integrate aspects of one subfield to the subject of another, or to explore the symbiotic relationship among elements of distinct subfields, adds multidimensional depth and understanding to those subjects, as evidenced by Walter Buenger's comprehensive look at Northeast Texas and the war-and-society studies mentioned above. Some significant factors, however, mitigate their more widespread use. Currently, it takes a special type of scholar with extensive training and diverse interests to produce such works, while the existing methods of graduate training often encourage much specialization. Few military scholars get extensive training in economic matters, for example, to develop coordinated war-and-economy studies. Few political historians become experts in advanced economic theory to feel comfortable tackling a truly integrated study of the political economy of Texas during a certain time period.

The postrevisionist strand that interconnects older approaches should have a good chance to endure. Not only do the adherents have merit by providing a more balanced coverage of topics through the inclusion of a multiplicity of perspectives, they also tend to be more acceptable to scholars and general readers of the traditional and revisionist stripes. Devout traditional military historians, for example, do not have many problems with campaign narratives that weave in the experiences of common soldiers within the general framework of the story. Likewise, many energetic economic revisionists should not be too troubled with a work exploring a particular industry that discusses top-level policy decisions of company leaders as long as ample attention is also given to the workers' perspective.

Ultimately, because they have different personal experiences and because of the fact that history writing is a human art form, it should not be surprising that differences exist among historians about the best way to approach their craft. Historians will continue to seek truths in ways reflecting their training, research interests, and exposure to new methods tempered by their upbringing, biases, and general outlook. Nevertheless, when one reviews the current crop of literature in its totality, one glaring omission within each subfield stands out: the lack of synthesis. The disparate approaches, themes, and interpretive trends existing within Texas political, economic, and military history demand a unifying look through twenty-first-century eyes. The commonalities and disparities that one can find within each subfield call out for a cohesive analysis to help scholars and eager students make better sense of it all.

Notes

1. Kenneth B. Hendrickson Jr. and Michael L. Collins, eds., *Profiles in Power: Twentieth-Century Texans in Washington* (Arlington Heights, Ill.: Harlan Davidson, 1993); Carolyn Barta, *Bill Clements: Texian to His Toenails* (Austin: Eakin Press, 1996). Other recent noteworthy biographies of state political leaders utilizing the standard approach include: James Reston Jr., *The Lone Star: The Life of John Connally* (New York: Harper and Row, 1989); Nancy Beck Young, *Wright Patman: Populism, Liberalism, and the American Dream* (Dallas: Southern Methodist University Press, 2000); Lewis L. Gould, *Alexander Watkins Terrell: Civil War Soldier, Texas Lawmaker, American Diplomat* (College Station: Texas A&M University Press, 2004); Godfrey Hodgson, *Woodrow Wilson's Right Hand: The Life of Colonel Edward M. House* (New Haven, Conn.: Yale University Press, 2006); Dorothy Blodgett, Terrell Blodgett, and David L. Scott, *The Land, the Law, and the Lord: The Life of Pat Neff* (Austin: Home Place Publishers, 2007).

2. Gregg Cantrell, *Kenneth and John B. Rayner and the Limits of Southern Dissent* (Urbana: University of Illinois Press, 1993) and *Feeding the Wolf: John B. Rayner and the Politics of Race, 1850–1918* (Wheeling, Ill.: Harlan Davidson, 2001); Ann Fears Crawford, *Frankie: Mrs. R. D. Randolph and Texas Liberal Politics* (Austin: Eakin Press, 2000); Darwin Payne, *Indomitable Sarah: The Life of Judge Sarah T. Hughes* (Dallas: Southern Methodist University Press, 2004); Nancy Baker Jones and Ruthe Winegarten, *Capitol Women: Texas Legislators, 1923–1999* (Austin: University of Texas Press, 2000); José Angel Gutiérrez, Michelle Meléndez, and Sonia Adriana Noyola, eds., *Chicanas in Charge: Texas Women in the Public Arena* (Lanham, Md.: AltaMira Press, 2006); Sonia R. García et al., eds., *Políticas: Latina Public Officials in Texas* (Austin: University of Texas Press, 2008); Mary Beth Rogers, *Barbara Jordan: American Hero* (Westminster, Md.: Bantam, 1998); Merline Pitre, *In Struggle against Jim Crow: Lulu B. White and the NAACP, 1900–1957* (College Station: Texas A&M University Press, 1999).

3. Joel H. Silbey, *Storm over Texas: The Annexation Controversy and the Road to Civil War* (New York: Oxford University Press, 2005). For a classic campaign narrative, see James D. Ivy, *No Saloon in the Valley: The Southern Strategy of Texas Prohibitionists in the 1880s* (Waco: Baylor University Press, 2003). Patrick G. Williams, *Beyond Redemption: Texas Democrats after Reconstruction* (College Station: Texas A&M University Press, 2007), provides an important new survey of the Texas "Redeemers" and their impact on state government once they assumed power.

4. Marion K. Barthelme, ed., *Women of the Texas Populist Movement: Letters to the Southern Mercury* (College Station: Texas A&M University Press, 1997).

5. Dale Baum, *The Shattering of Texas Unionism: Politics in the Lone Star State during the Civil War Era* (Baton Rouge: Louisiana State University Press, 1998). For another recent work of Civil War–era political history using quantitative analysis, see Clayton E. Jewett, *Texas in the Confederacy: An Experiment in Nation Building* (Columbia: University of Missouri Press, 2002). Other recent uses of advanced quan-

titative techniques to analyze aspects of Texas political history include Dale Baum and James L. Hailey, "Lyndon Johnson's Victory in the 1948 Texas Senate Race: A Reappraisal," *Political Science Quarterly* 109, no. 4 (1994): 595–613, and Chandler Davidson and Bernard Grofman, eds., *Quiet Revolution in the South: The Impact of the Voting Rights Act, 1965–1990* (Princeton, N.J.: Princeton University Press, 1994).

6. Robert C. McMath, *American Populism: A Social History, 1877–1898* (New York: Hill and Wang, 1993); Judith N. McArthur, *Creating the New Woman: The Rise of Southern Women's Progressive Culture in Texas, 1893–1918* (Urbana: University of Illinois Press, 1998). For other recent examples of works that discuss the use of strategies employed by Texas Progressive women, see Elizabeth Hayes Turner, *Women, Culture, and Community: Religion and Reform in Galveston, 1880–1920* (New York: Oxford University Press, 1997); Jacquelyn Masur McElhaney, *Pauline Periwinkle and Progressive Reform in Dallas* (College Station: Texas A&M University Press, 1998); Elizabeth York Enstam, "The Dallas Equal Suffrage Association, Political Style, and Popular Culture: Grassroots Strategies of the Woman Suffrage Movement, 1913–1919," *Journal of Southern History* 68 (November 2002): 817–48; Judith N. McArthur and Harold L. Smith, *Minnie Fisher Cunningham: A Suffragist's Life in Politics* (New York: Oxford University Press, 2003).

7. Chandler Davidson, *Race and Class in Texas Politics* (Princeton, N.J.: Princeton University Press, 1990).

8. Patrick J. Carroll, *Felix Longoria's Wake: Bereavement, Racism, and the Rise of Mexican American Activism* (Austin: University of Texas Press, 2003).

9. Craig A. Kaplowitz, *LULAC, Mexican Americans, and National Policy* (College Station: Texas A&M University Press, 2005). Another example discussed in other essays appearing in this volume but worth noting here is Emilio Zamora's *Claiming Rights and Righting Wrongs in Texas* (2009), in which the author focuses on the role played by the Fair Employment Practices Committee in combating discrimination against Mexican workers in Texas manufacturing firms during World War II. Zamora argues that as discrimination undermined job opportunities, the Mexican government intervened and challenged the American commitment to the Good Neighbor Policy. These protestations subsequently encouraged U.S. government agencies to address discrimination and created unprecedented political possibilities for Mexican American civil rights leaders and labor representatives to become major participants in domestic politics. Emilio Zamora, *Claiming Rights and Righting Wrongs in Texas: Mexican Workers and Job Politics during World War II* (College Station: Texas A&M University Press, 2009). See also Thomas A. Guglielmo, "Fighting for Caucasian Rights: Mexicans, Mexican Americans, and the Transnational Struggle for Civil Rights in World War II Texas," *Journal of American History* 92 (2006): 45–77.

10. Keith J. Volanto, *Texas, Cotton, and the New Deal* (College Station: Texas A&M University Press, 2005).

11. See, for example, Martin Kuhlman, "Direct Action at the University of Texas during the Civil Rights Movement, 1960–1965," *Southwestern Historical Quarterly* 98

(April 1995): 551–68; Glenn Linden, *Desegregating Schools in Dallas: Four Decades in the Federal Courts* (Dallas: Three Forks Press, 1995); Robyn Duff Ladino, *Desegregating Texas Schools: Eisenhower, Shivers, and the Crisis at Mansfield High* (Austin: University of Texas Press, 1996); Amilcar Shabazz, *Advancing Democracy: African Americans and the Struggle for Access and Equity in Higher Education in Texas* (Chapel Hill: University of North Carolina Press, 2004); Charles L. Zelden, *The Battle for the Black Ballot: Smith v. Allwright and the Defeat of the Texas All-White Primary* (Lawrence: University Press of Kansas, 2004).

12. Armando Navarro, *The Cristal Experiment: A Chicano Struggle for Community Control* (Madison: University of Wisconsin Press, 1998). See also José Angel Gutiérrez's autobiography: *The Making of a Chicano Militant: Lessons from Cristal* (Madison: University of Wisconsin Press, 1998).

13. Gregg Cantrell, *Stephen F. Austin: Empresario of Texas* (New Haven, Conn.: Yale University Press, 1999); James L. Haley, *Sam Houston* (Norman: University of Oklahoma Press, 2002).

14. Paul D. Lack, *The Texas Revolutionary Experience: A Political and Social History* (College Station: Texas A&M University Press, 1992).

15. James Marten, *Texas Divided: Loyalty and Dissent in the Lone Star State, 1856–1874* (Lexington: University of Kentucky Press, 1990). See also Richard B. McCaslin, "Wheat Growers in the Cotton Confederacy: The Suppression of Dissent in Collin County, Texas during the Civil War," *Southwestern Historical Quarterly* 96 (April 1993): 526–39, and *Tainted Breeze: The Great Gainesville Hanging, 1862* (Baton Rouge: Louisiana State University Press, 1997); David Pickering and Judy Falls, *Brush Men and Vigilantes: Civil War Dissent in Texas* (College Station: Texas A&M University Press, 2000).

16. Ignacio M. García, *Viva Kennedy: Mexican Americans in Search of Camelot* (College Station: Texas A&M University Press, 2000). Likewise, in *Claiming Citizenship* (2005), a work discussed in another essay appearing in this volume, Anthony Quiroz examines Tejano civil rights activities in his hometown of Victoria, Texas, and concludes that local Hispanics were neither docile nor militant. Instead, they organized to challenge the system through "consensual opposition," that is, they accepted the central tenets of society and simply sought inclusion within it. This finding, Quiroz readily acknowledges, was "a departure from the standard historiography on Tejano communities that argues that a questioning of mainstream institutional life and confrontational tactics were the norm, particularly during the 1960s and after." Anthony Quiroz, *Claiming Citizenship: Mexican Americans in Victoria, Texas* (College Station: Texas A&M University Press, 2005).

17. William Henry Kellar, *Make Haste Slowly: Moderates, Conservatives, and School Desegregation in Houston* (College Station: Texas A&M University Press, 1999). See also Michael Phillips, *White Metropolis: Race, Ethnicity, and Religion in Dallas, 1841–2001* (Austin: University of Texas Press, 2006); Brian D. Behnken. "The 'Dallas Way': Protest, Response, and the Civil Rights Experience in Big D and Beyond,"

Southwestern Historical Quarterly 111 (July 2007): 1–29; and the film documentary "The Strange Demise of Jim Crow" (San Francisco: California Newsreel, 1998), whose producers seek to reveal "the behind-the-scenes compromises, negotiations, and the controversial news black-outs which helped bring about the quiet desegregation of commercial establishments in Houston."

18. Randolph B. Campbell, *Grass-Roots Reconstruction in Texas, 1865–1880* (Baton Rouge: Louisiana State University Press, 1997); Barry A. Crouch and Donaly E. Brice, *Cullen Montgomery Baker, Reconstruction Desperado* (Baton Rouge: Louisiana State University Press, 1997); James M. Smallwood, Barry A. Crouch, and Larry Peacock, *Murder and Mayhem: The War of Reconstruction in Texas* (College Station: Texas A&M University Press, 2003). See also James M. Smallwood, *The Feud That Wasn't: The Taylor Ring, Bill Sutton, John Wesley Hardin, and Violence in Texas* (College Station: Texas A&M University Press, 2008).

19. James T. Patterson, *The New Deal and the States: Federalism in Transition* (Princeton, N.J.: Princeton University Press, 1969); John A. Adams Jr., *Damming the Colorado: The Rise of the Lower Colorado River Authority, 1933–1939* (College Station: Texas A&M University Press, 1990); Carl A. Weisenberger, *Dollars and Dreams: The National Youth Administration in Texas* (New York: Peter Lang, 1994); Kenneth E. Hendrickson Jr., "Replenishing the Soil and the Soul of Texas: The Civilian Conservation Corps in the Lone Star State as an Example of State-Federal Work Relief during the Great Depression," *The Historian* 65 (Summer 2003): 801–16; Phillip Parisi, *The Texas Post Office Murals: Art for the People* (College Station: Texas A&M University Press, 2004); Volanto, *Texas, Cotton, and the New Deal*.

20. Robert A. Caro, *The Years of Lyndon Johnson: The Path to Power* (New York: Alfred A. Knopf, 1982), *The Years of Lyndon Johnson: Means of Ascent* (New York: Alfred A. Knopf, 1990), and *The Years of Lyndon Johnson: Master of the Senate* (New York: Alfred A. Knopf, 2002). For a well-conceived and finely written critique of Caro's first two volumes, see Evan Anders, "Robert Caro's Lyndon Johnson and the Pitfalls of Political Biography: A Critical Evaluation of *The Years of Lyndon Johnson: The Path to Power and Means of Ascent*," *Southwestern Historical Quarterly* 94 (April 1991): 581–98.

21. Robert Dallek, *Lone Star Rising: Lyndon Johnson and His Times, 1908–1960* (New York: Oxford University Press, 1991), and *Flawed Giant: Lyndon B. Johnson, 1960–1973* (New York: Oxford University Press, 1998). For praise of Dallek's work, see Evan Anders, "Light at the End of the Tunnel: Evaluating the Major Biographies of Lyndon Johnson," *Southwestern Historical Quarterly* 98 (October 1994): 297–324. See also the well-received Randall B. Woods, *LBJ: Architect of American Ambition* (New York: Free Press, 2006), discussed in another essay appearing in this volume.

22. Walter L. Buenger, "Flight from Modernity: The Economic History of Texas since 1845," in *Texas Through Time: Evolving Interpretations,* ed. Walter L. Buenger and Robert A. Calvert (College Station: Texas A&M University Press, 1991), 310.

23. Robert W. McDaniel and Henry C. Dethloff, *Pattillo Higgins and the Search for Texas Oil* (College Station: Texas A&M University Press, 1989).

24. Steve Kelton, *Renderbrook: A Century under the Spade Brand* (Fort Worth: Texas Christian University Press, 1989); Christopher J. Castaneda and Joseph A. Pratt, *From Texas to the East: A Strategic History of Texas Eastern Corporation* (College Station: Texas A&M University Press, 1993).

25. Thad Sitton and Dan K. Utley, *From Can See to Can't: Texas Cotton Farmers on the Southern Prairies* (Austin: University of Texas Press, 1997). See also Rebecca Sharpless, *Fertile Ground, Narrow Choices: Women on Texas Cotton Farms, 1900–1940* (Chapel Hill: University of North Carolina Press, 1999); Thad Sitton, ed., *Harder than Hardscrabble: Oral Recollections of the Farming Life from the Edge of the Texas Hill Country* (Austin: University of Texas Press, 2003).

26. Don E. Carleton, *A Breed So Rare: The Life of J. R. Parten, Liberal Texas Oilman, 1896–1992* (Austin: Texas State Historical Association, 1999); Victoria Buenger and Walter L. Buenger, *Texas Merchant: Marvin Leonard and Fort Worth* (College Station: Texas A&M University Press, 1998).

27. Andrés Tijerina, *Tejano Empire: Life on the South Texas Ranchos* (College Station: Texas A&M University Press, 1998).

28. Neil Foley, *The White Scourge: Mexicans, Blacks, and Poor Whites in Texas Cotton Culture* (Berkeley: University of California Press, 1997).

29. Judith Walker Linsley, Ellen Walker Rienstra, and Jo Ann Stiles, *Giant under the Hill: A History of the Spindletop Oil Discovery at Beaumont, Texas, in 1901* (Austin: Texas State Historical Association, 2002).

30. Walter L. Buenger, *The Path to a Modern South: Northeast Texas between Reconstruction and the Great Depression* (Austin: University of Texas Press, 2001). Another recent innovative approach to Texas economic history, discussed in separate essays in this volume, involves the study of transnational economic issues, a technique applied by a growing number of Tejano labor historians. Emilio Zamora's *The World of the Mexican Worker in Texas* (1993) is probably the best example of this method. In his book, Zamora explains how early twentieth-century South Texas immigrant workers reacted to low wages, pitiable living conditions, and racial discrimination. Far from accepting their situation, they organized to protect themselves. How they organized, more specifically, where they received their inspiration to organize, is the key to Zamora's approach. The workers' membership in ethnic-based mutual aid societies, labor unions, patriotic societies, and sometimes even radical groups such as the Texas Socialist Party were not only attempts to further their aims but also hearkened to a traditional "Mexicanist" political identity derived from their homeland experiences. Emilio Zamora, *The World of the Mexican Worker in Texas* (College Station: Texas A&M University Press, 1993). See also Roberto R. Calderón, *Mexican Coal Mining Labor in Texas and Coahuila, 1880–1930* (College Station: Texas A&M University Press, 2000).

31. Riley Froh, *Edgar B. Davis and Sequences in Business Capitalism: From Shoes to Rubber to Oil* (New York: Garland Publishing, 1993).

32. William R. Childs, *The Texas Railroad Commission: Understanding Regula-

tion in America to the Mid-Twentieth Century (College Station: Texas A&M University Press, 2005).

33. C. Allan Jones, *Texas Roots: Agriculture and Rural Life before the Civil War* (College Station: Texas A&M University Press, 2005).

34. Examples of new works examining aspects of twentieth-century Texas economy include Caleb Pirtle III, *Engineering the World: Stories from the First 75 Years of Texas Instruments* (Dallas: Southern Methodist University Press, 2005); Darwin Payne and Kathy Fitzpatrick, *From Plains to Planes: How Dallas and Fort Worth Overcame Politics and Personalities to Build One of the World's Biggest and Busiest Airports* (Dallas: Three Forks Press, 1999); Kenneth B. Ragsdale, "Barnstormers, Businessmen, and High Hopes for the Future: Austin, Texas, Enters the Modern Air Age," *Southwestern Historical Quarterly* (April 2004): 534–57; Joseph A. Pratt and Christopher J. Castaneda, *Builders: Herman and George R. Brown* (College Station: Texas A&M University Press, 1999); Elizabeth Silverthorne and Geneva Fulgham, *Women Pioneers in Texas Medicine* (College Station: Texas A&M University Press, 1997); Henry C. Dethloff and Donald H. Dyal, *A Special Kind of Doctor: A History of Veterinary Medicine in Texas* (College Station: Texas A&M University Press, 1991); Ronald Garay, *Gordon McLendon: The Maverick of Radio* (Westport, Conn.: Greenwood Press, 1992); Richard Schroeder, *Texas Signs On: The Early Days of Radio and Television* (College Station: Texas A&M University Press, 1998); Carol Dawson and Carol Johnston, *House of Plenty: The Rise, Fall, and Revival of Luby's Cafeterias* (Austin: University of Texas Press, 2006); Karen Wright, *The Road to Dr Pepper, Texas: The Story of Dublin Dr. Pepper* (Austin: State House Press, 2006).

35. Kyle G. Wilkison, *Yeoman, Sharecroppers, and Socialists: Plain Folk Protest in Texas, 1870–1914* (College Station: Texas A&M University Press, 2008).

36. Robert Lee Maril, *The Bay Shrimpers of Texas: Rural Fishermen in a Global Economy* (Lawrence: University Press of Kansas, 1995).

37. Elizabeth Maret, *Women of the Range: Women's Roles in the Texas Beef Cattle Industry* (College Station: Texas A&M University Press, 1993); Sara R. Massey, ed., *Texas Women on the Cattle Trails* (College Station: Texas A&M University Press, 2006). Regarding women in Texas agriculture, Rebecca Sharpless's *Fertile Ground, Narrow Choices* (1999), discussed in another essay appearing in this volume, makes excellent use of oral history to recreate in vivid detail the social and economic lives of early twentieth-century Texas farmers. Because most farm families lacked modern amenities of home life enjoyed by many urban dwellers, the lives of farm women involved constant drudgery. They cooked on wood-burning stoves. Laundry cleaning involved the use of tubs filled with hot water followed by intense scrubbing on washboards. The interviews reveal that these time-consuming responsibilities were just a portion of farm women's overall duties. In addition to cooking and cleaning, farm women preserved food, sewed, tended gardens, raised poultry and livestock, and raised the children. Despite the social stigma, many also performed fieldwork when needed, usually around weed-chopping or cotton-picking time. One cannot put down

the book without an abiding respect for the hard work these women performed on a daily basis. Sharpless, *Fertile Ground, Narrow Choices: Women on Texas Cotton Farms, 1900–1940*. (Chapel Hill: University of North Carolina Press, 1999).

38. Marilyn D. Rhinehart, *A Way of Work and a Way of Life: Coal Mining in Thurber, Texas, 1888–1926* (College Station: Texas A&M University Press, 1992). For labor solidarity in Texas lumber company towns, see Thad Sitton and James H. Conrad, *Nameless Towns: Texas Sawmill Communities, 1880–1942* (Austin: University of Texas Press, 1998). A recent favorable review of oil company camp life is Diana Davids Hinton, "Creating Company Culture: Oil Company Camps in the Southwest," *Southwestern Historical Quarterly* 111 (April 2008): 369–88.

39. Paul H. Carlson, *"Pecos Bill": A Military Biography of William R. Shafter* (College Station: Texas A&M University Press, 1989).

40. Edward T. Cotham Jr., *Sabine Pass: The Confederacy's Thermopylae* (Austin: University of Texas Press, 2004).

41. The number of recently published diaries and correspondence of soldiers is vast, but among the more interesting are Charles D. Spurlin, *The Civil War Diary of Charles A. Leuschner* (Austin: Eakin Press, 1992); Richard Lowe, ed., *A Texas Cavalry Officer's Civil War: The Diary and Letters of James C. Bates* (Baton Rouge: Louisiana State University Press, 1999); Thomas W. Cutrer, ed., *Our Trust Is in the God of Battles: The Civil War Letters of Robert Franklin Bunting, Chaplain, Terry's Texas Rangers, C.S.A.* (Knoxville: University of Tennessee Press, 2006).

42. Robert S. La Forte and Ronald E. Marcello, *Building the Death Railway: The Ordeal of American POWs in Burma, 1942–1945* (Wilmington, Del.: SR Books, 1993); Kelly E. Crager, *Hell under the Rising Sun: Texan POWs and the Building of the Burma-Thailand Death Railway* (College Station: Texas A&M University Press, 2008); Frank Fujita, *Foo: A Japanese-American Prisoner of the Rising Sun; The Secret Prison Diary of Frank "Foo" Fujita* (Denton: University of North Texas Press, 1993).

43. William T. Hagan, *Quanah Parker, Comanche Chief* (Norman: University of Oklahoma Press, 1995); Charles M. Robinson III, *Satanta: The Life and Death of a War Chief* (Austin: State House Press, 1997).

44. José A. Ramírez, *To the Line of Fire! Mexican Texans and World War I* (College Station: Texas A&M University Press, 2009). See also Maggie Rivas-Rodríguez's edited volume, *Mexican Americans and World War II*, whose eleven essays include five dealing specifically with Tejano home front issues during the Second World War. Maggie Rivas-Rodríguez, ed., *Mexican Americans and World War II* (Austin: University of Texas Press, 2005).

45. William A. Dobak and Thomas D. Phillips, *The Black Regulars, 1866–1898* (Norman: University of Oklahoma Press, 2001); Garna L. Christian, *Black Soldiers in Jim Crow Texas, 1899–1917* (College Station: Texas A&M University Press, 1995).

46. Richard G. Lowe, *Walker's Texas Division, C.S.A.: Greyhounds of the Trans-Mississippi* (Baton Rouge: Louisiana State University Press, 2004). See also Anne J. Bailey, *Between the Enemy and Texas: Parsons's Texas Cavalry in the Civil War* (Fort

Worth: Texas Christian University Press, 1989); Douglas Hale, *The Third Texas Cavalry in the Civil War* (Norman: University of Oklahoma Press, 1993); M. Jane Johansson, *Peculiar Honor: A History of the 28th Texas Cavalry, 1862–1865* (Fayetteville: University of Arkansas Press, 1998).

47. Stephen L. Hardin, *Texian Iliad: A Military History of the Texas Revolution* (Austin: University of Texas Press, 1994); Gregg J. Dimmick, ed., *General Vicente Filisola's Analysis of José Urrea's Military Diary: A Forgotten 1838 Publication by an Eyewitness to the Texas Revolution,* trans. John Wheat (Austin: Texas State Historical Association, 2007).

48. Gregg J. Dimmick, *Sea of Mud: The Retreat of the Mexican Army after San Jacinto: An Archeological Investigation* (Austin: Texas State Historical Association, 2004). Michael Waters also makes good use of archaeological evidence to supplement interviews with former prisoners of war, guards, and local residents in his book on life at Camp Hearne. Michael R. Waters et al., *Lone Star Stalag: German Prisoners of War at Camp Hearne* (College Station: Texas A&M University Press, 2004).

49. Randy Roberts and James S. Olson, *A Line in the Sand: The Alamo in Blood and Memory* (New York: Free Press, 2001); Timothy Matovina, *The Alamo Remembered: Tejano Accounts and Perspectives* (Austin: University of Texas Press, 1995); Richard R. Flores, *Remembering the Alamo: Memory, Modernity, and Master Symbol* (Austin: University of Texas Press, 2002).

50. James E. Crisp, *Sleuthing the Alamo: Davy Crockett's Last Stand and Other Mysteries of the Texas Revolution* (New York: Oxford University Press, 2005); Bill Groneman, *Defense of a Legend: The Myth and Mystery Surrounding the Death of Davy Crockett* (Plano: Republic of Texas Press, 1999).

51. Quoted in Thomas Reid, *Spartan Band: Burnett's 13th Texas Cavalry in the Civil War* (Denton: University of North Texas Press, 2005), 191. See also Anne Bailey's introduction to *Between the Enemy and Texas.*

52. Richard V. Francaviglia, *From Sail to Steam: Four Centuries of Texas Maritime History, 1500–1900* (Austin: University of Texas Press, 1998); Jonathan W. Jordan, *Lone Star Navy* (Washington, D.C.: Potomac Books, 2005); John Powers, *The First Texas Navy* (Austin: Woodmont Books, 2006). For an informative historiographical overview of the Texas navy, see Jerry C. Drake, "The Cruise of a Forgotten Flotilla: An Historiographical Survey of the Texas Navy," at http://www.texasnavy.com/forgotten_flotilla.htm (August 1, 2008).

53. James Ward Lee, ed., *1941: Texas Goes to War* (Denton: University of North Texas Press, 1991). For some examples of World War II scholarship besides the prisoner-of-war studies listed above, see Anne Noggle, *For God, Country, and the Thrill of It: Women Airforce Service Pilots in World War II* (College Station: Texas A&M University Press, 1990); Louis Fairchild, *They Called It the War Effort: Oral Histories from World War II, Orange, Texas* (Austin: Eakin Press, 1993); Thomas E. Alexander, *The Stars Were Big and Bright: The United States Army Air Forces and Texas during World War II,* 2 vols. (Austin: Eakin Press, 2000 and 2001), and *Rattlesnake Bomber Base: Pyote Army*

Airfield in World War II (Abilene, Tex.: State House Press, 2005); Tom Killebrew, *The Royal Air Force in Texas: Training British Pilots in Terrell during World War II* (Denton: University of North Texas Press, 2003).

54. Michael L. Tate, *The Frontier Army in the Settlement of the West* (Norman: University of Oklahoma Press, 1999).

55. Thomas T. Smith, *The U.S. Army and the Texas Frontier Economy, 1845–1900* (College Station: Texas A&M University Press, 1999).

56. Robert Wooster, *Frontier Crossroads: Fort Davis and the West* (College Station: Texas A&M University Press, 2006).

Why Is Big Tex Still a White Cowboy?

Race, Gender, and the "Other Texans"

Michael Phillips

In 1952 the symbol most associated with the annual Texas State Fair in Dallas made a memorable debut. That year, workers erected the fifty-two-foot-high cowboy "Big Tex." In a previous life the imposing figure served as a "the world's largest Santa Claus," created to encourage Christmas shopping in the town of Kerens. In his new incarnation, Big Tex, with his size seventy boots and seventy-five-gallon hat, embodied the larger-than-life Texas myth.[1]

As historian Gregg Cantrell noted in his 2007 essay, "The Bones of Stephen F. Austin: History and Memory in Progressive-Era Texas," by the early twentieth century elite Texas Progressives embraced a Western, as opposed to Southern, identity for the Lone Star State. The cowboy image served an economic purpose. Linking Texas identity with the Confederacy meant tying the Lone Star State to the "Lost Cause," a past redolent of defeat, nostalgia, and sleepy rural rhythms. In contrast, the Progressives who came to dominate Texas politics in the early twentieth century wanted to attract outside investment by linking the state with a more triumphant, Western narrative of bold, independent mavericks conquering an untamed frontier. Free-spirited and independent cowboys gradually displaced defeated soldiers in gray in the state's mythology.[2]

The ideas Big Tex embodied rested on racist foundations. The West stood for triumph, which in the Anglo mind meant the victory of superior whites over Mexican and Indian barbarians. Meanwhile, by the time Big Tex arose over the Fair Park landscape, the state's historians, primarily from the University of Texas at Austin, had driven Mexican Americans and African Americans to the margins of the master narrative. Anglo writers erased the Indian and Mexican contributions to the culture of Texas, the role of black and brown labor in building the state, and the political importance of men like Texas revolutionary leader Lorenzo de Zavala and African American Republican Party activist Norris Wright Cuney in the 1870s and 1880s.

The collective memory that Big Tex represents still casts a giant shadow on historical consciousness in this state. In essence, there have been two big epics in race and gender historiography in Texas. Writers in the first epic, such as T. R. Fehrenbach, believed that the Texas story centered on the nineteenth century with its Anglo conquests of the land and the collapse of the old plantation order. Fehrenbach and others focused on the "great men"—Sam Houston, the heroes of the Alamo, Jim Hogg, and the like—they saw as the almost exclusive historical actors. Late nineteenth-century Populists, twentieth-century labor activists and political radicals, the African American and Mexican American civil rights movement, the rising politicization of gays, battles over abortion, and so on really did not concern the Fehrenbach generations. This group spun tales of battlefield heroism and Western romance, and the public imagination regarding the Texas past remains firmly gripped by this zeitgeist.

A second epic, spawned by the social justice movements of the post–World War II era, moved the focus from the Alamo and the Civil War to what was called in the 1970s the New Social History. This phase remains the dominant approach in Texas historiography today. To paraphrase Mao Zedong, Texas historians "let a thousand flowers bloom." Since the 1970s, historians have sought stories of those at the bottom of the social ladder and have pioneered ever-proliferating approaches to Afro-Texan, Tejano, and women's history. This approach captured the imagination of researchers and has even modified the Fehrenbach-influenced popular memory of Texas history, though, as will be argued later, that influence has been on the margins. Many Texas scholars still use traditional narrative history as they seek to "fill in the record" of the African Americans, Mexican Americans, Asian Americans, and women left out in the Big Tex script. This New Social History has made a profoundly positive impact on Texas historiography but has crowded out other approaches. Meanwhile, a third approach, postmodernism, has struggled to gain footing in the Texas history field.

Postmodernism significantly influenced the type of questions modern Texas historians ask, but has not been central to Texas scholars' analysis outside of a limited number of works on gender and so-called whiteness studies. It was not until the new century began that important works utilizing the concept of public memory emerged. Meanwhile, the gap grows between what scholars know of the Texas past and what Texas history buffs think they know. Cowboys continue to be fetishized, slavery minimized, and women marginalized at public history sites.

What accounts for this lag in historical consciousness? Examining the state of Texas history prior to the 1990s helps explain the continued grip writers like Fehrenbach have on public memory today. For decades Texas history was the work of amateurs. Forty years elapsed between the Texas Revolution in the 1830s and the establishment of the state's first public university, the Agricultural and Mechanical College of Texas (later renamed Texas A&M University) in 1876. The University of Texas at Austin did not open until 1883. The state's lack of credentialed historians created a vacuum filled by men like John Henry Brown, mayor of both Galveston and Dallas in the mid- and late nineteenth century, who authored *The History of Texas, from 1685 to 1892* (1893). The pro-Confederate and antisuffragist sentiments of would-be historians like Brown ensured that women and people of color would be marginalized in the state's master narrative. These parahistorians, not trained in nuanced readings of the past, produced crowd-pleasing tales with clearly defined heroes and villains. Both the University of Texas and Texas A&M remained segregated until the second half of the twentieth century, meaning that black and brown historians remained unheard outside their communities. Texas A&M also excluded women until the 1960s, resulting in a silencing of female scholars.[3]

The old racial attitudes endured in T. R. Fehrenbach's weighty *Lone Star: A History of Texas and the Texans*, published in 1968, which became perhaps the most popular rendition of Texas narrative history ever. Fehrenbach characterized Indians as warlike and "sadistic," and claimed the Indian male "seldom soiled his hand with labor." Of African Americans, Fehrenbach commented, "The Negro was never a prime mover, but always a dangerous catalyst in American life." Tejanos failed to record substantial achievements post-Texas independence, he wrote, because they embraced a culture that belittled hard labor. "Nowhere in the Mexican ethos were the bedrock assumptions, the value system that lay so close to the Anglo heart . . . work as a virtue, transcending all necessity; wealth as desirable, if not the only desirable, basis of status; the drive for status itself." Women were also largely invisible. Only twenty-six women appear in Fehrenbach's twenty-eight-page index, with many identified by their husband's names, such as "Mrs. James Bowie." Several of the identified women appear in the text only as victims of Native American and Mexican military attacks.[4]

As will be explained later, many of the core beliefs of the Fehrenbach generation of Texas historians survives in popular memory today: that Texas steadily becomes more powerful, wealthier, and more free as time goes on; that Texas prosperity derives solely from the efforts of Texans; that white men, if no longer seen as a the only historical actors, remain the central characters in the

Texas story; that the twentieth century of Texas history is less important and compelling than the nineteenth century; and that the state overcame past social defects such as slavery and that racial oppression is not an important component of the Texas experience today.

Even after the civil rights movement from the 1950s to the 1970s, Texas remained relatively overlooked by American scholars because the state's past did not fit easily within established historical niches. My description in *White Metropolis: Race, Ethnicity, and Religion in Dallas, 1841–2001* (2006) regarding the scholarly neglect of Dallas applies to Texas as a whole. "Too small [in population] in the 1860s and 1870s to merit extensive consideration in histories of the Civil War and Reconstruction, too Southern to be placed in the context of the great labor battles of the late nineteenth century, and too Western to be incorporated into monographs on the Southern desegregation struggle in the mid-twentieth century," Texas attracted little historical attention outside of the Lone Star State.[5]

Texas thus represented a missed opportunity for understanding how race and gender are constructed in American culture. As historian Amilcar Shabazz observes in *Advancing Democracy: African Americans and the Struggle for Access and Equity in Higher Education in Texas* (2004), Texas provides a fascinating contrast with other Southern states due to its status as "the South's most unique and diverse state. It is the only former slave state that was once a part of Mexico and that has a substantial Mexican American population. . . . The diversity only begins there. Texas is where the East meets the West." In addition, Texas provided the setting for one of the most important Supreme Court decisions in the civil rights era. As Shabazz observes, the Supreme Court's *Sweatt v. Painter* ruling (which desegregated the University of Texas at Austin law school) not only opened public colleges and universities to black students but also served as an important precedent for the more famous *Brown v. Board of Education* decision that ordered the desegregation of public schools. Historians were also slow to recognize how Texas provides an excellent case study for gender scholars. Conditions on the Texas frontier appeared to have softened the rigid gender roles imposed in other Southern states. Thus in 1925 Miriam "Ma" Ferguson, along with Nellie Tayloe Ross of Wyoming, became the first women governors in the United States. A Texas woman, Jessie Daniel Ames, led the Association of Southern Women for the Prevention of Lynching. Texas also provided the setting for the divisive *Roe v. Wade* decision, which legalized abortion in the first two trimesters of pregnancy.[6]

Yet these stories would not begin to be told until the last third of the twentieth century. Two historical developments changed Texas scholarship on race and gender in the 1970s. First of all, in the 1960s Gov. John Connally and Lt. Gov. Ben Barnes successfully lobbied the legislature to substantially increase university budgets, arguing this was needed to maintain the state's economic competitiveness. The pair hiked university and college faculty salaries, attracting more academic talent from out of state, improved and expanded the state's community colleges, added the University of Houston to the state system, and turned Angelo State College and Pan American College into four-year schools. In addition to an upgrade of the state's higher education system, the women's movement and the African American and Mexican American civil rights movement successfully battled to desegregate and break down gender barriers at Texas colleges and universities. On more diverse campuses, pressure mounted for more inclusive scholarship and diverse faculties, which in turn produced more sensitive and imaginative scholarship.[7]

Second, a new generation of race and gender scholars tapped into the revisionist zeitgeist of the 1960s. The political climate of that decade spawned the so-called New Social History. This approach rejected the "great man" paradigm that emphasized the lives and actions of the rich and powerful as the major force shaping the past. The New Social Historians created narratives from "the bottom up," emphasizing, for instance, the roles of slaves, migrant workers, child laborers, and union organizers in creating social norms and political discourse, and documenting how the oppressed resisted elite domination.

In Texas, the leading exponents of the New Social History included Lawrence D. Rice, Alwyn Barr, Cary D. Wintz, James M. SoRelle, Arnoldo De León, David Montejano, and Randolph B. Campbell. These scholars opened the first serious examination of black and Tejano history in Texas. They expanded what constituted history and who could be considered historical actors.[8] Works like De León's *They Called Them Greasers: Anglo Attitudes toward Mexicans in Texas, 1821–1900* (1983); Jacquelyn Dowd Hall's groundbreaking essay, "'The Mind That Burns in Each Body': Women, Rape, and Racial Violence" (1984); Montejano's *Anglos and Mexicans in the Making of Texas, 1836–1986* (1987); and Campbell's *An Empire for Slavery: The Peculiar Institution in Texas, 1821–1865* (1989) examined how racial and gender identities form; the relationship of racism to class politics; and how women, African Americans, and Tejanos created counterhegemonic cultures to resist white male oppression.[9] Even if the New Social History is a bit long in the tooth in the twenty-first-century's first decade, this approach continues to dominate Texas historiography, perhaps at the expense of newer approaches such as postmodernism.

The concerns raised by Campbell and his peers clearly informed the most nuanced work ever on the role racial ideology played in Texas politics: Chandler Davidson's *Race and Class in Texas Politics,* published in 1990.[10] Beginning with Dwight Eisenhower's two presidential campaigns against liberal, pro–civil rights Illinois Senator Adlai Stevenson, Davidson argues, the segregationist leadership of the Texas Democratic Party began ticket splitting, voting Republican in presidential races and for conservative Democrats in local races. Rightwing Democrats crossed the Rubicon and became Republicans in the 1970s and 1980s as the Democratic Party became an unstable coalition of African Americans, Mexican Americans, and left-of-center whites. Davidson argued that the ascendant Republican Party in Texas benefited from instigating Anglo resentments over issues like affirmative action and illegal immigration. According to Davidson, race became the grammar by which Texans engaged in political conflict.

Davidson, in addition to De León, Hall, Campbell, and Montejano, brought these insights into Texas history: that white supremacy and sexism formed a central part of Texas politics and culture; that African Americans, Mexican Americans, and women shaped and also were shaped by Texas history and culture; that the story of marginalized groups in Texas represents a contingent tale swinging from the extremes of compromise and accommodation on one hand to resistance on the other; and that gender and racial hierarchies in Texas uniquely derive from the state's ambiguous geographical position at the intersection of the South, the West, the Mexican borderlands and, some suggest, the southern extreme of the Midwest. These writers provided an alternative vision of Texas history, one no longer monochromatic.

The New Social History project, however, perhaps proved to be too successful. Unfortunately for the growth of Texas scholarship, much history written since Campbell, De León, and others, has built on, but not substantially revised or expanded, the work of these academic pioneers. As Texas race and gender scholars in the 1990s sought more and more untold "bottom-up" narratives, their research splintered into endless microcategories: Afro-Texan, Tejano, Native American, Asian American, and women's history;[11] biography;[12] racial and gender politics;[13] slavery;[14] racial violence;[15] immigration and ethnic studies;[16] histories of the various civil rights movements since World War II;[17] African Americans, Mexicans, and women in the labor movement;[18] and studies of nonwhite culture and values.[19] Social history has proved a boon to creative research but has also reduced analysis to ever-smaller universes ever further removed from the general public's historic consciousness. Meanwhile, one of Texas' two flagship universities, the University of Texas at Austin, has downplayed Texas history as a field, perhaps for fear of appearing too parochial.

The New Social History still enjoys a substantial constituency among historians themselves. The longtime, unbearable whiteness of Texas history bottled up scholarly frustration. For the scholars, history from the bottom up exhilarated in its freshness and its implicitly revolutionary politics. As familiar as some of the information has become to scholars, one still gets the excitement of discovery that must have come to writers like De León and Campbell in the 1970s and 1980s. One can almost sense when the "ah-ha" moments came in their groundbreaking work. Documenting the bravery of civil rights marchers and leaders of the suffrage campaign and recording the idealism of rural Populists inspired these historians. The emotional investment in this narrative proved as durable as the Fehrenbach generation's attraction to Davy Crockett.

An academic approach that swept American universities and dominated talk in graduate history seminars in the 1990s, postmodernism, lacked such an emotional punch. In contrast, the message of postmodernism disorients and strikes readers as grim. Its influence on Texas historiography still does not match the pervasive popularity of social history. Postmodernism arose in Europe after World War II, when any notions that Western civilization had brought the world progress drifted away in the smokestacks of Auschwitz and the radioactive furnaces of Hiroshima and Nagasaki. Primarily French scholars like Michel Foucault, Jean Baudrillard, and Jean-François Lyotard and American theorists like Thomas Kuhn[20] bitterly responded to the totalitarianism of both Adolf Hitler and Joseph Stalin by rejecting grand narratives. To these thinkers, the truth remains eternally elusive. Humans, postmodernists argued, cannot detach completely from their subjectivity when analyzing the physical, political, and social worlds. Furthermore, attempts to define philosophical truth, or to derive a universal meaning from events, so bind with an individual's race, class, nationality, and gender position that no sweeping interpretation of historical epics or societies can be completely trusted. Foucault, in particular, believed that power politics lies embedded in language. Historical actors forever manipulate language in Orwellian Newspeak fashion to legitimize oppression and maintain the existing social order. Yet these power discourses prove difficult to pin down because they are subject to constant redefinition and resistance.

Postmodernists view history as not primarily about class struggle, or an ever-forward battle for justice, or a confrontation between the powerful and the powerless. Instead, vaporous discourses control both those at the top of the social pyramid and those on the bottom. Ambiguity forever reigns. Outcomes such as desegregation or improvement in the lives of the working class cannot be automatically assumed to constitute progress, because each alteration of the power structure creates victims as well as victors.

Even though it provides powerful answers to mysteries, such as the pervasiveness of racism in American society, such an approach provides hard sledding. Diplomatic historians Colin Elman and Miriam Fendius Elman suggest that "although postmodernism has had a substantial influence on the philosophy of history, it has had less influence on the actual writing of history."[21] Postmodernism certainly has not reached a particularly large audience, at least, in part, because the concept itself is so slippery and difficult. As Karen Cox notes, "Postmodern theorists' approach to popular culture [and, it should be added, to history] can be valuable, but its jargon-laced language often makes the results inaccessible to a broad readership."[22] In the past twenty years, postmodernism has more often represented an influence rather than serving as a separate analytical category in Texas scholarship. Postmodernism, for instance, could be credited with reinforcing the New Social History approach. Since, as postmodernists contend, grand narratives cannot be fully trusted, the particularized perceptions of small groups within society become more relevant and more likely to be accurate. Scholars of all stripes have therefore placed more emphasis on the formation of individual identity. However, only one new research paradigm clearly owes its existence to postmodernist thought. So-called whiteness studies stemmed directly from postmodernism and became one of the most interesting and one of the most controversial academic trends in the past two decades.

Before the 1990s, most race scholars either accepted the reality of racial categories or, in the case of Marxists, saw class position as the base upon which society rested and race as a distracting superstructure diverting attention from the underlying economic conflict. With the collapse of ostensibly Marxist governments in Eastern Europe from 1989 to 1991, class struggle perceptibly retreated in the academic mind. Postmodernist historians saw race as a category worthy of analysis in and of itself. Beginning in the early 1990s, scholars of racial ideology like David R. Roediger, Noel Ignatiev, and Theodore W. Allen published major works that suggested that white racial identity did not represent a valid biological category and that the definition of whiteness varied over time. Like Chandler, whiteness scholars such as Roediger asked why white workers rallied around their racial identity and supported antiblack politics when they had potentially much more to gain by finding common ground with blacks, Latinos, and other economically oppressed groups in resistance to the power of rich whites.[23]

According to Roediger and his allies, nineteenth-century American culture defined many European immigrant groups, such as Jews, Italians, and the Irish, as nonwhite. Differences in language, religion, and culture from dominant Anglos marked these groups as outsiders. Elites created increasingly complex racial hierarchies that placed Northern and Western Europeans at the apex, and which defined Southern and Eastern Europeans, Middle Easterners, and Asians as neither white nor black.[24]

As nonwhites, groups such as the Irish in northeastern cities such as Boston, and Tejanos in South Texas, experienced their own taste of discrimination, though in most cases considerably less bitter than that endured by African Americans. As labor radicalism began to rise, these groups, consciously or not, struck a metaphorical bargain with traditional "native" Anglo-Saxon elites. Immigrants would gain membership within the white race provided they surrendered their ethnic identities, accepted white supremacy, and disavowed radicalism. In return, they would receive material benefits, such as better housing and schools than their black peers, in addition to the "psychological" wage of membership in a superior caste. Yet immigrant groups paid the wages of whiteness by alienating themselves from possible allies in their struggle for genuine political and economic power.

A second generation of whiteness scholars, many based in Texas, moved the focus on racial construction to the Old Confederacy. With the 1997 publication of *The White Scourge: Mexicans, Blacks, and Poor Whites in Texas Cotton Culture*, Neil Foley became the first Texas scholar to apply this paradigm to the Lone Star State.[25] Foley argues that Texas represents a unique opportunity for studying the mutability of whiteness. To Foley, Central Texas provides a particularly fascinating setting, given demographics that include Southern African Americans, Tejanos and Mexican immigrants, and poor whites from the Deep South. In this so-called shatterbelt, whites occupied both the highest and the lowest economic rungs, and the relative social position of poor whites, blacks, and Mexicans varied with the economic needs of the wealthy Anglo planters.

Foley and other Texas whiteness scholars built their arguments on the following propositions:

1. Each generation of Texans redefines racial categories as suits the political and social conditions of that time, and these definitions are tied to political and economic conditions.

2. Marginal white men in Texas often embraced racism because of their perceived shared identity with white elites, or their desire to join the ruling caste.

3. Race and gender discourses did not flow in one direction, from the social top to the bottom. Marginalized white workers, Mexican Americans, African Americans, and women used their own constructions of race and gender to resist domination by the wealthy white men who ran the state.

133

Foley contends that if a group never faced racial demotion, the urge to embrace white supremacy would diminish over time. He demonstrates, however, that impoverished Anglo sharecroppers in nineteenth- and twentieth-century Texas faced the loss of their racial position. Wealthy cotton growers began exploiting Mexican and black sharecroppers as cheaper sources of labor than white farmworkers flirting with political radicalism. Elite Anglos warned of the threat posed by "white trash" descended from inferior stock. Such whites faced exclusion from the racial ruling caste, and poor whites responded by re-committing to antiblack racism. The fluidity of racial categories gave whiteness both its allure and its power to coerce compliance with a social structure that provides few material benefits for poor whites.

Foley was among the first Texas historians to suggest that African Americans, Mexicans, and Indians do not alone possess race. Whiteness, too, is socially constructed, and its meaning faces continual opposition. Foley's work provided the groundwork for two other major studies of white racial identity in the state. In *Lynching to Belong: Claiming Whiteness through Racial Violence* (2007), Cynthia Skove Nevels corrected the notion promoted by earlier writers like Fehrenbach who depicted Texas' white population as uniformly Celtic in origin. Nevels pointed out that even the most thoughtful Southern historians like C. Vann Woodward paid virtually no attention to Southern and Eastern European immigrants in the former Confederate states. The number of these immigrants was low for the South as a whole in the late nineteenth and early twentieth centuries. "But if overall percentages look puny when considering the South as a region," Nevels writes, "they gain significance when one examines particular patterns of immigration settlement. . . . In certain areas of the post [Civil War] South, foreign immigration was by no means insubstantial." Nevels observed that while Mexican immigrants to Texas have been studied, other "marginal whites" have been neglected in Texas historiography.[26] Nevels makes a provocative argument that Italian, Irish, and Czech immigrants in late nineteenth-century Brazos County purchased membership in the white race through the brutal torture and killing of black men. Such rituals of racial oppression, she writes, were rites of passage for the growing number of marginal whites occupying Central Texas.

As Neil Foley's student, in *White Metropolis: Race, Ethnicity, and Religion in Dallas, 1841–2001* (2006), I applied the whiteness paradigm to an urban setting.[27] I compared the relative success of Mexican Americans and Jews in achieving white identity. I argued that elite Gentiles perceived their upper-class Jewish neighbors, the great merchant families such as the Marcuses and the Sangers, as a conduit for an ambitious city to achieve "world class" status. I noted that Christian eschatology, popularized in the United States by Dallas minister Cyrus Scofield, portrayed Jews as playing the key role in bringing about Jesus' Second Coming. Scofield's popularization of prophecy belief provided a path by which at least middle- and upper-income Jews could be accepted as subordinate members of the ruling white race. At the same time, Gentile powerbrokers re-Semitized lower-class Jews toiling in textile sweatshops or involved in union organizing in the 1930s. The quest for whiteness produced mixed results for Mexican Americans as well. A tiny number of Mexican Americans, if they were wealthy, light skinned, and sufficiently fluent in English, might have occupied the margins of whiteness, but most found that their working-class and poor backgrounds consigned them to a status at times indistinguishable from that of African Americans.[28]

Major academic trends prevailing in the rest of the country often take longer to affect Texas historiography. Here, whiteness studies remains a relatively new approach among Lone Star scholars and does not yet constitute a large body of work. Critics outside of the Texas history discipline have complained that whiteness scholars project twentieth-century ideas of race into the past, and that the conclusions of historians like Foley concerning an alleged choice by the European ethnic and Mexican working class to be "white" cannot be verified through objective documentation.[29] The harshest criticism of whiteness studies has come from scholars of Tejano history, such as Carlos Blanton[30] in this volume, who claim that works like Foley's and mine make too much of antiblack racism within the Mexican American community. Blanton has argued that citizenship was a more important issue than racial identity to Mexican Americans such as political activist and education professor George I. Sanchez, not acknowledging the degree to which whiteness subsumed American identity.[31] To Blanton, Mexican Americans simply put a higher priority on their own civil rights struggle than on the African American cause. To assume racism as a motivation is unfair.

"So far . . . this whiteness scholarship in Texas history disappoints more than it delivers," Blanton argues elsewhere in this book. "To the extent that Mexican Americans grappled with the whiteness branded upon them by law and fought different kinds of civil rights battles than African Americans, they are stridently condemned by whiteness studies as having engaged in 'Faustian pacts' or 'outright negrophobia.' Essentially criticizing Mexican Americans for not fighting African Americans' struggles first, these scholars ignore the real connections between both movements. . . . These works miscarry their great promise by choosing to ignore nuance, complexity, balance, and interpretive sophistication."[32]

Blanton mischaracterizes whiteness studies. First of all, he compares chronological apples to oranges. He castigates Foley for not mentioning Latino involvement in civil rights struggles of the post–World War II period, when *White Scourge*'s scope reaches only to the period ending at around 1940. In any case, whiteness scholars acknowledge the Latino involvement in the black civil rights movement. Whiteness researchers never depict black-brown relationships as uniformly defined by Mexican racism. In *White Scourge,* Foley describes how Mexicans in Texas helped runaway slaves, and he analyzes black-brown marriages and the shared experiences of African Americans and Mexican Americans in dealing with white supremacy.[33]

In *White Metropolis,* for instance, I explore the career of Dallas civil rights and labor leader Pancho Medrano, who was deeply and courageously supportive of the African American freedom struggle. At the same time, I note Medrano's anger at groups like LULAC, which Medrano accused of being often indifferent or hostile to the black civil rights movement.[34] Neither Foley's work nor mine suggests that Mexican Americans should have placed their struggle for justice on the back burner while they crusaded for black rights. Simple power politics dictate that, in a white supremacist society in which the police, the courts, the media, and the schools rest completely in the hands of a hostile Anglo ruling class, Mexican Americans, African Americans, and the white working class gain more by joining forces than by directing their anger and frustrations at one another. Anglo elites had money and power. All the black, white, and brown working class had on their side was numbers.

Scholars like Blanton seem to be unwilling to confront racism, or even milder racialism, unless it emanates from the Anglo power center. (The fact that I documented instances of Jewish collaboration with segregation apparently did not offend Blanton.) White supremacist thought has deeply marked Mexican history, as demonstrated by scholars such as Alan Knight.[35] Foley and I thoroughly documented the racism within groups such as LULAC. Critics like Blanton choose to ignore statements such as that made by American GI Forum (AGIF) supporter Manuel Avila who, in a letter to AGIF founder Hector García, insisted that Mexican Americans "have to establish we are white then be on the 'white side' then we'll become *'Americans'* otherwise never." To overlook the degree to which Mexican Americans may have embraced or rejected white identity ignores a key factor in community formation. Neil Foley's 2010 work, *Quest for Equality: The Failed Promise of Black-Brown Solidarity,* provides abundant documentation that Mexican American civil rights leaders like Carlos Castañeda used racist terms like "nigger" in his correspondence and that many in the LULAC leadership believed they would only lose clout if they spoke in favor of African American civil rights.[36]

Rather than assuming that Mexican Americans should have fought "African Americans' struggles first," whiteness scholars have illustrated why such an alliance never should have been assumed. Rather than ignoring "nuance, complexity, [and] balance," whiteness studies has captured the complexities of a Mexican American society caught in a racial crossfire, living at the intersection of two nationalities and experiencing life as both victim and victimizer. Acknowledging that racism played a role in dividing the black, brown, and Anglo working class may not lend itself to a heroic mythic past but demonstrates how a tiny, conservative, and white ruling clique has successfully held power in Texas for so many years.

While whiteness studies have come under sometimes harsh questioning, the thoughtful study of collective memory and its role in forming racial and gender identity shows signs of flourishing. Utilizing the concept of public memory, Harvey J. Graff wrote one of the most intellectually sophisticated works of Texas history in the past decade, *The Dallas Myth: The Making and Unmaking of an American City* (2008).[37] Graff demonstrates how Dallas's public spaces minimize the visibility of its nonwhite population and reinforce the highly hierarchical political leadership that characterizes the city. One collection, Gregg Cantrell and Elizabeth Hayes Turner's *Lone Star Pasts: Memory and History in Texas* (2007), makes great use of the insights provided by thinkers such as sociologist Maurice Halbwachs concerning collective memory, defined as the use of memorials such as the Alamo or the School Book Depository in Dallas, or public art and other representational forms that depict a widely shared experience. These historic sites more often capture the subjective emotional essence of a shared event rather than accurately document the past. Such sites, however, forge a common identity for an otherwise diverse population.

In the nineteenth century, collective memory primarily derived from word-of-mouth and folklore. As Cantrell and Turner note in their 2007 essay, "A Study of History, Memory, and Collective Memory in Texas," the folk recollection of the past has been shaped by "the history lessons taught in schools; visits to museums, monuments, historical sites, or public celebrations; and the viewing of historically themed art, television, and movies—to name a few."[38] In Texas that collective memory has generally served to reinforce the political and economic dominance of white men.

No work shows the power of collective memory as an analytical tool better than William D. Carrigan's *The Making of a Lynching Culture: Violence and*

Vigilantism in Central Texas (2004). In this work, collective memory played a key role in shaping the bloody race relations in the heart of the state. In part, lynching and other acts of mass public violence, according to Carrigan, derived from local folklore grounded in Central Texas' past as a frontier, where white colonizers engaged in warfare against Native Americans and outlaws. In the public memory, brave pioneers exploited the lack of political infrastructure to impose a crude order, and their supposed successes legitimized the tradition of violence. The experience of slavery, with its brutal discipline and its armed slave patrols, also bolstered latter-day vigilantism. Finally, memories of past resistance to constituted authorities on the part of African Americans, Mexicans and Mexican Americans, and poor whites—combined with myths concerning these groups' alleged propensity toward violence—incited the fear that lay at the heart of group retaliation.[39]

Scholarship on lynching, of course, sits at the intersection of race and gender studies. Therefore, in addition to Carrigan's probing work, students of racial violence should note the contribution by Patricia Bernstein's *The First Waco Horror: The Lynching of Jesse Washington and the Rise of the NAACP* (2006), which recounts the critical role played by a white NAACP investigator and suffragette, Elisabeth Freeman, in revealing the horror and injustice surrounding a particularly gruesome 1916 lynching in Central Texas, and how, in spite of her marginalization as a woman, she brought the nation's attention to the incident.[40]

Changing demographics, combined with more immediate local memories, ultimately racialized lynching, according to Carrigan. While whites accused of being abolitionists, Republicans, or criminals formerly suffered violent death at the hands of mobs, by the end of the nineteenth century the Central Texas victims increasingly became black men. Carrigan writes that increased Mexican immigration to Central Texas reduced the importance of black labor in the region. Also, the implementation of de jure segregation alienated blacks from whites, loosening whatever emotional bonds might have existed between the two groups. In addition, Carrigan says, local whites remembered the 1900–1901 murder case against Will King, an African American from Waco accused of killing a white police officer. King's white lawyers mounted an unusually spirited defense, and the court twice overturned King's conviction before he died at the gallows October 25, 1901. Whites perceived the King case as an example of excessive leniency toward African American criminals. This local collective memory, Carrigan argues, sparked later vigilantism, culminating in the gruesome 1916 murder of the teenaged Jesse Washington, who had been accused of the murder of a white woman.

Benedict Anderson echoes Halbwachs's work. Anderson deconstructs the idea of nationhood. The fluidity of national identity forms a lived daily experience for many Tejanos who in a single lifetime might glide from being members of the Mexican community to inclusion as Americans, to identity with the Mexican American community. Tejanos constructed a useful Mexican past as a means of coping with Anglo racism. As Michel Foucault once observed, "there are no relations of power without resistance."[41] Mexican Americans, caught betwixt and between the racial polarities of black and white, sought to maintain their own cultural identity while avoiding disenfranchisement. Powerful Anglos may have set the ground rules for racial discourse, but Mexican Americans and other marginalized groups waged an occasionally successful campaign to redefine terms such as "Mexican" and "brown" and "white." Meanwhile, their collective memories of Mexico, their experiences as strangers in a strange land, and the experience of watching their children come of age in the United States deeply shaped the community's self-perception.

Divided by class and color, the Mexican community in America constructed its imagined community, according to Richard A. Garcia, in his landmark study *Rise of the Mexican American Middle Class: San Antonio, 1929–1941* (1991), through national identity rather than racial identity. Garcia poses questions similar to those of Benedict Anderson. He questions the stability of national identities. He saw deep divides along generational lines within the Tejano community. In this, his approach overlaps postmodern linguistic analysis but also incorporates the study of public memory.

Garcia depicted Tejano identity politics as, to a large degree, a story of assimilation similar to the experience of other immigrants. "In many ways," Garcia writes, "this search for identity, educational opportunities, and political efficacy was not very different from the stories of the Irish in Boston, the Italians in Chicago, the blacks in the South, or the Jews in New York."[42] Mexico's proximity to the United States differentiated Mexican immigrants, Garcia suggested. The continuous and at times massive population surge from the home country left Mexican identity in never-ending flux.

According to Garcia, "Spanish" elites claiming little or no Indian heritage dominated San Antonio until Reconstruction. These elites related more to the *"Americano"* dominant class than to the *"Mexicano"* working class and poor. As white immigration to San Antonio increased after the Civil War, marriage between the Spanish elites and wealthy Anglos declined. With urbanization, segregation between the Mexican and Anglo communities deepened. At the same time, incomes in the Mexican neighborhoods of San Antonio declined. These factors led to an intensified "Mexican" identity in the community, an identity that only deepened as San Antonio industrialized through the first half of the twentieth century and drew increasing numbers of blue-collar workers from south of the Rio Grande. The number of "white Spanish" elites declined to the vanishing point as Anglos racialized almost the entire Mexican community. "For the Mexicans, geographical and cultural separation contributed to a heightened sense of ethnicity, since they continued to perceive themselves as others constantly identified them—as Mexicans," Garcia said.[43]

Unlike Foley, Garcia saw racial identity as a superstructure built upon a foundation of class politics within the Mexican American community in San Antonio and between the Mexican American and Anglo populations. The continued immigration of poor Mexicans to San Antonio, even during the mass deportations of Mexican immigrants in the Great Depression, moved many Anglos to associate Mexican identity with poverty, filth, crime, and illiteracy. Urbanization and industrialization, however, had created a Mexican middle class horrified by the image of their community in the eyes of their Anglo peers. Worried about their status, members of the Mexican middle class consciously distanced themselves from the Mexican poor and began calling themselves "Latin Americans" or "Americans of Latin descent." The middle class, Garcia suggests, embraced this identity for economic and political reasons. Rather than searching for whiteness, as Foley suggests, the Latin American middle class sought acceptance as a distinct ethnic group valuable to the city's economy.[44] While some whiteness scholars detected antiblack racism shaping Mexican identity politics, Garcia suggested that the middle-class Mexican Americans who formed groups like the League of United Latin American Citizens (or LULAC) were motivated by a genuine attraction to American society coupled with a pragmatic awareness that a racial identity separate from whites represented a handicap in the United States. "The ideology of this 'new consciousness' was clear: be proud of being Mexican in culture, but be American in politics, and most of all be industrious, efficient and productive," Garcia writes.[45] The middle class, Garcia argues, eased the community's transition from being Mexican to Mexican American to Americans of Mexican extraction.

Perhaps because Chicano historians experienced the scarring generational battles over social justice and the Vietnam War in the 1960s, Garcia's approach, with its emphasis on shifting identities tied to age groups, anticipated much Tejano historiography since 1991. For instance, Guadalupe San Miguel extends Garcia's argument in *Brown, Not White: School Integration and the Chicano Movement in Houston* (2001).[46] San Miguel adds a twist: Mexican American identity goes full circle. Influenced by the black liberation struggle and its fascination with Afro-centrism, San Miguel argues, young Mexican Americans in the 1960s and 1970s embraced the brown "Chicano" identity many of their grandparents brought with them from Mexico and which their "Mexican American" parents had rejected. This choice of identity with clear racial overtones, according to San Miguel, resulted in part as a reaction against a dominant Anglo society seen by Chicanos as racist and militaristic. San Miguel argues that the Chicanos' Mexican American elders ironically also redefined themselves as brown once they realized that antidiscrimination laws passed under Pres. Lyndon Johnson provided economic and educational opportunities for the Latino community if they forged a nonwhite identity.

Postmodern scholars generally decry the racism of workers who embraced white identity, since that choice derives from negative assumptions about African Americans. Yet while *Chicanismo* rejects whiteness and all its racist baggage, this ideology at its extremes substituted white power politics with a racialist Chicano supremacism. *Chicanismo,* like whiteness, essentialized and still rested on the idea that racial categories reflected real biological differences and that members of racial groups shared certain innate characteristics. San Miguel does not explore this important shortcoming in Chicano ideology. Also, while postmodernism emphasizes the fluidity of identity, San Miguel, Garcia, Ignacio García,[47] and other historians utilizing the generational approach to Tejano history portrayed the identity of the first Mexican Generation in America as relatively static, a major flaw in this scholarship.

While Richard Garcia discussed class conflict between *ricos* and *pobres* in San Antonio, he did not explore in much detail the ideas of race that Mexican immigrants of all classes brought with them to the United States. San Miguel noted the influence on the Chicano movement of the Mexican Revolution ideology of "la raza," the idea that Latinos represented the best traits of white, Native American, and African peoples. He ignored, however, the older Mexican concept of *blanqueamiento,* the idea that *Mexicanos* can advance only to the degree by which people of Northern and Western European heritage can be incorporated into Mexican society.[48] This concept divided *indios,* mestizos, and *criollos* in Mexico. Did these conflicts within the immigrant community survive in an American setting? Did Mexican *indios* share the same view of race as their mestizo peers? Were Mayans and Yaquis in the United States ever Mexicans, Mexican Americans, or Chicanos, or did they become Native Americans? Using postmodern theory, one might argue that racial identity among Mexican Americans was fluid not just between generations but also within generations. However, historians using the generational approach to Tejano history rarely address these questions.

In the 2001 edition of *Ethnicity in the Sunbelt: Mexican Americans in Hous-*

ton, Arnoldo De León argued that several racial identities—"Mexican," "Mexican American," "Chicano," and "Hispanic" exist side by side in the Bayou City. This model employs a more complex, multidimensional description of Mexican identity in Texas than Garcia's generational approach. De León suggested that after the 1910 Mexican Revolution a wave of immigrants joined the already established barrios in proudly preserving a Mexican identity. Like other historians of the Tejano community, De León suggested that the "Mexican American" second generation sought to retain its distinct culture while being accepted as a white ethnicity, as opposed to a separate racial group. De León, however, did not see the Mexican American generation as seeking whiteness. Referring to the Mexican American organization LULAC, De León noted that members of that group have "come under attack for advocating assimilation. This they did, but never at the expense of renouncing '*lo mexicano.*' Politically the LULACers were Americans, but they took pride in their cultural past."

This cultural past, of course, was filtered through collective memory. Even as Mexican Americans fiercely battled attempts by the Department of Public Safety and other institutions to classify them as nonwhites, they named their clubs and their institutions with reference to their Aztec heritage or to Mexican heroes like Benito Juárez with the same zest as later Chicanos. De León's research suggests that Houston's Mexican American community juggled several national identities at the same time. In the past two decades, however, middle- and upper-class Mexican Americans in particular experienced greater social interaction with other racial groups. This resulted in increased intermarriage with their Anglo peers. The multicultural environment Houston "Hispanics" experienced led to a moderate, more accommodating political approach to civil rights and a more full embrace of "whiteness."[49]

De León observes that "Americanization" coexisted in the barrio with "lo mexicano." Andrés Reséndez, in *Changing National Identities at the Frontier: Texas and New Mexico, 1800–1850* (2005),[50] demonstrates why such questions of national identity are important for race scholarship. He documents the extreme fluidity of national identities among Mexicans, Anglos, and Native Americans in the borderlands before Mexican independence and in the early national period. These national identities held clear racial implications. Two competing forces, the building of the Mexican state and the penetration of the American marketplace, pulled the population in Texas and New Mexico from 1800 to 1850 in opposite directions. Inhabitants of this volatile region traded national, and in some cases racial, identities with ease. Any number of alternative historical outcomes could have changed the later racial categorization of borderland inhabitants. On the one hand, Anglo residents could have been pulled closer politically to Mexico City, thereby making their "Mexican" identities more than a matter of convenience. Anglos could have found Tejanos useful allies in wars against Native Americans, and, perhaps, this affiliation might have paved a road to whiteness for Tejanos. On the other hand, Anglos may have found in local natives welcome allies in the struggle against Mexican domination, thus transforming whites' perception of Indians.

Tejano historians like De León, and Mexican American historians like Vicki L. Ruiz in *From Out of the Shadow: Mexican Women in Twentieth-Century America* (1998), argue that the Mexican community in the early twentieth-century Southwest forged a self-consciously multiracial self-image, expressed in the community's music.[51] As noted below, this racial self-definition resembles similar approaches taken by Comanches in Texas. Did Mexican immigrants and Tejanos redefine "Mexicanness" as time went by? Reséndez's and Ruiz's research suggests that national and racial identities are slippery, and that an individual's self-identification as a "Mexican" or a "Mexican American" or a "Chicano" raises as many questions as it answers. Historians like Richard Garcia and San Miguel, for all the brilliance of their work, should more closely interrogate those terms.

Perhaps because two important Hispanic organizations, LULAC and the American GI Forum, originated in Texas (in 1929 and 1948 respectively), the Mexican American experience in Texas has attracted national scholarly interest. Not so for the African American freedom struggle in Texas. Civil rights campaigns in the Deep South, and the leaders of the movement in that region such as Martin Luther King Jr., unfortunately overshadowed voting rights and integration battles in Texas. Texas should attract historians because the state offers an illustration of how geography and a multiracial environment uniquely shaped the Texas freedom struggle. Recent scholarship indicates that this state represented a key battleground in the fight against segregation and disenfranchisement, but the field remains underdeveloped. The civil rights struggle in Texas has been overlooked nationally probably because Texas elites in the twentieth century successfully divorced Texas from the rest of the South. Transformed in the public memory from part of Dixie to, as a Fort Worth motto puts it, "where the West begins," Texas may not have appeared Southern enough to be considered a case study in the battle over desegregation in the mid-twentieth century.

So far, Texas civil rights historiography has focused too narrowly on political and legal resistance to Jim Crow and to a large extent has ignored African American culture as a form of resistance. Afro-Texan history still largely reflects the techniques pioneered by Randolph Campbell and the rest of the

New Social History generation. Outside of Texas, Sterling Stuckey produced some of the most exciting research on African American history with his books *Slave Culture: Nationalist Theory and the Foundations of Black America* (1987) and *Going through the Storm: The Influence of African American Art in History* (1994.) Building on earlier work by the anthropologist Melville Herskovits, Stuckey documents how African cultural traditions survived within the slave community and strongly influenced the black identity in the United States and the political approach of the civil rights movement. Stuckey suggests that African folktales such as the B'rer Rabbit story cycle and West African religious practices such as the "ring shout," in which African Americans gathered in circles for religious purposes and in democratic fashion participated in a call and response form of worship, forged a community out of slaves kidnapped from diverse West African cultures. Black stories, rhymes, and songs, with themes of intelligence winning over brute force, of loyalty prevailing against greed, of mutual responsibility and the value of community, provided mental defenses against white racism for the African Americans. These cultural practices, Stuckey argues, constituted political resistance to white oppression.[52]

Unfortunately, Texas historians have yet to make full use of Stuckey's insights. Slave narratives collected by the Works Progress Administration in the 1930s, material uncovered by the Texas Folklore Society, and folktales collected by John Mason Brewer[53] serve as a rich record of African Americans' "reactions to the incidents and pressures in [their] environment."[54] Furthermore, Black Nationalists in the late 1960s sought to find a "useable past" and attempted to recreate their lost African culture in a Texas setting.[55] Yet little work has been done to analyze the uniquely Texas themes of the folklorist Brewer's story collections or to tie African-origin folklore to later expressions of black nationalism in the Texas civil rights movement.

Most monographs on the African American civil rights movement begin in or primarily focus on the twentieth century. A closer analysis of resistance in Afro-Texan culture would push back the origins of the black civil rights movement in this state deep into the nineteenth century. Afro-Texans, the evidence suggests, constructed an identity linked to the global African diaspora. The Afro-Texan viewpoint interpreted the struggle of blacks against American segregation as part of a global struggle against white racism, a complex task that perhaps inspired the black Texan emphasis on multilateral coalition building.

If nineteenth-century Black Nationalism in Texas has been underexplored, the contributions of Afro-Texans to the twentieth-century civil rights movement have been largely unexplored. William Henry Kellar, in his book *Make Haste Slowly: Moderates, Conservatives, and School Desegregation in Houston*

(1999), observes that Houston was the largest school district desegregated by the 1954 *Brown v. Board of Education* decision, but no works focused on the movement there until publication of Kellar's book forty-five years later. Taylor Branch does not mention Dallas once in his 1,064-page study of the civil rights movement, *Parting the Waters: America in the King Years, 1954–63* (1988). The civil rights campaign in San Antonio has received even less attention. Kellar believes that this oversight results from "the general perception that Texas is primarily a Western state, a land of cattle, cowboys, oil wells, and wide open spaces. Lost amid the western lore is the state's Southern heritage. . . . A second factor is that few historians have viewed Texas as a hotbed of civil rights activity."[56]

If postmodernism values the particular over the universal, then the Texas civil rights story needs to be more fully told. Authors like Dallas reporter Jim Schutze and historian Robert Weisbrot portrayed Afro-Texans as more accommodationist than their peers in the Deep South and have suggested that Texas blacks were largely quiescent during the rights revolution in the mid-twentieth century.[57] The lack of galvanizing incidents like the "Freedom Summer" in Mississippi in 1964 or the "Bloody Sunday" march at the Edmund Pettus Bridge in Selma, Alabama, on March 7, 1965, does not mean that equally compelling and enlightening episodes were absent in Texas. Kellar's work suggests that Houston provides an intriguing case study for civil rights historians, and he argues that black activists were far more assertive and on the cutting edge than earlier writers suggested.

The African American community faced a unique environment in triracial Houston, which included a growing Mexican American population and an ethnically diverse white population for most of the twentieth century. The city was more industrial and more economically diverse than most of the South, with petroleum supplanting cotton as a chief export. The presence in Houston of a black middle class not relying on white support and the critical mass of talented lawyers working in the African American community fueled the mid-twentieth-century courtroom assaults on Jim Crow, where legal battles generally took precedence over direct action. While the scholarly neglect of Houston suggests that little of note regarding desegregation happened there, to the contrary the civil rights movement arose early in that city. An NAACP chapter formed in Houston at least by 1918, just nine years after the founding of the national organization, with women such as Lulu B. White and Christa V. Adair serving as leaders during state government-sponsored repression of the organization in the 1920s and 1950s. Even as Houston's schools and its downtown businesses remained segregated, an African American woman, Hattie White, won a seat on the Houston school board in 1958, becoming only the second black elected official in Texas since Reconstruction. Students staged sit-in strikes at Houston's segregated lunch counters, restaurants, and department stores in March 1960, a little more than a month after the nation's first sit-in was staged in North Carolina. In Texas, the incident that came closest to a riot during the civil rights era happened in Houston during in 1967 when overly aggressive police fired bullets into a dorm occupied by Texas Southern University students. Such an active civil rights campaign clearly deserves more historical attention.[58]

Kellar convincingly argues that on the state's biggest integration battleground, blacks combined quiet methods with radical aims. Kellar, and Amilcar Shabazz in the previously mentioned *Advancing Democracy,* suggest that Texas' highly organized NAACP chapters won repeated victories through lawsuits rather than more visible street battles. Shabazz notes that by the end of the 1950s, half of the state-supported universities and colleges in Texas were "moderately desegregated," as opposed to South Carolina, Georgia, Mississippi, and Alabama, where higher education remained completely segregated.

If parts of Texas desegregated faster than the norm in the rest of Dixie, this difference possibly derived from a number of factors: Texas' ambiguous geographical position on the margins of the South and the West; the declining percentage of African Americans in the Texas population; the troubled sometimes alliance African Americans enjoyed with Mexican Americans; the high number of whites who immigrated to Texas from northern states after World War II; or the more industrialized economy of Texas and the increased demands for skilled labor following the Great Depression, or a combination of the above. Hopefully, in the coming years more local studies like Kellar's *Make Haste Slowly* and Robyn Duff Ladino's *Desegregating Texas Schools: Eisenhower, Shivers, and the Crisis at Mansfield High* (1996) will bring greater focus on Lone Star black politics in the mid-twentieth century. Researchers will undoubtedly find that black resistance has deeper historical roots than previously assumed.[59]

Afro-Texan scholarship still has to contend with a powerful "plantation myth," the idea that slave life served as an idyllic golden age for African Americans. In Texas the self-congratulatory, and false, claim that Texas slavery was milder than anywhere in the South reinforces the "moonlight and magnolias" legend. Furthermore, in Texas the Anglo population often embraces a willful amnesia concerning the peculiar institution. Minimizing the importance of slavery to Texas' economic and political development, of course, serves a political agenda as it whitewashes the guilt of the state's conservative hegemons. Brutal honesty about the tragedies attending the peculiar institution might also cloud white racial identity, which the dominant culture has always associated with "advanced civilization" as opposed to black, brown, and red "savagery." Elizabeth R. Rabe's heartbreaking essay, "Slave Children in Texas: A Qualitative and Quantitative Analysis," originally published in the *East Texas Historical Journal* in 2004, provided an important corrective. Campbell's monograph on Texas slavery did not gloss the cruelty of Texas slave owners, but Rabe's work became one of the earliest explorations of the impact of physical and mental abuse on the youngest African American slaves. Rabe's work not only provided ammunition against the stubbornly durable plantation myth, but it also directly confronted the modern right-wing attacks on the black family as she outlined how a communal approach to raising children evolved among African Americans out of necessity because slave owners often separated children from their parents via the auction block. A book-length study of the Afro-Texan family similar to Herbert G. Guttman's *The Black Family in Slavery and Freedom, 1750–1925* (1977) would be a major contribution to Texas race and gender scholarship, but Rabe's essay provides a good start. Race scholars in particular should investigate the family as a site where new generations learned racial definitions and the code of behavior expected of blacks, whites, Mexicans, and Asians.[60]

Similar to findings by researchers of the Chicano movement, Afro-Texan historians in the last two decades have noted the conflicts between race and class identity in the black community. James SoRelle has argued that across the Lone Star State, black teachers and entrepreneurs were divided among advocates of desegregation, those who saw in segregation an opportunity to promote self-reliance and economic independence, those who saw a collapse of Jim Crow as a threat to black-owned businesses, and those who saw the issue from a combination of these perspectives. Black businesses, however, faced hardships in obtaining badly needed credit, and black consumers at times undermined African American businesses because they believed that these enterprises lacked the quality and variety of similar businesses owned by whites. According to SoRelle, some African Americans also absorbed white racism and feared that black doctors and other professionals were less qualified than whites in those fields.[61] SoRelle's work complicates the vastly understudied field of civil rights history in Texas, and subsequent works will undoubtedly owe much to his nuanced approach. However, like the scholarship on Mexican American identity in Texas, the definition of "blackness" could be interrogated more closely to see if ethnic divides, as well as generational conflict, afflicted the Afro-Texan community. A spectrum of color exists within the so-called black community, which in recent years added new immigrants from the Caribbean and Africa. Have the imperatives of whiteness continued to forge the diverse

African American community into a unitary "blackness"? Scholars have yet to explore how different "black" groups relate to one another. Such research would unpack the concept of blackness, which has been seen to date as essentially monolithic.

Not only have perhaps differing racial self-identities within the black community been ignored, but also so have nonmainstream political movements among Afro-Texans. Outside of W. Marvin Dulaney's brilliant essay, "What Happened to the Civil Rights Movement in Dallas, Texas?" (1993), there has also been little exploration of black radicalism in Texas and the impact, or lack thereof, of groups such as Marcus Garvey's United Negro Improvement Association, the Black Panthers and their successors the New Black Panthers, the Nation of Islam, or the small Black Israelite cult. Kellar paid some attention to black nationalists in Houston, but much of the black political spectrum, right and left, has been ignored.[62]

Collective memory in Texas has left little room for the state's original inhabitants. Fortunately, some of the most intriguing work on race in the past twenty years has been done on Native Americans. Historians of Texas' indigenous peoples have, in particular, utilized an intriguing approach that shares much with both whiteness studies and the imagined communities approach taken by Garcia. Ethnogenesis traces how specific ethnic identities ebb and flow over time. Gary Clayton Anderson made the best use of this approach in his work *The Indian Southwest: Ethnogenesis and Reinvention, 1580–1830* (1999).[63] Anderson describes the Southwest as an "emerging ethnic stew" in which dynamic Indian cultures maintained dominance for more than two hundred years, even shaping the encroaching European cultures they encountered. Where Anglo historians traditionally have viewed Indian history from a teleological lens, depicting Indians as gradually worn down to the point of cultural or literal extinction, Anderson sees societies that, under the pressures of genocide and ecological and economic change, continually created new identities from the fragments of decimated nations. Instead of depicting them as clinging to the past, as some of the scholarship on Native Americans suggested, Anderson's historiographic perspective described the Southwest Indians as being cultural innovators up until the onslaught of European invaders overwhelmed them in the early nineteenth century.

The defeat, domination, and expulsion of Native Americans in Texas, and the racist ideology underlying this policy, raises questions that could perhaps be best answered by comparative history. Anderson, in *The Conquest of Texas: Ethnic Cleansing in the Promised Land, 1820–1875* (2005), explores whether the policies of the Texas Republic and the subsequent Texas state government toward Indians constitutes genocide. Anderson prefers the term "ethnic cleansing," first widely used to describe Serbian atrocities during the 1990s civil war in Bosnia-Herzegovina. "[T]he situation in Texas fails to rise to the level of genocide, if genocide means the intentional killing of nearly all of a racial, religious, or cultural group," Anderson writes. "Rather, Texans gradually endorsed . . . a policy of ethnic cleansing that had as its intention the forced removal of certain culturally defined groups from their lands. . . . Texans would have been pleased had the groups they wanted removed simply left without violence. But these groups did not. The conflict in Texas was over land; indiscriminate killing, while common during the fighting, never became prolonged, strategic, state policy on either side."[64] Anderson reduces this ethnic cleansing to a coldhearted campaign of greed, and one might think that racism was irrelevant to the Anglo-Texans' motives. One wonders, however, if the land Anglos desired had been filled with Czech or German immigrants, the ethnic cleansing would have been as bloody and ruthless.

Anderson made a reasonable case for not describing Texas' Indian policy as genocide. Unanswered, however, was why genocide did not occur. Here, comparative history might be instructive. How did Anglo-Texan attitudes toward the Native population compare to that of Afro-Texans or Tejanos? How does the "nongenocide" of Indians in Texas compare to genocides in places as diverse as Nazi-occupied Europe and the Darfur region of Sudan? How did Anglo-Texan policies regarding Native Americans compare with that of Canada, Mexico, or Central America? Was there a tipping point at which conflicts over land would have escalated to an Anglo desire to completely exterminate indigenous peoples? Any answer would be speculative, but without some theories ventured about the choices made by Texans, Anderson's work seems incomplete.

Texas scholars rarely acknowledge that the state's historians operate within a cultural framework that shapes their analysis. Pekka Hämäläinen, in his monograph *Comanche Empire* (2008), engages in this metahistory. He chides historians who continue to depict Indians from a colonial perspective, failing to acknowledge that groups like the Comanche rose as regional military and economic powers fully competitive with invading European armies and nation-states like Mexico and the United States. Just as Anderson demonstrates how Indians continually recreated their ethnic identity, Hämäläinen outlines how the Comanches dramatically transformed their economy as they spread to dominate the trans-Mississippi West from the plains to northern Mexico.

Rather than being merely a barrier to Anglo conquest as they have usually been portrayed by previous Western historians, Hämäläinen contends that "the

Comanche were the dominant people in the Southwest . . . [and] they extracted resources and labor from their Euro-American and Indian neighbors through thievery and tribute and incorporated foreign ethnicities into their ranks as adopted kinspeople, slaves, workers, dependents, and vassals. The Comanche empire was powered by violence, but, like most viable empires, it was first and foremost an economic arrangement. At its core was an extensive commercial network that allowed Comanches to control nearby border markets and long-distance trade, swing surrounding groups into their political orbit, and spread their language and culture across the mid-continent."[65] With the arrival of the horse, the Comanche reduced their dependence on gathering and created a complex economy based on buffalo hunting in which women "specialized in food and hide production; boys in animal herding; and adult men in raiding, trading, and hunting." This economic transformation helped the Comanche deal with the European and North American powers on an equal or dominant basis, a situation that transformed racial ideology on the American plains.[66]

In true Foucauldian fashion, Juliana Barr and Hämäläinen see the power discourses between Natives and Europeans as a dialogue. They inverted the long-standing portrayal of Western history, placing European powers and the emerging Mexican and American nations at the margins of a Native American imperial realm. In their texts, there is no frontier, only an Indian-controlled imperium. White traders, soldiers, and missionaries live on the margins of an Indio-centric world and must cope with Native demands and customs. Rather than seeing Native responses as part of a doomed survival strategy, Barr and Hämäläinen portray Indians as coequal or even dominant partners with Europeans, Mexicans, and Americans in creating the West. Hämäläinen makes a strong claim for depicting the Comanche as a regional superpower engaged in sophisticated diplomacy and making clever use of the terrain and natural resources. Lying "deep in the continental grasslands," the Comanche found themselves between Spanish and Mexican outposts to their south and west, and French and American colonies to the east. "This geopolitical setting permitted Comanches to use one imperial regime as a counterweight when negotiating with one another to enforce political and commercial agreements or to compel Euro-Americans to modify their aggressive policies."[67]

The Comanche proved both inclusive and self-aware of their separate identity. In the Comanche world, race rested on geopolitical considerations. Even while speaking with hatred and contempt toward Anglo-Texans, "Behaviors and beliefs, and not blood lineages, determined who would be accepted into Comanchería and could become a Comanche. If a newcomer of Hispanic, Anglo, Caddoan, or any other ethnic descent was willing and able to adopt to the proper code of behavior, he or she would be accepted as a member of the community."[68] The evidence presented in this work suggests that many Europeans and Anglo-Americans made just that choice, thereby suggesting instability in racial identity in the white community, where many might assume race would be seen as a matter of blood and not culture.

Famously, the Iroquois Confederation in the northeastern United States inspired Ben Franklin's "Albany Plan" for American colonial unity during the French-Indian War in the 1750s. While Hämäläinen's evidence suggests that the Comanches may have led Europeans and Americans to reexamine their notions of race, he does not explore how the rise of the Comanche empire may have influenced Anglo notions of nationhood. The Comanche clearly represented an organized and powerful polity but did not resemble a nation in the Euro-American mold. The Comanche did not build cities, and they led a combined settled and migratory existence built on horse breeding and hunting. Their nomadic ways encouraged the Comanche to fully engage with diverse people over a broad geographic expanse, which furthermore encouraged a broad degree of cultural borrowing. The Comanche system made efficient and effective use of the land without creating the ecological damage that later led to the 1930s Dust Bowl in the same region. Did Anglos living in contact with the Comanches ever consider their economy and government as worthy of imitation, or did white racism preclude such intellectual exchange? Hopefully, Hämäläinen and his colleagues will further examine the intellectual exchange among Natives, Anglos, and Mexicans on the plains.

As with much recent racial scholarship, most writing on gender in Texas seems stuck in the New Social History mode of the 1970s and 1980s. Biographies of important Mexican Americans; African Americans; and women in the arts, politics, the labor movement, and the civil rights struggle dominated the study of race and gender in Texas for much of the past twenty years. In particular, Ruthe Winegarten and Hollace Weiner staked a claim to the current biography-driven historical narrative that dominates Texas gender studies. Their emphasis on biography meant that these authors spent less time on racial and gender ideology and the social construction of identity. Nevertheless, their works, generally aimed at a popular audience, made an important contribution to the new Texas historiography rejecting the myth that white men alone served as historical actors in Texas.[69]

Still dominated by white men, the history discipline remains to a large degree phallocentric in its orientation, according to Juliana Barr in *Peace Came in the Form of a Woman: Indians and Spaniards in the Texas Borderlands* (2007). Barr points out that historians have routinely referred to the era of Texas history after Hernán Cortés's conquest of Mexico and before Mexican independence as the "colonial period." Barr argues that the Spanish, outside of a few small outposts like San Antonio, really only controlled land south of the Rio Grande. North of that line, politics could be negotiated only on Indian terms, she argues.[70] Similarly, Judith N. McArthur notes in her perceptive study, *Creating the New Woman: The Rise of Southern Women's Progressive Culture, 1893–1918* (1998), that in spite of the fact that women dominated the "social justice side of Progressivism," historians "emphasize the agency of farmers, organized labor, and politicians in pursuit of goals such as railroad and insurance industry regulation, electoral reform, labor safety laws, and prohibition. Only recently has research on the state's women begun to uncover female-inspired efforts to restrict child labor, reform the juvenile justice system, protect the food supply, secure minimum wage and maximum hour legislation for employed women, establish settlement houses, and abolish red-light districts."[71]

Even after the historical revisionism from the 1960s to the 1980s, the centrality of women to the Texas past continued to be neglected. Recent historians have noted the importance of female imagery in Mexican and Mexican American religion, from Toltec and Aztec deities with dual male/female identities to the Virgin of Guadalupe. Juliana Barr argues that historians have used race as the primary category of analysis in studying Spanish-Indian relations in Texas before Mexican independence, and this has caused them to overlook the importance of gender in the period before 1821. Barr suggests that this misinterpretation happened because historians overemphasized the Spanish view of events. As previously noted, political relations between the Spanish and native societies were conducted on Indian terms. Since the various Indian polities rested on kinship networks, women played a key part in negotiations between Spanish authorities and Native American leaders. Native societies associated men with war, while women played a critical role in political negotiations. Indian women not only served as peace emissaries to the Spanish, but also women and children customarily accompanied Indian men to greet European delegations. The presence of unarmed women and children served as a sign of trust in the good faith of visitors.

Conflicting concepts of gender created miscommunication between Spanish and Native American men with mixed results, Barr argues. Indian leaders worried when they saw the Spanish greet them without the presence of women, fearing this indicated hostile intent. Baffled by this absence, Texas Indians interpreted images of the Virgin Mary adorning Spanish banners as substitutes for the expected female diplomats. The relation between Spanish and French men with Native women also profoundly impacted the rival European powers' colonial projects. The absence of women in the Spanish camps often contributed to the rape of Indian women even as many Spanish men in Texas proved reluctant to enter into the Indian kinship networks necessary for peaceful relations. The French, meanwhile, enjoyed greater success in trade with the Caddo Indians and other Native American groups because of their willingness to assimilate into Indian culture, including marrying Native American woman and leaving French women and children in the adoptive care of Native American nations. The more woman-centered narrative that Barr constructed in 2007 provides a more postmodern look at fluid gender identity and serves as a more contingent, dynamic, and ultimately more interesting tale than the old conquistador-driven mythology.

Similarly, Roberto R. Treviño's research indicated that Tejanas played a key role in the community's folk religion, which in turn played a key part in Mexican Americans' racial identity. Tejanas served as traditional healers and created and maintained the home altars, the *altarcitos,* that became a central site of devotion in the "ethno-Catholicism" practiced by many *Tejanos* and *Tejanas,* according to Treviño in *The Church in the Barrio: Mexican American Ethno-Catholicism in Houston* (2006). For Tejanas, Treviño wrote, the church became a zone that empowered women and yet boxed them into prescribed gender roles. Treviño observes that the tradition of the *quinceañera,* the coming-of-age celebration held for girls when they reach age fifteen, "promoted ethnoreligious solidarity and reflected a woman's importance in her family and her culture, it also perpetuated the notion of women's inequality and constrained women's role in life as primarily mothers and caretakers—the guardians of home and faith." Nevertheless, Tejanas stretched the boundaries of their assigned station, constructing an identity that allowed them entrée into politics when issues were perceived as domestic and family oriented, such as health care and education. Even in as patriarchal an institution as the Catholic Church, nuns used the constructed identity of women as caregivers to prod the Galveston-Houston parish into fighting hunger and school segregation.[72]

Tejanas apparently played the same key diplomatic role as Indian women in mediating across cultures, genders, and class status. Tejana politics echo the national pattern outlined by Vicki Ruiz in her account, *From Out of the Shadows.* Ruiz illustrates the major role Latinas played in breaking down barriers between the Spanish and Mexican communities and between Mexicans and Native women in the 1700s and early 1800s. She suggests that these women created an alternative, nonhierarchical form of leadership within the emerging Mexican and Mexican American communities in Texas and other states. "Women's networks based on ties of blood and fictive kinship proved central to the settlement of the Spanish/Mexican frontier," she writes. "At times women acted as midwives to mission Indians and baptized sickly or stillborn babies. As godmothers for these infants, they established bonds of *compadrazgo* between Native Americans and Spanish/Mexican women."[73] Barr, Ruiz, Treviño, and Teresa Palomo Acosta and Ruthe Winegarten in *Las Tejanas: 300 Years of History* (2003)[74] move women from the political margins and assign them a central role in Spain's empire building in the Southwest and Mexico's nation building in Texas.

The networking style of leadership that Barr and Ruiz describe appears in the life stories recorded by José Angel Gutiérrez, Michael Meléndez, and Sonia Adriana Noyola in *Chicanas in Charge: Texas Women in the Public Arena* (2007). *Tejana* politicians like former Dallas city council member Anita N. Martínez, occupying the nexus of race and gender, tapped into grassroots feminist and Mexican American activists. At times such women faced accusations that as assertive women they were insufficiently focused on the Chicano cause, and as Chicanas they were charged with lacking commitment to women's issues. The authors of *Chicanas in Charge* suggest that many Mexican American women suffered from quadruple oppression, based on their race, gender, class, and position as a minority within the feminist movement. Chicanas, the writers suggest, almost uniquely understood the mutually reinforcing nature of elitism, racism and sexism.[75]

Race and gender scholars since the 1970s have debunked earlier notions that women, African Americans, Mexican Americans, Asians, the working class, and other marginalized groups were passive actors forced to live life on the terms imposed from above. Agreeing with Foucault that discourses of power generate opposition, feminist scholars in Texas have suggested that distinctions drawn between the choices of assimilation versus separatism or accommodation versus resistance lack authenticity. Elizabeth York Enstam, Judith N. McArthur, and Elizabeth Hayes Turner in particular have been inventive in demonstrating how Texas women subverted assigned gender roles while also seeming to submit to male-imposed limitations. These historians describe how late nineteenth- and early twentieth-century women redefined the boundaries between the spheres of private and public life, forged alliances across racial lines or helped draw the color line, used women's clubs as political vehicles, and responded to issues like lynching, Prohibition, segregation, public health, and school funding. McArthur's work was particularly sophisticated as she explores, in *Creating the New Woman,* how women utilized male politicians' neglect of food inspection, sanitation, and infant care to build a grassroots political network that laid a foundation for the later suffrage campaign.[76]

McArthur suggested that while "female consciousness" (an awareness by individual women of their common identity with other women) arose fairly early in Dixie, "feminist consciousness" (an awareness of male oppression and the need for women to organize to gain full rights) developed more slowly in the South because Southern women had no comparable experience to Northern women's abolitionist and temperance activism. Slavery created a politically oppressive atmosphere that suffocated all manner of political dissent, especially among already marginalized women. Conservatism among Texas male elites dampened not only an indigenous women's suffrage campaign but also even the spread of the Women's Christian Temperance Union (WCTU). Powerful male preachers attacked WCTU activists for violating gender norms by involving themselves in politics and speaking to audiences including both men and women.

McArthur argued that two events provided entrée for Texas women into the Progressive movement: the confederation of local women's clubs into national organizations, which put Texas women into more regular contact with their politically active peers in the North, and the involvement of women, including those from Texas, in creating a women's exhibit hall for the Columbian Exposition in Chicago in 1892. She suggested that women in Texas in particular benefited from the creation of new academic disciplines, including the rise of "scientific" housekeeping and child rearing. "Fired with the progressives' passion for efficiency and scientific rationalism, the first home economists sought to free women from drudgery and elevate traditional women's work into a professional co-equality with that of men," McArthur wrote. Women's "scientific" expertise in these traditionally female domains of concern gave women heightened credibility as they gradually nudged into mainstream politics.[77]

According to McArthur, professional housekeeping flowed naturally toward campaigning for cleaner cities. "Learning the dangers of living in a house that drained toward the well, carried drinking water in lead pipes, and lacked vents and fans to move airborne microbes that spread diseases such as tuberculosis was a first step," according to McArthur. "Discovering the interconnectedness of domestic and municipal sanitation followed."[78] Women forced open the door to the political world by focusing on so-called women's issues such as improving schools or increasing the accessibility of quality health care. The organizational experience from these "women's campaigns" smoothed the way for the successful women's suffrage campaign of the second decade of the twentieth century. Thus women exploited men's belief that women should concern themselves with hearth and home to stake a claim in the male-dominated world of public health.

Largely triumphant, McArthur's account nevertheless concedes that the club women she studied entered into municipal politics on the heels of segregation policies that allegedly made it safer for white women to plunge into the state's urban spaces. Such women, she also found, tapped into xenophobia, employing anti-German stereotypes to promote the temperance campaign. True to the postmodern perspective, the state's disenfranchised simultaneously act as the oppressed and as oppressors. In her biography of early twentieth-century grassroots suffragist Minnie Fisher Cunningham, McArthur found a woman who strode a "careful line between assertiveness and deference" as she exploited the popular image of Southern womanhood in order to manipulate male legislators to support women's right to vote in Texas.

Contemporary gender scholars have found that women in nineteenth- and twentieth-century rural Texas found symbolic power in unexpected places, power that gave them limited autonomy and allowed them to form bonds with other women. Rebecca Sharpless, in *Fertile Ground, Narrow Choices: Women on the Texas Cotton Farms, 1900–1940* (1999), argued that not only African American and Mexican American women, but also white ethnics such as Germans and Czechs faced prejudice and lived on the edge of poverty as their families struggled with the harsh demands of sharecropping. Sharpless makes remarkable use of oral histories she conducted as well as archived interviews and reports filed by the social workers sent to cotton farms in the Texas Blackland Prairie in North Central and Central Texas during the 1920s and 1930s. With these materials, she reconstructed the lives of black, Anglo, and Eastern and Southern European–descended rural women. As Sharpless points out, in spite of their relative absence in traditional archival sources, these women constituted a majority of the adult population in this region. Sharpless suggested that women contributed perhaps the most important labor to the cotton economy in three ways: their physical labor in the cotton fields; the domestic savings they created through their household work such as sewing and cooking; and their participation in the microeconomy through sales of surplus eggs, butter, and such.[79]

Women contributed significantly to their family income, Sharpless writes. Any food not prepared at home had to be bought on credit, an unsupportable burden for families already buried in debt. Meanwhile, preparation of dinners for holidays, church suppers, cooking contests, and the like allowed women the opportunity to form independent social networks in a context where social isolation posed a serious threat. In preparing meals, women also introduced technology to their sharecropping community, for instance, pooling their resources to obtain canning equipment for preserving food products. One of Sharpless's greatest contributions comes by demonstrating how common labor and the shared experience of sexism allowed Texas women to cross racial and ethnic lines. Also, while many gender historians note the contributions of women to the home economy, Sharpless documents the invaluable labor that women contributed to the American and global economies.

Sharpless, Ruiz, and Acosta and Winegarten confirmed the significant role Latinas played in the macroeconomy. Agricultural labor depended on the family unit with women pulling a double shift, working in the fields all day while they tended to household tasks when they returned home in the evening.[80] Latinas in the United States transformed gender roles within their communities, supporting Catholic parishes even as their importance to the family economy altered the construction of masculinity and femininity in the Mexican American community.

The new gender scholars portray Latinas from the 1930s on as utilizing their increasing self-awareness and their long-standing networks of kinship to lead the Mexican American labor movement and shape the state's politics. Women like Emma Tenayuca, the secretary of the Texas Communist Party, braved police tear gas and billy clubs while organizing a pecan shellers union in San Antonio between 1933 and 1938. A strike led by Tenayuca involved 6,000 to 8,000 workers, the largest strike in Texas as of that date.[81] Latinas' participation in church politics and volunteer organizations gave them an advantage in union organizing, argue recent gender scholars. These intricate female networks proved necessary because women labor organizers ran head first into more traditional ideas of sex roles. For instance, labor historian Patricia Hill found that when mostly Jewish female garment workers attempted to organize an International Ladies Garment Workers Union local in Dallas in the 1930s, middle-class men who had sympathized with male-led union organizing in the past refused to support the women's campaign for better working conditions. Local newspapers constructed female strikers as guilty of "unwomanly violence."[82]

Three decades later Latinas had to battle sexism even within the left, according to Acosta and Winegarten. The Chicano movement, they noted, relied on warlike masculine imagery, and Chicano leaders saw women's issues as an unimportant distraction. Chicanas active in *la causa* "were often castigated as a threat to the political unity of the Chicano movement," Acosta and Winegarten wrote. "They were identified as both anti-male and lesbian since, in some individuals' views, lesbianism was an extreme outcome of feminism." Chicana feminists faced similar disdain from their white peers who saw Mexican Americans as unsophisticated and lacking in political skills.[83]

Similar to Tejanas, the role of African American women in the state's civil rights movement was erased from the collective memory and has been uncovered by historians in the past twenty years. The absence of such stories from most Texas historical works perhaps accounts for why these monographs offer little in the way of scholarly innovation distinct from the social history techniques established in the 1970s and 1980s. Even though these writers do not take traditional gender roles as a given, many of these works, well-written and thoughtfully researched, still resemble a "great woman" approach to history. A more sophisticated account can be found with Merline Pitre's *In Struggle against Jim Crow: Lulu B. White and the NAACP, 1900–1957* (1999) and Stefanie Decker's *East Texas Historical Journal* essay, "Women in the Civil Rights Movement: Juanita Craft versus the Dallas Elite" (2001), present evidence that, like Tejanas, black women in the twentieth century also fought the four-front war against racial, gender, and class oppression as well as marginalization within the larger women's movements. "Within three decades following the civil rights movement, scholars have amassed a rich body of literature detailing the battle for racial and political struggle," Pitre observes in her eloquent account. "Yet, although black women were leaders and activists in crusades against lynching, poll taxes, and Jim Crow statutes, very few studies document the major role played by them in the modern movement for social change. . . . These women were not only supporters, fulfilling traditional female roles as nurturers and caretakers, but were also major leaders, organizers, and strategists."[84]

In analyzing the life of Lulu White, the one-time executive secretary of the NAACP's Houston branch, Pitre combines political socialization theory with the "theory of marginality." Pitre argues that black women never neatly fit within the socially constructed female roles assigned to their white peers. Under slavery, black women were reduced to sex objects by the white ruling class or were unsexed as "mammies." They toiled as the caretakers of not just their own children but those of their white masters, while whites at the same time demeaned them as jezebels. As mothers, daughters, and sisters in families that could be destroyed if the slave owner went into debt, died, got sued, or suffered gambling debts, African American women often found themselves thrust into roles as family heads and spokespersons for their community. Viewed through the lens of contradictory stereotypes and thrust, willingly or not, into a leadership role, African American women in the twentieth century inherited a tradition of independence and assertion that equipped them to battle sexist condescension. While political socialization theory suggests that the political behavior of adult men and women derives from childhood gender indoctrination, Pitre notes that for African American women this theoretical framework provides insight only when combined with the theory of marginalization. Under the latter approach, scholars acknowledge that highly visible political activism by marginalized groups already defies social expectations. It was seen as defiance to convention for any African Americans to demand justice, equal housing, and quality schools. In this context, hearing these demands from bold women like Lulu White was not as shocking. The situation faced by all blacks, men and women, required "some measure of unconventionality in thinking and the absence of a clear standard of conduct."[85]

In Texas historiography, to a large degree scholars have assumed that gender studies means women's history. Ironically, given the hypermacho nature of the mythic Texas past, little notable scholarship has appeared on the construction of masculinity in this state. One would not know it from the historic literature on Texas, but men have gender too, and the contested Texan definition of manliness has shaped debates about gay and abortion rights, the high rate of violence in Texas cities, decisions about war and peace vis-à-vis Mexico, and the politics of lynching. Strangely, scholars have not interrogated the instability of masculine identity in the same way they have examined racial identities. Perhaps this is because the gender field in Texas has been carried almost exclusively by women who might feel compelled to focus on the untold stories of suffragettes, pioneer wives, and other previously overlooked historical actors rather than shift focus to men who have dominated the historic texts of the last century.

Fascinating stories remain to be told concerning masculinity in Native American societies like the Karankawas. Karankawa society accepted, if it did not always embrace, *berdaches,* individuals born male who dressed as women and spent part of their days doing what was considered women's work, such as cooking, and serving as sexual partners or wives to men. One yearns to know how Spanish, Mexican, and Anglo men responded to such direct challenges to Western notions of gender. Scholars have yet to study why such a conservative state as Texas approved the Equal Rights Amendment in the 1970s and whether the governorships of Miriam "Ma" Ferguson in the 1920s and 1930s and of Ann Richards in the 1990s challenged dominant notions of maleness. The neglect of masculinity as a social construct by Texas historians embarrasses and will hopefully become a focus of substantial research in the next twenty years.

Built on whiteness studies, intergenerational analysis, and the examination of collective memory and created communities, race and gender studies in Texas historiography have expanded dramatically since the 1970s, and have grown in sophistication. Nevertheless, the literature on many other subtopics remains shockingly thin or completely neglected. To date, Asian Texans have been underresearched. Thoughtful scholarly debates on the relationship among different Asian communities and among those communities and Anglo, Mexican, and African Americans in Texas; on Japanese internment in Texas during World War II; on the impact of Asian immigration on Texas communities after the fall of South Vietnam, Laos, and Cambodia to the communists in 1975; and on Asian Texan political perspectives still await the future. Some of the most interesting work regarding Asian immigrants in Texas has come from University of Texas at Arlington historian Stephanie Cole, who found that, even with the intense anti-Chinese racism on the West Coast at the dawn of the twentieth century, the Chinese in Dallas enjoyed greater tolerance, in part because of their small numbers and in part because of a local fascination with Chinese culture and religion. Their experience compared favorably with white ethnics and Mexican immigrants who found that their status depended on the lightness of their skin, their mastery of English, and higher income. The specific experiences of Cambodian, Laotian, Vietnamese, Indian, and Indonesian immigrants to Texas, however, have not yet been adequately studied.[86]

Another subtopic of race and gender studies, sexuality in Texas, remains mostly overlooked, though Mark M. Carroll made an admirable start with his 2001 book *Homesteads Ungovernable: Families, Sex, Race, and the Law in Frontier Texas, 1823–1860*. Carroll emphasized the use of law by Texas' governing Anglos as a tool to prevent interracial sex and the birth of mixed-race children. Anglos sought to prevent a transfer of wealth to African Americans, Indians, and Mexicans and their multicultural offspring, Carroll argued, and thus used law to criminalize miscegenation and to, in the case of the children of black slave women and white men, render them as "bastards."[87]

Carroll built on the work of feminist historians like Joan Wallach Scott, a specialist in French history at the Institute for Advanced Studies in Princeton, New Jersey, who has suggested that constructions of masculinity and femininity do not translate across historical epochs.[88] Carroll also looks to Southern historians such as Victoria Bynum who has suggested that analysis of Southern gender and sexuality "built exclusively on planter hegemony and the cult of male honor are too blunt to account for the considerable variety in family relations within particular regions and among various groups."[89] Carroll suggested that frontier conditions loosened Texan attitudes toward interracial sex, gender roles, and definitions of the family. According to Carroll, "[S]tressful living conditions, institutional disarray, land-grant rules designed to promote rapid settlement, and a dysfunctional law of matrimony made settling Anglo-Texan families highly unstable as did the often self-indulgent and sexually promiscuous behavior of Texas men." These factors, he maintained, undermined plantation patriarchy and created spaces where women could on occasion exercise domestic authority and economic autonomy. "[P]ioneer conditions, land policy, and the Hispanic matrimonial property regime prompted homesteading spouses to work cooperatively and often ruthlessly as conjugal joint venturers, grounding their marriages in survival and economic imperatives rather than in republican family ideals," he concluded.[90]

While Carroll's work will probably shape how future Texas historians view the state's nineteenth-century heterosexual family life, Texas historiography since the late 1980s did not analyze the impact of the state's gay, lesbian, bisexual, and transgendered population. Comparisons among the black, brown, white, Asian, and Native American gay communities in Texas cry to be written. Nevertheless, there has been no Lone Star equivalent to George Chauncey's innovative *Gay New York: Gender, Urban Culture, and the Making of the Gay Male World, 1890–1940* (1995),[91] which made innovative use of police records, vice commission reports, oral histories, and other sources to uncover a world not usually covered in historical archives. Yet collections for studying gay/lesbian/bi/transgendered history in Texas exist in Texas. The Phil Johnson Historical Archives and Library houses such materials as interviews with gay activists at the John Thomas Gay and Lesbian Community Center in Dallas. Researchers can also access the Gay and Lesbian Archives of Texas in Houston. Such collections await exploration by a new generation of scholars.

Another field, reproductive politics and abortion, has received more attention but has been focused on individual participants in the pro-choice and pro-life movements. A history of those movements from the nineteenth century on, has of this date not been attempted. A sophisticated theoretical approach to the politics of reproduction, its relation to concepts like "race suicide" (in which Anglo leaders encouraged white women to reproduce in order to prevent people of color from "threatening" Western civilization as their numbers increased), the impact of Mexican immigration and the Catholic Church on the abortion debate in Texas, and differing perceptions of abortion among white women and black women remains to be offered. The role of eugenicists and their intellectual heirs in the state's psychology programs who study alleged differences in IQ between races and genders, in shaping Texan views of race, gender, and reproduction, and Texas feminists' attitudes toward the family have also not been adequately studied. Finally, the position of women in unconventional religious movements, such as the so-called fundamentalist polygamous Mormon sect in West Texas, and how reproductive ideology influences their identity as females, remains to be considered.

Inspired not just by postmodernism but also by post-1960s multiculturalism and feminism, Texas historians now acknowledge the diversity of historical actors key to the Texas past. More complex and inclusive scholarship, however, has not resulted in a more diverse body of scholars. As a result of globalism and immigration, the Texas population will in the future only encompass more national cultures, native languages, and religious traditions, increasingly multidimensional racial politics, and myriad new definitions of masculinity, femininity, and transgendered identities. Unfortunately, Texas historians remain overwhelmingly white and male, and the near future does not promise the rise of an academic rainbow coalition. According to the "National Science Foundation Survey of Earned Doctorates" records from 1997 to 2005, only 4.6 percent of new history Ph.D. recipients in the United States were African American, only 4 percent were Hispanic, fewer than 2 percent were Asian American, and just below 40 percent were women. I make this point not to question the ability of white scholars, the author included, to make intelligent inquiries regarding African Americans and others. However, the dominance in the past decade of white Ph.D. scholars in the history field means the questions asked and the conclusions reached by the historical profession will remain grounded in a too-narrow cultural perspective.[92]

A considerable gap exists between how scholars see the Texas past and how the general public perceives that history. To a large extent Big Tex still embodies Texas history for a large popular audience. Preparatory to his 2000 race for the presidency, Texas Gov. George W. Bush tapped into the state's colorful and mythic landscape, buying a ranch in the small town of Crawford near Waco in Central Texas in 1999. Bush did little actual ranching but frequently participated in photo opportunities centered on the president engaged in the manly toil of clearing brush. Texas intellectuals could see through the guise. "Texans responded [to] the forty-third president's accent with a wink and a nod," wrote historian Ricky Floyd Dobbs. "We know the truth. Crawford ranch aside, George W. Bush is no agrarian. He's a city boy. Just like most of the rest of us."[93] Nevertheless, Bush's political gurus like Karl Rove saw political benefit, perhaps mostly outside of Texas, in bedecking Bush in a western-style hat as he portrayed for the cameras a macho white frontiersman. According to *Vanity Fair* writer Christopher Bateman, "George W. Bush's ranch in Crawford, Texas, will forever be one of the symbols of his presidency—the place where the Connecticut-born, Andover- and Yale-educated scion honed his cowboy image."[94]

Texans embraced the western cowboy identity embodied by Big Tex and imitated by Bush in part because it sells well to tourists and because it cleanses the Anglo public memory of the state's Southern past. For much of its history,

Texas was "rural, backward, segregated and poor," as Dobbs notes. "Many present-day Texans would rather not think on such things, even if they knew about them. Modern automobile license plates feature the space shuttle, a cowboy, a cactus, and an oilrig. Where's the cotton? The lynching tree? The soup line?"[95] Texas myth continues to weigh heavily on local scholarship. Even as the rise of new approaches in the history field such as postmodernism and the study of collective memory flourished outside the state as early as the 1980s, these new paradigms did not become a feature of Texas historiography until a decade later.

White audiences can no longer completely ignore black, brown, and red people, but once they genuflect to diversity, they shove what they see as bit players aside so they can marvel at the daring deeds of Jim Bowie, William Travis, and company. Audiences much preferred John Wayne's 1960 film *The Alamo* to the more racially inclusive 2004 version starring Dennis Quaid and Billy Bob Thornton. Even with a greater number of brown and black faces in the cast, and the prominent role given the Mexican American hero of the Texas Revolution, Juan Seguín, the 2004 film in many ways emotionally echoed the tone of Texas history texts before the civil rights movement. Texas film historian Don Graham notes how makers of the 2004 version of *The Alamo* tacked on a coda featuring Sam Houston's victory at the Battle of San Jacinto. "The filmmakers seemingly bowed to the collective memory of their audience, a memory that (they believed) required the battle [of the Alamo] to be cast in heroic—and thus victorious—terms," Graham wrote.[96] Twenty-first-century audiences still like their T. R. Fehrenbach fables in which white civilization triumphs over dark-skinned barbarism.

Ironically, New Left politics lay behind much of New Social History, but this approach, as mistranslated in popular historical memory, has simply reified the old power structure. To a certain extent, the still dominant not-so-New Social History in Texas seeks a useable past in which African Americans, Mexican Americans, immigrants, and women are not seen as simple victims but as heroic revolutionaries, maintaining cultural integrity even in the face of oppressive Anglo violence and white supremacist propaganda. These empowering narratives, however, run the risk of minimizing the degree to which white supremacy still shapes Texas, and American, culture, even in the supposedly postracial era of Pres. Barack Obama. In public history sites, the still-regnant social history approach influences the popular imagination of the Texas past only insofar as the story of nonwhites and women serves a larger positive spin on the Texas past, in which blacks, browns, and women overcome obstacles and achieve equality. This take makes the hard social justice struggles of marginalized groups a credit to the ultimate fair-mindedness of the white majority.

Such a narrative marks the mish-mash that shapes the popular tourist destination, the Bob Bullock Texas History Museum that borders the University of Texas at Austin. Opened in 2001 and funded in part by polluting oil industries and the famously corrupt and extinct Enron Corporation, the museum attracts more than 500,000 visitors a year, according to its Web site, a far larger audience than enjoyed by books produced by Texas historians.[97] Visitors to the Bob Bullock Museum in 2009 were treated to a popular understanding of multiculturalism. Exhibits, dioramas, and narrative plaques include Native Americans, African Americans, Mexicans and Mexican Americans, and women in a sweeping tale of Texas' rise to greatness. At the Bob Bullock Museum as of December 2009, one ascends staircases as one moves from Indians on the first floor to Mexicans and Anglos on the second floor to a third floor overwhelmingly dominated by the economic and scientific achievements of white Texans. This organization implies racial hierarchy, with visitors ascending from the world of dark-skinned people toward a heavenly realm at the top in which people of color play only bit parts.

A subtle white supremacy, and a more obvious sexism, marks the entire museum. An effigy of an armored conquistador on horseback guards the entry to the first-floor exhibits. Texas history thus begins when Europeans arrive. An interactive map highlights the movements of European explorers against a map of the American South depicting the territories held by Indian nations as static. The map suggests Indians and Indian identity forever frozen before the European conquest. The role of disease in destroying Native communities receives far more space than specific instances of European mass violence. When wars between Europeans and Natives receive attention, the text on wall plaques joins this information with descriptions of conflicts between Indian nations and European "settlers." Thus, rarely acknowledged racial violence becomes the shared responsibility of whites and Indians. Throughout the museum, the narrative texts that adorn exhibits describe Europeans seizing land from the Native population with the morally neutral term "settler" rather than with the more accurate "invader." Spanish missionaries "rely on peoples they encountered for . . . labor" rather than enslaving them. Plaques claim that Indian demographics "changed dramatically," with the few details explaining the causes of that change scattered widely on the first floor. Only a film projected on a screen inside a teepee and treating Comanche resistance to the United States captures the poignancy of the Anglo onslaught on Texas' Native peoples.

The Native American section largely amounts to a whitewash, but African Americans suffer worse treatment in the exhibit. Just as the museum uses wars between Indians to minimize the scope of Spanish and Anglo violence against

Native Americans, virtually every exhibit plaque that notes Texas slavery pairs that information with a description of Texas' small free black population before the Civil War. One of the few life-sized representations of African Americans consists of a mannequin representing a free woman, Fanny McFarland, who lived in Texas before the Civil War. Washing laundry, the mannequin bows so visitors cannot see her face. A plaque notes without explanation that the Congress of the Texas Republic refused her petition to be allowed to stay, but observed, "she stayed here anyway." The museum thus refuses an opportunity to explore the role of racism in Texas history. Instead, visitors enjoy another happy tale detailing McFarland's successful laundry business leading to a career as "one of Houston's first real estate developers, acquiring and selling land for a profit." If McFarland and her descendants experienced ugly racism at any point in their lives, patrons can only guess.

One of the Bullock Museum's major storytelling techniques involves using Mexican Americans to narrate historical chapters dominated by white racism. For instance, a film screened at a minitheater with an Alamo-style entrance on the second floor has an actor reading the diary of Tejano revolutionary hero Juan Seguín describing the Anglo revolt against Mexico in 1835–36. The script never alludes to the dominant role in the Texas Revolution played by slave owners who wanted to separate from Mexico, which earlier outlawed slavery. Over and over again, viewers hear Seguín describe the revolution as being a fight for "freedom." Although discussing massacres of surrendered soldiers by the Mexican Army at Goliad, the Battle of the Alamo, and the Mier expedition (which had attacked the Mexican border town of Ciudad Mier in 1842), museum plaques cover up the Anglo slaughter of Mexican troops after the Battle of San Jacinto in April 1836. A plaque covers the Battle of San Jacinto this way:

> *The decisive battle of the Revolution opened with shouts of "Remember the Alamo!" and "Remember Goliad!" After 18 minutes, the fighting was over. The Mexican army lost 630 men and the Texans nine in the battle that won Texas Independence from Mexico.*

Visitors relying on the museum for their understanding of history would never know it, but most of those 630 Mexican casualties happened after the Mexican army surrendered. As historian Rodolfo Acuña notes, "Few Mexican prisoners were taken at the battle of San Jacinto. Those who surrendered 'were clubbed and stabbed, some on their knees. The slaughter . . . became methodical; the Texan riflemen knelt and poured a steady fire into the packed, jostling ranks.' They shot the 'Meskins' down as they fled."[98]

Seguín describes Anglo revolutionaries in glowing terms in the film *Revolution!* Meanwhile, Seguín portrays Mexican leader Santa Anna as "like the cold hand of death." The movie ends with Texas triumphant in its revolutionary struggle. Anyone who only saw the movie and ignored a more obscure plaque later in the museum would not know what happened to Seguín after the revolution. A plaque notes that "*Tejanos* found life in Texas increasingly difficult." The museum plaques provide little information for visitors on the nature of these difficulties. Just as the Spanish murder and enslavement of Mexicans gets short shrift on the first floor, the museum obscures the Anglo lynching and physical assaults against Tejanos. "Despite the service of Juan Seguín, Lorenzo de Zavala, and others during the revolution, newly arrived Anglos were suspicious of anyone of Mexican ancestry," the plaque continues. Thus, "real" Texans accepted Mexicans, but those vague outsiders arriving after the revolution caused the racial strife of the 1840s. "When the Mexican Army invaded San Antonio in 1842, attitudes hardened, forcing many *Tejanos* to flee to Mexico," the plaque says. "Among them was Juan Seguín." The plaque then declares that Seguín faced false accusations of collaborating with the Mexican enemy when it attacked San Antonio. In this section of the museum narrative, the blame for anti-Tejano racism and violence ultimately rests on Mexico. Although highly flawed as a historical text, this plaque still gives a more realistic view of how Tejanos experienced life in Texas during the 1830s and 1840s, but it remains much harder to find than the *Revolution!* film, portraying collegiality between Anglos and Mexicans, displayed behind a big Alamo facade.

The museum glosses Texas Reconstruction, an era in which whites murdered 1 percent of the black population between ages fifteen and forty-nine from 1865 to 1868, in this passive-voice manner: "In this period called Reconstruction there were clashes over politics, land, education, race and work. But many people, in the process of rebuilding their daily lives, contributed to the slow, sometimes painful process of redefining the Lone Star identity." Other plaques celebrate the achievement of Africans Americans during Reconstruction. The museum text's feel-good tale obscures the common experience during Reconstruction of black men, women, boys, and girls like Dolla Jackson of Bosque County, raped and robbed of 25 cents by a gang of white men who faced no prosecution, or Limestone County freedwoman Jo Ann Brooks, who suffered the cutting off of her ears and arms, which were then burned to a crisp, for no apparent reason other than her blackness.[99] Despite the widespread nature of such racially motivated violence during Reconstruction-era Texas, the museum's creators find this to be an "inconvenient truth" that would dampen the endless cheeriness of the exhibits and thus chose to shroud such crimes with vague allusions to "clashes." Bad acts are attributed to "extremists," thus misleading patrons about how many Texans participated in antiblack violence and lesser acts of oppression.

Texas ranked third among all states in the number of lynchings between 1882 and 1930, but this horrid chapter receives no attention from the museum. Other notable omissions in the museum narrative include the Populist movement, which represented a rare chapter of biracialism in Texas, and the Ku Klux Klan's political dominance of the state in the first half of the 1920s. Throughout, women disappear to the point of invisibility, and the black civil rights struggle gets significantly less attention than the Texas Revolution. Based on the museum exhibits, one would conclude that gays do not exist in the Lone Star State. Like Fehrenbach, the museum suggests that most of the big stories in Texas history happened in the nineteenth century. Cattle drives and the space program in Houston assume exaggerated emphasis. The overall effect is one of narrative tokenism.

Prominent blacks, browns, and women simply serve as evidence of how justice inevitably "triumphs" in Texas and how the state today is better than yesterday, and that tomorrow will, undoubtedly, be even sunnier.

At the beginning of a new century, Texas historians and the much larger Texas history audience occupy the same planet, but different worlds. Like it or not, weaving a historical narrative out of a chaotic, confusing past constitutes a political act. The Bob Bullock narrative represents an archconservative spin on history only slightly more inclusive than the image of Big Tex. Historians know the falseness of the Texas image captured by Big Tex and could easily deconstruct each exhibit in the Bob Bullock Museum, but they have not found a way to share this knowledge with the public. At least in the academy, the mountain of research into the construction of identity in the last twenty years transformed and inverted the larger myths of the Texas past. Events once hailed as triumphs, such as the Battle of San Jacinto, now appear as atrocities. Old heroes like William Travis, Jim Bowie, and Davy Crockett have morphed into genocidal imperialists. Texas under the Confederacy no longer represents a flowering of independent spirit but stands as the desperate gamble of a slave empire. Reconstruction no longer appears in scholarly pages as a period of corruption and "Negro Rule" but as a false spring of inclusive democracy destroyed by domestic terrorists like the Klan. Cowboys have retreated to the margins, and triumphant tales of Anglo "civilization" prevailing over dark-skinned backwardness have transformed into an often-tragic collusion of cultures that produced not homogeneity but hybridization. Finally, if historians once regarded the dawn of the twentieth century as the end of Texas history (or at least of its most interesting stories), more modern scholars have placed battles over modernization, integration, and sexual discrimination alongside the set-piece conflicts between Sam Houston and Santa Anna as the most important conflicts of the Texas past. The old Whiggish narrative of Texas history as an unending tale of progress receded, replaced by a confused zigzag journey producing as many losers as winners. Conflict, rather than consensus, rules in the postmodern narrative.

From the standpoint of scholarly integrity, social history and the postmodernist project and other modern approaches continue to be hampered by the still too small number of African American, Mexican American, Asian American, and women historians examining Texas history. The audience for Texas history, however, remains largely white and male. The new race and gender historiography represents a repudiation of the public memory nurtured by that audience and groups like the Daughters of the Texas Republic. The postmodern take on the Lone Star State stands at a distance from how most Texan citizens probably view their past. The new history is too fractured and too particularized to profoundly shape collective memory as did the old white supremacist myths, and Whiggish myths celebrating the triumph of Western civilization still reign supreme. Historians increasingly work in alienation from their potential audience. As Randolph Campbell noted, in a state where its citizens view Texas as "an exceptional place in the world, the home of the Alamo where selfless patriots fought to the last man for freedom, a noble defender of states' rights against northern aggression, a long-suffering victim of carpetbagger corruption, and in the end a place of heroic western values," then historians have to work harder to "write accounts of the past that entertain, inform, and instruct but at the same time are critical, analytical, and true to the sources." Even if he seems more like a cartoon than an icon to historians, until historians find a way to make their messier and less optimistic stories compelling to the average reader, Big Tex will still rule over the State Fair of Texas every year.[100]

Notes

1. Nancy Wiley, *The Great State Fair of Texas: An Illustrated History* (Dallas: Taylor Publishing, 1985), 157.

2. Gregg Cantrell, "The Bones of Stephen F. Austin: History and Memory in Progressive-Era Texas," in *Lone Star Pasts: Memory and History in Texas,* ed. Gregg Cantrell and Elizabeth Hayes Turner (College Station: Texas A&M University Press, 2007), 39–68.

3. Michael Phillips, *White Metropolis: Race, Ethnicity, and Religion in Dallas, 1841–2001* (Austin: University of Texas Press, 2006), 20; John Henry Brown, *A History of Texas, from 1685 to 1892* (St. Louis: L. E. Daniell, 1893).

4. T. R. Fehrenbach, *Lone Star: A History of Texas and Texans* (1968; New York: Collier Books, 1985), 6, 679, 699, 733–61.

5. Phillips, *White Metropolis*, 1.

6. Amilcar Shabazz, *Advancing Democracy: African Americans and the Struggle for Access and Equity in Higher Education in Texas* (Chapel Hill: University of North Carolina Press, 2004), 5.

7. Robert A. Calvert and Arnoldo De León, *The History of Texas* (Wheeling, Ill: Harland Davidson, 1996), 396. For more on the impact of the civil rights movement on higher education in Texas, consult Shabazz, *Advancing Democracy*.

8. See Lawrence D. Rice, *The Negro in Texas, 1874 to 1900* (Baton Rouge: Louisiana State University Press, 1971); Alwyn Barr, *Black Texans: A History of African Americans in Texas, 1528–1995* (1973; Norman: University of Oklahoma Press, 1996); James M. SoRelle, "The Darker Side of 'Heaven': The Black Community in Houston, Texas, 1917–1945" (Ph.D. diss., Kent State University, 1980); Arnoldo De León, *They Called Them Greasers: Anglo Attitudes toward Mexicans in Texas, 1821–1900* (Austin: University of Texas Press, 1983); David Montejano, *Anglos and Mexicans in the Making of Texas, 1836–1986* (Austin: University of Texas Press, 1987); and Randolph B. Campbell, *An Empire for Slavery: The Peculiar Institution in Texas, 1821–1865* (Baton Rouge: Louisiana State University Press, 1989).

9. Jacquelyn Dowd Hall, "'The Mind That Burns in Each Body': Women, Rape, and Racial Violence," *Southern Exposure* 12, no. 6 (1984).

10. Chandler Davidson, *Race and Class in Texas Politics* (Princeton, N.J.: Princeton University Press, 1990).

11. Notable examples include Dianna Everett, *The Texas Cherokees: A People between Two Fires, 1819–1840* (Norman: University of Oklahoma Press, 1990); Morris W. Foster, *Being Comanche: A Social History of an American Indian Community* (Tucson: University of Arizona Press, 1991); Gerald E. Poyo and Gilberto Hinojosa, eds., *Tejano Origins in Eighteenth-Century San Antonio* (Austin: University of Texas Press, 1991); Barry A. Crouch, *The Freedman's Bureau and Black Texans* (Austin: University of Texas Press, 1992); Timothy K. Perttula, *"The Caddo Nation": Archaeological and Ethnohistoric Perspectives* (Austin: University of Texas Press, 1992); Kenneth L. Stewart and Arnoldo De León, *Not Room Enough: Mexicans, Anglos, and Socioeconomic Change in Texas, 1850–1900* (Albuquerque: University of New Mexico Press, 1993); Andrés Tijerina, *Tejanos and Texas under the Mexican Flag, 1821–1836* (College Station: Texas A&M University Press, 1994); Garna L. Christian, *Black Soldiers in Jim Crow Texas, 1899–1917* (College Station: Texas A&M University Press, 1995); Timothy Matovina, *Tejano Religion and Ethnicity in San Antonio, 1821–1860* (Austin: University of Texas Press, 1995); F. Todd Smith, *The Caddo Indians: Tribes at the Convergence of Empires, 1542–1854* (College Station: Texas A&M University Press, 1995); F. Todd Smith, *The Caddos, the Wichitas, and the United States, 1846–1901* (College Station: Texas A&M University Press, 1996); Walter Struve, *Germans and Texans: Commerce, Migration, and Culture in the Days of the Lone Star Republic* (Austin: University

of Texas Press, 1996); James L. Haley, *Apaches: A History and Culture Portrait* (Norman: University of Oklahoma Press, 1997); Paul Howard Carlson, *The Plains Indians* (College Station: Texas A&M University Press, 1998); Ann Fears Crawford and Crystal Sasse Ragsdale, *Texas Women: Frontier to Future* (Austin: State House Press, 1998); David La Vere, *The Caddo Chiefdoms: Caddo Economics and Politics, 1700–1835* (Lincoln: University of Nebraska Press, 1998); Andrés Tijerina, *Tejano Empire: Life on the South Texas Ranchos* (College Station: Texas A&M University Press, 1998); Gary Clayton Anderson, *The Indian Southwest, 1580–1830: Ethnogenesis and Reinvention* (Norman: University of Oklahoma Press, 1999); Arnoldo De León, *Mexican Americans in Texas: A Brief History* (Wheeling, Ill.: Harlan Davidson, 2009); Rebecca Sharpless, *Fertile Ground, Narrow Choices: Women on Texas Cotton Farms, 1900–1940* (Chapel Hill: University of North Carolina Press, 1999); Sara R. Massey, *Black Cowboys of Texas* (College Station: Texas A&M University Press, 2000); Emilio Zamora, Cynthia Orozco, and Rodolfo Rocha, eds., *Mexican Americans in Texas History: Selected Essays* (Austin: Texas State Historical Association, 2000); Angela Boswell, *Her Act and Deed: Women's Lives in a Rural Southern County, 1837–1873* (College Station: Texas A&M University Press, 2001); Arnoldo De León, *Ethnicity in the Sunbelt: Mexican Americans in Houston* (College Station: Texas A&M University Press, 2001); Gerald Betty, *Comanche Society before the Reservation* (College Station: Texas A&M University Press, 2002); Arnoldo De León, *Racial Frontiers: Africans, Chinese, and Mexicans in Western America, 1848–1890* (Albuquerque: University of New Mexico Press, 2002); Carlos E. Cuéllar, *Stories from the Barrio: A History of Mexican Fort Worth* (Fort Worth: Texas Christian University Press, 2003); Marilyn Dell Brady, *The Asian Texans* (College Station: Texas A&M University Press, 2004); David La Vere, *The Texas Indians* (College Station: Texas A&M University Press, 2004); Phyllis McKenzie, *The Mexican Texans* (College Station: Texas A&M University Press, 2004); James Smallwood, *The Indian Texans* (College Station: Texas A&M University Press, 2004); F. Todd Smith, *From Dominance to Disappearance: The Indians of Texas and the Near Southwest, 1786–1859* (Lincoln: University of Nebraska Press, 2005); Donald Willett and Stephen Curley, eds., *Invisible Texans: Women and Minorities in Texas History* (Boston: McGraw-Hill, 2005); William C. Foster, *Historic Native Peoples of Texas* (Austin: University of Texas Press, 2008); Bruce Glasrud and Merline Pitre, eds., *Black Women in Texas History* (College Station: Texas A&M University Press, 2008); and Bruce A. Glasrud and Paul H. Carlson, *Slavery to Integration: Black Americans in West Texas* (Abilene, Tex.: State House Press, 2008).

12. Consult May Nelson Paulissen and Car McQuery, *Miriam: The Southern Belle Who Became the First Woman Governor of Texas* (Austin: Eakin Press, 1995); Eddie "Sarge" Stimpson Jr., *My Remembers: A Black Sharecropper's Recollections of the Depression* (Denton: University of North Texas Press, 1996); Elizabeth Silverthorne and Geneva Fulgham, *Women Pioneers in Texas Medicine* (College Station: Texas A&M University Press, 1997); Zaragosa Vargas, "Tejana Radical: Emma Tenayuca and the San Antonio Labor Movement during the Great Depression," *Pacific Historical Review*

66 (1997); Nancy Beck Young and Lewis L. Gould, *Texas, Her Texas: The Life and Times of Frances Goff* (Austin: Published for the Center for American History by the Texas State Historical Association, 1997); Jacquelyn Masur McElhaney, *Pauline Periwinkle and Progressive Reform in Dallas* (College Station: Texas A&M University Press, 1998); Merline Pitre, *In Struggle against Jim Crow: Lulu B. White and the NAACP, 1900–1957* (College Station: Texas A&M University Press, 1999); Rob Fink, "Hermine Toblowsky, the Texas ELRA, and the Political Struggle for Women's Equal Rights," *Journal of the American West* 42, no. 3 (2003); Darwin Payne, *Indomitable Sarah: The Life of Judge Sarah T. Hughes* (Dallas: Southern Methodist University Press, 2004); Rachel Burrow, "Juanita Craft: Desegregating the State Fair of Texas," *Legacies: A History Journal for Dallas and North Central Texas* 16, no. 1 (2005); and Sarah Ragland Jackson, *Texas Woman of Letters, Karle Wilson Baker* (College Station: Texas A&M University Press, 2005).

    13. See Crouch, *The Freedman's Bureau and Black Texans*; Elizabeth Hayes Turner, "'White-Gloved Ladies' and 'New Women' in the Texas Woman's Suffrage Movement," in *Southern Women: Histories and Identities*, ed. Virginia Bernhard, Betty Brandon, Elizabeth Fox-Genovese, and Theda Perdue (Columbia: University of Missouri Press, 1992); Judith N. McArthur, "Saving the Children: The Clubwomen's Crusade against Child Labor, 1902–1918," in *Women and Texas History: Selected Essays*, ed. Fane Downs and Nancy Baker Jones (Austin: Texas State Historical Association, 1993); Elizabeth York Enstam, "They Called It 'Motherhood': Dallas Women and Public Life, 1895–1918," in *Hidden Histories of Women in the New South*, ed. Virginia Bernhard et al. (Columbia: University of Missouri Press, 1994); Sue Tolleson-Rinehart and Jeanie R. Stanley, *Claytie and the Lady: Ann Richards, Gender, and Politics in Texas* (Austin: University of Texas Press, 1994); Judith N. McArthur, "Minnie Fisher Cunningham's Back-Door Lobby in Texas: Political Maneuvering in a One-Party State," in *One Woman, One Vote*, ed. Marjorie Spruill Wheeler (Troutdale, Ore.: NewSage Press, 1995); Emily Honig, "Women at Farah Revisited: Political Mobilization and Its Aftermath among Chicano Workers at El Paso," *Feminist Studies* 22, no. 2 (1996); Julie Leininger Pycior, *LBJ and Mexican Americans: The Paradox of Power* (Austin: University of Texas Press, 1997); Elizabeth Hayes Turner, *Women, Culture, and Community: Religion and Reform in Galveston, 1880–1920* (New York: Oxford University Press, 1997); Ignacio García, *Viva Kennedy: Mexican Americans in Search of Camelot* (College Station: University of Texas A&M Press, 2000); Rodolfo Rosales, *The Illusion of Inclusion: The Untold Political Story of San Antonio* (Austin: University of Texas Press, 2000); Patrick J. Carroll, *Felix Longoria's Wake: Bereavement, Racism, and the Rise of Mexican American Activism* (Austin: University of Texas Press, 2003); and Charles L. Zelden, *The Battle for the Black Ballot: Smith v. Allwright and the Defeat of the Texas All-White Primary* (Lawrence: University Press of Kansas, 2004).

    14. Recent works in this field include T. Lindsay Baker and Julie P. Baker, *Till Freedom Cried Out: Memories of Texas Slave Life* (College Station: Texas A&M University Press, 1997); and James F. Brooks, *Captives and Cousins: Slavery, Kinship, and*

Community in the Southwest Borderlands (Chapel Hill: University of North Carolina Press for the Omohundro Institute of Early American History and Culture, 2002).

15. Included in this category are Monte Akers, *Flames after Midnight: Murder, Vengeance, and the Desolation of a Texas Community* (Austin: University of Texas Press, 1999); Paul Howard Carlson, *The Buffalo Soldier Tragedy of 1877* (College Station: Texas A&M University Press, 2003); Benjamin Heber Johnson, *Revolution in Texas: How a Forgotten Rebellion and Its Bloody Suppression Turned Mexicans into Americans* (New Haven, Conn.: Yale University Press, 2003); Ricardo Ainslie, with photographs by Sarah Wilson, *Long Dark Road: Bill King and Murder in Jasper, Texas* (Austin: University of Texas Press, 2004); Patricia Bernstein, *The First Waco Horror: The Lynching of Jesse Washington and the Rise of the NAACP* (College Station: Texas A&M University Press, 2005); Gary B. A. Borders, *A Hanging in Nacogdoches: Murder, Race, Politics, and Polemics in Texas's Oldest Town, 1870–1916* (Austin: University of Texas Press, 2006); Stephen L. Moore, *Savage Frontier: Rangers, Riflemen, and Indian Wars in Texas*, 3 vols. (Denton: University of North Texas Press, 2006); and Donald E. Reynolds, *Texas Terror: The Slave Insurrection Panic of 1860 and the Secession of the Lower South* (Baton Rouge: Louisiana State University Press, 2007).

16. Examples include Ruthe Winegarten and Cathy Schecter, *Deep in the Heart: The Lives and Legends of Texas Jews; A Photographic Legacy* (Austin: Eakin Press, 1990); Walter Stuve, *Germans and Texans: Commerce, Migration, and Culture in the Days of the Lone Star Republic* (Austin: University of Texas Press, 1996); Gerry Cristol and Jonathan Sarna, *A Light in the Prairie: Temple Emanu-El of Dallas, 1872–1997* (Fort Worth: Texas Christian University Press, 1998); Clinton Machann, ed., *Czech-Americans in Transition* (Austin: Eakin Press, 1999); François Lagarde, ed., *The French in Texas: History, Migration, Culture* (Austin: University of Texas Press, 2003); Barbara J. Rozek, *Come to Texas: Attracting Immigrants, 1865–1915* (College Station: Texas A&M University Press, 2003); Lawrence H. Konecny and Clinton Machann, eds., *Perilous Voyages: Czech and English Immigrants to Texas in the 1870s* (College Station: Texas A&M University Press, 2004); Allan O. Kownslar, *The European Texans* (College Station: Texas A&M University Press, 2004); Gary Clayton Anderson, *The Conquest of Texas: Ethnic Cleansing in the Promised Land, 1820–1875* (Norman: University of Oklahoma Press, 2005); and Charles H. Russell, *Undaunted: A Norwegian Woman in Frontier Texas* (College Station: Texas A&M University Press, 2006).

17. See Robin Duff Ladino, *Desegregating Texas Schools: Eisenhower, Shivers, and the Crisis at Mansfield High* (Austin: University of Texas Press, 1996); Ignacio M. García, *Chicanismo: The Forging of a Militant Ethos among Mexican Americans* (Tucson: University of Arizona Press, 1997); William Henry Kellar, *Make Haste Slowly: Moderates, Conservatives, and School Desegregation in Houston* (College Station: Texas A&M University Press, 1999); Ignacio M. García, *Hector P. García: In Relentless Pursuit of Justice* (Houston: Arte Público Press, 2002); Anthony Quiroz, *Claiming Citizenship: Mexican Americans in Victoria, Texas* (College Station: Texas A&M University Press, 2005); Robert J. Robertson, *Fairways: How Six Black Golfers Won Civil Rights in*

Beaumont, Texas (College Station: Texas A&M University Press, 2005); and Emilio Zamora, *Claiming Rights and Righting Wrongs in Texas: Mexican Workers and Job Politics during World War II* (College Station: Texas A&M University Press, 2009).

18. This genre includes Rick Halpern, "Interracial Unionism in the Southwest: Fort Worth's Packinghouse Workers, 1937–1954," in *Organized Labor in the Twentieth-Century South*, ed. Robert Zieger (Knoxville: University of Tennessee Press, 1991); Irene Ledesma, "Unlikely Strikers: Mexican American Women and Strike Activity in Texas, 1919–1974" (Ph.D. diss., Ohio State University, 1992); Patricia Evridge Hill, "Real Women and True Womanhood: Grassroots Organizing among Dallas Dressmakers in 1935," *Labor's Heritage* 5 (Spring 1994); Toni Marie Herrera, "Constructed and Contested Meanings of the Tex-Son Strike in San Antonio, Texas, 1959: Representing Mexican American Workers" (master's thesis, University of Texas at Austin, 1997); Thad Sitton and Dan K. Utley, *From Can See to Can't: Texas Cotton Farmers on the Southern Prairies* (Austin: University of Texas Press, 1997); Scott Cook, *Mexican Brick Culture in the Building of Texas, 1800s–1980s* (College Station: Texas A&M University Press, 1998); Roberto R. Calderón, *Mexican Coal Mining Labor in Texas and Coahuila, 1880–1930* (College Station: Texas A&M University Press, 2000); Ernest Obadele-Starks, *Black Unionism in the Industrial South* (College Station: Texas A&M University Press, 2000); Michael R. Botson Jr., *Labor, Civil Rights, and the Hughes Tool Company* (College Station: Texas A&M University Press, 2005); Clifford Farrington, *Biracial Unions on Galveston's Waterfront, 1865–1926* (Austin: Texas State Historical Association, 2007); and Debra A. Reid, *Reaping a Greater Harvest: African Americans, the Extension Service, and Rural Reform in Jim Crow Texas* (College Station: Texas A&M University Press, 2007).

19. Noteworthy examples include Joe S. Graham, ed., *Hecho en Tejas: Texas-Mexican Folk Arts and Crafts* (Denton: University of North Texas Press, 1991); Alan B. Govenar and Jay F. Brakefield, *Deep Ellum and Central Track: Where the Black and White Worlds of Dallas Converged* (Denton: University of North Texas Press, 1998); Guadalupe San Miguel, *Tejano Proud: Tex-Mex Music in the Twentieth Century* (College Station: Texas A&M University Press, 2002); and Julia Kirk Blackwelder, *Styling Jim Crow: African American Beauty Training during Segregation* (College Station: Texas A&M University Press, 2003).

20. See Michel Foucault, *The Essential Works of Michel Foucault, 1954–1984* (New York: New Press, 1997); Jean Baudrillard, edited and introduced by Mark Poster, *Selected Writings* (Stanford, Calif.: Stanford University Press, 1988); Jean-François Lyotard, *The Postmodern Condition: A Report on Knowledge,* Theory and History of Literature, vol. 10 (Minneapolis: University of Minnesota Press, 1984); and Thomas Kuhn, *The Structure of Scientific Revolutions,* 2nd ed., enlarged (Chicago: University of Chicago Press, 1970).

21. Colin Elman and Miriam Fendius Elman, *Bridges and Boundaries: Historians, Political Scientists, and the Study of International Relations* (Cambridge, Mass.: MIT Press, 2001), 75.

22. Karen Cox, "The South and Mass Culture," *Journal of Southern History* (August 2009), at http://www.highbeam.com/doc/1G1-206533085.html, accessed December 14, 2009.

23. See David R. Roediger, *The Wages of Whiteness: Race and the Making of the American Working Class* (New York: Verso, 1991), and *Toward the Abolition of Whiteness: Essays on Race, Class, and the American Working Class* (New York: Verso, 1994); Noel Ignatiev, *How the Irish Became White* (New York: Routledge, 1996); and Theodore Allen, *The Invention of the White Race*, vol. 1, *Racial Oppression and Social Control* (New York: Verso Records, 1990).

24. See Stephen Jay Gould, *The Mismeasure of Man* (New York: W. W. Norton, 1981); and Thomas F. Gossett, *Race: The History of an Idea in America* (New York: Oxford University Press, 1997).

25. Neil Foley, *The White Scourge: Mexicans, Blacks, and Poor Whites in Texas Cotton Culture* (Berkeley: University of California Press, 1997).

26. Cynthia Skove Nevels, *Lynching to Belong: Claiming Whiteness through Racial Violence* (College Station: Texas A&M University, 2007), 3–4.

27. Phillips, *White Metropolis*.

28. My thesis that second-generation Mexican Americans sought white identity has been challenged by Bianca Mercado in her master's thesis, "With Their Hearts in Their Hands: Forging a Mexican American Community in Dallas, 1900–1925" (master's thesis, University of North Texas, 2008).

29. The *International Labor and Working Class History* no. 60 (Fall 2001) devoted an entire edition to criticism of "whiteness" as an interpretive paradigm, led off by Eric Arneson's essay, "Whiteness and the Historians' Imagination," 4–32.

30. Blanton has written *The Strange Career of Bilingual Education in Texas, 1836–1981* (College Station: Texas A&M University Press, 2007).

31. Carlos K. Blanton, "George I Sanchez, Ideology and Whiteness in the Making of the Mexican American Civil Rights Movement, 1930–1960," *Journal of Southern History* (August 2006), at http://www.highbeam.com/doc/1G1-149769041.html, accessed December 18, 2009.

32. See Blanton's essay, "Deconstructing Texas: The Diversity of People, Place, and Historical Imagination in Recent Texas History," in this volume.

33. Foley, *White Scourge*, 19, 24–25, 40, 54, 60–61, 208–209.

34. Phillips, *White Metropolis*, 164–65.

35. See Alan Knight, "Racism, Revolution, and *Indigenismo*: Mexico, 1910–1940," in *The Idea of Race in Latin America, 1870–1940*, ed. Richard Graham (Austin: University of Texas Press, 1990), 71–113.

36. Neil Foley, *The Quest for Equality: The Failed Promise of Black-Brown Solidarity* (Cambridge, Mass.: Harvard University Press, 2010).

37. Harvey J. Graff, *The Dallas Myth: The Making and Unmaking of an American City* (Minneapolis: University of Minnesota Press, 2008).

38. Gregg Cantrell and Elizabeth Hayes Turner, "A Study of History, Memory, and Collective Memory in Texas," in *Lone Star Pasts*, ed. Cantrell and Turner, 2.

39. William D. Carrigan, *The Making of a Lynching Culture: Violence and Vigilantism in Central Texas, 1836–1916* (Urbana: University of Illinois Press, 2004).

40. Bernstein, *The First Waco Horror*.

41. See Foucault, *The Essential Works of Michel Foucault;* "Dictionary for the Study of the Works of Michel Foucault," at http://users.sfo.com/~rathbone/foucau10.html, accessed June 21, 2008; "Michel-Foucault.com," at http://www.michel-foucault.com/concepts/index.html, accessed June 21, 2008.

42. Richard A. Garcia, *Rise of the Mexican American Middle Class: San Antonio, 1929–1941* (College Station: Texas A&M University Press, 1991), 7.

43. Garcia, *Rise of the Mexican American Middle Class*, 28.

44. Ibid., 42–43.

45. Ibid., 258.

46. Guadalupe San Miguel Jr., *Brown, Not White: School Integration and the Chicano Movement in Houston* (College Station: Texas A&M University Press, 2001).

47. See Ignacio García, *Viva Kennedy: Mexican Americans in Search of Camelot* (College Station: Texas A&M University Press, 2000), and *White But Not Equal: Mexican Americans, Jury Discrimination, and the Supreme Court* (Tucson: University of Arizona Press, 2008).

48. See Eduardo Bonilla-Silva and David R. Deitrich, "The Latin Americanization of Racial Stratification in the U.S.," in *Racism in the 21st Century: An Empirical Analysis of Skin Color,* ed. Ronald Hall (New York: Springer, 2008), 151–70.

49. Arnoldo De León, *Ethnicity in the Sunbelt: Mexican Americans in Houston* (College Station: Texas A&M University Press, 2001), xii–xiii, 69–71, 94.

50. Andrés Reséndez, *Changing National Identities at the Frontier: Texas and New Mexico, 1800–1850* (Cambridge: Cambridge University Press, 2005).

51. Vicki L. Ruiz, *From Out of the Shadows: Mexican Women in Twentieth-Century America* (Oxford: Oxford University Press, 1998).

52. Sterling Stuckey, *Slave Culture: Nationalist Theory and the Foundations of Black America* (New York: Oxford University Press, 1987), and *Going through the Storm: The Influence of African American Art in History* (New York: Oxford University Press, 1994); Melville J. Herskovits, *The Myth of the Negro Past* (Boston: Beacon Press, 1941).

53. For example, see John Mason Brewer, *The Word on the Brazos: Negro Preacher Tales from the Brazos Bottoms of Texas* (Austin: University of Texas Press, 1953); *Aunt Dicy Tales: Snuff-Dipping Tales of the Texas Negro* (Austin: Privately published, 1956); *Dog Ghosts and Other Texas Negro Folk Tales* (Austin: University of Texas Press, 1958); and *American Negro Folklore* (Chicago: Quadrangle Books, 1968).

54. Lorenzo Thomas, "The African-American Folktale and J. Mason Brewer," in *Juneteenth Texas: Essays in African American Folklore,* ed. Francis Edward Abernathy et al. (Denton: University of North Texas Press, 1996), 224.

55. Cary D. Wintz, *Blacks in Houston* (Houston: Houston Center for the Humanities, National Endowment for the Humanities, 1982); Cary D. Wintz and Howard Beeth, eds., *Black Dixie: Afro-Texan History and Culture in Houston* (College Station: Texas A&M University Press, 1992); James M. SoRelle, "The Emergence of Black Business in Houston, Texas: A Study of Race and Ideology, 1919–1945," in Wintz and Beeth, eds., *Black Dixie,* 103–15.

56. Taylor Branch, *Parting the Waters: America in the King Years, 1954–63* (New York: Simon and Schuster, 1988); Kellar, *Make Haste Slowly,* 3.

57. See Jim Schutze, *The Accommodation: The Politics of Race in an American City* (Secaucus, N.J.: Citadel Press, 1986); Robert Weisbrot, *Freedom Bound: A History of America's Civil Rights Movement* (New York: W. W. Norton, 1990), 39–40.

58. Kellar, *Make Haste Slowly,* 41, 106, 152–54.

59. Ladino, *Desegregating Texas Schools.*

60. Herbert G. Gutman, *The Black Family in Slavery and Freedom, 1750–1925* (New York: Vintage Books, 1977).

61. See SoRelle, "The Emergence of Black Business in Houston," and Michael Lowery Gillette, "The NAACP in Texas, 1937–1957" (Ph.D. diss., University of Texas at Austin, 1984).

62. W. Marvin Dulaney, "Whatever Happened to the Civil Rights Movement in Dallas, Texas?" in *Essays on the American Civil Rights Movement,* ed. Dulaney and Kathleen Underwood (College Station: Published for the University of Texas at Arlington by Texas A&M University Press, 1993), 66–95.

63. Anderson, *The Indian Southwest.*

64. Anderson, *The Conquest of Texas,* 7.

65. Pekka Hämäläinen, *Comanche Empire* (New Haven, Conn.: Yale University Press, 2008), 2.

66. Hämäläinen, *Comanche Empire,* 347.

67. Ibid., 346; Juliana Barr, *Peace Came in the Form of a Woman: Indians and Spaniards in the Texas Borderlands* (Chapel Hill: University of North Carolina Press, 2007).

68. Hämäläinen, *Comanche Empire,* 177.

69. Among Winegartens's works in this genre are Ruthe Winegarten and William Bedford Clark, eds., *Katherine Anne Porter and Texas: An Uneasy Relationship* (College Station: Texas A&M University Press, 1990); Winegarten and Cathy Schechter, *Deep in the Heart: The Lives and Legends of Texas Jews: a Photographic History* (Austin: Eakin Press, 1990); Winegarten, *Black Texas Women: 150 Years of Trial and Triumph* (Austin: University of Texas Press, 1995); Winegarten, *Black Texas Women: A Sourcebook—Documents, Biographies, Timeline* (Austin: University of Texas Press, 1996); Winegarten and Sharon Kahn, *Brave Black Women: From Slavery to the Space Shuttle* (Austin: University of Texas Press, 1997); Winegarten and Nancy Baker Jones, *Capitol Women: Texas Female Legislators, 1923–1999* (Austin: University of Texas Press, 2000); Winegarten and Marc Sanders, *The Lives and Times of Black Dallas Women* (Austin:

Eakin Press, 2002); and Winegarten and Teresa Palomo Acosta, *Las Tejanas: 300 Years of History* (Austin: University of Texas Press, 2003). Weiner's works include *Jewish Stars in Texas: Rabbis and Their Work* (College Station: Texas A&M University Press, 2006); Weiner and Kenneth D. Roseman, eds., *Lone Stars of David: The Jews of Texas* (Waltham, Mass.: Brandeis University Press; Hanover, N.H.: In association with the Texas Jewish Historical Society published by University Press of New England, 2007); and *Jewish Junior League: The Rise and Demise of the Fort Worth Council of Jewish Women* (College Station: Texas A&M University Press, 2008).

70. Barr, *Peace Came in the Form of a Woman*, 2–3.

71. Judith N. McArthur, *Creating the New Woman: The Rise of Southern Women's Progressive Culture in Texas, 1893–1918* (Urbana: University of Illinois Press, 1998), 2.

72. Roberto R. Treviño, *The Church in the Barrio: Mexican American Ethno-Catholicism in Houston* (Chapel Hill: University of North Carolina Press, 2006), 52–57, 159–61, 183–85.

73. Ruiz, *Out of the Shadows*, 4.

74. Acosta and Winegarten, *Las Tejanas: 300 Years of History.*

75. José Angel Gutiérrez, Michael Meléndez, and Sonia Adriana Noyola, *Chicanas in Charge: Texas Women in the Public Arena* (Lanham, Md.: AltaMira Press, 2007).

76. See Elizabeth York Enstam, *Women and the Creation of Urban Life: Dallas, Texas, 1843–1920* (College Station: Texas A&M University Press, 1998); Douglas Hales, *A Southern Family in White and Black: The Cuneys of Texas* (College Station: Texas A&M University Press, 2003); Jacquelyn Dowd Hall, *Revolt Against Chivalry: Jessie Daniel Ames and the Women's Campaign Against Lynching* (New York: Columbia University Press, 1993); Elizabeth Hayes Turner, *Women, Culture, and Community: Religion and Reform in Galveston, 1880–1920* (Oxford: Oxford University Press, 2002); Turner, "Juneteenth: Emancipation and Memory," in *Lone Star Pasts,* ed. Cantrell and Turner, 143–75; Judith N. McArthur and Harold L. Smith, *Minnie Fisher Cunningham: A Suffragist's Life in Politics* (New York: Oxford University Press, 2003), and Angela Boswell and Judith N. McArthur, eds., *Women Shaping the South: Creating and Confronting Change* (Columbia: University of Missouri Press, 2006).

77. McArthur, *Creating the New Woman*, 31.

78. Ibid., 33–34.

79. Sharpless, *Fertile Ground, Narrow Choices*, 3.

80. Ruiz, *From Out of the Shadows*, 17.

81. Acosta and Winegarten, *Las Tejanas,* 118, 143–45, 319, 328

82. Patricia Evridge Hill, *Dallas: The Making of a Modern City* (Austin: University of Texas Press, 1996), 129–45.

83. Acosta and Winegarten, *Las Tejanas,* 234.

84. Pitre, *In Struggle against Jim Crow;* Stefanie Decker, "Women in the Civil Rights Movement: Juanita Craft versus the Dallas Elite," *East Texas Historical Journal* 39, no. 1 (2001): 33–42.

85. Pitre, *In Struggle against Jim Crow,* xi, 130–31.

86. Stephanie Cole, "Finding Race in Turn-of-the-Century Dallas," in *Beyond Black and White: Race, Ethnicity, and Gender in the U.S. South and Southwest,* ed. Stephanie Cole and Alison M. Parker (College Station: Texas A&M University Press, 2004), 75–96.

87. Mark M. Carroll, *Homesteads Ungovernable: Families, Sex, Race, and the Law in Frontier Texas, 1823–1860* (Austin: University of Texas Press, 2001).

88. See Joan Wallach Scott, *Gender and the Politics of History* (New York: Columbia University Press, 1999).

89. Carroll, *Homesteads Ungovernable,* xv.

90. Ibid., xix.

91. George Chauncey, *New York: Gender, Urban Culture, and the Making of the Gay Male World, 1890–1940* (New York: Basic Books, 1995).

92. "National Science Foundation Survey of Earned Doctorates/Doctorate Records File by Field and Gender, 10-year Trend and the NSF Survey of Earned Doctorates Filed by Field and Race, 10-year Trend," at http://webcaspar.nsf.gov/index.jsp?subheader=WebCASPAR Home%ShowHelp=false, accessed October 9, 2008.

93. Ricky Lee Dobbs, "Lyndon, We Hardly Remember Ye: LBJ in the Memory of Modern Texas," in *Lone Star Pasts,* ed. Cantrell and Turner, 236.

94. Christopher Bateman, "Counting Down until Bush Sells the Ranch," *Vanity Fair,* August 12, 2009, at http://www.vanityfair.com/online/politics/2008/08/counting-down-till-bush-sells-the-ranch.html, accessed December 14, 2009.

95. Dobbs, "Lyndon, We Hardly Remember Ye," in *Lone Star Pasts,* ed. Cantrell and Turner, 236.

96. Don Graham, "Mission Statement: The Alamo and the Fallacy of Historical Accuracy in Epic Filmmaking," in *Lone Star Pasts,* ed. Cantrell and Turner, 255.

97. "Get Involved: The Bob Bullock Texas State History Museum," at http://www.thestoryoftexas.com/get_involved/tshm_foundation.html, accessed December 21, 2009.

98. Rodolfo Acuña, *Occupied America: A History of Chicanos* (New York: HarperCollins, 1988), 11.

99. Barry A. Crouch and Larry Madaras, *The Dance of Freedom: Texas African Americans during Reconstruction* (Austin: University of Texas Press, 2007), 106.

100. Randolph B. Campbell, "History and Collective Memory in Texas: The Entangled Stories of the Lone Star State," in *Lone Star Pasts,* ed. Cantrell and Turner, 279–80.

Deconstructing Texas

The Diversity of People, Place, and Historical Imagination in Recent Texas History

Carlos Kevin Blanton

The volume in which this essay appears testifies to the fact that Texas has no shortage of professional commentators. For example, in 1961 John Steinbeck remarked, "Texas is a state of mind. Texas is an obsession. Above all, Texas is a nation in every sense of the word. . . . A Texan outside of Texas is a foreigner." He was on the mark. As others have noted time and again, Texans possess a peculiar attachment to a dual, though precociously compatible, national identity. One of the roots of this biculturalism, this binationalism, is the state's singular past, which Steinbeck also referred to as "its own private history based on, but not limited by, facts."[1] Historians of Texas, it seems, have struggled mightily to fairly and accurately document the state's rich, diverse, yet oddly obscured past on the one hand, and on the other hand to grapple daily with the popular, powerful, emotionally charged historical myths that make up so much of Texan identity. The original *Texas Through Time: Evolving Interpretations* (1991), edited by Walter L. Buenger and the late Robert A. "Bob" Calvert twenty years ago, was entirely devoted to combating old, chauvinistic, triumphalist myths in a manner more resembling a barroom brawl than a genteel academic dispute. Its overwhelming focus on myth, however, was more than justified. Myth is a peculiarly strong problem in Texas history. While historical documents and sources are capable of multiple kinds of intellectual interrogation, Texas myth demands the opposite. It brooks no critical engagement. It, like any myth, depends on uncritical submission. Myths are handed down and accepted, not put under any scholar's microscope. They cannot withstand that kind of scrutiny; therefore, to attempt to unearth, catalog, and analyze them invites vague, unformed, yet undeniably passionate charges of disloyalty, of bad taste, and of foreignness. So despite any and all contrary evidence, Texas myth insists that slaves must be happy, women must be cheerful yet silent helpmates, Mexicans must be treacherous, and Indians must be deadly, implacable foes. The influence of Texas myth, an exaggeration of the broader U.S. frontier myth, is that such ideas are "known" without evidence.

These myths, particularly in their more traditional forms, are enmeshed with age-old power relations and attitudes that today would surely be considered racist, nativist, sexist, and classist.[2] By no means are they neutral, inconsequential notions. Interpretations emanating from a creation myth around the Alamo and its Anglo defenders as slain martyrs, as blood sacrifices to the creation of a new utopia, also invoke rugged frontiersmen who heroically reclaimed the land from the alleged savagery of its Indian and Mexican inhabitants; they also invoke the supposed cultural superiority of Anglo, Protestant frontiersmen over everyone else, and the sacrosanct belief in Texan independence as a preordained chapter of manifest destiny. But even these origin myths have origins themselves. Forged in the nineteenth century by amateur scholars, these myths were greatly extended into the realm of academic and popular knowledge by professional twentieth-century scholars such as (but not limited to) George P. Garrison, Walter Prescott Webb, J. Frank Dobie, Charles W. Ramsdell, and Eugene C. Barker. The crystallization of fictive myth into officially sanctioned history occurred at a time of great change in Texas. In the aftermath of Civil War defeat and the arrival of Jim Crow, these myths created a separate, unique identity by substituting a culturally homogenous, heroic, and sacred past in place of the state's actual unruly, untidy, diverse past.[3]

This essay owes a great debt to the first *Texas Through Time*. Its intellectual guidance to any scholar working on Texas history is incalculable. And of course, the original *Texas Through Time* also had a style! *Texas Through Time*'s critical, no-nonsense, unsentimentality expected as much from its readers as from its authors. Its keynote essay demanded that the state's historians "challenge the cultural heritage received from previous generations with an intellectual toughness and an honesty based on the point of view of the present one." This essay takes up how historians have answered that call. It focuses first on how historians since the late 1980s have directly addressed and engaged the origins of these seemingly irrefutable, irreducible myths that are so much a part of the Texas "cultural heritage." Second, the essay examines how historians view the people of this state, especially the interpretive evolution of traditionally marginalized groups such as African Americans, Mexican Americans, immigrants, women, as well as white people regardless of power and influence.

Third, this essay will demonstrate that a diversity of ideas on how to view Texas has shaped modern historiography from the contributions of fictional literature, the concept of borderlands, urban studies, works that focus on the natural environment and Texans' shaping of it, as well as studies of place within Texas. Such topics lend themselves to different kinds of historical imagination that open up entirely new lines of inquiry. All these interpretive changes continue to diminish the power of older myths.[4]

This essay finds that scholars of late have deconstructed the traditional telling of Texas history and are reassembling the pieces of this shattered narrative. The unifying theme to this larger intellectual project is an attempt to more critically deal with the state's diverse past. If the scholars of distant eras constructed "useable pasts" that assembled mythic historical narratives around the ideological and social assumptions of their own times, then modern historians have attacked these ways of perceiving Texas history with narratives indebted to more socially egalitarian attitudes and postmodern intellectual trends: a greater concern for gender equality and racial/ethnic diversity, an interest in various types of oppression and resistance, a preference for more situational notions of individual and group identity, a greater comfort with multicausality, a fascination with language and its contended meaning, and a predisposition to less sweeping interpretative conclusions.[5]

The Deconstruction of Texas Myth

But before an extended discussion of how this new Texas history addresses the state's diverse peoples and places, "Texas myth" must be further examined. Texas historical myth has proven a durable component to a kind of swaggering Texan identity that, oddly enough, non-Texans seem to find exotically authentic. It reminds one of Larry L. King's essay about Texans "playing Texan" to rapt audiences outside the state. Indeed, at times non-Texans seem to feel as if they "know" Texanness, or at least know what to expect—enter King's playacting. This notion that non-Texans might be as invested (or more) as native Texans in what constitutes Texan identity is not terribly surprising; as Karen L. Cox has recently written of Southern history, the images that are sold to national consumers through film, television, radio, and other mass-media mechanisms throughout the twentieth century have been produced from afar in New York City or Los Angeles, making the images' "authenticity" inherently problematical.[6]

So the connection between a strong sense of identity and some degree of mythic understanding is actually quite strong. So strong, in fact, that the idea of Texan exceptionalism is often carried far enough that, somewhat resonant with Steinbeck's remarks about a sense of dual Texan nationalism, it is often conflated with hyper-Americanism. In an interesting parallel Laura Edwards writes of Southern exceptionality and nationalism that on the eve of the Civil War southerners had convinced themselves of an odd, mythic logic in justifying rebellion to a government they professed to cherish: "the South was southern because it was more American than anywhere else in the United States." Substitute "Texas" and "Texan" for "South" and "Southern" and this *Journal of Southern History* essay could very well fit in this volume. Concern with the overlap of myth and identity is not simply an interest of Texas scholars.[7]

But many other authors in the field of Texas history have remarked upon such notions for years. In the last *Texas Through Time* Ronald L. Davis pointedly connected myth to identity: "Self-conscious and schizophrenic, Texas clings to its frontier heritage, viewing it in heroic terms, fearful that should the past be lost, with its courage and risk taking lifted to epic proportions, so will the state's uniqueness." In a more recent essay, Randolph Campbell warns against the dangers of blurring history with memory. He notes that today's postmodern adherents of the use of memory and its multiplicity of perspectives as a way to abandon the idea of objectivity can be just as dangerous as traditional memories owing to older social attitudes: "Historians of Texas should not give up their discipline to reactionaries or romantics—speaking in the name of memory."[8]

Traditional myths of Texas history still very much define the field in support or opposition, though they themselves have undergone some change lately. Most recent upholders of the mythic narratives eschew the directly offensive interpretations of past decades. Borrowing from Walter Buenger's appraisal in this volume's introductory essay, the "updated traditionalists" of Texas history for ideological or moral ends propagate a modified, more sanitized extension of the old-fashioned interpretations of the exclusionary, mythic past. The other Texas history camps, the "persistent revisionists" and "cultural constructionists," take issue in their own way with how traditionalist narratives leave out nonmales, non-Anglos, and nonconformists, or disparage them through moralistic judgments. While Buenger views these latter two camps as having significant differences, neither displays support for traditionalist interpretations. While revisionists are usually centered upon directly challenging older myth, cultural constructionists also challenge them, but in more theoretically informed ways that often posit oblique interpretations that reflect an interest in getting beyond older interpretive battle lines. Most recent Texas history takes on older assumptions and produces new knowledge that goes beyond a staid emphasis upon colorful, two-dimensional heroes or simplified narratives.[9]

The focus on marginalized groups began in the 1960s and 1970s due to sweeping changes in society and in the history profession. But not all revisionists engaged myth, even though they opposed it. As Paul Lack noted, while revisionists by the 1980s acknowledged that older, traditional historians viewed Texas history as "the march of Anglo-American democracy westward in triumph over inferior races," few cared to take on more precisely the ideological assumptions undergirding those interpretations.[10] One of the most fascinating aspects of recent historiographical trends in Texas history has been the way in which scholars are directly addressing the construction of those older myths. Laura McLemore's *Inventing Texas: Early Historians of the Lone Star State* (2004) locates the idea of a romantic, heroic, mythic past as an invention of amateur scholars of the nineteenth century with attitudes about race and nationality that hopefully most modern readers of Texas history will not share. Instead of these early impressions and attitudes being corrected or at least modified with the advent of trained, professional scholars early in the twentieth century, they were uncritically amplified to younger generations. McLemore offers a thought-provoking assessment of the peculiar doggedness of certain myths central to Texas history and identity: "In the face of disillusioning and humiliating defeat and the erosion of the agrarian ideal at a time of rapid industrialization, Texans reached back to a pre–Civil War paradigm in an effort to create and preserve for themselves a unique identity, a world apart. They saw history as a way to redeem Texas from the debacle of the Lost Cause, as something they could use as a means of positively confronting the future."[11]

Recently, a great deal of scholarship has emerged on the subject of myth and Texas. In one essay Gregg Cantrell excavates the meaning of state history during the Progressive era as it pertained to the disinterment of the corpse of Stephen F. Austin, the "Father of Texas." Following the interpretive lead of Buenger, and echoing McLemore, Cantrell notes that the Progressive era in Texas was the site of the consolidation of oral traditions and loose myths from the nineteenth century—little more than the victor's tales of the immediate postrevolutionary period—into a master narrative that would become intellectually entrenched in the ways that Texans constructed their own sense of identity and memory. If the nineteenth century created the outsized Texan myth out of the loose threads of oral tradition and common social attitudes, as McLemore holds, then the Progressive era institutionalized it through academic and governmental sponsorship.[12] The interest in myth and memory in Texas history has culminated recently in a sophisticated collection, *Lone Star Pasts: Memory and History in Texas* (2007), edited by Cantrell and Elizabeth Hayes Turner. This volume focuses on how and why "Texas identity, in many regards, is an exaggeration of purported American traits. Mythic Texas is loud, brash, extravagant, and rustic, like the pint-sized, fabulously rich, and mustachioed oil barons who drive immense Cadillacs (with cattle horns on the radiator) through Bugs Bunny cartoons."[13]

The challenge to traditional Texas history is evidenced by the discovery of forgotten narratives that, due to their different spin on the same mythic events, were once ignored. The 1996 recovery of Adina de Zavala's *History and Legends of the Alamo and Other Missions in and around San Antonio* (1917) is an example of one of the alternative narratives of Texas history that was silently shelved as the myth of Anglo superiority was institutionalized through a master narrative. Although perhaps seen by some traditionalists as politically correct babble, such lost narratives demonstrate how the traditionalist interpretation of Texas history is based on a selective, exclusionary reading of available texts. While de Zavala's work is no paragon of twenty-first-century multiculturalism, it must be noted, its rediscovery by scholars is indicative of the current interest in competing narratives of the past and how the "one" Texas history was selectively assembled. Many decades ago scholarly efforts to confound the accepted narrative with different portrayals of people of Mexican descent, as with those of University of Texas–trained folklorist Jovita González, were neglected by the academic community. Even González's own advisors, Dobie and Barker, held such work in little regard. Recent scholars have begun to explore the literary and historical narratives of early Tejano writers as they directly dealt with the Progressive-inspired and academically sanctioned myths of white supremacy. The Mexican American response to the Texas Centennial of 1936 and its vilification of Mexican-origin peoples, for example, illustrates a fascinating vein of artistic and political resistance.[14]

Scholars also critically assess the writings of earlier, academic twentieth-century historians and the institutionalization of Texas history as a professional field. Félix Almaráz's *Knight without Armor: Carlos Eduardo Castañeda, 1896–1958* (1999), for example, documents the life and career of a historian who is commonly read as the starting point for the history of Spanish Texas. Castañeda, who faced racism at the University of Texas from the 1920s to the 1950s, not only was a political activist within the Mexican American community, but he also aimed to correct interpretive imbalances about the colonial past, particularly the age-old "Black Legend" of Spanish cruelty in the academic community. That he discounted Native American peoples and their cultures reminds students, as does the de Zavala text, that even "progressive" efforts at interpretive reform can exhibit other interpretive blind spots. And in the interest of fair play, it should be noted that Webb and Dobie, who wrote disparagingly about Mexican Americans, and Ramsdell, who was similarly insensitive toward African Americans, were also political progressives who championed the liberal wing of the Texas Democratic Party, which was occasionally pro–civil rights. Ahhh . . . the "left" in Texas![15]

The most potent, mythic subjects of Texas history are generally the Texas Revolution and more specifically the Battle of the Alamo. Indeed, the 1830s are crucial in Texas history. The first *Texas Through Time*'s introduction takes special note of this brief period's role as a lodestone of Texas myth. It was here (so the story goes) that heroic men sacrificed for the birth of a new nation, unassuming women supported them wholeheartedly (and without comment), dissenters from sure martyrdom were no-account cowards, and African Americans and Tejanos were "good" only when they supported the revolution in a clearly subservient role. Buenger and Calvert write, "The creation myth of the nation—the Texas Republic—separates the Texas myth from the Anglo North American myth and gives to the culture a Texas nationalism and romantic vision that transcends geography and creates, as Willie Nelson sings, a Texas state of mind." Confronting that ancient, uncritical, mythic sense of memory so central to modern Texas identity is then the task of all state historians. In that sense, the very reality of today's modern Texas is an affront to such myth.[16]

Some fruitfully write about what the Alamo means to people and why. Richard Flores's *Remembering the Alamo: Memory, Modernity, and the Master Symbol* (2002) fleshes out how the small, bloody battle became a mythic event of outsized proportions in how Texans came to identify themselves: "The Alamo backlash against Mexicans not only serves a social purpose but an economic one as well. To this end, the Alamo fixes a narrative against Mexicans that 'naturalizes' the class identities that erupted at this time. Understanding Mexicans through the story of the Alamo is a strategy that normalizes what otherwise could not be stated—that the economic reorganization of South Texas was based on a system of social dominance." James Crisp's *Sleuthing the Alamo: Davy Crockett's Last Stand and Other Mysteries of the Texas Revolution* (2005) is a wonderful meditation on the controversies of interpreting the period as well as the social attitudes behind some of its enduring myths. It autobiographically captures how writing Texas history is as personal as it is political. These and other works implicitly challenge the simplistic "us versus them" narrative structure.[17] Yet, other works still seek to propagate the old myths and to "defend" its heroes at any and all costs. The Alamo, above all other topics in Texas history, is where traditionalists often *draw a line in the sand*. While the popularity of such an unvarnished interpretive resistance to change does call into question the impact academically trained historians have on the shaping of popular historical consciousness, such examples of updated traditionalists are fewer every year and are hardly ever associated with university presses and other rigorous publishers.[18]

One of the finest monographs of recent decades takes the Texas Revolution head on. Paul Lack brilliantly observes, in *The Texas Revolutionary Experience: A Political and Social History, 1835–1836* (1992), that the old, heroic yarns informing Texan identity willfully erase the confusing, combustible political matrix of the state's past: "the legend became *the* Revolution, but not *a* revolution, cleansed of its political turbulence, regional disharmonies, conflicts of interest, social turbulence, and racial or ethnic strife. Essentially, the Texas Revolution was transformed into little more than a staple for the swaggering boastfulness of the archetypal Texan." Lack documents the crucial yet willfully forgotten roles of Tejano revolutionaries and how their sacrifices were subordinated to the eventual cartoonish understanding of white supermen conquering barbarian races against overwhelming odds. By reexamining the Texas Revolution, Lack also excavates the roots of Texan identity.[19]

A Diversity of People

The notion that Texas is a diverse place should not be startling. The state's polyglot heritage has been known to scholars for quite some time and formed the theme of D. W. Meinig's forty-year-old classic *Imperial Texas: An Interpretive Essay in Cultural Geography* (1969).[20] One of the most pressing difficulties in teaching Texas history has to do with complicating an already understood historical narrative, incomplete and exclusive though it may be, with the perspectives of different groups and ways of viewing the past. Traditionalists believe that historians spread disunity by the very act of teaching complexity, and that stressing the diversity of the past mocks the very foundations of the present. Such worldviews are informed by an early twentieth-century, social Darwinist outlook, holding that a superior Anglo culture/race triumphed over other deficient cultures/races (African, Mexican, and Native American), thus rendering as unnecessary pandering any attention to such groups.[21] Such heritage-minded orthodoxy stubbornly persists despite the state's rapidly changing demographic makeup. In 2003, state demographer Steve Murdock and his research team warned that the state's racialized wealth and education gap means that Texas is becoming poorer, less educated, and less economically competitive. Murdock and his team recommend closing the educational gap between whites and non-whites—in other words, to deal more effectively with Texas' cultural diversity and regard it as the treasure it is rather than a handicap to be endured.[22]

Recently, Barbara Rozek has reminded us that the state has wrestled with the same issues of diversity for well over a century. She illustrates the degree to which Texans of the nineteenth century encouraged immigration and sold the state to prospective immigrants. In what must be a fascinating moment of historical déjà vu, state policy makers in the nineteenth century acknowledged and even trumpeted Texas' then-teeming diversity through census and agricultural data from state agencies to encourage the arrival of more newcomers. So interest in statistical measures of health, wealth, and social divisions has been a going concern of public officials long before the state's recent transition to majority-minority demographic status. Barring a few exceptions since Terry Jordan's excellent work on demography and cultural geography of the 1970s and 1980s, however, historians of the Lone Star State have generally neglected such fascinating, wide-ranging, and inherently interdisciplinary demographic topics.[23]

Until recently, one of the groups most neglected by historians was Native Americans. And to the extent that Native Americans were included in Texas history, they were dimly perceived as "savage" obstacles to the progress of American/white "civilization." Even relatively progressive historians who sought to include other traditionally ignored minority groups often discounted Native Americans. It was not so very long ago that respected works in the field bore such unblinkingly offensive titles as *The Comanche Barrier to South Plains Settlement: A Century and a Half of Savage Resistance to the Advancing White Frontier* (1933).[24] But there has been a renaissance of interest in Texas' Native American history. These new approaches teach that the original inhabitants of the land, though they suffered disasters and displacement by the imperial expansion of successive European groups, were still major factors to be contended with. The recent history of Native Americans of Texas can be characterized as one of discovery; new theoretical perspectives and more advanced techniques of analyzing the potential evidence of Native American culture promise exciting times for this field in the years to come. Pekka Hämäläinen's essay in this collection ably and thoroughly documents these impressive developments. So while I defer analysis of this field to his expertise, I would be remiss if I did not at least mention that recent work by Hämäläinen, Gary Anderson, F. Todd Smith, David La Vere, and Juliana Barr outstandingly contribute to what is promising to be one of the most exciting fields in Texas history.[25]

Other Texans enjoying boom years of historical interpretation are Mexican Americans. Research on this group has moved far beyond the stereotype of the lying, thieving, treacherous Mexican echoed by Webb and Dobie. After groundbreaking historical conceptualizations by Arnoldo De León and David

Montejano in the 1980s, recent work continues to both fill the extant gaps and theoretically push the field in new and exciting directions.[26] Prior to the 1980s very little existed on Tejanos. As De León noted in a 2003 state-of-the-field essay, up to then Tejanos generated little interest, because "like women and other minorities, Mexican Americans did not fit into the triumphalist myth that gripped Texas history until the last few decades of the twentieth century. Historians seemed bent solely on affirming the virtues of the Texas war for independence, the Republic of Texas, and the frontier. This 'Ideals of the Republic' approach to history cast Mexican Americans in unflattering roles (generally as bandits) or dismissed them altogether as active players in the state's development."[27]

Studies of Spanish exploration and colonialism remain popular. In particular, the legendary odyssey of Álvar Núñez Cabeza de Vaca and his few surviving crewmates who wandered through Texas and northern Mexico in the 1530s has lately inspired several books. The works of noted colonialists David Weber and Donald Chipman have refreshed our narrative of the Spanish world of the American Southwest as well as that of Texas with their respective books *The Spanish Frontier in North America* (1992) and *Spanish Texas, 1519–1821* (1992).[28] Jesús F. de la Teja, in *San Antonio de Béxar: A Community on New Spain's Northern Frontier* (1995), brings to life a vibrant, multicultural frontier community. Breaking away from traditional interpretive schemes centering upon the survival and transmission of Spanish institutions along the frontier, de la Teja examines the isolated community's adaptability to its surroundings over time. This places the historical gaze not on abstract similarities of static laws and structures inherited from Spain, but on the lived experiences of a wide variety of people who shared an identity and participated in a community of their own. This is history "from the bottom up" and an important model for future colonial studies.[29]

The Mexican period of nineteenth-century Texas is similarly undergoing a rich transformation in scope and perspective and has directly squared off against the most mythic parts of Texas history: Mexican governance and Texas independence. In a revolutionary reinterpretation, Andrés Reséndez's *Changing National Identities at the Frontier: Texas and New Mexico, 1800–1850* (2005) investigates the stateless nature of northern Mexico. He argues that the nationalizing project of Mexico's independence from Spain was disastrously unfinished in its northern frontier. Tejanos, Native Americans, and Anglo immigrants crafted fluid identities that enabled them to adopt and cast aside various allegiances with different imperial systems, incipient nation-states, and all manner of secessionist movements. Reséndez reminds us that while nations may lay claim to land, they only truly possess it when the inhabitants accept that claim in ways that alter their own identity. Constant chaos in the Texas borderlands from Spanish independence to the U.S. Civil War created fleeting, impermanent conceptions of national identity in the minds of all Texans, regardless of ethnicity. In other words, the Texas Revolution was not about unstoppable Anglo destiny; it was about Mexican statelessness, which was different from the level of statelessness on the U.S. frontier only in degree. Reséndez's comparative, internationally framed work has influenced not only Texas history, but borderlands and Latin American history as well.[30]

Tejano research on the last half of the nineteenth century investigates the survival and adaptability of the community in the face of larger, impersonal forces working against them. Kenneth Stewart and De León's *Not Room Enough: Mexicans, Anglos, and Socioeconomic Change in Texas, 1850–1900* (1993) documents the challenges of economic modernization and industrialization for Tejanos who, due to structural racism, faced stark downward mobility. The few opportunities that did exist for Mexican Americans were racially bound to low-paying, backbreaking, dead-end labor. But others argue that not all Tejanos slipped quite so far. Armando Alonzo's *Tejano Legacy: Rancheros and Settlers in South Texas, 1734–1900* (1998) illustrates that, contrary to the assertions of earlier Chicano scholars, not all Mexican Americans lost their land. He argues that while Anglos often tried to dispossess Tejanos in the nineteenth century, many elite and middling Tejano ranchers tenaciously retained and even expanded their lands.[31]

Nationally, Mexican American history of the twentieth century is bound together through the interpretive net of self-defining generations: the Mexicanist generation of the early twentieth century, the Mexican American generation of the mid-twentieth century, and the Chicano generation of the late twentieth century. Tejano history follows the same pattern; in fact, Tejano history in part *set* this national pattern. The outstanding work on the early twentieth century is Emilio Zamora's influential *The World of the Mexican Worker in Texas* (1993). Zamora reconceptualizes the cultural and political identity of early twentieth-century Tejanos as Mexicanist, entailing a primary cultural affinity with Mexico. A cross-border sharing of ideas and identities is paramount in this work. Zamora recovers the Mexicanist world of *mutualistas* (mutual aid societies) as well as the radical politics of proletarianized, economically exploited Tejanos. He also documents the shift that took place in the 1920s when Tejano leaders began to discard Mexicanist orientations and grope toward a Mexican American ideology that had at its core a primary affinity for U.S. citizenship, civil rights, economic incorporation, and cultural assimilation. Very recent work on the Tejano community and its soldiers during World War I, José A. Ramírez's *To the Line of Fire! Mexican Texans and World War I* (2009) also makes a groundbreaking national impact.[32]

The Mexican American generation between the New Deal and the Great Society exerts more scholarly interest. Historians have recently documented the role that prominent Mexican American civic activists played in state and national politics from the formation of LULAC in the late 1920s, the American GI Forum in the late 1940s, and PASSO in the early 1960s. But in theoretical contributions, Anthony Quiroz's *Claiming Citizenship: Mexican Americans in Victoria, Texas* (2005) enlivens the traditional understanding of the Mexican American generation through its analytical focus on the driving ideological category of U.S. citizenship and how activism over civil rights, economic justice, and immigration was filtered through it. Quiroz marks the rhetorical and ideological parameters derived from the Mexican American generation's acceptance of a guiding ideological principle of citizenship. This urges a fresh conceptualization of Mexican American civil rights as well as notions of assimilation and acculturation in ways that are ideologically consistent rather than simply pejorative.[33] Very recent work by a number of scholars foreshadows an even greater level of sustained engagement with the Mexican American generation in the years to come.[34]

One of the least developed aspects of the history of Tejanos in the twentieth century examines the Chicano era. Not only did a Chicano identity entail different notions of assimilation, immigration, patriotism, civic action, and ideological beliefs concerning capitalism, but it also ushered in new articulations of racial identity. No longer identifying themselves as "Caucasian" or "white," young Chicanos referred to themselves as a separate "brown" race. Guadalupe San Miguel's *Brown, Not White: School Integration and the Chicano Movement in Houston* (2001) explores the origins of a local Chicano movement and emphasizes how the shift in one's identity, initially the product of a strategic, legal attempt to counter racist public officials, then triggered a whole range of other shifts involving tactics, strategy, and ideology.[35]

More specialized studies on Tejanos have also garnered some attention. For example, my book *The Strange Career of Bilingual Education in Texas, 1836–1981* (2004) examines the Mexican American community's nineteenth- and twentieth-century responses to the language issue in education. It discovers a wealth of engagement that complicates easy interpretive characterizations of the generational approach. Another recent collection edited by Jorge Iber and Samuel Regalado, *Mexican Americans and Sports: A Reader on Athletics and Barrio Life* (2007), examines Mexican American involvement in organized sports in the American Southwest, and especially in Texas with regard to track, boxing, and football.[36]

The field of Mexican Americans in Texas is opening up in new and interesting ways since its inception out of resistance to racial oppression just a few decades ago. Tejano history is one of the most vital subfields in Texas history today. And it also thrives among the Tejano public, notes Andrés Tijerina, with regard to the growth of Hispanic statues and other memorial projects of recent years. This is a dependable growth industry in Texas history. Of this vital subject, De León writes, "Without argument, it can be said that Tejano history has been written with a passion equal to that which permeates institutional Texas history."[37]

One cannot write a historical essay on the many Texas groups and cultures without discussing whites or Anglos. Both terms are slippery. *White* can mean almost anything and *Anglo* is often used as a synonym for white, even when applied to groups who could be more properly viewed as *ethnic* whites. The lazy wag will point out that since whites/Anglos have exercised dominance in politics, economics, and the intellectual production of Texas myth and memory, any historical approach not expressly about race or ethnicity is inherently about whites. But scholarly interest in whiteness does not stop at such a negatively derived, incurious perspective. Instead, some have begun to seriously ask what there is to the concept of being white. What does it mean if not just an absence of color? Building upon the pioneering work of David Roediger, Neil Foley and Michael Phillips have introduced such considerations to Texas history. In *The White Scourge: Mexicans, Blacks, and Poor Whites in Texas Cotton Culture* (1997), Foley holds that notions of whiteness in the twentieth century were intimately bound with the control of agricultural labor. Phillips, in *White Metropolis: Race, Ethnicity, and Religion in Dallas, 1841–2001* (2006), argues that the city of Dallas has a record of racial divisiveness that belies its widespread, propagandistic assertions of harmony. He argues that ethnic groups in Dallas, particularly African Americans, Mexican Americans, and Jewish Americans, were set against one another by racism and whiteness.[38]

This new whiteness scholarship is cutting edge. It is an entirely new line of inquiry relatively unconcerned with traditional Texas history. It has the promise to move beyond stale interpretive traditions to a truly comparative analysis of the power of racism as well as the more subtle workings of ideas of race. So far, however, this whiteness scholarship in Texas disappoints more than it delivers. This is especially noticeable in these works' characterizations of Tejanos, for centuries a thorny group to racially pigeonhole. To the extent that Mexican Americans grappled with the whiteness branded upon them by law and fought different kinds of civil rights battles from what African Americans fought, they are stridently condemned in some whiteness studies as having engaged in "Faustian pacts" or "outright negrophobia." Essentially criticizing Mexican Americans for not fighting African Americans' struggles first, these scholars ignore the real connections between both movements. Were historians to scold the African American civil rights movement for an insufficient deference to the Mexican American civil rights movement, it would be equally unfair and condescending. In these studies the theoretically fueled abstraction of whiteness is advanced relentlessly to the exclusion of all else, especially power. These works miscarry their great promise by choosing to ignore nuance, complexity, balance, and interpretive sophistication, and thus they mirror a wider, national reassessment of whiteness studies in recent years.[39]

Scholars do analyze race and racism, however, beyond the existence of discourse. Outstanding lynching scholarship by William Carrigan represents the first systematic analysis in Texas of the horrors of racial violence against African Americans and Mexican Americans. Even the old myths of Texas held the state to be a particularly violent place. Carrigan's *The Making of a Lynching Culture: Violence and Vigilantism in Central Texas, 1836–1918* (2006) places the onus of this violence not on its victims but on the dominant society. Carrigan connects the Texas tradition of lynching and violence to the rest of the U.S. South. Lynching in Texas was a glue for different classes of whites to assert not only a sense of belonging with one another but also an assurance of power and dominance over others on the simple basis of being white. Whiteness had tangible benefits, and the lack of whiteness had terrible costs. This lynching scholarship documents the chillingly real power of racism; it packs more punch than teasing out the discursive imaginings of race. *Making of a Lynching Culture* reminds historians that racial identity in a not-so-distant past involved more than which box to check in a census form or the minute shifts in how an idea of race could be expressed through newspaper editorials—it could mean the difference between justice and horror, between life and death.[40]

Certainly not all work focusing on white Texans centers upon racial oppression and violence. Ironically, biographies of those dead, white men that seem such an albatross for the more ridiculous advocates of curricular diversity have been wonderful vehicles for exhuming the profound uncertainty of identity and allegiance during the revolutionary era. These were not simplistic racial partisans, but complicated individuals weighing conflicting, contradictory beliefs in nation, community, and kin. Gregg Cantrell's thoughtful and nuanced *Stephen F. Austin: Empresario of Texas* (1999) revises an important figure of Texas history ignored since Barker's classic 1925 biography. This is especially noteworthy because Austin's story presents interpretive dilemmas to uncritical, flag-waving adherents to traditional Texas nationalism. Jack Jackson's *Indian Agent: Peter Ellis Bean in Mexican Texas* (2005) rediscovers a forgotten Anglo powerbroker whose life demonstrates how unbelievably complicated the Texas Revolution was for its participants. The traditionalist thinking of easy, if not automatic, allegiances to one's own race quickly crumbles as these new biographies explore the fragility of allegiances and identities among early Anglo pioneers.[41]

White women of the nineteenth century have inspired impressive scholarship, and in doing so have overcome obstacles. Traditional historical myths of Texas are as slighting to women as they are to racial and ethnic minorities. Fane Downs stipulated in *Texas Through Time,* "Texas women's history must be conducted within the context of the suffocating Texas macho myth."[42] Recent work on Texas women stresses agency and recovers forgotten aspects of daily life. Angela Boswell's *Her Act and Her Deed: Women's Lives in a Rural Southern County, 1837–1873* (2001) traces the lives of women through court records of Colorado County in the early and middle nineteenth century, discovering a more fluid, dynamic social reality of work and class relations. What wealthy white women shared with poor white and African American women was having to bear an intense patriarchy that was heightened by the existence of slavery and its influence on slaveholding men to recreate in their homes the ultimate, at times frightening, authority they exerted in the fields. Rebecca Sharpless's *Fertile Ground, Narrow Choices: Women on Texas Cotton Farms, 1900–1940* (1999) is a painstaking and moving recreation of the social world of women on Texas farms, their daily lives, their attitudes, their beliefs, and their memories.[43] Other work on Texas women in the eighteenth and nineteenth centuries demonstrates their participation in the intellectual imaginings of the manifest destiny craze in the years leading up the Civil War, the role of gender in early Texas law derived from medieval Spain, and women of the Texas Populist movement and how they viewed their activism.[44]

Much of the explosive growth of women's history in Texas has taken the form of biography of elite figures, particularly Progressive activists who sought to transform society as well as their own lives. Scholarship on Texas poet and writer Karle Wilson Baker, Texas governor Miriam "Ma" Ferguson, state superintendent of public instruction Annie Webb Blanton, suffrage proponent and liberal Democrat Minnie Fisher Cunningham, and Dallas civic activist and journalist Isadore Miner Callaway have begun the process of reconstructing a fascinating world that for years went untold by many earlier (and yes, male) historians who regarded the Lone Star State's knack for producing incredible women as somehow less worthy of study than yet another second-rate, male politician.[45] In the Progressive-era world of women and politics, however, Judith McArthur's *Creating a New Woman: The Rise of Southern Women's Progressive Culture in Texas, 1893-1918* (1998) and Elizabeth Hayes Turner's *Women, Culture, and Community: Religion and Reform in Galveston, 1880-1920* (1997) stand out in their outstanding depth and penetration of a separate sphere of heretofore neglected women's activity, thus placing it at the center of deliberations as to the very meaning of the Progressive era.[46]

The combination of race and gender is less commonly studied. Complementing recent work by Leticia Garza-Falcón, Teresa Palomo Acosta and Ruthe Winegarten bring the subject of Tejanas into a larger focus with an ambitious synthesis of current published material and their own archival knowledge of sources documenting the hidden life of Mexican American women. Dale Baum has very recently discovered the remarkable narrative of Azeline Hearne, a former slave who was bequeathed a large estate by her prior owner and their mulatto son shortly after the Civil War, and her courageous attempts to keep her inheritance from predatory whites seeking to exploit the Reconstruction politics of race for their own selfish ends.[47]

Recent work on gender in Spanish–Native American relations also commands attention. Juliana Barr's *Peace Came in the Form of a Woman: Indians and Spaniards in the Texas Borderlands* (2007) focuses not just on women but also on the role of gender in Texas history. This work explores the kinship-based social organization of Native American tribes in which men and women contributed relatively equally. Europeans learned from Native Americans that to arrange for peace treaties or trading rights meant acknowledging the political importance of gender. Whether functioning as captive bargaining chips or crucial intermediaries in the diplomatic process, women were integral to the waging of peace in Spanish Texas. In these societies gender generated its own degree of power and authority.[48]

Examinations of masculinity or sexual politics, for example, all involve the category of gender in ways that build upon and go beyond a more traditional conception of women's history. Barr's *Peace Came in the Form of a Woman,* for example, hinges its analysis of Spanish-Indian diplomacy and social interaction upon the way in which gender structured decision making. Boswell's *Her Act and Her Deed* documents how women understood an idealized image of femininity and attempted to achieve it even in the most trying and hardscrabble of frontier conditions. Mark Carroll's *Homesteads Ungovernable: Families, Sex, Race, and the Law in Frontier Texas, 1832-1860* (2001) examines how male policy makers responded to demographic realities in early Texas history—high rates of interracial/interethnic marriage, oddly reconsolidated families, and a more casual approach to marriage—and in the process unintentionally created a more imaginative and permissive, some might say "progressive," legal system pertaining to gender and family.[49]

One recent essay's focus on gay southerners uses as its starting point the 2003 *Lawrence v. Texas* decision of the U.S. Supreme Court. *Lawrence,* which arose out of the arrest of two consenting gay men engaged in sex in Houston, struck down sodomy statutes across the United States. *Lawrence* was hailed as momentous a decision for the gay community as was the *Brown v. Board of Education* decision for African Americans and for other minorities. Unfortunately, state historians have contributed no surveys of gays and lesbians in Texas, or sexuality for that matter, a shortcoming that time will have to address. One wonders if in the next iteration of the *Texas Through Time* franchise decades from now one of the biggest criticisms will be the current lack of development on the subject of gays and lesbians. This is not a far-fetched thought given the community's prominence in the Lone Star State, whose largest city elected as mayor a lesbian candidate in 2009. There is more than enough room in Texas history for queer studies.[50]

African American history in Texas is also richly studied. Ironically, given the sad legacy of Jim Crow, the story of African Americans and Anglos in Texas are actually inseparable. In fact, one of the more important economic histories of Anglos in Texas up to the Civil War is Randolph Campbell's *An Empire for Slavery: The Peculiar Institution in Texas, 1821–1865* (1989). This magisterial book is also the definitive account of the development of slavery in Texas, "that peculiar institution's" role in independence from Mexico, and its economic influence on the politics of the state. Campbell brilliantly reappraises the daily lives of slaves, including their accommodation and resistance to bondage's insidiousness. *Empire for Slavery* takes Texas historians that much further away from Barker's and Ramsdell's old stereotypes of childish bondsmen cheerfully laboring in a system of benign slavery, a trend already noted by Alwyn Barr in his review of the field in *Texas Through Time*.[51]

The history of African Americans in postbellum Texas centers upon African American agency. Work by Gregg Cantrell on Kenneth and John B. Rayner, a unique southern slaveholder and his illegitimate mulatto son, analyzes how both men dissented from the dominant political ethos of their day. The father opposed political orthodoxy by supporting the Whig Party in North Carolina, and the son consistently opposed the Democratic Party in Texas as a Republican and Populist leader. Other historical studies on the period of Reconstruction demonstrate how African Americans and white Freedmen's Bureau agents worked together against depressingly insurmountable racism, as well as important differences among themselves, to transform freedom from a word into a reality. Historians also explore how African Americans remembered their emancipation. This trend in the literature places African Americans at the center of the historical narrative and highlights their role in shaping the meaning of freedom. These works communicate how important, honorable, and decent were those early attempts at black-white cooperation, whatever their limitations and failures.[52]

The era of segregation and African American adaptations to it are also hot topics. African American agency again emerges as the dominant interpretive thread. Small, rural African American communities throughout Texas that formed during the Jim Crow era endure with a remarkable sense of cohesiveness and identity. In addition to protests against Jim Crow, which tend to gain more notice from historians, African Americans also worked within the system of segregation in an attempt to force government agencies to offer services to their communities. Debra Reid's *Reaping a Greater Harvest: African Americans, the Extension Service, and Rural Reform in Jim Crow Texas* (2007) explores this tension between repression and reform. Reid examines how the Negro Division of the Texas Agricultural Extension Service "reflected black agency as well as black subjugation" and "grew because of black talent as well as white racism." Others discover how the power to legislate Jim Crow did not always entail an easy or effective enforcement. Executing a strict racial separation in romantic matters, for example, proved a challenging headache to white supremacists.[53]

The history of African American workers generates much attention from scholars. Black workers consistently struggled for better pay, conditions, and respect. Ernest Obadele-Starks's *Black Unionism in the Industrial South* (2000) demonstrates that although routinely denied admittance into white unions, African American men nevertheless created their own labor brotherhoods and devised successful alliances across class divisions within their community. Obadele-Starks stresses the impermeability of the color line among the white working class.[54] However, a spate of other historians have countered that the common cause proffered by labor unions had the potential, as with Reconstruction, to occasionally bridge the racial divide that came to seem ever more insurmountable as the nineteenth century ambled into the twentieth century. As with Reconstruction, some labor historians hold that such fragmentary moments are notable for their potential, not just their ultimate failure.[55]

The subject of civil rights among Texas historians has grown immensely in recent years. There are many new studies of activist organizations, legal cases, courts, attorneys, judges, and political figures who all played their part in the drama of civil rights in the Lone Star State. Such traditional desegregation and civil rights topics have flourished and continue to shed new light into the complicated, slow process by which the harsher aspects of Jim Crow were, at least partially, lifted from the state's public life.[56] But civil rights historians of Texas have also moved beyond what some scholars term the "black-white binary" in their conception of race and racism. Recent work not only includes the social justice activism of women and Mexican Americans in addition to African Americans as a part of a larger conception of civil rights, but also how these movements compared, interacted, and influenced one another. This more comparative and additive approach is well represented in Debra Reid's edited volume *Seeking Inalienable Rights: Texans and Their Quests for Justice* (2009).[57]

But two trailblazing works especially define the history of African American civil rights in Texas. Amilcar Shabazz's *Advancing Democracy: African Americans and the Struggle for Access and Equity in Higher Education in Texas* (2004) expands the usual civil rights story by offering crucial attention to local grassroots activists as well as the struggle to desegregate institutions other than the University of Texas. Shabazz's sensitivity to tensions within the African American community over the direction of the movement transforms a simple, almost mythic narrative to a more complicated reality that is every bit as compelling (if not more) in its depiction of the unsung heroism of otherwise forgotten people in their daily lives. And Dwonna Goldstone's *Integrating the 40 Acres: The 50-Year Struggle for Racial Equality at the University of Texas* (2006) eschews a narrow legal history for a fresh, innovative look at the hard work of actually integrating the campus once black students arrived. This, unlike other civil rights narratives of courtrooms, attorneys, strategies, politicians, and the dry, abstract reading of judicial opinions, is very much a social history of students, faculty, and administrators each dealing with racial integration in their own way as they conducted their daily responsibilities within the university. This more critical, less triumphalist shift in the scholarship of civil rights by younger scholars is perhaps indicative of a generational shift in attitudes toward the civil rights movements and the role of race in American society, explains Yvonne Davis Frear.[58]

European immigrants came to Texas in large numbers during the nineteenth and early twentieth centuries. Much of the work on European ethnic groups is influenced by the "new" immigration history that stresses the persistent lingering of ethnicity, the gradual evolution of identity, and the substantial degree to which immigrants themselves were decisive agents in their own lives; the older, traditional interpretive approach portrayed immigrants as hapless victims who were ignorant of the world around them and brutalized at every turn.⁵⁹ Texas historians have definitely begun to embrace the new immigrant history as exemplified by Zamora's *World of the Mexican Worker*. One flaw in this field, however, is that few works analyze multiple European immigrant groups in any sustained manner. My *Strange Career of Bilingual Education* briefly analyzes the educational administration, teaching techniques, and languages in schools for Germans, Czechs, and Tejanos of the nineteenth and early twentieth centuries, discovering that the supposedly modern practice of bilingual education dates far into the Texas past due to the constant efforts by ethnic parents to find for their children a better education than their own. But aside from a few chapters in this work, there are very few other studies that rigorously analyze, compare, and attempt to interpret the larger immigrant experience in Texas during the nineteenth and twentieth centuries. The general acclaim and popularity of the 2009 exhibit, *Forgotten Gateway: Coming to America through Galveston Island,* at the Bob Bullock State History Museum (now traveling the country) testifies to a great interest in the broader Texas immigrant experience.⁶⁰

German immigrants came to Texas in the largest numbers and thus garner more of this small puddle of ink. Walter Struve's *Germans of Texas: Commerce, Migration, and Culture in the Days of the Lone Star Republic* (1996) discards the old stereotypes of penniless, destitute immigrants arriving to the New World with little in the way of skills or opportunities. True to the new immigration scholarship, Struve demonstrates that this German migration was undertaken not on a lark or by accident, but rather as the result of an expanding, international, capitalistic ethos that connected energetic, entrepreneurial migrants in emerging capitalist regions throughout Europe to the farthest reaches of the American frontier in Texas. Struve's focus on German American small businessmen also adds a unique and valuable perspective on the Texas Republic era.⁶¹

Most of the best recent work on European immigrants to Texas, however, is in article form. Walter Kamphoefner has contributed two essays that offer significant reconsiderations of historical interpretations of German Texans. One counters the revisionist interpretation of recent decades holding that German antislavery reputations are overinflated. Another explores the Klan menace toward German Americans during World War I and finds that such intimidation did not much impact their use of the German language or otherwise accelerate their glacial rate of acculturation. These essays exemplify the new immigrant history in showing that German Americans accommodated to their surroundings, yet always kept vital elements of their ethnic and immigrant identity alive, heedless of periodic waves of intolerance or inconvenience. German Americans were not powerless, voiceless victims; they had agency and used it.⁶²

Recent works on other ethnic groups have expanded our understanding of the European immigrant experience beyond Germans. Charles Russell's *Undaunted: A Norwegian Woman in Frontier Texas* (2006) is a marvelous exploration of the life of nineteenth-century, antislavery, and feminist immigrant Elise Waerenskjold. From her small Norwegian community in northeast Texas, Waerenskjold wrote letters to sell Texas as a final destination to her Scandinavian countrymen, which in turn confirms for immigration historians the degree to which prospective immigrants had knowledge about their ultimate destinations and made informed decisions. Other works on the Czech, French, and Irish experiences advance similar interpretations.[63] Works on Jewish Texans particularly stand out. For example, Harold Hyman's *Oleander Odyssey: The Kempners of Galveston, Texas, 1854–1980s* (1990) offers the compelling story of a Jewish immigrant who fled czarist oppression in the 1850s to build a Texas family fortune. Also, the works of Hollace Ava Weiner introduce the Jewish experience throughout the state.[64]

But what of more recent immigrants? Texas historians would be well served to take their cue from social scientists and some historians outside the state who have delved into immigrant groups of more recent vintage. The new wave of Latino, Asian, and African immigration to Texas cities and towns since the 1960s has changed the face of the state in a way that historians have yet to document. Such historical treatments would nudge the state's history ever closer to the global reality of the cosmopolitan Texas cities of today. What little work there is intriguingly points out that as of the 2000 census Texas led the South in immigrants from Asia; its numerical increase in immigrants in the 2000s is nearly twice as large as the next southern state, Florida. Dallas and Houston were among the top metropolitan destinations in the country for Asian and Latino immigrants in the 1990s and 2000s. Other essays on immigrant explosions in the Texas suburbs demonstrate the depth and richness of the topic for enterprising historians eager to update the narrative of Texas immigration and demographic history. In the field of immigration, with the older groups of the nineteenth and early twentieth century and with newer immigrant groups, Texas historians have their work cut out for them.[65]

A Diversity of Historical Imagination

This portion of the essay dwells on new aspects of historical imagination in Texas. By imagination I mean the way historians see history, how we structure our examinations of Texas. One of the most profound changes in history writing about Texas is that the state is no longer seen as merely a modern geographical entity. Recent scholarship tends to view Texas much more ambitiously: the way in which literature in the 1960s and 1970s opened up Texans to a new level of self-awareness; the idea of borderlands and how Texas fits several different kinds of borderlands constructions; in the cities of Texas and their role in state history; in the natural environment in its bounty, its destructiveness, and Texans' positive and negative adaptations to it; and in the way a sense of place influences Texan identity.

Interestingly, the state's literary figures, not its historians, were often the first to attempt to shake Texans out of thralldom to their own origin myths. By the late 1950s and early 1960s several young authors urged readers to think of the state as a cauldron of ideological turmoil, fantastic wealth and poverty coexisting all too happily, and sprawling cities of amoral, economic power. This was a modern Texas these writers depicted through their fiction and journalism. Larry L. King, Billy Lee Brammer, Larry McMurtry, Gary Cartwright, Edwin "Bud" Shrake, and other writers fired first upon mythic Texas, well before most historians. In his *Texas Literary Outlaws: Six Writers in the Sixties and Beyond* (2004), Steven Davis argues of this literary pack, "They helped Texans attain a new awareness of their state. Taken as a whole, their work establishes an authentic Texas vision, one far removed from the fanciful notions promulgated by outsiders and the state's dewy-eyed sentimentalists." Given the Texas media's infamous reputation for complacency, Davis rightly notes that with hot-button topics such as poverty, racism, and politics, twentieth-century fiction can be more useful to historians than newspapers of the time, echoing Hemingway's dictum that good fiction must always be truer than true.[66]

Texan literary figures from the late 1950s through the 1970s did not attack Texas myth only through their stories. Some went after Texas myth more directly. The most critically acclaimed and commercially successful of these authors, Larry McMurtry, had by the late 1960s trenchantly criticized some of the mythmakers of Texas history such as Webb and Dobie as intellectually sterile in his *In a Narrow Grave* (1968). Ironically, though, McMurtry's blockbuster *Lonesome Dove* series of books and television movies has probably done more to replicate and maintain those mythic images of the wild Texas frontier and vigilante justice (the "good" kind meted out by irascible Texas Rangers, no less) in the public consciousness than any modern reading of the old Texas myth itself. Scholar Don Graham, in *Giant Country: Essays on Texas* (1999), explores the meaning of the Lone Star State, its myths, and the way in which it sees itself. Other writers have devoted considerable energy in the collection of anthologies for Texas writers of all backgrounds, including Tejanos and women.[67]

The notion of borders and the borderlands, both in the literal sense of the

U.S.-Mexico border and in more abstract conceptualizations, are of late in considerable vogue in the history profession. Indeed, several institutions within the state that offer the Ph.D. in history list as a major point of emphasis comparative borders generally or the southwestern borderland in particular. The area of South Texas easily lends itself to intellectual projects inspired by notions of borders. Daniel Arreola explores this border region as a unique cultural homeland for the entire Mexican American community of the Southwest in *Tejano South Texas: A Mexican American Cultural Province* (2002). He argues that the Tejanos of this sprawling land mass the size of Pennsylvania represent a crucial native culture that has endured, constantly absorbing outside influences from Anglo and Mexican immigrants while tenaciously preserving its homegrown traditions.[68]

Other works on the South Texas borderlands stress the fluid, sometimes confusing loyalties and identities that swirl through both sides. Benjamin Johnson's *Revolution in Texas: How a Forgotten Rebellion and Its Bloody Suppression Turned Mexicans into Americans* (2003) excavates the transnational traffic of ideas on culture, nationality, race, and ideology. He analyzes the 1915 irredentist movement and resulting atrocities by Texas Rangers that provided the impetus for Tejanos to begin to explore new, more formal and deliberate ways to identify with the United States. *Building the Borderlands: A Transnational History of Irrigated Cotton along the Mexico-Texas Border* (2008), by Casey Walsh, is an outstanding example of an interdisciplinary historical analysis of the intellectual, economic, political, and demographic exchanges that flowed back and forth across the Rio Grande, connecting a wide array of experiences and people to one another through the common medium of growing cotton.[69]

The conception of East Texas as a colonial borderland arises from *Colonial Natchitoches: A Creole Community on the Louisiana-Texas Frontier* (2008), by H. Sophie Burton and F. Todd Smith. Although the village was technically on the French side, this study casts light on the entire borderland, including the Spanish residents of East Texas in Nacogdoches, the local Native American tribes that played one empire off against the other, and the steep level of racial, ethnic, and cultural blending. This open eighteenth-century borderland vitally contributed to transatlantic trade. Although an ever-present reality to be negotiated, the border artificially divides in most of these works. Thus, South and East Texas are not only a part of a larger U.S. conceptualization, but a part of a Latin American and Atlantic World historical framework as well. Such perspectives reflect larger trends in the profession in which historians seek to re-center what might earlier have been classified as regional studies, such as Texas or southern history, into more global contexts that better reflect our own times.

For example, southern labor historian Jacqueline Jones recently explored this very phenomenon of how a more sustained engagement with Latin American, Caribbean, Atlantic World, and Asian histories is now more imperative than ever to gain an accurate picture of her central field: "neither the southern economy nor the people whose labor fuels it can be studied in isolation from the rest of the world. Just as the Atlantic basin provides new perspectives on early southern labor history, so too the global economy offers new perspectives on southern labor over the last four decades or so. And again, the vulnerability of dark-skinned peoples to the authority of landed and monied interests sounds a recurring theme throughout history."[70]

Texas urban histories have multiplied in recent years. And given that Texas boasts three of the top ten largest cities in the nation (Texans are still quite impressed with size, after all), the focus on urban Texas is neither provincial nor novel, but national and, yes, even global in significance. Despite this daily reality, urban histories of Texas still feel compelled to make the case that their subject is important. Perhaps this is because the field of urban history is an obvious affront to the traditionalist obsession with the state's rural, Jeffersonian, early nineteenth-century roots. The romantic, sentimental influences of the Texas origin myth has had a far-reaching influence on the state's urban development according to Char Miller: "Planning in Texas? Perish the thought. One need but view how its men are portrayed in countless westerns—images of stalwart and quiet men who, to succeed, must be disengaged from the very community that they defend so heroically—to know that this is not a place that would cotton to communal restrictions on individual freedoms."[71]

Perhaps unsurprisingly given its less than bashful reputation, Dallas garners a disproportionate share of the ink. Numerous books on Dallas (and Fort Worth) have appeared since *Texas Through Time*. This sprawling urban space holds a special place in Texan identity. For example, the personal connections to Dallas and Fort Worth of prominent literary figures, especially after the Kennedy assassination, influenced them to write of Texas as a modern, urban, diverse place where stereotypes of cowboys and Indians were but mere fanciful memories of a distant past. Phillips's *White Metropolis* succeeds in presenting a very different kind of history of Dallas, emphasizing conflict over consensus. Elizabeth York Enstam's *Women and the Creation of Urban Life: Dallas, Texas, 1843–1920* (1998) sheds much light on women's roles in Dallas as activists for education and suffrage. And neither have civil rights in "Big D" been neglected.[72]

Urban history on Houston emphasizes the city's multicultural roots. Arnoldo De León's *Ethnicity in the Sunbelt: Mexican Americans in Houston*

(2001), Roberto Treviño's *The Church in the Barrio: Mexican American Ethno-Catholicism in Houston* (2006), and Howard Beeth and Cary Wintz's collection *Black Dixie: Afro-Texan History and Culture in Houston* (1992), plumb the demographic treasure that is Houston. De León and Treviño revise our understanding of what has in the past been conceptually regarded as a quintessentially southern city. They present a more ethnically complex Houston that goes far beyond a binary, black-white understanding of race. De León covers the socioeconomic position of Mexican Americans in Houston, the trends toward greater participation and inclusion, and the recent arrival of other Latinos from Central America, South America, and the Caribbean. Treviño documents how Houston's Mexican American Catholics were systematically ignored by church officials, as they were in most other parts of the country; he also shows how folk practices of the faith, heavily influenced by a mixture of pre-Reformation Catholicism and indigenous religiosity, flourished as a substitute for more formal church participation. Beeth and Wintz's collection deepens and revises our understanding of African American life in the Bayou City.[73]

Recent work on San Antonio connects that city's historical relationship with its natural environment. Char Miller's volume, *On the Border: An Environmental History of San Antonio* (2005), argues that despite its incredible natural resources and favorable geography, the governing elites of San Antonio consistently sought to build the city "on the cheap" and, thus, sorely mismanaged the city's growth in comparison to other Texas cities with less favorable natural advantages such as Houston and Dallas. This is a sophisticated interjection of environmental issues into the standard narratives of urban development from the Spanish colonial period to the present day. In another work on San Antonio, Miller notes the consequences of the city's miserly attitude toward an economic growth that is more widely distributed among the populace by mentioning that San Antonio consistently vies with the devastatingly hollowed-out city of Detroit in various measures of urban poverty.[74]

Smaller Texas cities offer productive lenses from which to engage mythic notions of the Lone Star past that also include Texans' responses to their environmental inheritance. Paul Carlson's *Amarillo: The Story of a Western Town* (2006) studies the dominant city of the Texas Panhandle from its founding as a part of the expanding agricultural frontier of the southern plains, but goes beyond the pioneer heritage of the region to explain its twentieth-century, urban development. Likewise, studies of Corpus Christi go beyond mythical, nineteenth-century emphases upon cattle ranches and colorful pioneers to modern narratives of urban development, planning, and infrastructure. Recent works, including Mary Jo O'Rear's *Storm over the Bay: The People of Corpus Christi and Their Port* (2009), conceptualize Corpus Christi as a twentieth-century, industrial city that, after a disastrous 1919 hurricane, capitalized on federal aid to rebuild its port in such a way as to spur its eventual growth into a major port of the Gulf Coast that, even before Katrina, had displaced the Port of New Orleans in the cargo volume it ships.[75]

But of the state's smaller cities, Galveston has for a variety of reasons inspired the most impressive scholarly effort. Of course, in the nineteenth century Galveston was one of the largest cities of the state. Its rebuilding effort after the calamitous 1900 storm that nearly wiped it off the face of the earth expectedly attracts a great deal of scholarly interest. For example, Turner's *Women, Culture, and Community* traces the laborious efforts of Galveston's women in the rebuilding. White and African American women, often through churches, participated mightily in the city's reconstruction as well as with the Progressive civic reforms of later years. Susan Wiley Hardwick's *Mythic Galveston: Reinventing America's Third Coast* (2002) locates Galveston as an essential component of the nation's "Creole Coast" stretching from Texas to Florida. This area, she provocatively argues, has more in common with the Caribbean and the broader Atlantic World than the rest of the U.S. South.[76]

One interesting new type of inquiry opened up by historians studying place and environment are natural and human-made disasters. Those histories of Texas coastal cities like Galveston and Corpus Christi, not so coincidentally, all deal with hurricanes. Galveston obviously lends itself to the role of storms in history. The popular, studiously researched *Isaac's Storm: A Man, a Time, and the Deadliest Hurricane in History* (1999) grippingly chronicles the tragic 1900 Galveston hurricane through the eyes of U.S. Weather Bureau employee Isaac Monroe Cline. The recent storms that have ravaged the Texas coast, particularly hurricanes Rita in 2005 and Ike of 2008, as well as Louisiana's infamous Katrina of 2005 that deposited a large number of temporary and permanent refugees in the state, remain strongly imprinted upon the public consciousness and make Galveston's past destruction and reconstruction anxiously topical.[77]

But human-inspired disasters have also stirred historians' interests. Hugh Stephens's *The Texas City Disaster, 1947* (1997) terrifyingly documents one of the worst industrial accidents in U.S. history: the explosion of the Texas City docks from a ship laden with ammunition and ammonium nitrate. This accident killed over five hundred and injured several thousand. It stands as a stark reminder of the costs that can accompany careless industrial growth and development. Houston's infamous national reputation for poor air quality, a major theme in the 2000 presidential election, has also caught historians' attention. Martin Melosi and Joseph Pratt's *Energy Metropolis: An Environmental History of Houston and the Gulf Coast* (2007) offers a wealth of fresh ideas on human-environmental interactions in the Houston area including industrial pollution, the impact of air-conditioning technology, roads and highways, deforestation, environmental racism, and environmental activism. Environmental racism in Texas is a central topic of Robert Bullard's *Dumping in Dixie: Race, Class, and Environmental Quality* (1990) as well as a recent article on lead contamination in El Paso by Monica Perales.[78]

Of course, there is more to the environmental history of Texas than hurricanes, industrial accidents, and pollution. John Adams's *Damming the Colorado: The Rise of the Lower Colorado River Authority, 1933–1939* (1990) analyzes Central Texas' history of devastating floods, particularly in Austin, that spurred creation of the Lower Colorado River Authority. Widely regarded as "Texas' Little TVA," this agency owed much to the New Deal as well as to politicos Alvin Wirtz and Lyndon B. Johnson. The damming of the Colorado River not only stabilized Central Texas for rapid urban development, but it also created jobs and spread electricity throughout the area. Recent work on the development of Williamson County from a leading agricultural area to an extension of the Austin metropolis also credits federal dam- and road-building projects of the New Deal and liberal politicians of Texas, making predictably ironic the county's subsequent transformation into a reliably Republican and ideologically conservative area.[79]

When asked to visualize Texas, many might picture plains, deserts, brush country, and beaches before they think of forests. But Richard Francaviglia's *The Cast Iron Forest: A Natural and Cultural History of the North American Cross Timbers* (2000) examines the wide expanse of the Cross Timbers forests existing only in the plains of North Texas, Central Oklahoma, and South Kansas. This is not the southern Great Plains of Walter Prescott Webb's vision. These tightly packed, hardy oaks offered sustenance to Native Americans and early pioneers. Yet, they often frightened farmers who preferred open prairies as well as eastern migrants used to bigger, lusher, more penetrable forests. Francaviglia warns about the deterioration of this unique natural habitat. He somberly concludes that the Cross Timbers forests, under constant pressure from urban growth and agriculture, represent a little understood or appreciated natural ecosystem.[80]

The increased attention to disease and health care as a topic of analysis involves people, places, cities, and the environment. The Lone Star State has been justifiably proud of its hospitals, its veterinary professionals, and its health care providers throughout its history, and that pride is reflected in recent scholarship. James S. Olson's *Making Cancer History: Disease and Discovery at the University of Texas M.D. Anderson Cancer Center* (2009) introduces one globally recognized

Texas institution in the fight against a most dreaded disease. The social history of polio, its treatment, its survivors, and the widespread societal panic it engendered in practically every corner of the state, is the subject of Heather Green Wooten's *The Polio Years in Texas: Battling a Terrifying Unknown* (2009). It reminds modern Texans that before AIDS and other more recent public health scares, the specter of polio struck a daily fear into the people of this state that cannot be forgotten or minimized.[81]

The notion of regionalism within Texas is, seemingly, as important to Texas identity as is ethnicity. Texas boasts a state historical society that publishes a journal, the Texas State Historical Association's *Southwestern Historical Quarterly*. However, unlike many other states, Texas also possesses intrastate, regional historical societies that publish their own academic journals. The South Texas Historical Association's *Journal of South Texas,* the East Texas Historical Association's *East Texas Historical Journal,* the West Texas Historical Association's *West Texas Historical Association Yearbook,* and a host of other publications over the years have valuably contributed distinctively regional approaches to Texas history. Texas lends itself to intrastate studies as often as statewide studies. And these studies of place within Texas also connect it with much wider national and international conceptualizations involving the U.S. South, West, and Great Plains, as well as Latin America and the Atlantic World. This development addresses a criticism from the first *Texas Through Time* that "often deservedly, historians from outside the state minimize the work done on Texas, because it fails both to draw comparisons between Texas and other similar places and to set Texas in a larger national focus." Studies in Texas history that focus on place utilize different analytical perspectives; they engage historical debates far beyond the space between the rivers Sabine and Red and Rio Grande.[82]

New studies and approaches do not mean that older imaginings of place are forgotten. Historians still engage the southern Great Plains written of by Walter Prescott Webb, particularly his notions about human settlement patterns and aridity. But the endless American fascination with the "West" still occupies a good deal of myth-busting attention from historians. Ty Cashion's *A Texas Frontier: The Clear Fork Country and Fort Griffin, 1849–1887* (1996) challenges the wild-west myths of nineteenth-century West Texas. Cashion doggedly argues that the Clear Fork region was not as luridly violent as subsequent writers' fantasies. Also, the region was decidedly southern in outlook prior to the Civil War; only in the postwar era did its residents begin politically and economically defining themselves in more westerly directions. John Jameson's *The Story of Big Bend National Park* (1996) illuminates the creation of and controversies with the state's most spectacular natural treasure. Not one to let the park's connection to other touchstones of Texas myth go by without mention, Jameson also documents the explorations of the park by Walter Prescott Webb in the 1930s and Lady Bird Johnson during her first lady years in the 1960s.[83]

In one of the finer works recently published on any region of Texas, John Miller Morris's *El Llano Estacado: Exploration and Imagination on the High Plains of Texas and New Mexico, 1536–1860* (1997) poignantly traces the human exploration and habitation of the great staked plains. Morris unpacks the semiotic meaning of the narratives European explorers imposed on El Llano through an examination of their understanding of science and art, their ideological backgrounds, and the ways in which their personal stories of exploration fit other narrative structures of the time. Morris successfully deconstructs the idea of exploration narratives by explaining how such journeys were not simply physical exertions but exercises in the imagination as well: "How we perceive the Llano Estacado environment is not only historical but also geographical, literary, and artistic, requiring interdisciplinary exploration of texts, translations, maps, and iconography. . . . To this end *El Llano Estacado* illustrates the role of mind and culture in the invention of the Southwest."[84]

Scholarly conceptions of East Texas engage the age-old debate as to what degree Texas is southern or western. Contrary to myths that prioritized Texas' frontier, western experience, Walter Buenger's *The Path to a Modern South: Northeast Texas between Reconstruction and the Great Depression* (2001) adeptly explores how this rural, East Texas region, the most "southern" area of the state, prepared itself in the early twentieth century for the economic modernization that many reflexively attribute to the New Deal. He demonstrates how East Texans had by the 1930s replaced their leftover cultural reverence of the Confederate, slaveholding past for a romanticized historical tradition emphasizing the western, frontier experience: "Northeast Texans abandoned the limited possibilities implicit in the Lost Cause and adopted the mantle of progress of the Texas Revolution." *The Path to a Modern South* persuasively demonstrates how historical interpretations and identities are connected to a wider ideological, economic, and political matrix. Buenger extends this thesis elsewhere to provocatively suggest that North, West, and South Texas are, by many measures, profoundly southern.[85]

In conclusion, the state's history in the last twenty years has moved away from uncritical notions of Texan identity to a more sophisticated, nuanced understanding of how that identity has been constructed, with what, and what has been left out. Historians are recapturing the reality of Texas' early diversity, something that was erased during the late nineteenth and early twentieth centuries when mythmaking scholars imposed a culturally homogenous, heroic, sacred past. For an ambitious society that was simultaneously embracing a new level of intolerance toward immigrants and racial and ethnic minorities in expanding Jim Crow to its fullest form, looking backward toward a handful of easily digestible mythic tales was preferable to a critical examination of the otherwise awkward facts. State apologists who were a part of such societal racism and nativism were little interested in writing into the historical narrative Texas' polyglot past.

Since the advent of more modern, egalitarian notions of gender, race, ethnicity, and class as well as the continued professional training of a legion of new historians searching for inclusivity, complexity, and a more critical perspective since the 1960s, the old myths that once defined Texas history, indeed the history of this nation, are slowly and surely crumbling. Such notions in academia now hardly exist, and their reproduction is mostly as popularly written history that, with the passage of additional time, will appear to ever more modern readers as dull and intellectually arid as they do now to trained historians. And if all this sounds hubristic or somehow lacking in humility, I am positive that by then Texas historians will have moved on to entirely new myths and errors that we are all unwittingly (or unapologetically) replicating in this very volume. Writing history is humbling, and I, of course, anxiously wonder at the ways in which these words will be criticized days, years, decades from now. Yet in the spirit of the original *Texas Through Time*, we historians must not flinch at our responsibility to interpret the past, whatever our fears at sometimes being wrong.

Yet this essay, perhaps jarringly to some scholars, remains stubbornly positive. As Buenger noticed in this volume, some myths do continue to exert a troubling influence that persists despite historians' scowls. However, the trend toward recognizing and analyzing the state's rich diversity of people, places, and ideas is real and, in my estimation, continuing to gain speed. The works cited here represent but a mere sample of a larger flood of published works that are changing the way we understand and teach Texas history. As Richard McCaslin's timely *At the Heart of Texas* reminds us, even the institutional bedrock of Texas history, the Texas State Historical Association and its *Southwestern Historical Quarterly*, were in 2008 uprooted from their century-old home at the University of Texas. So change in Texas history is at hand in a very literal, physical manner as well as in a broader intellectual sense.[86] The deconstruction of traditional Texas history has led to new historical imaginations. One hopes that this larger effort will counter Steinbeck's observations of the state's private history that is not limited by fact with a more public, accessible history based above all on fact and intelligent analysis. As documented by *Texas Through Time* some twenty years ago, I think it already has and will continue to do so.

Notes

1. John Steinbeck, *Travels with Charley: In Search of America* (New York: Curtis Publishing, 1961; New York: Penguin Books, 2002), 173 (first quotation), 174 (second quotation).

2. An obvious, some might say glaring, example of these offensive attitudes and their intended replication to mass audiences, especially children, is represented in the old *Texas History Movies* originally published in the 1920s and continually reissued for decades. Historian and cartoonist, Jack Jackson, recently updated the project with an eye toward eliminating insensitivities from an earlier age. See Jack Jackson, *The New Texas History Movies* (Austin: Texas State Historical Association Press, 2007).

3. Laura Lyons McLemore, *Inventing Texas: Early Historians of the Lone Star State* (College Station: Texas A&M University Press, 2004), 94–95; Walter L. Buenger and Robert A. Calvert, "Introduction: The Shelf Life of Truth in Texas," in *Texas Through Time: Evolving Interpretations,* ed. Walter L. Buenger and Robert A. Calvert (College Station: Texas A&M University Press, 1991), xiv–xxiii. For more on these early historians, see Richard B. McCaslin, *At the Heart of Texas: One Hundred Years of the State Historical Association, 1896–1996* (Austin: Texas State Historical Association, 2007). Also consult the *Handbook of Texas Online* at http://www.tshaonline.org/handbook/online/.

4. Buenger and Calvert, "Introduction: The Shelf Life of Truth in Texas," xiv. My essay focuses on a selected pool of published books except for instances where articles and chapters better illustrate an important development. A discussion of Native Americans will mostly be left for Pekka Hämäläinen's essay in this volume.

5. For a good introduction of the impact of new theoretical perspectives in the historical profession these last few decades, see Elizabeth A. Clark, *History, Theory, Text: Historians and the Linguistic Turn* (Cambridge, Mass.: Harvard University Press, 2004).

6. Larry L. King, *Of Outlaws, Con Men, Whores, Politicians, and Other Artists* (New York: Viking Press, 1980), 60; Karen L. Cox, "The South and Mass Culture," *Journal of Southern History* 75, August (2009): 680–81. The essays of this seventy-fifth commemorative issue of the *Journal of Southern History* seek to examine new ways of studying southern history and to explain recent advancements in the field, much as the contributors of this edited volume aspire. Not coincidentally, several works from this edition of the *Journal of Southern History* appear in this essay.

7. Laura F. Edwards, "Southern History as U.S. History," *Journal of Southern History* 75, August (2009): 544.

8. Ronald L. Davis, "Modernization and Distinctiveness: Twentieth-Century Cultural Life in Texas," in *Texas Through Time,* ed. Buenger and Calvert, 4 (first quotation); Randolph B. Campbell, "History and Collective Memory in Texas: The Entangled Stories of the Lone Star State," in *Lone Star Pasts: Memory and History in Texas,* ed. Gregg Cantrell and Elizabeth Hayes Turner (College Station: Texas A&M University Press, 2007), 280 (second quotation).

9. See Buenger's "Three Truths in Texas," in this volume. For the purposes of this essay Buenger's "persistent revisionist" and "cultural constructionist" camps will not be pursued further. I find them of less use here. Most of the works in this essay stand out in their opposition to traditionalist interpretations, whether direct or implied. They only differ in whether they fall into older, antitraditionalist fields and interpretations that were already noted in *Texas Through Time,* or if they offer entirely new ways of interpreting the past that have since arisen. I strongly suspect that what Buenger calls cultural constructionists are not so far removed from revisionists as to warrant a separate category. I wonder if this third group is really not just an "updated" form of revisionist history? I feel we are all postrevisionists now in our attempts to both decry pernicious myth and to go beyond it. It is perhaps no coincidence that this volume's title begins with *Beyond*. However one sees this issue, much more debate is needed on Buenger's stimulating thesis, to be sure.

10. Paul D. Lack, "In the Long Shadow of Eugene C. Barker: The Revolution and the Republic," in *Texas Through Time,* ed. Buenger and Calvert, 135 (quotation) and 136.

11. McLemore, *Inventing Texas,* 99–100. See also McLemore, "Early Historians and the Shaping of Texas Memory," in *Lone Star Pasts,* ed. Cantrell and Turner, 15–38.

12. Gregg Cantrell, "The Bones of Stephen F. Austin: History and Memory in Progressive-Era Texas," *Southwestern Historical Quarterly* 108, (October 2004): 144–78.

13. Cantrell and Turner, *Lone Star Pasts,* xiii. This volume contains several contributors whose works on historical consciousness dot this essay.

14. Adina de Zavala, *History and Legends of the Alamo and Other Missions in and around San Antonio,* ed. Richard Flores (San Antonio, 1917; Houston: Arte Público Press, 1996); Leticia Magda Garza-Falcón, *Gente Decente: A Borderlands Response to the Rhetoric of Dominance* (Austin: University of Texas Press, 1998); John Morán González, *Border Renaissance: The Texas Centennial and the Emergence of Mexican American Literature* (Austin: University of Texas Press, 2009).

15. Félix D. Almaráz, *Knight without Armor: Carlos Eduardo Castañeda, 1896–1958* (College Station: Texas A&M University Press, 1999); Angus Lauchlan, "The Texas Liberal Press and the Image of White Texas Masculinity, 1938–1963," *Southwestern Historical Quarterly* 110, (April 2007): 486–512. See also McCaslin, *At the Heart of Texas.*

16. Buenger and Calvert, "Introduction: The Shelf Life of Truth in Texas," in *Texas Through Time,* ed. Buenger and Calvert, xii.

17. Richard R. Flores, *Remembering the Alamo: Memory, Modernity, and the Master Symbol* (Austin: University of Texas Press, 2002), 33; James E. Crisp, *Sleuthing the Alamo: Davy Crockett's Last Stand and Other Mysteries of the Texas Revolution* (New York: Oxford University Press, 2005); Holly Beachley Brear, *Inherit the Alamo: Myth and Ritual at an American Shrine* (Austin: University of Texas Press, 1995).

18. For an "updated traditionalist" book on the Alamo, see Bill Groneman, *Defense of a Legend: Crockett and the de la Peña Diary* (Plano: Republic of Texas Press, 1994).

19. Paul D. Lack, *The Texas Revolutionary Experience: A Political and Social History, 1835–1836* (College Station: Texas A&M University Press, 1992), 266.

20. D. W. Meinig, *Imperial Texas: An Interpretive Essay in Cultural Geography* (Austin: University of Texas Press, 1969).

21. Buenger and Calvert, "Introduction: The Shelf Life of Truth in Texas," *Texas Through Time,* ed. Buenger and Calvert, xiv–xv.

22. Steve H. Murdock, Steve White, Md. Nazrul Hoque, Beverly Pecotte, Xuihong You, and Jennifer Balkan, *The New Texas Challenge: Population Change and the Future of Texas* (College Station: Texas A&M University Press, 2003). This is an updated version of the original book based on 1990 census data.

23. L. L. Foster, Introduction by Barbara J. Rozek, *Forgotten Texas Census: First Annual Report of the Agricultural Bureau of the Department of Agriculture, Insurance, Statistics, and History, 1887–88* (Austin: Texas State Historical Association, 2001); Barbara J. Rozek, *Come to Texas: Attracting Immigrants, 1865–1915* (College Station: Texas A&M University Press, 2003). For examples of Jordan's earlier work on such topics, see Terry G. Jordan, "A Century and a Half of Ethnic Change in Texas, 1836–1986," *Southwestern Historical Quarterly* 89 (April 1986): 385–422; Jordan, *German Seed in Texas Soil: Immigrant Farmers in Nineteenth-Century Texas* (Austin: University of Texas Press, 1975).

24. F. Todd Smith, *From Dominance to Disappearance: The Indians of Texas and the Near Southwest, 1786–1859* (Lincoln: University of Nebraska Press, 2005), xi. For the book in question, see also Rupert Norval Richardson, *The Comanche Barrier to South Plains Settlement: A Century and a Half of Savage Resistance to the Advancing White Frontier* (Glendale, CA: Arthur H. Clarke, 1933).

25. For a sample of these works, see F. Todd Smith, *From Dominance to Disappearance;* Smith, *The Wichita Indians: Traders of Texas and the Southern Plains, 1540–1845* (College Station: Texas A&M University Press, 2000); David La Vere, *The Texas Indians* (College Station: Texas A&M University Press, 2004), La Vere, *The Caddo Chieftains: Caddo Economics and Politics, 700–1835* (Lincoln: University of Nebraska Press, 1998); Pekka Hämäläinen, *The Comanche Empire* (New Haven, Conn.: Yale University Press, 2008); Juliana Barr, *Peace Came in the Form of a Woman: Indians and Spaniards in the Texas Borderlands* (Chapel Hill: University of North Carolina Press, 2007); Gary Clayton Anderson, *The Indian Southwest: Ethnogenesis and Reinvention, 1580–1830* (Norman: University of Oklahoma Press, 1998); Anderson, *The Conquest of Texas: Ethnic Cleansing in the Promised Land, 1820–1875* (Norman: University of Oklahoma Press, 2005).

26. Arnoldo De León, *The Tejano Community, 1836–1900* (Albuquerque: University of New Mexico Press, 1982; Dallas: Southern Methodist University Press, 1997); De León, *They Called Them Greasers: Anglo Attitudes toward Mexicans in Texas, 1821–1900* (Austin: University of Texas Press, 1983); David Montejano, *Anglos and Mexicans in the Making of Texas, 1836–1981* (Austin: University of Texas Press, 1987).

27. Arnoldo De León, "Whither Tejano History: Origins, Development, and Status," *Southwestern Historical Quarterly* 106, (January 2003): 350–51. For an example

of the growing importance of Tejanos to institutional Texas history, papers from the 1991 Texas State Historical Association conference "Mexican Americans in Texas History" were published as a groundbreaking collection. See Emilio Zamora, Cynthia Orozco, and Rodolfo Rocha, eds., *Mexican Americans in Texas History: Selected Essays* (Austin: Texas State Historical Association Press, 2000).

28. David J. Weber, *The Spanish Frontier in North America* (New Haven, Conn.: Yale University Press, 1992); Donald E. Chipman, *Spanish Texas, 1519-1821* (Austin: University of Texas Press, 1992). See also David J. Weber, *Bárbaros: Spaniards and Their Savages in the Age of Enlightenment* (New Haven, Conn.: Yale University Press, 2005). For the most recent book on Cabeza de Vaca, see Andrés Reséndez, *A Land So Strange: The Epic Journey of Cabeza de Vaca* (New York: Basic Books, 2007).

29. Jesús F. de la Teja, *San Antonio de Béxar: A Community on New Spain's Northern Frontier* (Albuquerque: University of New Mexico Press, 1995). See also de la Teja, "Why Urbano and María Trinidad Can't Get Married: Social Relations in Late Colonial San Antonio," *Southwestern Historical Quarterly* 112, (October 2008): 120–46.

30. Andrés Reséndez, *Changing National Identities at the Frontier: Texas and New Mexico, 1800-1850* (New York: Cambridge University Press, 2005). See also Raúl A. Ramos, *Beyond the Alamo: Forging Mexican Ethnicity in San Antonio, 1821-1861* (Chapel Hill: University of North Carolina Press, 2008); Andrés Tijerina, *Tejanos and Texas under the Mexican Flag, 1821-1836* (College Station: Texas A&M University Press, 1994); Ana Carolina Castillo Crimm, *De León: A Tejano Family History* (Austin: University of Texas Press, 2003); Timothy M. Matovina, ed., *The Alamo Remembered: Tejano Accounts and Perspectives* (Austin: University of Texas Press, 1995).

31. Kenneth L. Stewart and Arnoldo De León, *Not Room Enough: Mexicans, Anglos, and Socioeconomic Change in Texas, 1850-1900* (Albuquerque: University of New Mexico Press, 1993); Armando C. Alonzo, *Tejano Legacy: Rancheros and Settlers in South Texas, 1734-1900* (Albuquerque: University of New Mexico Press, 1998).

32. Emilio Zamora, *The World of the Mexican Worker in Texas* (College Station: Texas A&M University Press, 1993); José A. Ramírez, *To the Line of Fire! Mexican Texans and World War I* (College Station: Texas A&M University Press, 2009).

33. Anthony Quiroz, *Claiming Citizenship: Mexican Americans in Victoria, Texas* (College Station: Texas A&M University Press, 2005). See also Ignacio García, *Viva Kennedy: Mexican Americans in Search of Camelot* (College Station: Texas A&M University Press, 2000); Ignacio García, *Hector P. García: In Relentless Pursuit of Justice* (Houston: Arte Público Press, 2002); Julie Leininger Pycior, *LBJ and Mexican Americans: The Paradox of Power* (Austin: University of Texas Press, 1997); Thomas H. Kreneck, *Mexican American Odyssey: Felix Tijerina, Entrepreneur and Civic Leader, 1905-1965* (College Station: Texas A&M University Press, 2001); Richard A. Garcia, *Rise of the Mexican American Middle Class: San Antonio, 1929-1941* (College Station: Texas A&M University Press, 1991); Zaragosa Vargas, "Tejana Radical: Emma Tenayuca and the San Antonio Labor Movement during the Great Depression," *Pacific Historical Review* 66, (November 1997): 553–80.

34. Cynthia Orozco, *No Mexicans, Women, or Dogs Allowed: The Rise of the Mexican American Civil Rights Movement* (Austin: University of Texas Press, 2009); Emilio Zamora, *Claiming Rights and Righting Wrongs: Mexican Workers and Job Politics during World War II* (College Station: Texas A&M University Press, 2009); Ignacio M. García, *White, But Not Equal: Mexican Americans, Jury Discrimination, and the Supreme Court* (Tucson: University of Arizona Press, 2009); Carlos Kevin Blanton, "The Citizenship Sacrifice: Mexican Americans, the Saunders-Leonard Report, and the Politics of Immigration, 1951–1952," *Western Historical Quarterly* 40, (Autumn 2009): 299–320.

35. Guadalupe San Miguel Jr., *Brown, Not White: School Integration and the Chicano Movement in Houston* (College Station: Texas A&M University Press, 2001). See also Ignacio García, *Chicanismo: The Forging of a Militant Ethos among Mexican Americans* (Tucson: University of Arizona Press, 1997); Armando Navarro, *Mexican American Youth Organization: Avant-Garde of the Chicano Movement in Texas* (Austin: University of Texas Press, 1995).

36. Carlos Kevin Blanton, *The Strange Career of Bilingual Education in Texas, 1836–1981* (College Station: Texas A&M University Press, 2004); Jorge Iber and Samuel O. Regalado, eds., *Mexican Americans and Sports: A Reader on Athletics and Barrio Life* (College Station: Texas A&M University Press, 2007).

37. Andrés Tijerina, "Constructing Tejano Memory," in *Lone Star Pasts*, ed. Cantrell and Turner, 176–202; De León, "Whither Tejano History," in *Texas Through Time*, ed. Buenger and Calvert, 363 (quotation).

38. Neil Foley, *The White Scourge: Mexicans, Blacks, and Poor Whites in Texas Cotton Culture* (Berkeley: University of California Press, 1997); Michael Phillips, *White Metropolis: Race, Ethnicity, and Religion in Dallas, 1841–2001* (Austin: University of Texas Press, 2006). For foundational texts in this emerging field, see David R. Roediger, *The Wages of Whiteness: Race and the Making of the American Working Class* (New York: Verso, 1991); Roediger, *Towards the Abolition of Whiteness: Essays on Race, Politics, and Working Class History* (New York: Verso, 1994).

39. Neil Foley, "Becoming Hispanic: Mexican Americans and the Faustian Pact with Whiteness" in Foley, ed., *Reflexiones 1997: New Directions in Mexican American Studies* (Austin: University of Texas Press, 1998), 53 (first quotation); Phillips, *White Metropolis,* 133 (second quotation). For a refutation of such interpretations, see Carlos Kevin Blanton, "George I. Sánchez, Ideology, and Whiteness in the Making of the Mexican American Civil Rights Movement, 1930–1960," *Journal of Southern History* 72, (August 2006): 569–604; Zamora, *Claiming Rights and Righting Wrongs in Texas,* 9–11, 247–48, nn. 24–26. For recent national critiques that raise similar questions, see Barbara J. Fields, "Whiteness, Racism, and Identity," *International Labor and Working-Class History* 60, no. 2 (2001): 48–56; Peter Kolchin, "Whiteness Studies: The New History of Race in America," *Journal of American History* 89, (June 2002): 154–73; Ronald H. Bayor, "Another Look at 'Whiteness': The Persistence of Ethnicity in American Life," *Journal of American Ethnic History* 29, (Fall 2009): 13–30.

40. William D. Carrigan, *The Making of a Lynching Culture: Violence and Vigilantism in Central Texas, 1836–1918* (Urbana: University of Illinois Press, 2006). See also Patricia Bernstein, *The First Waco Horror: The Lynching of Jesse Washington and the Rise of the NAACP* (College Station: Texas A&M University Press, 2005); Cynthia Nevels Skove, *Lynching to Belong: Claiming Whiteness through Racial Violence* (College Station: Texas A&M University Press, 2007). For the role of memory and notions of race and gender in the rise of the Ku Klux Klan in Texas shortly after World War I, see Walter L. Buenger, "Memory and the 1920s Ku Klux Klan in Texas," in *Lone Star Pasts*, ed. Cantrell and Turner, 119–42.

41. Gregg Cantrell, *Stephen F. Austin: Empresario of Texas* (New Haven, Conn.: Yale University Press, 1999); Jack Jackson, *Indian Agent: Peter Ellis Bean in Mexican Texas* (College Station: Texas A&M University Press, 2005).

42. Fane Downs, "Texas Women: History at the Edges," in *Texas Through Time*, ed. Buenger and Calvert, 100.

43. Angela Boswell, *Her Act and Her Deed: Women's Lives in a Rural Southern County, 1837–1873* (College Station: Texas A&M University Press, 2001); Rebecca Sharpless, *Fertile Ground, Narrow Choices: Women on Texas Cotton Farms, 1900–1940* (Chapel Hill: University of North Carolina Press, 1999).

44. Adrienne Caughfield, *True Women and Westward Expansion* (College Station: Texas A&M University Press, 2005); Jean A. Stuntz, *Hers, His, and Theirs: Community Property Law in Spain and Early Texas* (Lubbock: Texas Tech University Press, 2005); Marion K. Barthelme, ed., *Women in the Texas Populist Movement: Letters to the Southern Mercury* (College Station: Texas A&M University Press, 1997).

45. Sarah Ragland Jackson, *Texas Woman of Letters, Karle Wilson Baker* (College Station: Texas A&M University Press, 2005); Shelley Sallee, "'The Woman of It': Governor Miriam Ferguson's 1924 Election," *Southwestern Historical Quarterly* 100, (July 1996), 1–16; Debbie Mauldin Cottrell, *Pioneer Woman Educators: The Progressive Spirit of Annie Webb Blanton* (College Station: Texas A&M University Press, 1993); Judith N. McArthur and Harold L. Smith, *Minnie Fisher Cunningham: A Suffragist's Life in Politics* (New York: Oxford University Press, 2003); Jacquelyn Masur McElhaney, *Pauline Periwinkle and Progressive Reform in Dallas* (College Station: Texas A&M University Press, 1998); Elizabeth York Enstam, "The Dallas Equal Suffrage Association, Political Style, and Popular Culture: Grassroots Strategies of the Woman Suffrage Movement, 1913–1919," *Journal of Southern History* 68, (November 2002): 817–48. For a notable biography that reaches much later into the twentieth century, see Darwin Payne, *Indomitable Sarah: The Life of Judge Sarah T. Hughes* (Dallas: Southern Methodist University Press, 2004).

46. Judith N. McArthur, *Creating the New Woman: The Rise of Southern Women's Progressive Culture in Texas, 1893–1918* (Urbana: University of Illinois Press, 1998); Elizabeth Hayes Turner, *Women, Culture, and Community: Religion and Reform in Galveston, 1880–1920* (New York: Oxford University Press, 1997).

47. Teresa Palomo Acosta and Ruthe Winegarten, *Las Tejanas: 300 Years of His-*

tory (Austin: University of Texas Press, 2003); Dale Baum, *Counterfeit Justice: The Judicial Odyssey of Texas Freedwoman Azeline Hearne* (Baton Rouge: Louisiana State University Press, 2009); Garza-Falcón, *Gente Decente*. See also Vicki Howard, "The Courtship Letters of an African American Couple: Race, Gender, Class, and the Cult of True Womanhood," *Southwestern Historical Quarterly* 100, no. 1 (1996): 65–80.

48. Barr, *Peace Came in the Form of a Woman*.

49. Ibid.; Boswell, *Her Word and Her Deed*; Mark M. Carroll, *Homesteads Ungovernable: Families, Sex, Race, and the Law in Frontier Texas, 1823–1860* (Austin: University of Texas Press, 2001); Lauchlan, "The Texas Liberal Press," 486–512.

50. John Howard, "Southern Sodomy; or, What the Coppers Saw," in *Southern Masculinity: Perspectives on Manhood in the South Since Reconstruction*, ed. Craig Thompson Friend (Athens: University of Georgia Press, 2009), 196–218.

51. Randolph B. Campbell, *An Empire for Slavery: The Peculiar Institution in Texas, 1821–1865* (Baton Rouge: Louisiana State University Press, 1989); Alwyn Barr, "African Americans in Texas: From Stereotypes to Diverse Roles," in *Texas Through Time*, ed. Buenger and Calvert, 50. See also Kevin Mulroy, *Freedom on the Border: The Seminole Maroons in Florida, the Indian Territory, Coahuila, and Texas* (Lubbock: Texas Tech University Press, 1993).

52. Gregg Cantrell, *Kenneth and John B. Rayner and the Limits of Southern Dissent* (Urbana: University of Illinois Press, 1993); Cantrell, *Feeding the Wolf: John B. Rayner and the Politics of Race, 1850–1918* (Wheeling, Ill.: Harlan Davidson, 2001); Barry A. Crouch, *The Freedmen's Bureau and Black Texans* (Austin: University of Texas Press, 1992); Randolph B. Campbell, *Grass-Roots Reconstruction in Texas, 1865–1880* (Baton Rouge: Louisiana State University Press, 1998); Dale Baum, *The Shattering of Texas Unionism: Politics in the Lone Star State during the Civil War Era* (Baton Rouge: Louisiana State University Press, 1998); Elizabeth Hayes Turner, "Juneteenth: Emancipation and Memory," in *Lone Star Pasts*, ed. Cantrell and Turner, 143–73.

53. Debra A. Reid, *Reaping a Greater Harvest: African Americans, the Extension Service, and Rural Reform in Jim Crow Texas* (College Station: Texas A&M University Press, 2007), xxiv (quotations); Thad Sitton and James H. Conrad, *Freedom Colonies: Independent Black Texans in the Time of Jim Crow* (Austin: University of Texas Press, 2005); Charles F. Robinson II, "Legislated Love in the Lone Star State: Texas and Miscegenation," *Southwestern Historical Quarterly* 108, (July 2004): 65–86. For the military experience of African Americans in Texas, see also James N. Leiker, *Racial Borders: Black Soldiers along the Rio Grande* (College Station: Texas A&M University Press, 2002); Garna L. Christian, *Black Soldiers in Jim Crow Texas, 1899–1917* (College Station: Texas A&M University Press, 1995).

54. Ernest Obadele-Starks, *Black Unionism in the Industrial South* (College Station: Texas A&M University Press, 2000); Obadele-Starks, "Black Labor, the Black Middle Class, and Organized Protest along the Upper Gulf Coast, 1883–1945," *Southwestern Historical Quarterly* 103, (July 1999): 52–65; Michael R. Botson Jr., *Labor, Civil Rights, and the Hughes Tool Company* (College Station: Texas A&M University Press, 2005).

55. Robert S. Shelton, "'Which Ox Is in the Mire': Race and Class in the Galveston Longshoreman's Strike of 1898," *Southwestern Historical Quarterly* 110, (October 2006): 218–39; Joseph Abel, "Opening the Closed Shop: The Galveston Longshoremen's Strike of 1920–1921," *Southwestern Historical Quarterly* 110, (January 2007): 316–47; Gregg Andrews, "Black Working-Class Political Activism and Biracial Unionism: Galveston Longshoremen in Jim Crow Texas, 1919–1921," *Journal of Southern History* 74, (August 2008): 627–68.

56. Steven Harmon Wilson, *The Rise of Judicial Management in the U.S. District Court, Southern District of Texas, 1955–2000* (Athens: University of Georgia Press, 2003); Melissa Kean, *Desegregating Private Higher Education in the South: Duke, Emory, Rice, Tulane, and Vanderbilt* (Baton Rouge: Louisiana State University Press, 2008); Charles L. Zelden, *The Battle for the Black Ballot: Smith v. Allwright and the Defeat of the Texas All-White Primary* (Lawrence: University Press of Kansas, 2004); William Henry Kellar, *Make Haste Slowly: Moderates, Conservatives, and School Desegregation in Houston* (College Station: Texas A&M University Press, 1999); Robyn Duff Ladino, *Desegregating Texas Schools: Eisenhower, Shivers, and the Crisis at Mansfield High* (Austin: University of Texas Press, 1996); Dwight Watson, *Race and the Houston Police Department, 1930–1990: A Change Did Come* (College Station: Texas A&M University Press, 2005); Robert J. Robertson, *Fair Ways: How Six Black Golfers Won Civil Rights in Beaumont, Texas* (College Station: Texas A&M University Press, 2005).

57. Steven Harmon Wilson, "Brown over 'Other White': Mexican Americans' Legal Arguments and Litigation Strategy in School Segregation Lawsuits," *Law and History Review* 21 (Spring 2003): 145–94; Blanton, "George I. Sánchez," 569–604; Debra A. Reid, ed., *Seeking Inalienable Rights: Texans and Their Quests for Justice* (College Station: Texas A&M University Press, 2009). This collection, composed of several former students, is warmly dedicated to the memory of Bob Calvert, coeditor of the first *Texas Through Time*.

58. Amilcar Shabazz, *Advancing Democracy: African Americans and the Struggle for Access and Equity in Higher Education in Texas* (Chapel Hill: University of North Carolina Press, 2004); Dwonna Goldstone, *Integrating the 40 Acres: The 50-Year Struggle for Racial Equality at the University of Texas* (Athens: University of Georgia Press, 2006); Yvonne Davis Frear, "Generation versus Generation: African Americans in Texas Remember the Civil Rights Movement," in *Lone Star Pasts,* ed. Cantrell and Turner, 203–19.

59. For foundational texts of traditional and new immigration scholarship, see Oscar Handlin, *The Uprooted* (Boston: Little, Brown, 1951); John Bodnar, *The Transplanted: A History of Immigrants in Urban America* (Bloomington: Indiana University Press, 1987).

60. Zamora, *World of the Mexican Worker;* Blanton, *Strange Career of Bilingual Education.* See also Allen O. Kownslar, *The European Texans* (College Station: Texas A&M University Press, 2004); Thad Sitton and Dan K. Utley, *From Can See to Can't: Texas Cotton Farmers on the Southern Prairies* (Austin: University of Texas Press,

1997); Marilyn D. Rhinehart, *A Way of Work and a Way of Life: Coal Mining in Thurber, Texas, 1888–1926* (College Station: Texas A&M University Press, 1992).

61. Walter Struve, *Germans of Texas: Commerce, Migration, and Culture in the Days of the Lone Star Republic* (Austin: University of Texas Press, 1996).

62. Walter D. Kamphoefner, "New Perspectives on Texas Germans and the Confederacy," *Southwestern Historical Quarterly* 102, (April 1999): 441–55; Kamphoefner, "The Handwriting on the Wall: The Klan, Language Issues, and Prohibition in the German Settlements of Eastern Texas," *Southwestern Historical Quarterly* 112, (July 2008): 52–66. See also Karl A. Hoerig, "The Relationship between German Immigrants and the Native Peoples in Western Texas," *Southwestern Historical Quarterly* 97, (January 1994): 422–51; Benjamin Paul Hegi, "'Old Time Good Germans': German-Americans in Cook County, Texas, during World War I," *Southwestern Historical Quarterly* 109, (October 2005): 234–57.

63. Charles H. Russell, *Undaunted: A Norwegian Woman in Frontier Texas* (College Station: Texas A&M University Press, 2006); Clinton Machann and James W. Mendl Jr., trans. and eds., *Czech Voices: Stories from Texas in the Americán Národní Kalendář* (College Station: Texas A&M University, 1991); François Lagarde, ed., *The French in Texas: History, Migration, Culture* (Austin: University of Texas Press, 2003); Graham Davis, "Models of Migration: The Historiography of the Irish Pioneers in South Texas," *Southwestern Historical Quarterly* 99 no. 3 (1996): 326–48.

64. Harold M. Hyman, *Oleander Odyssey: The Kempners of Galveston, Texas, 1854–1980s* (College Station: Texas A&M University Press, 1990); Hollace Ava Weiner, *Jewish Stars in Texas: Rabbis and Their Work* (College Station: Texas A&M University Press, 1999); Weiner, *Jewish "Junior League": The Rise and Demise of the Fort Worth Council of Jewish Women* (College Station: Texas A&M University Press, 2008). See also Hollace Ava Weiner and Kenneth D. Roseman, eds., *Lone Stars of David: The Jews of Texas* (Waltham, Mass.: Brandeis University Press, 2007).

65. David M. Reimers, "Asian Immigrants in the South," in *Globalization and the American South,* ed. James C. Cobb and William Stueck (Athens: University of Georgia Press, 2005), 100–134; Audrey Singer, Susan W. Hardwick, and Caroline B. Brettell, eds., *Twenty-First-Century Gateways: Immigrant Incorporation in Suburban America* (Washington, D.C.: Brookings Institution Press, 2008).

66. Steven L. Davis, *Texas Literary Outlaws: Six Writers in the Sixties and Beyond* (Fort Worth: Texas Christian University Press, 2004), 6 (quotation), 278. Davis cites the novels of Brammer, Shrake, Américo Paredes, and Elmer Kelton as examples. For a more recent study of McMurtry, see Mark Busby, *Larry McMurtry and the West: An Ambivalent Relationship* (Denton: University of North Texas Press, 1995). See also Ernest Hemingway, "Old Newsman Writes: A Letter from Cuba," *Esquire,* December 1934, 26.

67. Larry McMurtry, *In a Narrow Grave* (Austin: Encino Press, 1968); Don Graham, *Giant Country: Essays on Texas* (Fort Worth: Texas Christian University Press, 1999); Ronald L. Davis, "Modernization and Distinctiveness: Twentieth-Century

Cultural Life in Texas," in *Texas Through Time,* ed. Buenger and Calvert, 5–6; Sylvia Ann Grider and Lou Halsell Rodenberger, eds., *Let's Hear It: Stories by Texas Women Writers* (College Station: Texas A&M University Press, 2003); Dagoberto Gilb, ed., *Hecho en Tejas: An Anthology of Texas Mexican Literature* (Albuquerque: University of New Mexico Press, 2008); Don Graham and Larry McMurtry, eds., *Lone Star Literature from the Red River to the Rio Grande: A Texas Anthology* (New York: W. W. Norton, 2003).

68. Daniel D. Arreola, *Tejano South Texas: A Mexican American Cultural Province* (Austin: University of Texas Press, 2002).

69. Benjamin Heber Johnson, *Revolution in Texas: How a Forgotten Rebellion and Its Bloody Suppression Turned Mexicans into Mexican Americans* (New Haven, Conn.: Yale University Press, 2003); Casey Walsh, *Building the Borderlands: A Transnational History of Irrigated Cotton along the Mexico-Texas Border* (College Station: Texas A&M University Press, 2008). See also Elliott Young, *Catarino Garza's Revolution on the Texas-Mexico Border* (Durham, N.C.: Duke University Press, 2004).

70. H. Sophie Burton and F. Todd Smith, *Colonial Natchitoches: A Creole Community on the Louisiana-Texas Frontier* (College Station: Texas A&M University Press, 2008); Jacqueline Jones, "Labor and the Idea of Race in the American South," *Journal of Southern History* 75, (August 2009): 625.

71. Char Miller, "Sunbelt Texas," in *Texas Through Time,* ed. Buenger and Calvert, 284–85.

72. Davis, *Texas Literary Outlaws;* Phillips, *White Metropolis;* Elizabeth York Enstam, *Women and the Creation of Urban Life: Dallas, Texas, 1843–1920* (College Station: Texas A&M University Press, 1998); Brian Behnken, "The 'Dallas Way': Protest, Response, and the Civil Rights Experience in Big D and Beyond," *Southwestern Historical Quarterly* 111, (July 2007): 1–29.

73. Arnoldo De León, *Ethnicity in the Sunbelt: Mexican Americans in Houston* (College Station: Texas A&M University Press, 2001); Roberto R. Treviño, *The Church in the Barrio: Mexican American Ethno-Catholicism in Houston* (Chapel Hill: University of North Carolina Press, 2006); Howard Beeth and Cary D. Wintz, eds., *Black Dixie: Afro-Texan History and Culture in Houston* (College Station: Texas A&M University Press, 1992).

74. Char Miller, ed., *On the Border: An Environmental History of San Antonio* (San Antonio: Trinity University Press, 2005), 243; Miller, *Deep in the Heart of San Antonio: Land and Life in South Texas* (San Antonio: Trinity University Press, 2004). For an urban study of San Antonio focusing more on race and ethnicity, see Rodolfo Rosales, *The Illusion of Inclusion: The Political Story of San Antonio, Texas* (Austin: University of Texas Press, 2000).

75. Paul H. Carlson, *Amarillo: The Story of a Western Town* (Lubbock: Texas Tech University Press, 2006); Mary Jo O'Rear, *Storm over the Bay: The People of Corpus Christi and Their Port* (College Station: Texas A&M University Press, 2009); O'Rear, "Silver-Lined Storm: The Impact of the 1919 Hurricane on the Port of Corpus Christi,"

Southwestern Historical Quarterly 108, (January 2005): 312–43; Alan Lessoff, "A Texas City and the Texas Myth: Urban Historical Identity in Corpus Christi," *Southwestern Historical Quarterly* 100, (January 1997): 304–29.

76. Turner, *Women, Culture, and Community*; Susan Wiley Hardwick, *Mythic Galveston: Reinventing America's Third Coast* (Baltimore: Johns Hopkins University Press, 2002).

77. Erik Larson, *Isaac's Storm: A Man, a Time, and the Deadliest Hurricane in History* (New York: Crown Publishers, 1999); Turner, *Women, Culture, and Community*; Hardwick, *Mythic Galveston*; O'Rear, *Storm over the Bay*; O'Rear, "Silver Lined Storm."

78. Hugh W. Stephens, *The Texas City Disaster, 1947* (Austin: University of Texas Press, 1997); Martin V. Melosi and Joseph A. Pratt, eds., *Energy Metropolis: An Environmental History of Houston and the Gulf Coast* (Pittsburgh: University of Pittsburgh Press, 2007); Robert D. Bullard, *Dumping in Dixie: Race, Class, and Environmental Quality* (Boulder, Colo.: Westview Press, 1990); Monica Perales, "Fighting to Stay in Smeltertown: Lead Contamination and Environmental Justice in a Mexican American Community," *Western Historical Quarterly* 39, (Spring 2008): 41–63. See also Bill Minutaglio, *City on Fire: The Forgotten Disaster That Devastated a Town and Ignited a Landmark Legal Battle* (New York: HarperCollins, 2003); James B. McSwain, "Urban Government and Environmental Policies: Regulating the Storage and Distribution of Fuel Oil in Houston, Texas 1901–1915," *Journal of Southern History* 71, (May 2005): 279–320.

79. John A. Adams Jr., *Damming the Colorado: The Rise of the Lower Colorado River Authority, 1933–1939* (College Station: Texas A&M University Press, 1990); Ken Kesselus, *Alvin Wirtz: The Senator, LBJ, and LCRA* (Austin: Eakin Press, 2002); Linda Scarbrough, *Road, River, and Ol' Boy Politics: A Texas County's Path from Farm to Supersuburb* (Austin: Texas State Historical Association Press, 2005).

80. Richard V. Francaviglia, *The Cast Iron Forest: A Natural and Cultural History of the North American Cross Timbers* (Austin: University of Texas Press, 2000).

81. Elizabeth Silverthorne and Geneva Fulgham, *Women Pioneers in Texas Medicine* (College Station: Texas A&M University Press, 1997); Henry C. Dethloff and Donald H. Dyal, *Special Kind of Doctor: A History of Veterinary Medicine in Texas* (College Station: Texas A&M University Press, 1991); James S. Olson, *Making Cancer History: Disease and Discovery at the M.D. Anderson Cancer Center* (Baltimore: Johns Hopkins University Press, 2009); Claire Strom, "Texas Fever and the Dispossession of the Southern Yeoman Farmer," *Journal of Southern History* 66, (February 2000): 49–74; Heather Green Wooten, *The Polio Years in Texas: Battling a Terrifying Unknown* (College Station: Texas A&M University Press, 2009).

82. Buenger and Calvert, "Introduction: The Shelf Life of Truth in Texas," in *Texas Through Time*, ed. Buenger and Calvert, xxxi.

83. Myron P. Gutmann and Christie G. Sample, "Land, Climate, and Settlement on the Texas Frontier," *Southwestern Historical Quarterly* 99, (October 1995), 136–72; Ty Cashion, *A Texas Frontier: The Clear Fork Country and Fort Griffin, 1849–1887*

(Norman: University of Oklahoma Press, 1996); John Jameson, *The Story of Big Bend National Park* (Austin: University of Texas Press, 1996). For the mythic Texas cattle industry, see Terry G. Jordan, *North American Cattle-Ranching: Origins, Diffusion, and Differentiation* (Albuquerque: University of New Mexico Press, 1993); David L. Wheeler, "The Blizzard of 1886 and Its Effect on the Range Cattle Industry in the Southern Plains," *Southwestern Historical Quarterly* 94, (January 1991): 415-32.

84. John Miller Morris, *El Llano Estacado: Exploration and Imagination on the High Plains of Texas and New Mexico, 1536-1860* (Austin: Texas State Historical Association, 1997), 342.

85. Walter L. Buenger, *The Path to a Modern South: Northeast Texas between Reconstruction and the Great Depression* (Austin: University of Texas Press, 2001), 258 (quotation); Buenger, "Texas and the South," *Southwestern Historical Quarterly* 103, (January 2000): 308-24.

86. McCaslin, *At the Heart of Texas.*

Beyond Parochialism
Modernization and Texas Historiography

Nancy Beck Young

The *Oxford English Dictionary* defines parochialism as a "Parochial character or tendency; *esp.* confinement of one's interests to the local sphere; lack of global perspective; narrowness of view; petty provincialism." Similarly, it defines modernization as "The action or an act of modernizing something; the state of being modernized. Also: a modernized version."[1] Scholars of Texas history have in the past been charged with parochialism for exploring isolated topics not relevant to the larger narrative of the United States and its role in the world, but that criticism is inaccurate for the writings of the last twenty or so years. Instead, many historians have argued about three things, including when modernization began, the processes by which Texas became modern, and how and why Texas became more integrated into the world beyond its borders.

Just what has changed in the last two decades since the creation and publication of the essays in *Texas Through Time* (1991)?[2] Just as the borders between Texas scholarship and national scholarship have diminished, so too has the border between what is local and what is national in Texas history. Historians now focus on the connections between Texas and beyond. Texas historians now often lead the field rather than trailing it. This has resulted in large part because Texas historians interested in the various aspects of modernization have moved beyond the paradigm described in *Texas Through Time,* which pitted heroic revisionists against defenders of a traditional, celebratory literature, and have begun asking new questions. Thus, whereas the national profession motivated historians twenty years ago, that is less true in the early twenty-first century. The foci of scholarly inquiry have enlarged in the last two decades, when the New Social History and race and class were the dominant trends. In the years since, scholars have engaged wholly new modes of analysis, including gender, modernization, the new political history, and cultural history. Because so many historians working on modernization questions in Texas history have crossed these boundaries with the work on larger regions of the United States and the nation as a whole, a richer and more nuanced history of Texas has emerged.

Texas historians have in the last two decades been asking questions that merge the Lone Star State's story with the regional or national or international story. This trend toward seeing Texans and Texas history as part of something larger and in some cases as architects of national and international currents characterizes much of the recent work on Lone Star State topics and is most apparent in scholarship in the borderlands and the study of national politicians from Texas. Embedded within this work is the theme of modernization, which encompasses many different fields and is reflected in the arguments of much of the literature written about recent Texas topics. The two main trends then, in the historiography have been the effort to situate Texas history within American history and to assert when and how Texas became modern.

Put simply, since 1988 Texas history has changed from being too parochial to being focused on crossing borders between the state and the nation. As recent scholars have debated modernization processes they have merged the study of Texas with larger national historical trends. There is a double way of looking at this development: while the scholarship of the last two decades is far less parochial and far more integrated into the mainstream of U.S. history, a most desirable development, it is also less uniquely interested in the Texas experience as an end point. Much of the recent literature has a larger thematic purpose beyond explicating and celebrating things Texan. Instead, work on Texas modernization, regardless of topic, focuses on the move of Texas and Texans into national politics, economics, culture, and society. Histories of Texas now more closely follow national trends, indeed in the case of at least Mexican American civil rights, they lead national trends. The fit though, of Texas history with U.S. history remains somewhat askew, but this is not necessarily a problem. Just as Texans stood within and outside the circle of the larger United States, writings on Texas history are increasingly mirroring this fact, existing both within but also outside, even ahead of, the circle of the larger historical profession.

When *Texas Through Time* was first published, Walter L. Buenger and Robert A. Calvert contended that the scholarship on modern Texas was so underdeveloped that work in all fields was needed. Likewise, authors in that volume identified parochialism as a problem for students of Texas history.[3] The scholarly renaissance on Texas topics in the last two decades or so has begun a process of remediation. Perhaps the overall profession's bias against state history as amateurish and antithetical to the work of academic historians combined with the difficult reputation Texas and Texans have earned—loud, braggadocios, and exaggerated—ensures that the parochial perceptions about Texas history will remain a problem for serious scholars working in the field. While individual authors working since 1988 have addressed the parochialism problem and have begun to understand the nuanced complexity of modern Texas history, the field of Texas history still remains saddled with the reputation of narrowness. The freshest, best recent work on Texas traces to the scholarly revolutions in U.S. history dating back to the 1960s with the implosion of consensus historiography; the introduction of the New Social History; the emergence of race, class, and gender as analytic tools; and the revitalization of political history, historiographical trends that absorbed the profession in the last four decades of the twentieth century. Recent work on Texas topics has been situated within the larger discourse about U.S. history. With time, the strength of this new work will override the now-outmoded stereotypes about Texas history. That the process is not complete, though, is symptomatic of the slow filtration speed of new research findings into the more generalized manner in which historians think about fields and subfields.

While historians have worked to overcome the charges of parochialism, much less progress has been made on the question of how to conceptualize the twentieth century in Texas chronologically. The problem is even more apparent when juxtaposed against the more obvious divisions of the nineteenth century. The work considered in this chapter only begins the process of suggesting how historians might periodize modern Texas history. With the exception of the discussion of modernization, such matters so far have been a secondary concern at best for scholars in the field. The historiographic concentration on thematically driven scholarship as explored in other chapters in this volume combined with the longer trends away from political history, the latter having faded in the past decade, has generated little interest in defining and exploring political periods in Texas history.

When thought has been given to periodizing modern Texas history, the tendency has been to borrow chronological divisions from modern U.S. history, an obvious solution given the concomitant integration of Texas into the mainstream of American life, but one fraught with problems. There is an overall trend away from chronological configurations of U.S. history and toward thematic configurations. This process has been linked to the long move away from political history and the tendency at least a generation or so ago to employ a political lens when writing about defined chronological periods. Furthermore, thematic configurations offer a more ready opportunity for analysis and the application of theory to the study of the past than do chronological studies. Once the dividing mark of World War II is crossed, finding subdivisions according

223

to the calendar becomes difficult if only because they shift when the focus of scholarship moves from politics to society or to the economy or to culture or to race and ethnicity and so on. Within Texas, this problem is even more acute.

Distance, or the lack thereof, though, might be the most important factor in the failure of scholars to successfully periodize the recent past. Put simply, the proximity of scholars to the modern history of Texas makes more difficult the determination of more manageable chronological eras. The extant literature taken collectively does suggest that the 1930s should be viewed as a period of protomodernization. Similarly, the 1940s have attracted significant attention as a distinct chronological era and as a point of departure for thematic inquiries. The postwar social, economic, and political changes, especially when viewed in totality, were so significant that in many ways the better dividing line for understanding the evolution of modern Texas is the end of World War II, not the onset of the Great Depression. The years of depression and war were prologue, as most of the authors evaluated in this essay contend. More recent postwar historians, though, have shown much less interest in sorting out the chronology of Texas since 1945, but the work that has been done suggests there was another important shift in the late 1960s and early 1970s.

When Did Texas Start Modernizing?

The question of when Texas started modernizing is a deceptively complex one that initially suggests an easy answer, but when the multitude of historical approaches are brought to bear, the conclusions become much more nuanced. Indeed, modernization was not something that happened quickly or evenly. Nor were its results wholly positive. Some of the most sophisticated works to come out in the last twenty years have evaluated the uneven and undesirable results of modernization. In part, how one answers this question is guided by the periodization used to understand the Texas past. Did the modern era begin with the depression era, World War II, the advent of civil rights, or perhaps should an earlier date be considered, such as the discovery and development of the oil industry in Texas? However, a more basic determination needs to be made about the historical meanings of modernization and how they do and do not follow the dictionary definition quoted above. Here again different scholars have reached conflicting conclusions about modernization in Texas.

In *The Path to a Modern South: Northeast Texas between Reconstruction and the Great Depression* (2001), Walter Buenger finds early signs of modernization in northeast Texas in the years between Reconstruction and the 1930s, specifically the economic development of the timber and oil industries and the proliferation of railroads. His story of modernization is not wholly celebratory, though, as he also accounts for the racial violence that was all too common in northeast Texas and that intensified even as the region became more like the rest of the United States and less like the South in terms of its economic development. Some of the other signs of modernization that he discerned included the development of a class hierarchy in farming communities between landowners and sharecroppers and the emergence of booming small-town economies. Indeed, Buenger contended, "Statistical similarity and other similarities with the South before 1887 and greater dissimilarity after 1930 suggest that the years in between hold the key to the emergence of modern Texas."[4] Buenger finds that this modernization was not just economic but also was cultural in that the subjects examined in his book ceased thinking of themselves as southerners and began seeing themselves as Texan in the early twentieth century.

Patrick Cox's study, *The First Texas News Barons* (2005), covers the period from the late nineteenth century through 1940. His work bears consideration because of his argument that Texas modernization predated World War II and was the product of the journalistic boosters. He argued: "For Texas to achieve a modern economy, the state would have to move away from the South's defeatist moonlight-and-magnolia nostalgia to a more forward-looking self-image. Texas newspapers served as chief agents in transforming Texas' regional identity from a frontier outpost where Dixie petered out to 'where the West begins,' as the Fort Worth city motto puts it."[5]

Furthermore, Cox was sensitive to the balance of a regional study against the backdrop of national trends. He found the daily independent papers in the Lone Star State during this period to have performed much better than was true in the country as a whole, showing Texas to be a leader in an important national trend toward modernization, that is, the manner in which journalists conceived and reported the news. Because Cox has juxtaposed his account of the newspaper barons against the business and political history of the state, there was ample context and evidence offered to sustain the thesis. This final point suggests one other important aspect in understanding Cox's historiographic contribution: he has privileged the study of elites, in this case the newspaper barons who played a key role in shaping how nonelites viewed the world, and in the process suggests the importance of this socioeconomic class to understanding how and why modernization happened when it did in Texas and the nation.

The shifts in the oil business unfolded over several decades, as the scholars examined in this chapter suggested. Indeed, within the subfield of modern economic history in Texas, there has been substantial work on the oil industry as a business that perhaps more than anything else remade and modernized

Texas.[6] Diana Davids Hinton (then Olien) and Roger M. Olien published an important book, *Oil in Texas: The Gusher Age, 1895–1945* (2002), that took the story of Texas modernization back to the late nineteenth century and ended with the Second World War, suggesting the important divide that the war had for the history of the petroleum industry. They link modernization of the state to the emergence of the oil industry, asserting, "Texas without oil? The notion is near inconceivable. One might as easily image Los Angeles without freeways, Manhattan without skyscrapers, or Washington, D.C., without politics. Oil is central to the economic and social identity of modern Texas."[7] Because their study took as its topic the oil industry in Texas during its infancy, and because they convincingly demonstrated oil's centrality to Texas' modernization, this study made the periodization of Texas modernization difficult. Suggested in this work is the artificiality and even academic bias of any attempt to subdivide as complex and interconnected a period as the twentieth century. Their nuanced account will force a historiographic debate about the following question: Had the modern era in Texas begun as early as the discovery of the first commercial oil field in Texas in Corsicana in the 1890s, or the boom that followed Spindletop in 1901, or were the early decades of the twentieth century merely prologue or rehearsal for the Texas that would emerge after World War II?

This question requires consideration of the problem that drives Hinton and Olien's book: why did the petroleum industry flourish as it did in Texas? Part of the contribution that this book made, then, is the careful description the authors give to the discovery of the important oil fields in Texas: Corsicana, Spindletop, the East Texas field, and those in West Texas. Hinton and Olien showed that the processes begun in the late nineteenth century had a rolling as opposed to an immediately transformative impact on Texas, putting their work in line with other scholars who are interested in when and how Texas modernized and who have argued modernization was a gradual process. Among the major shifts were the transformation of the state from a rural, agrarian economy to a more urban but still extractive economy, and a tremendous flow of people out of the countryside to more prosperous lives in the city, either directly in the oil industry or in one of the many businesses that developed to serve it. Other important measures of this process include the proliferation of oil and gas wells throughout the state, covering about two-thirds of the counties in Texas, and the tax revenue—about half of all such monies collected in the state—generated by the industry. None of these processes occurred quickly, and it took the dramatic events of World War II, the authors contended, to cement modernization. Until World War II, though, the market for oil and gas was not equal to the productive capacity of the Texas fields, especially with regard to pipeline accessibility to transport petroleum products to market. Still, the authors find that Texas throughout its history was far from the victim in a colonial economic relationship with the rest of the United States but instead used its oil resources to exploit outside capitalists interested in investing in the petroleum industry. This finding is a major challenge to earlier scholarship on Texas, notably the work of Walter Prescott Webb, who argued that the state functioned as a colony to the rest of the nation. Instead, Texas oil interests engaged in smart political and economic negotiating to maintain high prices that benefited the overall growth of the Texas economy.

Because the oil industry was crucial to the modernization of Texas and the shifting boundaries between state and national concerns, scholars working in business history have attempted to understand the Texas Railroad Commission, the agency charged with regulating the Texas oil industry. William R. Childs's *The Texas Railroad Commission* (2005), which looks at the history of that regulatory agency from its 1891 founding through the mid-1960s, is concerned less with dramatic fights about regulation and more about the daily work of regulators, in itself an important topic because it suggests much about the changing expectations for the intervention of the state into the economy. Childs coined the term "pragmatic federalism" to describe how the Texas Railroad Commission worked with federal regulators. This nuanced historiographic development contributed to the wider understanding of how the state and the nation functioned in tandem in the twentieth century. In the end, Childs saw the war years as the turning point in this longitudinal study because they marked the apex of commission-style regulation. Furthermore, by this juncture the Texas Railroad Commission had completed its expansion of responsibility to include a host of industries.

Indeed, because Childs ranged over approximately seventy years of history his conclusions about the modernization of Texas into the national mainstream are particularly valuable. His book provided a perspective lacking from other scholarship on the topic. It also questioned how and in what way Texas was a leader in the development of the regulatory state, especially commission regulation of the oil industry. Because the Texas Railroad Commission exerted inordinate power over the price of oil and gas on the world market until the oil crises of the 1970s, this book is a perfect example of how to take a Texas topic and tell a story of wider national, and even international, interest. Childs explained, "This book interweaves the institutional history of the Texas Railroad Commission with the national story of regulation to present a fuller understanding of regulation in America, at least to the mid-twentieth century."[8] He also suggested that as the twentieth century wore on and global trade patterns emerged in the postwar era, the question became whether state level regulatory bodies such as the Texas Railroad Commission remained viable.

The book attempted to understand the multifaceted work of the Texas Railroad Commission while also making larger, more important points about the intersection of business, government, and the economy in a period of growth and industrial innovation. This chronological break is important because, as Childs noted, a cooperative model of business-government relations had emerged in the years between World War I and World War II. Furthermore, the expanding consumer economy of the nation demanded new regulatory strategies to support this culture of consumption, explaining the growing jurisdiction of the Texas Railroad Commission in the interwar years. Childs explained that during this period the progressive ethos, which had sustained the commission in its earliest years, was replaced with a more personality-driven style of regulation that encouraged cronyism. In this deeply researched, crisply written, and thoughtfully argued book, Childs contended, "The process of pragmatic federalism persisted, however, and the Washington lawmakers insisted in every extension of regulation that the state and national commissioners cooperate with one another in administrating the new laws."[9]

There are as yet few synthetic treatments of modern Texas. Leaving aside textbooks and overviews of the state's entire history, there has been little truly synthetic work on modern Texas since the publication of *Texas Through Time* in 1991. In addition to the problems already discussed, the historical processes of modernization occurred too recently for the scholarship of this crucial development to reach maturity. A further problem, true for historians of modern America as well as students of modern Texas, is the overall messiness of the twentieth century. Unlike the Civil War and the nineteenth century there is not one central event that demarcated the century, inviting the chronological subdivisions that make for easier periodization necessary since modernization was a process and not a single event. Instead, the twentieth century was marked with a number of significant turning points—for example, World War I, the Great Depression, World War II, the civil rights movement, the Vietnam War, and the rise of modern conservatism—that rise and fall in importance depending on whether the historian's focus is on political, social, diplomatic, economic, or cultural questions related to modernization.

In a popular, pictorial history driven by vignettes, James L. Haley provided the only single-authored overview of Texas history for this era published after *Texas Through Time.* His book, *Texas: From Spindletop through World War II* (1993), was not written for an academic audience. While in itself not analytical in its approach to the past, the most important historiographic contribution of the book was its plea for scholars to pay more attention to the twentieth century, which has been happening for the past several decades. A rudimentary examination of the scholarship on Texas history written since 1988 suggests that 27 percent has been focused on the modernization of Texas, a story of the twentieth century and a decided change from the earlier bias toward the nineteenth century. This book is most important for what it suggests about the value of twentieth-century history to a popular audience in Texas, which is a portion of the problem retarding academic study of these years. In his preface, Haley identified, fell into, then somewhat refuted the trap of privileging nineteenth-century Texas over twentieth-century Texas. He revealed that among the popular and textbook treatment of the totality of Texas history, the nineteenth century always garnered more ink. Haley explained, "And I guess that is as it should be, but in a way it is unfortunate, because the history of Texas in the twentieth century has gotten a bum rap. It does not become less interesting. On the contrary, it becomes more complex, and provides a greater variety of ways for a greater diversity of people to make a mark on a wider range of issues and topics."[10]

The paucity of truly synthetic work on modern Texas history is lessened somewhat by a provocative edited volume that drew out the important theme of memory as a topic. *Lone Star Pasts* (2007), edited by Gregg Cantrell and Elizabeth Hayes Turner, challenges scholars to think more carefully about new and old problems in Texas history. In using memory as a historiographic device Cantrell and Turner were in keeping with an important trend in the study of American history in the last few decades. While scholars have used the notion of memory to study a host of topics, prior to the publication of *Lone Star Pasts* few had applied the method to Texas history.[11] There is an important historiographic point to be derived from this approach, namely, the differing ways successive generations understand and know the same set of historical facts, especially with regard to modernization.

Cantrell and Turner asked their contributors to develop essays that engage the growing field of historical memory and the problem of how individuals and groups used the past for contemporary political and social purposes. Much of the work in this volume is about nineteenth-century Texas and the memory of topics from those years in the twentieth century. Key examples are the Alamo, Civil War monuments, and Juneteenth. In this way, nineteenth-century topics also become of direct interest to scholars of modern Texas. For example, in her essay on Juneteenth, Turner showed how a nineteenth-century event has seen its meaning shift with the passage of time. She wrote: "By the 1960s slavery, however, presented a shadow shame, a memory best forgotten. Juneteenth celebrations seemed old fashioned and quaint by modern standards. The civil rights movement more adequately expressed black aspirations. Thus, Juneteenth celebrations went underground to reemerge in new form. Juneteenth in collective memory today has new associations, with greater expression in artistic endeavors and less focus on recalling emancipation."[12]

Other chapters explored topics specific to the twentieth century, including the Ku Klux Klan, the civil rights movement, and Lyndon B. Johnson. What is revealed about memory's role in history is not entirely positive. Indeed, Ricky F. Dobbs's thoughtful essay about the forgetting of Johnson should be read as a cautionary tale. In it, he argued, "Lyndon Johnson no longer seems relevant to modern Texas." Later in the essay, Dobbs addressed the problem suggested by this quote—if the majority of the people do not remember something then it was not important. Dobbs asserted, "collective memory is not history and should not be allowed to become history."[13] This work on memory and history, in addition to suggesting fresh approaches to the study of Texas, provides important hints about using natural generational divides to periodize Texas history. For example, Yvonne Davis Frear noted that very problem in the stark differences among how civil rights participants and their children and grandchildren recall that momentous era. Maybe the complexity of twentieth-century Texas, which so far has defied scholarly synthesis and periodization, is best understood in a more ambiguous, generational fashion with the different historical approaches imposing different chronological divides. If this volume is any indication, topics that are thematically joined can be linked even when they fall in different centuries. More important, because there are no overviews that help conceive of periods and modernization, the study of memory helps by providing guideposts about the differing legacies of the past.

Two scholars in particular have looked at the critics of modernization. Whereas Kyle G. Wilkison, in *Yeomen, Sharecroppers, and Socialists: Plain Folk Protest in Texas, 1870–1914* (2008), examines the protests of small farmers against economic modernization, especially as it brought changes to agricultural life in Texas, my *Wright Patman: Populism, Liberalism, and the American Dream* (2000) treats the political career of one member of Congress who fought hard to mitigate the impact of modernization on the economic periphery of the United States. Wilkison looks at the reasons why yeomen farmers lost their land in the late nineteenth and early twentieth centuries and what such developments meant for communities dependent on the neighborliness of people joined together in subsistence agriculture. Indeed, modernization was responsible for the changes Wilkison explored, and in his telling the development was not a positive one for the people of Hunt County, Texas, his chosen case study.

Wilkison locates the economic modernization of East Texas with several interrelated factors—migration into the region from the rest of the South, increased land values, increased cotton production, and increased farm tenancy rates—none of which were positive for the individuals he studied in this book. Ironically, he argues that economic modernization did not cause changes to the values of his subjects even as it made mutuality more difficult to achieve. Hence the adherence to rural socialism, so found Wilkison. He concluded, "Texas farmers had long given more support than town-dwellers to structural critiques of the rapidly changing post–Civil War economy. . . . [T]he Texas plain folk community contained a consistently dissenting minority, occasionally swelling to a majority, fighting a dogged but doomed rearguard action against dependence and inequality."[14]

Wilkison's conclusions buttress the findings of my biography of Patman, which was published earlier in the decade. Although Wright Patman was not from Hunt County, the county's demographic makeup was not entirely unlike the far northeast corner of Texas that he represented. I argued that Patman's various political crusades for the early payment of the World War I soldiers' bonus and against chain stores and the Federal Reserve Board all aimed to even out the rough patches left in the wake of modernization. For Patman, politics, especially the federal government, functioned to make sure the losers were not completely destroyed by modernization. "In many of his endeavors, Congressman Patman was the voice for the people who were left behind by the progress of the twentieth century," I argued. "Patman spent his forty-seven years in Washington trying to reduce the negative impact of modernity on rural and small-town America. . . . [H]is greatest accomplishment came when he gave voice to a version of the American Dream that highlighted those very same rural values that were the bedrock of American civilization."[15] Not only is my biography important for the manner in which it complicates the understanding of modernity's origins and impact, but also it is a model for how to research and write political biography.

Texas in the 1930s

Historiographically, the construction of modernity in Texas has been an evolving process. As such, the 1930s can best be considered, according to the literature of the decade and the years following, as protomodern or a prologue to the recent past. The scholars who have written about the 1930s or who have ended their thematic explorations of Texas in that decade have noted important shifts to state politics, society, economics, and culture, enough to acknowledge the process of modernity at work, but when the 1930s are explored comparatively with what followed, qualifications are required. Collectively, historians have revealed that looking for modernization in the 1930s was wise, for these protomodern years contain much that bridged to the future.

Scholars have given attention to the rise of broadcasting in understanding the emergence of modern Texas. Richard Schroeder published *Texas Signs On: The Early Days of Radio and Television* (1998). In it, he claimed, "Texas broadcast history has been prolific, unique, revolutionary, colorful, interesting, and 'cutting edge.'"[16] He looked to innate factors regarding Texas, its social and economic conditions, that explain the pioneering developments of broadcasters in Texas. As rich as the material on radio and television broadcasting in Texas is, the book provided little in the way of needed context to understand the larger import of the story being told. For example, his discussion of WBAP's decision to introduce baseball broadcasting over the radio with play-by-play commentary was fascinating but was not connected analytically to larger trends in either sport history or media history. Still, when Schroeder is read in conjunction with other authors looking at components of cultural and media modernization in Texas, namely Cox, his work is historiographically important if for no other reason than its revelations of Texan leadership in broadcasting, a vital component of state and national modernization. Taken together, these works show Texas as a consistent consumer and sometimes leader of social and cultural modernity.

Scholars have produced numerous thoughtful political histories and policy studies of the 1930s. Collectively these works have advanced the historiography in two ways. They suggest the role of bureaucracy in making for a more modern Texas, and they also show the process by which politicians closed the gap between state and national concerns in the twentieth century. Indeed, the policy development and implementation process crossed borders more seamlessly by the 1930s. This change was a crucial prerequisite for the postwar modernization of the state.

In *Texas, Cotton, and the New Deal* (2005), Keith J. Volanto has produced a thoughtful and important case study of a transformational moment in the application of federal policy on the state of Texas. Volanto's book is representative of one of several newer approaches to understanding the New Deal. Some scholars have used thematic frames to reconsider the meaning and legacy of the New Deal, while others like Volanto have focused on case studies of specific programs as they functioned in a particular state.[17] This case study revealed, in a way that national studies cannot, how the bureaucratic revolution of the 1930s unfolded, especially its impact on remaking the political culture of state-federal relations. To this end, Volanto suggested, "Investigation of the [Agricultural Adjustment Administration] AAA's cotton programs has additional significance as a case study of the New Deal itself. The AAA provides an excellent example of how the New Deal attempted to solve national problems in a largely experimental fashion."[18]

Volanto's work provided thoughtful and substantive detail about how Texas had become central to the success of New Deal agricultural policy and thus the New Deal. This factual argument, drawing on the challenges of implementing the crop control program in one state, albeit one that grew almost 40 percent of the nation's cotton crop, is also relevant historiographically because it suggests the relocation of the national political balance of power to Texas. Looked at from this perspective, a study of the program in Texas is integral to understanding the fate of this key New Deal program. Put simply, had the Texas farm community—landowners as well as processors, ginners, sharecroppers, and tenant farmers—not acquiesced, the AAA would have been a failure. In explaining how and why the AAA worked in Texas, Volanto is also deepening our understanding of how and why a key New Deal program succeeded.

Because his approach to the topic is from the perspective of policy makers, Volanto explained in convincing fashion that while the plight of tenant farmers and sharecroppers under New Deal agricultural programs was grim, there were few other options. Officials in Washington were divided on how best to address the most marginalized sector of the agricultural economy, and southern politicians did not welcome a federal program that would introduce social engineering in the region, especially given that a high percentage of the sharecroppers were African American. A more aggressive strategy, would, in other words, have brought the demise of the AAA. Thus, Volanto's work provided rich insight into the nexus of several issues marking the origins of modern Texas in the 1930s: the emergence of a powerful federal bureaucracy, the height of Texas as a cotton-producing economy, and the contradictions between southern demands for economic liberalism and the limits of southern tolerance for an activist federal government. *Texas, Cotton, and the New Deal* implied the manner in which Texas and southern racial conservatism remade the policies of the federal government when liberals were most ascendant. This historiographical point speaks volumes about the merger of Texas into the mainstream of American political life but also suggests just how much and how fast Texas was able to shift priorities within that mainstream. Volanto asserted, "The saga of the AAA cotton programs in Texas is a multifaceted story involving great men and common people coming together to overcome an alarming economic emergency. In addition to being a fascinating tale of cooperative experimentation in the face of tremendous uncertainty, it is also a compelling chronicle of competing ideologies and clashing interest groups."[19]

Water power projects in the 1930s served two important functions: they facilitated modernization and crossing borders within the United States and between the nation's core and its periphery. The policy history of water power in Texas was no different. Another thoughtful book on the public policy shifts within Texas comes from John A. Adams Jr., who wrote *Damming the Colorado* (1990), an exploration of the rise of the Lower Colorado River Authority (LCRA) in the 1930s. While much is known about the major river development project of the New Deal years, the Tennessee Valley Authority, less well understood are the other initiatives of that era, including the LCRA, which Adams described as "the most extensive multidam project west of the Mississippi River."[20]

In *Damming the Colorado,* Adams demonstrated just how much the LCRA transformed that part of Texas in the Colorado River's watershed. Adams also crossed several fields in history. In addition to its focus on politics in Texas, *Damming the Colorado* is also of interest to business, environmental, Western, and Southern historians as well as students of U.S. public policy. By showing the confluence of these different fields, Adams spoke to the federal-state policy partnerships of the 1930s, the limits on what private business could accomplish, the environmental aspects of policy innovation, and the changing notions of regional identity, all central to the process of modernization as it unfolded in Texas.

Ultimately, though, Adams told a political story that provides subtle and nuanced historiographical elaboration of what modernization meant and what it did not mean. Adams contended that at the nexus of business and the government, successful modernization required government intervention. This important historiographic point gets beyond the somewhat stale question of when Texas modernized and to the much more interesting and important question of why and how Texas modernized and crossed borders into the life of the nation. To this end, Adams engaged the two relevant debates about water power that were extant in the 1930s: the contest between private and public power and economic development, and the conflict over whether federal or state authorities should control interstate waterways. He described the failure of private companies to develop the Texas river. It took federal government intervention to bring this important component of modernization to one key region of Texas. The LCRA project began as a flood control measure but evolved into much more, including reclamation and hydroelectric power, even as a series of floods in 1935, 1936, and 1938 reminded officials of the importance of the project's original purpose.

Adams's story at its essence is one of transformation. He showed convincingly how electricity revolutionized life in the West, was a necessary component of modernization, and ultimately merged Texas into the national mainstream. Indeed, the LCRA remade the Texas Hill Country from a barren, economically deprived region into a prosperous retreat for the wealthy and the upper middle classes over the course of the twentieth century. Adams concluded, "the New Deal in the West *did* foster prosperity. Prior to 1933, water projects, in the hands of local concerns, had limited use and scope. New Deal programs stressed better planning and multipurpose projects, ensured large-scale employment, attracted new industry to the West, and stimulated extensive agriculture. The LCRA is a good case in point."[21] This book suggested in a fresh way the efficacy of large federal government expenditures on infrastructure as well as the various ways Texas topics can be used to tell large stories of regional and national importance.

James Wright Steely's *Parks for Texas: Enduring Landscapes of the New Deal* (1999) should be read as something of a companion piece to *Damming the Colorado* and to *Texas, Cotton, and the New Deal*.[22] Like the first two, it addressed a larger point about modernization and crossing borders, namely how the development of parks was a luxury not possible prior to modernization of Texas. Its focus was also on public policy, and it linked a story centered in Texas with larger regional and national trends, in this case dealing with national politics. Here Steely revealed that park development in Texas was directly connected to the presence of powerful Texans in Washington, D.C. In developing these historiographic points, Steely answered several related questions: Who originated the idea for state parks? Who planned and funded them? When were they put into a system? How were the park locations determined? Why have the parks endured?

Focusing on the political, Steely showed how the Texas park system could not have developed without an alignment of Texas political concerns with national political concerns. Texans in Washington—including a powerful triumvirate of Vice President John Nance Garner; Sam Rayburn, who initially was chair of the powerful Committee on Interstate and Foreign Commerce, then Majority Leader, and finally Speaker of the House during this period; and rising Texas political star Lyndon Johnson—secured $20 million in federal funds for Texas parks while lawmakers in Austin only had to provide $40,000. This disparate rate of funding is the evidentiary basis for the important historiographic point about the widening shadow Washington, D.C., cast over state politics in the 1930s. Steely's narrative, then, gave substantive backing to much of the political history written about twentieth-century Texans in Washington, D.C., namely, the tremendous power they wielded in the federal government and the meaning of those actions for the state of Texas. Historiographically, the point of Steely's book is what it revealed about the growing proximity of state and national politics and what that meant for modernization of the Lone Star State. Finally, while Volanto, Adams, and Steely did not explicitly address the question of when modern Texas began, the information described here would seem most unfamiliar to a twenty-first-century Texan. Instead, these policy studies about the 1930s reveal the transitional nature of the decade.

Other recent scholars have focused more on the Texas activists who have lobbied for change in Austin and Washington but have not themselves held elected office.[23] This choice of topic to understand politics has itself had historiographic implications. The more inclusive scholarship of the last two decades has revealed the crucial role of women and minorities as political players in Texas, a vital prerequisite to the modernization of Texas in both fact and in the historiographic overthrow of the parochial past. Indeed, examination of this scholarship suggests a much more complex view of Texas politics in the modern era, because many of the actors were not white males but were either females or people of color or both. One of the best books in this genre is a biography of the left feminist Minnie Fisher Cunningham (2003), who began her career as a suffrage activist in Texas and remained involved in liberal causes until her death in 1964. The authors, Judith N. McArthur and Harold L. Smith, have done a remarkable job of piecing together the story of Cunningham's life, especially since the bulk of her papers are not available for research.

The most important accomplishment of this book is the manner in which it makes more complex the reality of gendered politics in the postsuffrage era. Most women's historians argue that female activists either worked in partisan politics or through women's voluntary associations, but not both. Cunningham was active in every type of organization and at every level. Careful examination of her life serves as an object lesson regarding the importance of learning the varieties of activism practiced at the local level in order to create richer, more satisfying, and more accurate synthetic interpretations at the national level. Indeed, McArthur and Smith argue: "Cunningham's forty years of activism after gaining the vote illustrates in bold relief the obstacles women encountered in politics, notably the difficulty of winning office and marginalization within the parties. Equally important, her story helps fill in the still-emerging narrative of women's political activism between the demise of the first women's movement after 1920 and the rebirth of feminism in the 1960s."[24]

McArthur and Smith's biography provides further evidence of modernization emerging in the 1920s and 1930s, not the postwar years. The victory in the suffrage fight marked a sharp divide in the history of Texas women as exemplified in the account of Cunningham. Still, for as helpful as this book is, *Minnie Fisher Cunningham* (2003) only begins to tell the convoluted story of women and Texas politics. If further work on twentieth-century women follows the example of McArthur and Smith and contextualizes the results within the larger literature on women's history, then perhaps a thoughtful, alternative chronology of modern Texas history can be fashioned.

Another key component of modernization is the process by which a society polices itself to ensure orderly behavior. Robert M. Utley has written extensively on the Texas Rangers, and his most recent book, *Lone Star Lawmen* (2007), found the iconic Rangers to have undergone significant shifts by the 1930s from their nineteenth-century frontier exploits. Utley's twentieth-century Rangers became professional law enforcement officers because the modernization of Texas demanded it. As Utley noted regarding the 1935 transformation, "Population growth, urbanization, and industrialization spawned spiraling crime rates, mainly in East Texas. The Rangers scattered thinly over this part of the state had to deal with a variety and profusion of crimes their predecessors rarely encountered. In the western part of the state, however, duties remained much the same, both in the type of crime and the methods of fighting it."[25] This book contributes to the historiography, understanding not only how modernization happened in Texas but also why not all parts of the state modernized at the same time.

The modernization of Texas involved more than just politics. In fact, if the trends were limited to the political realm there would be much less to the story. Equally significant developments occurred in the arts and have been reflected in the literature of Texas history produced in the last twenty years. Just as Texas politics used local and regional views to reshape national politics, Texas artists used the regional arts movement to suggest a much more complex definition of the American art scene.

Much has been written about the modern history of the fine arts in Texas. The work on the painter Jerry Bywaters is especially rich and important.[26] Francine Carraro has written the best biography of Bywaters (1994). She located his career within the state, but she also showed the process by which national and international artists influenced Bywaters as well as his impact on the art world outside of Texas.

As such, *Jerry Bywaters: A Life in Art* is a stellar example of how to weave local, regional, and national threads into one compelling account. The work also suggested much about how modern Texas became a focal point in the regional art movement of the Depression years. Here again is an example of a

Texan dominating his field and helping to drive the way it evolved in and out of the state. Carraro contended, "local subject matter was a means to identify what is intrinsically American." Furthermore, Bywaters shared the belief that art should be "relevant" and "accessible." Finally, Bywaters and the artists of his era used their understanding of the environment to foster "a new sense of nationalism."[27]

Thus, the Bywaters biography, read in conjunction with the literature of modern Texas, suggests not a story of continued exceptionalism, as the nineteenth-century narrative of the state would have it, but a story of contribution and leadership to national movements and reconfiguration of those movements. Put differently, the artistic trends with which Bywaters was associated resonated throughout the nation because of the unique intersection of ideas and concerns during the Depression era and not necessarily because of developments unique to Texas. Still, Carraro's book is an important contribution to recent Texas historiography. It reinforced and complexified trends apparent in the politics and economics of the state. It also suggested that modernization, at least in the field of art, also required a redefinition of the field in Texas and in the nation.

There is an equally rich literature looking at more general art and art history topics in recent Texas history. Like the biographical work on Bywaters, these books dispelled the notion of Texas exceptionalism, suggested a more nuanced treatment of the arts in modern Texas, and contributed to an understanding of how and why Texas modernized and moved beyond its older parochial borders into the mainstream of the United States. Two works especially should be read in conjunction with the Bywaters literature: Philip Parisi's *Texas Post Office Murals* (2004) and Scott Grant Barker and Jane Myers's *Intimate Modernism: Fort Worth Circle Artists in the 1940s* (2008). Parisi's book was located at the nexus of art and politics. In key ways it paralleled the work of Volanto, Adams, and Steely in that it explored the impact of a New Deal program within Texas, but it also has historiographic goals within the arts. Parisi's biggest aim was to show how a government program privileged one form of art in Texas and the nation. Here is a moving together of state and national concerns, but also this process suggested, in Texas, the importance of the state's history to the construction of its new modernized identity. The post office murals of the New Deal era captured the edicts of regionalism in that the purpose of the program was to democratize art while providing federally funded relief for artists impoverished during the Great Depression.

Parisi explained, "The Texas post office murals portray Texans' values embodied in such characters as the revered Indian chief Quanah Parker, cowboys,

Beyond Parochialism

the bandit and folk hero Sam Bass, Texas Rangers, and historical figures Davy Crockett and Sam Houston." Approximately a third of the Texas post office murals depict historical subjects, and the majority of the murals are heroic and positive, suggesting that "Americans would overcome existing challenges. History thus fulfilled the psychological need for stability and continuity."[28] Thus, according to Parisi, the past was prologue for understanding the path to modernization in Texas.

Meanwhile, Barker and Myers revealed that the art scene in Fort Worth remained staid and traditional through the 1930s compared to the developments in Dallas and in the rest of the country. Historiographically, the significance of this book is its finding that modernization was an evolving process in Texas. At least within the world of art, the authors contended, a necessary prerequisite for modernization was a shift in the type of art produced, again privileging the how over the when. By the World War II era, though, conditions had changed significantly in Cowtown with the artists who identified themselves as the Fort Worth Circle being "the state's first colony of artists to embrace and manifest a clearly nonregional aesthetic," putting their vision in direct contradiction with Bywaters and his followers. Because the artists in the Fort Worth Circle approached modernism from so many different perspectives—including as disparate forms as portraiture and abstraction—and with a host of mediums, suggests that these artists should not be viewed as a school but should be considered collectively for their shared views of what art should accomplish. By the mid-1950s, the Fort Worth Circle had been surpassed by the flourishing art scene in Houston, where modernist works were more unsentimental. While the authors showed how members of the Fort Worth Circle understood the wider world of art, this volume ultimately is more focused on the creation of art in Texas. As Barker and Myers conclude, "the Circle brought a cosmopolitan outlook to a local setting, marking a progressive turning point in Texas art history."[29]

The recent work on performing arts in modern Texas history falls into one of two categories: biography or exploration of a genre of music.[30] One of the more interesting of these books is *Texan Jazz* (1996) by Dave Oliphant.[31] A recovery project, Oliphant depicted for his readers why Texas jazz artists should be considered alongside the likes of those who hailed from New Orleans, New York, Los Angeles, Kansas City, and Chicago. Among the artists who can be traced back to Texas are Scott Joplin, Blind Lemon Jefferson, Jack Teagarden, and Ornette Coleman. Furthermore, most of the artists Oliphant discussed were African American. While Oliphant's narrative spanned the twentieth century and even dug back into the late nineteenth century to talk about artists like Joplin, much of his history unfolded in the 1930s. While arguing that Texans played an inordinate role in the evolution of each subgenre of jazz in each of its five major U.S. locations, he also acknowledged that there was no Texas center for jazz creativity. Ironically, or perhaps by necessity, Oliphant grouped the major parts of his book by the places to which Texas artists immigrated, showing how Texas and Texans crossed boundaries to merge with the rest of the nation. It is required reading for anyone interested in the cultural or racial history of how Texans have operated on a larger, regional or national stage.

World War II and the Modernization of Texas

For as many scholars who found elements of modernization in the 1930s, there are those more likely to lodge the locus for change in the 1940s. World War II was a crucial era in U.S. and Texas history. Within the Lone Star State, the global war secured the oil industry's dominant and determinant role in the state and national political economy. It also encouraged the first victories of the civil rights revolution. Finally, during the immediate postwar years, a rightward shift in state politics became obvious. These characteristics of Texas modernization have attracted much attention from scholars, who have used such trends to argue the 1940s were a significant moment of division in Texas history.

Of these examples, the developments in the oil industry are both the most significant and the most difficult to evaluate. Don E. Carleton, the director of the Center for American History at the University of Texas at Austin, has written a very smart, well-researched book about oilman J. R. Parten. This biography provided a reminder that individuals made history by crossing old boundaries, and certainly the modernization of Texas could not have happened without a diverse cast of forceful, colorful, and sometimes contradictory characters. Carleton's Parten is not a character from central casting but instead an aggressive businessman who also carved a place for himself in the world of public policy. In *A Breed So Rare* (1998), Carleton revealed the myriad ways Parten defied the stereotype of the conservative oilman. Carleton concluded that it was in the realm of public affairs, not business, where Parten made his historical reputation, helping to shape the nation's energy policy at midcentury when energy was key to the emergence of the American century.

Such policy views seemingly contradicted his politics. Carleton argued: "J. R. Parten was more than an influential businessman and public servant; his life of accomplishment and influence is also a study in apparent contradictions. He led his life against the grain, behaving in ways that transcended the expected. He was a wealthy Texas businessman with conservative economic views who remained to the end of his life a vocal advocate for liberal social principles."³² Within state and national politics, Parten inserted himself as a powerful antidote to the conservative forces that tried to take over the political economy in the postwar years. Parten's activities thus require a more complex historiographical understanding of mid-twentieth-century Texas, suggestive of actors with diverse ideological perspectives, goals, and understandings of what was meant by modernization.

The literature examining the intersection of race in Texas is as nuanced and mature as that on the oil industry and the state. Two scholars in particular, Neil Foley and Charles L. Zelden, have looked at issues of race and equality in Texas in the 1940s. Borderlands scholar Neil Foley wrote *The White Scourge* (1997), which treated the years between Reconstruction and the 1940s. Foley provided important context for understanding the midcentury transformations in the Lone Star State. Foley's book was historiographically important as it substantiated the argument that the modern era of Texas began with the war years.

In *The White Scourge,* Foley looked at the convergence of Anglos, African Americans, Mexican Americans, and Mexicans in central Texas cotton culture. He argued that by the 1940s, "Mexican identity, like whiteness itself, fissured along lines of class, nationality, language, and culture. Few of their immigrant parents identified themselves as whites; they were always mexicanos. Many middle class Texas Mexicans, however, were moving out of the ethnoracial borderlands between blackness and whiteness by constructing identities as Americans and embracing whiteness. The ethnoracial position of African Americans did not change substantially throughout this period."³³ This book nonetheless added further weight to the argument that the modern era of Texas history begins with the war years, not the Depression years. For Foley, the crux of modernization is not with business practices or political behavior but evolving concepts of racial identity. There was not substantial change regarding the latter until the war years to justify arguments for modernization.

Various aspects of the political struggle to end Jim Crow have received substantial attention.³⁴ Charles L. Zelden's recent offering, *The Battle for the Black Ballot* (2004), told the compelling story of Dr. Lonnie Smith, the Houston dentist who challenged the white primary in Texas. While the outlines of this civil rights victory in Texas political history are well known, Zelden revealed the litigation for *Smith v. Allwright* to be a significant turning point in the NAACP's struggle against segregation, and thus a historiographic foothold for studying the modernization of Texas. Put simply, the state could not claim that designation without ameliorating its past racial discrimination. In the introduction, Zelden contended, "Up to this point, most court victories, when they occurred, had little practical impact on the fight for equal rights.... Within a few years or so of the Supreme Court's 1944 decision, however, it was clear that *Smith* was different, and this difference heartened everyone associated with the fight for civil rights."[35] Thus, the Supreme Court decision in the *Smith* case provided still more evidence of why the mid-1940s are an important turning point in Texas history. Read this way, the Foley and the Zelden books are mutually reinforcing. They focus on the same decade as transformative but for very different reasons. In Foley's scholarship, the answer is found within individual identity formation, but for Zelden's work, the answer is a macroapplication of changed legal circumstances. Both are right.

The Postwar Political Economy and Society: From World War II through the Wars of Lyndon Johnson

The years between the mid-1940s and the late 1960s were dynamic in Texas. The state had claimed its place as modern, and historians who study Texas have recognized that fact. The tension in the historiography, then, became less about the coming of modernity and the crossing of boundaries between the state and the nation and more about what form modernity would take and how Texans would assert themselves as national leaders. These shifts became apparent in a range of otherwise disparate books that explore more aspects of the oil economy, football culture, Mexican American politics, the rise of conservatism, and Lyndon Johnson.

Joseph A. Pratt and Christopher J. Castaneda have been collaborating on a loosely drawn historical trilogy that tells the story of Brown & Root's important role in the political economy of the twentieth century. Their work is historiographically significant because the engineering and construction company, Brown & Root, mushroomed from its Texas origins to become an international player with tremendous impact on foreign policy from the 1960s through the early twenty-first century. Here, then, in the work of Pratt and Castaneda is a nuanced account of how a modern Texas came to exist within the national economic sphere and dominate one key component of it. Their first shared publishing venture in this effort was *From Texas to the East* (1993). Because it established the tone for the works that followed and because it, more than the other two, revealed how the war years changed the nature of economic life in Texas, it deserves in-depth consideration in this essay. Next, Pratt and Castaneda teamed with Tyler Priest to write *Offshore Pioneers: Brown & Root and the History of Offshore Oil and Gas* (1997).[36] Finally, in *Builders: Herman and George R. Brown* (1999), Pratt and Castaneda evaluate the careers of the

Houston-based brothers who established the preeminent construction company in the state.[37]

Despite the tremendous impact of Brown & Root, the Texas Eastern Corporation met with mixed success. When Pratt and Castaneda made this point, they suggested much that is historiographically significant about the years between 1945 and the late twentieth century. *From Texas to the East* detailed the history of the Texas Eastern Corporation from the 1940s through the late 1980s, when the Panhandle Eastern Corporation purchased it in 1989. From the late 1940s through the late 1960s, Texas Eastern Corporation was successful not only in the pipeline business, its major focus, but also in a host of subsidiary investments. Pratt and Castaneda noted that the oil shocks that began in the 1970s ultimately removed Texas Eastern Corporation's operating cushion and threatened the economic viability of the company. This factual evidence is suggestive of a larger historiographical point about recent Texas history and a crucial line of demarcation for subdividing the modern era of Texas history. Looked at from the perspective of energy history, not only is 1945 a key moment in the emergence of modern Texas, but also the 1970s are an equally crucial turning point in the redefinition of modernity in the state and the nation.

Pratt and Castaneda end their story with Texas Eastern Corporation's failure in the late 1980s. They write in the introduction that diversification within the energy industry "did not present serious difficulties as long as energy prices stayed high, but the collapse of oil prices in the mid-1980s undermined the company's short-term prosperity."[38] Their book, especially given its provocative beginning and ending moments, suggested that the process by which Texas modernized was directly linked to the history of the energy sector of the marketplace and the late twentieth-century crisis of capitalism.

Scholars working in other vineyards have reached similar conclusions about the arc of modernization but have attributed different causal factors to the process. Sport history is a growing and important subfield of the discipline. It would be impossible to understand modern Texas history without considering the role of sport.[39] Here is a topic that is vital to the lifeblood of the state, but is also one that transcends region. Here also is a topic that can wrongly yield itself to charges of parochialism no matter how the work is conceived just because of rivalries and biases about certain teams. Nonetheless, sports at all levels have come to play a dominant role in the social and cultural lives of Texans. The recent literature on sports in Texas suggests the richness of the topic, but much more work remains to be done both on individual topics in Texas sport history and on integrating this story with an understanding of modern Texas.

Perhaps the best recent book on sport in Texas at any level is Ty Cashion's *Pigskin Pulpit* (1998). Driven by theme, this book is also uniquely about the culture of place. Based on extensive oral history interviews with high school football coaches, *Pigskin Pulpit* argued that high school football became "one of the state's identifying institutions" in the twentieth century.[40] It achieved its dominant status because of early century modernizations, including infrastructure construction and school consolidation, and it ultimately faded in importance because of later modernizations, including urbanization and globalization of the Texas population. When future scholars try to synthesize the modern Texas story they will need to consider the ramifications of this point.

Cashion's work suggested the importance of the 1960s as a cultural division in modern Texas history. The coaches he has studied began their careers at the midcentury mark and coached at least through the 1960s. The upheavals of the 1960s remade the sport in Texas, reducing some of the authority coaches had over their charges, and ironically lessened its impact on the state in large part because of unrelated demographic shifts away from a rural culture toward an urban culture with a nonnative population. With the proliferation of activities for youth, the high school football coach lost more of his hegemony over young men in the state.

Just as with the petroleum economy and football culture, racial politics also experienced key transformations in the postwar years that speak to the modernization of Texas into the mainstream of American life. *Border Boss: Manuel B. Bravo and Zapata County* (1999), by J. Gilberto Quezada, is a model of how to construct a biography of a local political official and make an argument with regional and national thematic importance. Quezada's Bravo, who was a long-serving county judge and political boss from the late 1930s through the late 1950s, revealed the permutations to the all-important political boss system in South Texas. By understanding boss politics as geographically and historically driven, not racially driven, Quezada provided a more accurate reconstruction of Mexican American politics in South Texas and its regional centrality to the emergence of modern Texas. Put differently, by rejecting older scholarly constructs of a white or Anglo boss system, Quezada located Mexican American political integration earlier than some scholars. Indeed, Quezada contended that historians should adopt a more nuanced understanding of the political bosses who functioned along the Rio Grande in Texas. Previous scholars have understood such political developments as being racial in character, and George Parr, the boss of Duval County, was often incorrectly credited with control of the entire region. Quezada argued, "The Bravo story does much to bolster the case that bossism was rooted more in historical situations than anything inherent to ethnic culture. Unique circumstances in Zapata County helped promote and nurture this type of political governance. A major contributing cause of bossism was Zapata County's isolation from the hustle and bustle of South Texas social and economic activities."[41]

Quezada presented for his readers the story of an empowered and powerful Mexican American politician of a generation where too many historians assume that Anglos dominated the politics of the borderlands. In doing so, he also suggested that Bravo did not always use his power for the benefit of his Mexican American constituents. This more sophisticated reading of Bravo revealed a mature understanding of how politics functioned and moved beyond the binary of white, Anglo oppressors and, in this case, Mexican American victims, a finding that is new to the post-1988 literature and promised to inspire a more sophisticated historiography of both race and politics in modern Texas. While Bravo used his influence as a political boss to gain patronage and infrastructure improvements that otherwise would not have been available to such an isolated region, he also traded for favors with the oil companies and the large ranchers that operated in the region. Bravo's biography revealed how political history in the modern period of Texas history is less about elite white males than the standard story suggested. This historiographic finding is in keeping with the work of other scholars identified in this chapter, including McArthur and Smith. *Border Boss* is an excellent model for future historians wishing to explore the post-1945 inroads of minorities and women into the Texas political power structure.

Chandler Davidson, author of *Race and Class in Texas Politics* (1990), took as his problem the contention that political scientist V. O. Key Jr. made in his seminal book, *Southern Politics in State and Nation*, originally published in 1949: "The maintenance of southern Democratic solidarity has depended fundamentally on a willingness to subordinate to the race question all great social and economic issues that tend to divide people into opposing parties." Key argued that class-based politics would soon trump race-based politics in the South.[42] But Texas modernization did not follow Key's predictive model, and Davidson helped explain why.

Davidson mined the secondary literature on Texas politics to tell a familiar story with a fresh analysis. The weaknesses of the book rest with the lack of any archival research to test the standard, insufficiently studied story of midcentury politics and the perhaps naive assumption that were it not for the politics of race, Texas would have a much more liberal social welfare system. He posited this assumption on counterfactual reasoning: what if Texas was not one of the fifty states but was an independent nation. Using data from 1980, he then looked at the economic resources that Texas as a nation would enjoy and suggested that it would in terms of land mass, personal income, urban development, and oil production "be one of the major nations of the world."[43] Perhaps.

Using social science methodologies of the disciplines of sociology and political science, Davidson examined Texas political history from the late 1940s through the late 1980s. He advanced the provocative argument that race did not so much disappear as a political issue in Texas after the 1940s but that it assumed a new functionality. There had been a period of political calm during the 1930s, but animosity toward Franklin D. Roosevelt and the New Deal ushered in a new, vitriolic era of factionalism in Texas politics in the 1940s. He revealed the subtle, and perhaps more dangerous, racial political style of politicians such as Beauford Jester, Allan Shivers, Price Daniel, John Connally, Preston Smith, Dolph Briscoe, John Tower, and Bill Clements. For example, Tower, a Republican, had worked against civil rights within his party at least since the *Brown v. Board of Education* decision by the Supreme Court in 1954. Nor had the many conservative Democrats in Texas supported the national party on civil rights. These politicians, though, were not demagogic in the way of earlier Texas conservatives. Davidson correctly concluded: "V. O. Key's hoped-for realignment along economic cleavage planes did not occur. Instead, the spirit of the Old South reasserted itself to prove once more, if proof were needed, that racial hatreds die hard. Realignment did occur. Many white Texans at all socioeconomic levels moved toward the Republicans."[44] Davidson's book should be a clarion call for further scholarship on this crucial period, but the new work needs to draw on the rich archival sources and explore how the racialized politics of mid- and late twentieth-century Texas functioned in tandem with modernization. Were the two forces cooperative or contradictory?

Students more interested in state-level political leaders have had a big challenge in presenting their work as nuanced, thoughtful, and not parochial. To the sector of the historical profession that has prejudged state history as parochial there is perhaps nothing more parochial than state-level political history. Perhaps for that reason there has been less attention to governors and the history of politics in the state capital in recent years. Still, there has been some scholarly progress since 1988 in the study of modern Texas governors and leaders in the state house, and this work has not only helped debunk notions of state politics as parochial, but also has contributed to the scholarly conversation about Texas modernization.[45] The standard view of Texas governors is that they lacked very little real power, and while there is some constitutional truth to this assertion, some recent scholarship suggested how particularly charismatic governors can and have used the office to redirect the ideological compass of the state in the 1950s. Ricky F. Dobbs's biography of Allan Shivers, *Yellow Dogs and Republicans* (2005), was not only an important contribution to the history of modern Texas but also to twentieth-century U.S. political history. *Yellow Dogs and Republicans* provided a thoughtful contribution to the debate about the origins of modern conservatism, a political development directly related to the permutations modernity took in both Texas and the nation. While the emergence of conservatism was not a prerequisite for modernization, it became a key characteristic of what modernity looked like as it evolved in the state. More important, Texans were primary architects of conservatism on the national level, and this book will be a foundational study for unpackaging these late twentieth-century developments. Indeed, Dobbs's treatment of the early stages of conservatism in Texas was masterful and will influence future scholars who grapple with related problems.

In Dobbs's view, Shivers, who was governor of Texas between 1949 and 1957, led Texas and the South toward the Republican Party. He did so while making himself the "most powerful governor since Reconstruction" who was "the closest representation of a machine 'boss' in modern state politics." Although a Democrat, Shivers campaigned for Dwight D. Eisenhower in his two successful presidential races in 1952 and 1956. The political culture of Texas and the South as it existed at midcentury has become the political culture of the nation by century's end in that a conservative ideology of low taxes and inadequate public services dominated in both. In another important way, Shivers telescoped what would become, in slightly altered form, the featured strategy of conservative Republicans in the late twentieth and early twenty-first centuries: he used popular issues to distract voters—specifically the debate over who controlled the offshore Tidelands, and postwar anticommunism—while providing favorable treatment to business interests. Indeed, Dobbs concluded, "Shivers's reforms served primarily to humanize a business-dominated state government bent upon licensing rapacity."[46]

There has been a convergence of the major themes of Texas and American political history in the last seventy years of the twentieth century: the economic liberalism of the 1930s, the military capitalism of the 1940s, the uncomfortable but nascent conservatism of the postwar era, the contest over civil rights, and the conflicts between the cultures of liberalism and conservatism in the last three decades of the century. This historiographical point is subtly and sophisticatedly developed in the literature on Texans who served in Washington, D.C., and who were crucial actors in the process by which the Texas orbit and the national orbit merged. Indeed, careful consideration of political history generally and the Texans who served in Washington specifically will help answer the questions about how and why Texas modernized and crossed old boundaries into the national mainstream. Several good examples of this literature can be found in the biographies of Rep. Henry B. Gonzalez (2008) by Robert D. Auerbach, Rep. Wright Patman (2000) by me, and Sen. Ralph Yarborough (2001) by Patrick Cox.[47]

The most important Texan in Washington during these years was Lyndon Johnson. In the years since 1988, the literature on Johnson has both ballooned and matured, with more and more sources at the Lyndon B. Johnson Library in Austin, Texas, being opened for research.[48] Perhaps the most important development in Johnson scholarship has been the opening of the recordings of his White House telephone conversations.[49] This source ameliorates a major dilemma for Johnson-era scholars: the inability to find the authentic Johnson in textual documents.

Three of Johnson's biographers deserve extended consideration. In the last twenty years, Robert Caro remains a widely read and cited journalistic biographer, and he has published two more volumes in his multivolume study of Johnson, taking his subject through his career in the U.S. Senate. During the same time period, Robert Dallek produced a two-volume biography of Johnson that struck a more academic tone. Finally, Randall B. Woods recently published a one-volume, scholarly treatment of Johnson that is the only major biography to date to employ the telephone tapes in a meaningful fashion (Dallek used them selectively for his volume on the presidency).

Caro's book merits evaluation only because many nonspecialists regard him as definitive. In reality, his work has negative historiographical significance. Caro's Johnson biography is flawed, problematic, and replete with incorrect interpretations of Johnson. Nonetheless, Caro has acquired credence with not only the general public but also with too many historians. From that perspective, Caro requires analysis, not for what should be learned from his argument but what should be rejected. In contrast, the Johnson that emerged from the Dallek and Woods volumes suggested the centrality of understanding the role of Texans in Washington for the modernization of the state and the significant socioeconomic and political shifts that became apparent in the postwar years when Texas became more wealthy than poor, more urban than rural, and more conservative than liberal. Indeed, the policies of Johnson and other leading Texans in Washington, as revealed in the growing biographical literature, were central to this development.

The merger of Caro's journalistic, breezy writing style combined with his disparagement of Johnson has been attractive to academics and nonacademics alike who focus more on the contemptible aspects of Johnson's presidency, the Vietnam War, than either the positive or the debatable aspects of his administration, the civil rights reforms and the Great Society programs. Caro's Johnson became a cartoonish figure, always the villain juxtaposed against a heroic figure, Gov. Coke Stevenson, for example, in *Means of Ascent* (1990).[50] Put simply, Caro never let the facts stand in the way of telling a good story. In *Means of Ascent,* Caro explored the period after Johnson's defeat in a special U.S. senatorial election in 1941 through his victory in the 1948 U.S. Senate race. The entire book built to this climactic and close electoral victory for Johnson over Stevenson. Johnson was shown to be a Machiavellian politician with little or no core ethics, while Stevenson was painted as a personification of all that was good about Texas. This argument became Caro's negative historiographic contribution, and it must be abandoned because it presented a false picture of midcentury Texas politics, and it hindered any effort to understand significant changes at work in Texas and the nation for which Johnson was a principal architect. In reality, the truth of both Stevenson and Johnson was much more nuanced than Caro allowed. Stevenson was a racist, union-bating ideologue of the emerging conservative faction in the state's complex Democratic Party. At the same time, while Johnson could brutalize those who challenged him, the scholars who fail to understand that Johnson's ambition for his state and his nation was inextricably linked with his ambition for himself will never fully grasp his impact on Texas and the United States. In addition to large errors of interpretation, Caro also misused supporting evidence. Little that is presented as fact in Caro's works can or should be trusted as such without independent verification.

Caro's *Master of the Senate* (2002) was no better.[51] In this volume, he took on the twelve years that Johnson spent in the U.S. Senate. Here Caro found more to admire about Johnson, specifically his efforts to gain passage of civil rights legislation, but Caro's sympathy had its limits and was flawed by the continuation of problematic research methodologies found in his first two books about Johnson. In over a thousand pages, Caro made the passage of the 1957 Civil Rights Act the focal point of his story, slighting much of the important work Johnson did as a member of the U.S. Senate and as the majority leader of that body beginning in 1955. Furthermore, Caro never satisfactorily explained Johnson's meteoric rise in the Senate, which was occasioned by his ability to work equally well with the old guard southerners and the new generation of northern liberals. By turning the Johnson story into a rumination on good versus evil, in any case not a useful device for understanding the complexities of modern politics, and by remaining a popularly acclaimed biography of Johnson with invitations to speak on college campuses and before the public, Caro is a most problematic participant in the academic discourse about Lyndon Johnson. His simplistic and incorrect interpretations and his fraudulent research

249

methodologies have gained too wide a following, and in the process he has made it more not less difficult to understand the already complex Johnson.

Robert Dallek's two-volume biography of Johnson, *Lone Star Rising: Lyndon Johnson and His Times, 1908-1960* (1991) and *Flawed Giant: Lyndon Johnson and His Times, 1961-1973* (1998), will likely stand the test of time as the best multivolume account of the Johnson era in Texas and American history. Dallek is a thoughtful and talented historian who thoroughly researched his subject and allowed the sources to lead him to his conclusions as opposed to selectively using sources to prove a predetermined argument. If there are any major flaws in his work they rest with his use of earlier Johnson biographies about which he is critical, especially in the first volume, as a form of historical shorthand to advance his narrative.[52]

In *Lone Star Rising*, Dallek presented Johnson as a liberal nationalist, which he defined as unique for politicians from the South and the West in the 1930s. "Johnson's part in the nationalization of the South and the West or his conscious efforts to integrate the southern and western economies into the national life is a neglected piece of American history," Dallek argued. "Johnson saw the economic transformation of both sections as essential to their well-being." Dallek's concept of liberal nationalism was crucially important for understanding the end of Texas parochialism and exceptionalism and the beginning of the modern era in the Lone Star State, a new theme that emerged after 1988 and an important corrective to the work of Caro, who began publishing on Johnson before Dallek. Johnson for Dallek served as a major actor in the process of modernizing Texas and moving its political economy into alignment with the national political economy. Johnson more than anyone else was the central figure in changing the political and economic dynamic in Texas, and indeed from his earliest days in Congress Johnson became adept at using the state capitalism of the New Deal to shift Texas away from its historic position as a colonial economy of dependence and toward a diversified economy of independence. In the process, Dallek rejected previous amoral interpretations of Johnson's rightward shift during his House and Senate years and instead saw Johnson's political pragmatism as a necessary compromise for his electoral survival and the successful implementation of his liberal nationalism for the benefit of Texas, the South, the West, and the United States.[53]

Dallek's *Flawed Giant* is the concluding volume in his biography of Lyndon Johnson. In it, Dallek explained the juxtaposition of LBJ's tremendous successes in the domestic reform arena and his equally tremendous failures in the foreign policy arena. Regarding the former, Dallek took as his purpose the redemption of Johnson's political legacy. While finding much to admire about Johnson's Great Society, Dallek remained ambivalent about how his subject should be rated in comparison with other presidents. In the preface, Dallek acknowledged, "His contradictions—flaws and virtues, successes and failures—are on full display and will both enhance and detract from his historical reputation." This treatment of Johnson's presidency suggested that personality cannot be separated from politics. The debacle of Vietnam and the mixed longevity of Great Society programs—with civil rights remaking the political and social landscape of the nation but the War on Poverty fizzling because of the lack of a public commitment—can be traced to Johnson's unwillingness to explain to the American people the sacrifices necessary to win against communists in Vietnam and poverty at home.[54] This factual argument contributes to a larger historiographical point, that is, the shifting of direction within Texas (and the nation). Dallek implied correctly that Johnson's mixed record carried with it a significant legacy for public attitudes toward what a modern political economy should look like. The end of the Johnson era meant a shift away from the liberal political economy he fought so hard to implement.

For the purposes of this essay, though, the problem is as much one of determining how Johnson changed the way Texans thought about national politics. Certainly, Johnson remade the way Americans thought about things such as race relations, the environment, and health care. Dallek noted that while Johnson's solutions were flawed, never would the country be able to retreat back to a 1950s mindset regarding such domestic policy matters. *Flawed Giant* both challenged readers more than *Lone Star Rising* and left them feeling the need for closure. Indeed, Johnson's presidency is a complex topic that is difficult to grasp. Dallek hinted at his own incomplete solution to the riddle of Lyndon Johnson, arguing that "only one thing seems certain: Lyndon Johnson will not join the many obscure—almost nameless, faceless—Presidents whose terms of office register on most Americans as blank slates. He will not be forgotten."[55] Tragically, from Johnson's perspective, at least in Texas he has, as Ricky F. Dobbs noted in his essay described above. On a drive through the Texas Hill Country in the fall of 2008, I noticed far more signs of prosperity, and of Republican political allegiances to the McCain-Palin ticket, than Lyndon Johnson would appreciate. The transformation, though, was nothing if not a measure of the tremendous success of his years in Washington, D.C., for the rugged Hill Country would not have attracted such settlement without the midcentury federal programs of electrification and dam construction. Put simply, the political modernization of Texas also made possible its rightward political shift.

Randall Woods is much less ambivalent in his book *LBJ: Architect of American Ambition* (2006). His Johnson is much more altruistic and much less Machiavellian and manipulative than portraits of the thirty-sixth president in the other biographies that have been published. Woods credited Johnson's father and grandfather for instilling young Lyndon with a Populist's outrage about economic inequity in America. Indeed, it is no secret that Johnson's ambition as president was to surpass the liberal reforms of Franklin Roosevelt's New Deal. Woods contended that he did, vastly improving the lot in life for those Americans who were left untouched by the New Deal. Woods concluded his massive tome with a quote from the African American intellectual, Ralph Ellison, who explained that while conservatives and the liberal intelligentsia both disdained LBJ, Johnson would "have to settle for being recognized as the greatest American President for the poor and for the Negroes, but that, as I see it, is a very great honor indeed."[56] Thus, to understand Woods's Johnson is to understand the Texas in which he was born and raised. It was that Texas that shaped Johnson's politics. Those politicians, as explored in the fine books by Dallek and Woods, though, so changed Texas that citizens of the state were no longer intersected in the liberal nationalism Johnson developed and perfected, which was perhaps his biggest tragedy.

Post-1970: Recent Texas Historiography

Modern Texas underwent another slow transformation in the 1970s, and scholars are just beginning to identify these important developments. A preliminary but foundational literature has emerged, and it provides a rough definition of recent Texas historiography. Ideologically more conservative, the period nonetheless was characterized by further civil rights integration and a new level of identity politics among ethnic minorities in the state. The nascent scholarship on the Bush era is another important development. This period, not surprisingly given its proximity to the present, is not yet well developed.

The politics of desegregation, a topic that both suggests one aspect of modernization and perhaps the key manner in which Texans challenged the parochialism of their state, has attracted much scholarly attention in the last two decades with most of the work focused on the issue in the public school system. Desegregation was a crucial component of modernization in Texas and merging the state within the national mainstream. Given the racial and ethnic dynamics of the Texas population, the story of desegregation was not just about African Americans but also Mexican Americans. Especially those who study Chicano/a activism have led national historiographical trends in attempting to paint a more complex picture of racial integration. Indeed, the racial and ethnic diversity of Texas has meant that the scholarship on desegregation has not just been about the black-white binary but has also explored the impact of segregation on Tejanos and Latinos and the effort to end same. In this way, the historiography of desegregation in Texas is more advanced and sophisticated than what is commonly found in treatments of the topic located elsewhere in the United States.[57]

Guadalupe San Miguel Jr. has written one of the best books on the struggle to remedy segregation's impact on Mexican Americans. In *Brown, Not White* (2001), San Miguel explores the juxtaposition of the school integration movement and Chicano activism in Houston. Selecting Houston for this study was a wise decision, for the city has the largest Mexican-descent population of any city in Texas, and outside of Atlanta it has the largest African American population in the South. The most important contribution of this book to understanding the themes of modern Texas history is its contention that there was a decided shift in outlook within the community away from the older political, cultural, and social priorities of the Mexican American generation toward the preferences of the Chicano generation. The time period for this shift, the 1970s, demanded that scholars consider whether or not the 1970s be viewed as a breaking point for Texas history as a whole. Using evidence of generational division regarding civil rights issues, San Miguel made a strong argument that an important shift in political identity was underway in the early 1970s. Indeed, his findings suggested that a new era dawned in Texas in those years.[58]

A number of scholars have explored Latino/a politics.[59] In *United We Win* (1989), Ignacio M. García examined La Raza Unida Party, a significant component of the Chicano Movement of the 1960s and 1970s.[60] This account of La Raza suggested another transformative moment in modern Texas history. While not as dramatic as the impact of World War II on Texas, the turmoil of the civil rights era refashioned both political and social divisions in the Lone Star State. The Democratic Party became decidedly more liberal during this era, in part responding to the demands of social protesters in the civil rights movement, the women's rights movement, and the Chicano movement and in part the result of realigning processes within state politics. Regarding the latter, moderates and liberals were taking over the machinery of the Democratic Party, arguing that in a competitive, two-party system if the conservatives who had dominated midcentury state politics moved over to the Republican Party a liberal ideology would prevail. The events depicted in *United We Win* were just one piece of this much more complicated story and like San Miguel's study suggested why the 1970s was another important turning point in the long story of Texas modernization.

Standing in juxtaposition to the new contentiousness of Chicano/a activism is the other major historiographical development about recent Texas history topics: examination of the Bush political dynasty. The Texas of the other two presidents hailing from the Lone Star State was a very different place, and the nascent scholarship on George H. W. Bush and George W. Bush recognized this point. Ironically, more has been written about George W. Bush than George H. W. Bush. The books that treat the younger Bush are almost without exception partisan efforts to address the tumultuous politics of the early twenty-first century. These accounts will no doubt be useful to future scholars of the forty-third president as sources reflective of the political milieu of his term, but they cannot function as scholarship because they do not bring academic judgment and distance to their treatment of the topic.[61]

Work on the older Bush is less vitriolic and divisive by contrast, and there have been a few thoughtful treatments to emerge.[62] The best book yet that considers Bush 41 in and out of Texas is *George Bush: The Life of a Lone Star Yankee* (1997), by Herbert S. Parmet. The early career of the elder Bush merged the midcentury political and economic transformation of the state with the late century rise of conservatism in Texas. Just as with the culture of deprivation and liberal nationalism from which Johnson emerged earlier in the century, Bush identified early on with the postwar political changes in Texas, and his conservatism, as Parmet showed, was the result of such developments. In this narrative biography, Parmet is largely sensitive to his subject, debunking the most common myth about Bush, namely, that he was a wimp. Parmet's biography, though, does not solve the other major charge against Bush 41, that is, that he held few political convictions but instead yielded to the prevailing political currents to advance his career. Parmet provided further evidence to sustain this characterization, namely, Bush's retreat from his 1988 campaign promise not to raise taxes. In the end, Parmet's sympathy ran headlong into his evidence of Bush's presidency. This dilemma is to be expected given the nature of the forty-first president's administration. Parmet's book is a helpful academic introduction to George H. W. Bush, but likely not the final word.[63] Nonetheless, this charitable account of the political ambivalence Bush practiced is crucial to the historiographical understanding of how Texans in Washington, increasingly the centerpiece of modernity in Texas, had changed by the late twentieth century from the expansiveness of the Johnsonian era. In this way Parmet made an important initial point about the historiographic development of what post-1970s Texas political history looked like.

The younger Bush's Texas is a mutation of the one his father populated as a young man. By the dawn of the twenty-first century, Texas was even more a polyglot society with a highly diversified postindustrial economy, at least in its urban environs, but it also retained notions of the expansive mentality that has threaded throughout its history. By the early twenty-first century, that expansiveness had been merged with a sometimes obnoxious bombast (at least to the ears of those living elsewhere in the world). Work on the two Bushes is in its infancy, especially the younger Bush. The overwhelming bulk of the material is either journalistic, partisan, or memoir. There has been little that is thoughtful, reflective, or scholarly.

So far the best work that considers Bush 43 at least in part within the context of Texas is actually a longitudinal study of the Bush family's role in American politics. Written by Kevin Phillips, *American Dynasty* (2004) is a critical, sometimes polemical account of what the author saw as a lust for power that has driven four generations of the Bush family. The presentation of the topic in this fashion mixes the realities of East Coast politics at midcentury with Texas politics from that period to the present to understand some macrotrends in national politics, namely, the rise of the dynastic presidency, a development that Phillips decried as dangerous for American democracy. He saw the Bush version of political dynasty as the most dangerous to appear in the United States, not the Kennedys (John F., Robert, and Edward) or the Adamses (John and John Quincy), the Harrisons (William Henry and Benjamin), or the Roosevelts (Theodore and Franklin D.). Phillips contended that the Bush family behavior was just the most obvious of a larger American pattern at the turn of the twenty-first century, citing eight U.S. senators with relatives who had previously held prominent political office. Despite Phillips's best efforts, *American Dynasty* is less a historical biography that will stand the test of time and more a judicious contemporary affairs book timed according to the quadrennial cycle of presidential elections. There are too many overly broad comparisons across time for historians to be entirely comfortable with this book.

Still, at the earliest stages of scholarship on the Bushes and Texas, the Phillips book will hold value until historians provide a critical account of the origins and impact of Bush 41 and Bush 43. Phillips rooted the rise of the Bush family squarely in the postwar Texas political and economic culture, contending, "Texas residence imbued its own Middle Eastern focus. Oil-fixated Houston and Midland were much closer psychologically to Saudi Arabia and the Persian Gulf than other parts of the United States were. At the postwar center of the global petroleum industry, Texas had already begun luring Arabs and Iranians during the 1960s."[64] Phillips found a dangerous parallel between the business cronyism practiced in the Bush family with the political cronyism practiced in the Bush 43 White House. His often sweeping generalizations will await the rigorous testing of future scholars interested in this momentous juncture in history, but for now Phillips's arguments provided a point of departure for understanding what very well might prove itself as another crucial generational divide in the understanding of the historiography of modern Texas.

Place and Modernization

Perhaps a consideration of place is the most appropriate manner to conclude the evaluation of the literature about recent Texas history. Here the problem comes full circle with the question of whether geography—place—still matters, overlapping those works that contend directly or at least suggest implicitly that it does. Several questions bear consideration. What is the meaning of place and its importance when studying a state's history, especially a state as diverse as Texas? Does this question change as the history of Texas changes? In other words, should the concept of place hold the same significance for understanding modern Texas history as it has for understanding earlier periods of Texas history? Finally, do the decline of Texas exceptionalism and the rise of Texas modernization in recent American history render consideration of place unimportant for analysis of the Texas topics? These are difficult and divisive questions that beg attention. Several recent books about place in Texas help to frame these questions. Those that merit significant attention have either focused on the urban evolution of Texas or its fading rural identity. Other studies of place have looked at institutions ranging from colleges and universities to medical facilities and to the San Antonio River Walk and even the Fort Worth Stockyards and the Southwestern Exposition and Livestock Show. Put simply, the subject of place produced much innovative scholarship.[65]

A few scholars have looked at architecture as place in the recent history of Texas. Jay C. Henry's *Architecture in Texas: 1895–1945* (1993) touched only the first seven years of the period considered by this essay, but students of modern Texas will nonetheless be interested in this work because it suggested that the urban strivings of Texas builders predated the more recognized period of modernization in the state. Still, the encyclopedic style of writing gave the author little time to evaluate and understand some of the more significant structures completed in Texas in the first half of the twentieth century.[66]

Texas' largest cities have become laboratories for much innovative, new scholarship. Efforts to understand Houston's history have led authors to a diverse array of topics from religion to the environment and energy to the police and race.[67] In *Energy Metropolis* (2007), University of Houston historians Martin V. Melosi and Joseph A. Pratt have produced a provocative collection of essays that tell of the intersection between energy and environmental history in Houston, Texas, and the Gulf Coast region. The essays range widely, treating a host of topics: the Houston Ship Channel, ozone pollution, air conditioning, sanitation, freeways, deforestation, the relationship between Houston and Galveston, race, environmental justice and activism, and superfund sites. In their introduction, Melosi and Pratt argued, "Yet despite the Houston area's capacity to 'absorb' the oil industry, using its oil wealth to sustain long-term economic growth, one significant part of the 'curse of oil-led development' around the world proved most difficult: the management of the environmental impacts of the production and use of petroleum."[68]

Taken together the topics described and evaluated in *Energy Metropolis* reflect an important truth about environmental history, that is, the centrality of place to the study of man's interaction with nature. Indeed, the manner in which the volume's contributors conceptualized place, and the fact that their evidence and analysis ranged across much of the twentieth century, suggest that the location in which events took place cannot be separated from the historical, and the historiographical, analysis to be derived from such evidence. *Energy Metropolis* is compelling in another way central to the problem of this essay, that is, the question of what modernization meant for Texas and how that process should be understood. Studies of environmentalism gave different meanings to what was meant by modernization in that scholars working in this field of history do not necessarily tell a celebratory story.

Indeed, the contributors to this volume paint a decidedly mixed picture of modernization's meanings for Houston. Robert S. Thompson revealed that "access to air-conditioning became a leading indicator of which people were the winners and losers in Houston's cycle of growth, and most of those at the bottom remained in the city's economically forgotten neighborhoods."[69] Similarly, Tom Watson McKinney noted contradictory results of the construction of the Gulf Freeway—growth along its corridor and increased air pollution. Elizabeth D. Blum found a long-standing history of African American female involvement in the environmental justice movement, and she suggested a much more complex understanding of the movement, typically understood to originate in the 1980s and to be at odds with a more elitist environmental movement supposedly not interested in the intersection of race, class, and gender with the problem of pollution. Taken together, the essays in this volume offer a rich and layered history of important concepts not typically incorporated into the mainstream of Texas history but that contend modernization sometimes was a problematic development.

Other scholars have studied topics related to the history of Dallas.[70] Just as with Houston, the scholarship about Dallas ranged across a host of fields, including race and religion. For the purposes of this essay, Robert M. Fairbanks's book, *For the City as a Whole* (1998), deserves special attention. Fairbanks has examined twentieth-century politics and urban planning, using Dallas as case study, because it is representative of how southern and western cities used these concepts to abet faster growth, a trend important to twentieth-century modernization. Fairbanks explored the first half of the twentieth century when urban thinkers and planners still considered the "city as a whole" rather than later twentieth-century trends toward breaking analysis of cities into their constituent parts. He found the decline of "city as a whole" thinking about urban problems to be in the 1950s, not the 1960s as most urban historians contend. While he saw civil rights activism of the 1960s as important to this process, he also argued that in the case of Dallas the far right-wing politics of the 1950s negated support for the boosterism of earlier in the century.

Fairbanks found that between the crucial decades of the 1920s and the 1950s, Dallas leaders were primarily civic boosters and not southerners or westerners, or perhaps even Texans. An urban ethos, not a regional ethos, shaped the decisions about how to run the city in the first half of the century. He located the opposition of the business community to the Ku Klux Klan in the 1920s and its support, thirty years later, for court rulings demanding integration of the school system. In both cases, he argued that while the leaders certainly shared the racist belief system of many white Texans they were more committed to advancing the reputation of Dallas nationally.

At first glance the chronology of this book might suggest backdating the modern era in Texas history. Instead, *For the City as a Whole* can better be used to justify the war years as the point at which modern Texas emerged. The years between the 1920s and the early 1940s should be seen as period of preparation for the rise of Dallas in the years after World War II. Fairbanks argued, "Dallas in 1960 seemed a very different place than the Dallas that planning and political activists sought to tame in 1930. . . . The automobile, now established as the dominant mode of transportation in Dallas, helped reshape spatial relationships throughout the city and between city and suburb. The postwar central business district's building boom also completely refashioned the downtown area, as significant population shifts in the city's residential sections altered the social geography of the city."[71] Dallas and Houston have not been the only Texas cities and suburban areas to gain critical analysis. There have also been thoughtful studies of Amarillo, Austin, Fort Worth, Galveston, San Antonio, and Williamson County.[72]

Scholars looking at the South as a whole have contended that there is a strong linkage between place and politics, specifically with regard to the rise of modern conservatism. Studies of southern suburbs have shown a decided correlation between suburbanization and the rise of the Republican Party in the South.[73] As yet, there is not much of a historiography exploring Texas suburbs. Linda Scarbrough's *Road, River, and Ol' Boy Politics: A Texas County's Path from Farm to Supersuburb* (2005) is an exception. She evaluates the transformation of Williamson County in the last half of the twentieth century from rural, agrarian, and Democratic to suburban, high-tech, and Republican. Local politicians, she demonstrates, secured this form of modernization by federal public works projects to the county, an interstate highway and a dam. Her book is a cautionary tale about the impact of modernization on the environment.

"After World War II, as a deluge of new dams, pipelines, and canals concentrated water in certain portions of the nation's arid zones, and interstate highways linked formerly isolated 'oasis' cities, hypergrowth followed," according to Scarbrough. She disputes the assumed historiographic wisdom that the credit or fault for such developments belongs with national politicians and Washington, D.C. bureaucrats but instead with "local 'bosses'— savvy rural leaders—in places like Williamson County who conceived many of the projects." Arguing that the recipients of this federal largesse abandoned "their agricultural identities and became suburban megalopolises on a scale never before contemplated."[74] No wonder such economic and cultural developments remade the places where they were located and the politics that dominated those locales.

Other recent students of place in Texas have gravitated toward the more traditional and stereotypical notions of rural place. For most of its history, Texas has been identified as rural, either the plantation economy of cotton and slavery that was transplanted to East Texas in the middle nineteenth century or the frontier of western expansion. During the twentieth century this identity shifted in fact, but not necessarily in the minds of Texans. In the past few decades, though, scholars have reconceptualized the notion of place in Texas to fit the reality of most Texans, the urban world. As such, there has been less such work on rural topics. In *Nameless Towns* (1998), Thad Sitton and James H. Conrad explored the intricacies of Texas sawmill towns from the late nineteenth century through the early 1940s. Like so many other works that encompass several decades before 1930, this volume showed the essential continuity between the late nineteenth century and the World War II era, when the nature of the timber industry in East Texas changed. Although others, namely Robert S. Maxwell and Robert D. Baker in *Sawdust Empire* (1983), had written about the timber industry, Sitton and Conrad contended that none had followed the social historian's edict to explain how average people lived their lives in this universe.[75]

Sitton and Conrad have focused on the towns that were part of the Kirby Lumber Company empire simply because there were more records available for these communities. They explain that the sawmills drew their workers from local agriculture, including poor whites, African Americans, and Mexican Americans. The multiracial workforce was managed in a hierarchical fashion that paralleled the racial ideology of Jim Crow Texas, a structure that was possible before Texas modernized, but less so after the midcentury modernization and integration of the state into the national mainstream. Sitton and Conrad provided a finely drawn assessment of the feudalistic company policies that governed workers in and out of the mill.[76]

Sitton and Conrad's description and analysis of the "cut and get out" policies, predicated on cheap labor and little capital investment, revealed that the Great Depression hastened the demise of this phase of the timber industry in East Texas, and by the early 1940s the timber industry had evolved toward management of perpetual forests. The latter survived while the "cut and get out" operators did not. Heavy on the use of oral history and memoirs as evidence, *Nameless Towns* helped scholars understand the impact of place on the emergence of modern Texas. Texas cannot be considered modern as long as the economic and social functionality of place continued to be conceived in late nineteenth- early twentieth-century fashion. The transformation in the timber industry that came in the 1940s, then, was another marker in the emergence of modern Texas, and in the changing conception of place in studies of the state.

Another of the books about place is *The Story of Big Bend National Park* (1996). Big Bend was the first national park carved from Texas territory. Its inclusion in the National Park Service followed a unique path dictated by the absence of any federal land in Texas. In his case study of the park, John Jameson detailed the history of the region from the earliest efforts in the late nineteenth century to establish a park through the late twentieth century. His story should be of interest not only to environmental and public historians but also to political historians, scholars of U.S.-Mexican relations, and social and cultural historians interested in the leisure pursuits of Americans. Well researched, this book is as much an extended and thoughtful park manual as a work of scholarship.

Jameson's discussion in his conclusion of the park's problems in the late twentieth century encapsulated the major issues for modern Texas historians regardless of their focus—drug smuggling, increased air pollution, the passage of NAFTA, rising crime rates—and suggested the degree to which even rural topics have gained a focus that transcended state and even national boundaries. For Big Bend, Jameson contended, the challenges go to the heart of the park's survival, which he concludes will "reveal much about the human species' values, quality of life, and ability to adapt and survive in a global community."[77] Ultimately though, the contributions of this book to the project of understanding in more nuanced ways the tensions between parochialism and modernization in recent Texas history are implicit and not explicit. Jameson did not intend his case study as a substantive, analytical tome but more an academic paean to a national park for which he has much admiration.

Conclusion

As the books evaluated in this essay suggest, the story of twentieth-century Texas parallels the story of twentieth-century America in that the forces of modernization have produced a multiplicity of threads that need to be untangled. Unlike nineteenth-century U.S. and Texas history, there is less of the grand narrative in twentieth-century U.S. and Texas history and more of a competition among subfields for being understood as the central or driving force that explains the century as a whole. A significant point to remember is that while scholars have offered a range of different explanations and arguments for how, when, and why Texas modernized, there has been little in the way of historiographical arguments among subfields.

As such, it is too much to expect consensus regarding the major chronological divisions in the modern period of Texas history. Instead different fields, suggest different chronologies and thus different perspectives on when, how, and why Texas modernized as well as whether modernization was positive or negative. Still, at this juncture in the historiographic development of recent Texas history it is possible to discern several key turning points. Some scholars have found ample evidence of modernization by the early 1930s, but because enough other scholars do not locate such transformations until the war years or later, it makes sense to consider the 1890s through the mid-1940s as a period of protomodernization. With the Second World War wholesale changes to the Texas economy, political culture, and race relations became apparent. Other shifts, most notably in race relations, the economy, and politics, became apparent in the late 1960s and early 1970s. Until the scholarship on Texas modernization reaches maturity, though, the fuzzy definition of chronological dividing points will likely remain true.

The agenda for the next generation of scholars is threefold. First, more work needs to be done in each of the areas described above. Second, there are other significant topics that have been almost wholly ignored that future scholars of Texas should address: for example, post-1965 immigration and the changed demographic identity of the state; globalization of the Texas economy;

and the emergence of Texas as an international center of space, technological, and medical research. Work on these and other topics promises to make the understanding of modernization—its timeline, its sources, and its consequences—even more nuanced. Finally, scholars need to develop synthetic works about the modern era in Texas history. While addressing these challenges the scholars who work on Texas topics, though, still face the problem of parochialism common to any state historian, not just those who study Texas, who writes books that do not address larger regional or national issues.

Historians working in the last two decades have produced a body of scholarship that has moved the field away from the old parochialism of the Texas traditionalists who wrote celebratory books about the nineteenth century. Instead, Texas historians working on modernization have taken leadership roles in certain fields—especially Chicano/a history—and have demonstrated how Texas and Texans in Washington have led in the analysis of modernization in the United States. If the historiography of Texas modernization is to mature, scholars working on such topics need to continue in the vein of solid, analytical work that foregrounds topic over place (unless place is central to the topic) and further merges the Texas of the twentieth century with the nation. Texas historians need to take note of the trend toward globalizing U.S. history and make similar connections regarding state and local topics with the national and international story. If these challenges are not met, the literature will again stagnate, much like the celebratory and parochial literature of past generations. For the historiography of any given subject to thrive it must continually be prodded and challenged to move beyond accepted wisdoms to new visions.

Notes

1. Oxford English Dictionary, at http://dictionary.oed.com.

2. Walter L. Buenger and Robert A. Calvert, eds., *Texas Through Time: Evolving Interpretations* (College Station: Texas A&M University Press, 1991).

3. Buenger and Calvert, *Texas Through Time.*

4. Walter L. Buenger, *The Path to a Modern South: Northeast Texas between Reconstruction and the Great Depression* (Austin: University of Texas Press, 2001), xvii.

5. Patrick Cox, *The First Texas News Barons* (Austin: University of Texas Press, 2005), 6–7.

6. See, for example, Lawrence Goodwyn, *Texas Oil, American Dreams: A Study of the Texas Independent Producers and Royalty Owners Association* (Austin: Published for the Center for American History by the Texas State Historical Association, 1996);

Don Woodard, *Black Diamonds! Black Gold! The Saga of Texas Pacific Coal and Oil Company* (Lubbock: Texas Tech University Press, 1998).

7. Diana Davids Olien and Roger M. Olien, *Oil in Texas: The Gusher Age, 1895–1945* (Austin: University of Texas Press, 2002), vii.

8. William R. Childs, *The Texas Railroad Commission: Understanding Regulation in America to the Mid-Twentieth Century* (College Station: Texas A&M University Press, 2005), 4.

9. Childs, *Texas Railroad Commission,* 146.

10. James L. Haley, *Texas: From Spindletop through World War II* (New York: St. Martin's Press, 1993), xi.

11. See, for example, Richard R. Flores, "Memory-Place, Meaning, and the Alamo," *American Literary History* 10 (Fall 1998): 428–45; Holly Beachley Brear, *Inherit the Alamo: Myth and Ritual at an American Shrine* (Austin: University of Texas Press, 1995); Buenger, *The Path to a Modern South.*

12. Gregg Cantrell and Elizabeth Hayes Turner, eds., *Lone Star Pasts: Memory and History in Texas* (College Station: Texas A&M University Press, 2007), 166.

13. *Lone Star Pasts,* ed. Cantrell and Turner, 221, 227.

14. Kyle G. Wilkison, *Yeomen, Sharecroppers, and Socialists: Plain Folk Protest in Texas, 1870–1914* (College Station: Texas A&M University Press, 2008), 209.

15. Nancy Beck Young, *Wright Patman: Populism, Liberalism, and the American Dream* (Dallas: Southern Methodist University Press, 2000), 304–305.

16. Richard Schroeder, *Texas Signs On: The Early Days of Radio and Television* (College Station: Texas A&M University Press, 1998), xii.

17. Two pertinent examples of the former are Sarah T. Phillips, *This Land, This Nation: Conservation, Rural America, and the New Deal* (New York: Cambridge University Press, 2007); and Jason Scott Smith, *Building New Deal Liberalism: The Political Economy of Public Works, 1933–1956* (New York: Cambridge University Press, 2006).

18. Keith J. Volanto, *Texas, Cotton, and the New Deal* (College Station: Texas A&M University Press, 2005), xiii.

19. Volanto, *Texas, Cotton, and the New Deal,* xiv.

20. John A. Adams Jr., *Damming the Colorado: The Rise of the Lower Colorado River Authority, 1933–1939* (College Station: Texas A&M University Press, 1990), xvii.

21. Adams, *Damming the Colorado,* 112.

22. James Wright Steely, *Parks for Texas: Enduring Landscapes of the New Deal* (Austin: University of Texas Press, 1999).

23. See, for example, Ann Fears Crawford, *Frankie: Mrs. R. D. Randolph and Texas Liberal Politics* (Austin: Eakin Press, 2000); Ignacio M. García, *Hector P. García: In Relentless Pursuit of Justice* (Houston: Arte Público Press, 2002); Thomas H. Kreneck, *Mexican American Odyssey: Felix Tijerina, Entrepreneur and Civil Leader, 1905–1965* (College Station: Texas A&M University Press, 2001); Merline Pitre, *In Struggle against Jim Crow: Lulu B. White and the NAACP, 1900–1957* (College Station: Texas A&M University Press, 1999).

24. Judith N. McArthur and Harold L. Smith, *Minnie Fisher Cunningham: A Suffragist's Life in Politics* (New York: Oxford University Press, 2003), 6.

25. Robert M. Utley, *Lone Star Justice: The First Century of the Texas Rangers* (New York: Oxford University Press, 2002), 337–38.

26. Francine Carraro, *Jerry Bywaters: A Life in Art* (Austin: University of Texas Press, 1994), xv.

27. Carraro, *Jerry Bywaters,* 75–76.

28. Philip Parisi, *The Texas Post Office Murals: Art for the People* (College Station: Texas A&M University Press, 2004), 3, 8.

29. Scott Grant Barker and Jane Myers, *Intimate Modernism: Fort Worth Circle Artists in the 1940s* (Fort Worth, Tex.: Amon Carter Museum, 2008), 11, 66.

30. Joe Carr and Alan Munde, *Prairie Nights to Neon Lights: The Story of Country Music in West Texas* (Lubbock: Texas Tech University Press, 1995); John Mark Dempsey, *The Light Crust Doughboys Are on the Air: Celebrating Seventy Years of Texas Music* (Denton: University of North Texas Press, 2002); Robert Earl Hardy, *A Deeper Blue: The Life and Music of Townes Van Zandt* (Denton: University of North Texas Press, 2008); Dave Oliphant, *Texan Jazz* (Austin: University of Texas Press, 1996); Bill O'Neal, *Tex Ritter: American's Most Beloved Cowboy* (Austin: Eakin Press, 1998); Joe Nick Patoski, *Willie Nelson: An Epic Life* (New York: Little, Brown, 2008); Ronnie Pugh, *Ernest Tubb: The Texas Troubadour* (Durham, N.C.: Duke University Press, 1996); Guadalupe San Miguel, *Tejano Proud: Tex Mex Music in the Twentieth Century* (College Station: Texas A&M University Press, 2002); Richard Schroeder, *Lone Star Picture Shows* (College Station: Texas A&M University Press, 2001); Robert Uzzel, *Blind Lemon Jefferson: His Life, His Death, and His Legacy* (Austin: Eakin Press, 2002).

31. Oliphant, *Texan Jazz,* 4–5.

32. Don E. Carleton, *A Breed So Rare: The Life of J. R. Parten, Liberal Texas Oil Man, 1896–1992* (Austin: Texas State Historical Association Press, 1998), 571.

33. Neil Foley, *The White Scourge: Mexicans, Blacks, and Poor Whites in Texas Cotton Culture* (Berkeley: University of California Press, 1997), 211.

34. See, for example, Darlene Clark Hine, *Black Victory: The Rise and Fall of the White Primary in Texas,* new ed. (Columbia: University of Missouri Press, 2003).

35. Charles L. Zelden, *The Battle for the Black Ballot:* Smith v. Allwright *and the Defeat of the Texas All-White Primary* (Lawrence: University Press of Kansas, 2004), 3–4.

36. Joseph A. Pratt, Tyler Priest, and Christopher J. Castaneda, *Offshore Pioneers: Brown and Root and the History of Offshore Oil and Gas* (Houston: Gulf Publishing, 1997).

37. Joseph A. Pratt and Christopher J. Castaneda, *Builders: Herman and George R. Brown* (College Station: Texas A&M University Press, 1999).

38. Christopher J. Castaneda and Joseph A. Pratt, *From Texas to the East: A Strategic History of Texas Eastern Corporation* (College Station: Texas A&M University Press, 1993), 10.

39. Among the sport history books written about Texas since 1988, see Susan E. Cayleff, *Babe: The Life and Legend of Babe Didrikson Zaharias* (Urbana: University of Illinois Press, 1995); Jeff Guinn with Bobby Bragan, *When Panthers Roared: The Fort Worth Cats and Minor League Baseball* (Fort Worth: Texas Christian University Press, 1999); and Tom Kayser and David King, *Baseball in the Lone Star State: The Texas League's Greatest Hits* (San Antonio: Trinity University Press, 2005).

40. Ty Cashion, *Pigskin Pulpit: A Social History of Texas High School Football Coaches* (Austin: Texas State Historical Association, 1998), 1.

41. J. Gilberto Quezada, *Border Boss: Manuel B. Bravo and Zapata County* (College Station: Texas A&M University Press, 1999), 220.

42. V. O. Key Jr. with the assistance of Alexander Heard, *Southern Politics in State and Nation*, new ed. (Knoxville: University of Tennessee Press, 1984), 315–16.

43. Chandler Davidson, *Race and Class in Texas Politics* (Princeton, N.J.: Princeton University Press, 1990), xv.

44. Davidson, *Race and Class in Texas Politics*, 239.

45. There are a few books worth noting on Texas governors, gubernatorial candidates, and state political leaders. See, for example, Carolyn Barta, *Bill Clements: Texian to His Toenails* (Austin: Eakin Press, 1996); Mike Cochran, *Claytie: The Roller-Coaster Life of a Texas Wildcatter* (College Station: Texas A&M University Press, 2007); Bill Crawford, *Please Pass the Biscuits, Pappy: Pictures of Governor W. Lee "Pappy" O'Daniel* (Austin: University of Texas Press, 2004); Kenneth B. Hendrickson Jr., *The Chief Executives of Texas: From Stephen F. Austin to John B. Connally Jr.* (College Station: Texas A&M University Press, 1995); Mickey Herskowitz, *Sharpstown Revisited: Frank Sharp and a Tale of Dirty Politics in Texas* (Austin: Eakin Press, 1994); Nancy Baker Jones and Ruthe Winegarten, *Capitol Women: Texas Female Legislators, 1923–1999* (Austin: University of Texas Press, 2000); Kenneth Kesselus, *Alvin Wirtz: The Senator, LBJ, and LCRA* (Austin: Eakin Press, 2005); Dave McNeely and Jim Henderson, *Bob Bullock: God Bless Texas* (Austin: University of Texas Press, 2008); May Nelson Paulissen and Carl McQueary, *Miriam: The Southern Belle Who Became the First Woman Governor of Texas* (Austin: Eakin Press, 1995); David Richards, *Once upon a Time in Texas: A Liberal in the Lone Star State* (Austin: University of Texas Press, 2002); Sue Tolleson-Rinehart and Jeanie R. Stanley, *Claytie and the Lady: Ann Richards, Gender, and Politics in Texas* (Austin: University of Texas Press, 1994).

46. Ricky F. Dobbs, *Yellow Dogs and Republicans: Allan Shivers and Two-Party Texas Politics* (College Station: Texas A&M University Press, 2005), 148, 149.

47. See Robert D. Auerbach, *Deception and Abuse at the Fed: Henry B. Gonzalez Battles Alan Greenspan's Bank* (Austin: University of Texas Press, 2008); Patrick Cox, *Ralph Yarborough: The People's Senator* (Austin: University of Texas Press, 2001); and Young, *Wright Patman*. For additional recent literature on Texans in Washington, see Louise Ann Fisch, *All Rise: Reynaldo G. Garza: The First Mexican American Federal Judge* (College Station: Texas A&M University Press, 1996); Lewis L. Gould, *Lady Bird Johnson and the Environment* (Lawrence: University Press of Kansas, 1988); Gould,

Lady Bird Johnson: Our Environmental First Lady (Lawrence: University Press of Kansas, 1999); Kenneth B. Hendrickson Jr. and Michael L. Collins, eds., *Profiles in Power: Twentieth-Century Texans in Washington* (Arlington Heights, Ill.: Harlan Davidson, 1993); Gary A. Keith, *Eckhardt: There Once Was a Congressman from Texas* (Austin: University of Texas Press, 2007); Dan Murph, *Texas Giant: The Life of Price Daniel* (Austin: Eakin Press, 2002); Darwin Payne, *Indomitable Sarah: The Life of Judge Sarah T. Hughes* (Dallas: Southern Methodist University Press, 2004); James Reston Jr., *The Lone Star: The Life of John Connally* (New York: Harper and Row, 1989); Mary Beth Rogers, *Barbara Jordan, American Hero* (New York: Bantam Books, 1998); Jan Jarboe Russell, *Lady Bird: A Biography of Mrs. Johnson* (New York: Scribner, 1999); Steven Hamon Wilson, *The Rise of Judicial Management in the U.S. District Court, Southern District of Texas, 1955–2000* (Athens: University of Georgia Press, 2002); Charles L. Zelden, *Justice Lies in the District: The U.S. District Court, Southern District of Texas, 1902–1960* (College Station: Texas A&M University Press, 1993).

48. Among the more important recent books on the Johnson years are John A. Andrew, *Lyndon Johnson and the Great Society* (Chicago: Ivan R. Dee, 1998); Larry Berman, *Lyndon Johnson's War: The Road to Stalemate in Vietnam* (New York: Norton, 1989); Irving Bernstein, *Guns or Butter: The Presidency of Lyndon Johnson* (New York: Oxford University Press, 1996); H. W. Brands, *The Wages of Globalism: Lyndon Johnson and the Limits of American Power* (New York: Oxford University Press, 1995); John L. Bullion, *Lyndon B. Johnson and the Transformation of American Politics* (New York: Pearson Longman, 2008); Thomas Clarkin, *Federal Indian Policy in the Kennedy and Johnson Administrations, 1961–1969* (Albuquerque: University of New Mexico Press, 2001); Lloyd C. Gardner, *Pay Any Price: Lyndon Johnson and the Wars for Vietnam* (Chicago: Ivan R. Dee, 1995); Michael Janeway, *The Fall of the House of Roosevelt: Brokers of Ideas and Power from FDR to LBJ* (New York: Columbia University Press, 2004); David E. Kaiser, *American Tragedy: Kennedy, Johnson, and the Origins of the Vietnam War* (Cambridge, Mass.: Harvard University Press, 2000); Mitchell B. Lerner, ed., *Looking Back at LBJ: White House Politics in a New Light* (Lawrence: University Press of Kansas, 2005); Julie Leininger Pycior, *LBJ and Mexican Americans: The Paradox of Power* (Austin: University of Texas Press, 1997); Hal K. Rothman, *LBJ's Texas White House: "Our Heart's Home"* (College Station: Texas A&M University Press, 2001); Irwin Unger and Debi Unger, *LBJ: A Life* (New York: Wiley, 1999); Mark Stern, *Calculating Visions: Kennedy, Johnson, and Civil Rights* (New Brunswick, N.J.: Rutgers University Press, 1992); Brian VanDeMark, *Into the Quagmire: Lyndon Johnson and the Escalation of the Vietnam War* (New York: Oxford University Press, 1991).

49. The volumes edited by Michael R. Beschloss omit many conversations and also delete long sections of the conversations that are included, sometimes changing the meaning of these records. As a result they should be used selectively. Michael R. Beschloss, ed., *Taking Charge: The Johnson White House Tapes, 1963–1964* (New York: Simon and Schuster, 1997); Beschloss, ed., *Reaching for Glory: Lyndon Johnson's Secret White House Tapes, 1964–1965* (New York: Simon and Schuster, 2001). Far better are

the comprehensive volumes being produced by the Miller Center at the University of Virginia. These volumes contain every conversation in which Johnson was a participant or a subject, and the only omissions were conversations between Secret Service agents and the like that briefly noted the need to attend to this or that duty. These volumes are also useful because they provide detailed contextual notes. See *Lyndon B. Johnson: The Kennedy Assassination and the Transfer of Power, November 1963–January 1964,* vol. 1, November 22–30, 1963, edited by Max Holland; vol. 2, December 1963, edited by Robert David Johnson and David Shreve; vol. 3, January 1964, edited by Kent B. Germany and Robert David Johnson (New York: W. W. Norton, 2005). *Lyndon B. Johnson: Toward the Great Society, February 1, 1964–May 31, 1964,* vol. 4, February 1, 1964–March 8, 1964, edited by Robert David Johnson and Kent B. Germany; vol. 5, March 9, 1964–April 13, 1964, edited by David Shreve and Robert David Johnson; vol. 6, April 14, 1964–May 31, 1964, edited by Guian A. McKee (New York: W. W. Norton, 2007).

50. Robert Caro, *The Years of Lyndon Johnson: Means of Ascent* (New York: Knopf, 1990).

51. Robert Caro, *The Years of Lyndon Johnson: Master of the Senate* (New York: Knopf, 2002).

52. The biographies in question include Robert Caro, *The Years of Lyndon Johnson: The Path to Power* (New York: Knopf, 1982); Ronnie Dugger, *The Politician; The Life and Times of Lyndon Johnson: The Drive for Power, from the Frontier to Master of the Senate* (New York: Norton, 1982); and Doris Kearns, *Lyndon Johnson and the American Dream* (New York: Harper and Row, 1976).

53. Robert Dallek, *Lone Star Rising: Lyndon Johnson and His Times, 1908–1960* (New York: Oxford University Press, 1991), 7.

54. Robert Dallek, *Flawed Giant: Lyndon Johnson and His Times, 1961–1973* (New York: Oxford University Press, 1998), ix.

55. Dallek, *Flawed Giant,* 628.

56. Randall B. Woods, *LBJ: Architect of American Ambition* (New York: Free Press, 2006), 884.

57. Other examples of the recent literature on desegregation include William Henry Kellar, *Make Haste Slowly: Moderates, Conservatives, and School Desegregation in Houston* (College Station: Texas A&M University Press, 1999); Roby Duff Ladino, *Desegregating Texas Schools: Eisenhower, Shivers, and the Crisis at Mansfield High* (Austin: University of Texas Press, 1996); Glenn Linden, *Desegregating Schools in Dallas: Four Decades in the Federal Courts* (Dallas: Three Forks Press, 1995); Robert J. Robertson, *Fair Ways: How Six Black Golfers Won Civil Rights in Beaumont, Texas* (College Station: Texas A&M University Press, 2005); Amilcar Shabazz, *Advancing Democracy: African Americans and the Struggle for Access and Equity in Higher Education in Texas* (Chapel Hill: University of North Carolina Press, 2004); Paul A. Sracic, *San Antonio v. Rodríguez and the Pursuit of Equal Education: The Debate over Discrimination and School Funding* (Lawrence: University Press of Kansas, 2007).

58. Guadalupe San Miguel Jr., *Brown, Not White: School Integration and the Chicano Movement in Houston* (College Station: Texas A&M University Press, 2001).

59. See, for example, Benjamin Márquez, *LULAC: The Evolution of a Mexican American Political Organization* (Austin: University of Texas Press, 1993); Armando Navarro, *The Cristal Experiment: A Chicano Struggle for Community Control* (Madison: University of Wisconsin Press, 1998); Navarro, *La Raza Unida Party: A Chicano Challenge to the U.S. Two Party Dictatorship* (Philadelphia: Temple University Press, 2000); Henry A. J. Ramos, *The American G.I. Forum: In Pursuit of the Dream, 1948–1983* (Houston: Arte Público Press, 1998).

60. Ignacio M. García, *United We Win: The Rise and Fall of La Raza Unida Party* (Tucson: University of Arizona Press, 1989), xi.

61. One of the few exceptions to this rule is a thoughtful and well-researched evaluation of George W. Bush's war cabinet. While little is said about the nexus between Bush and Texas, the account is the best yet on the Bush 43 presidency. See James Mann, *Rise of the Vulcans: The History of Bush's War Cabinet* (New York: Viking, 2004).

62. See, for example, Ryan J. Barilleaux and Mark J. Rozell, *Power and Prudence: The Presidency of George H. W. Bush* (College Station: Texas A&M University Press, 2004); John Robert Greene, *The Presidency of George Bush* (Lawrence: University Press of Kansas, 2000); Michael Schaller, *Right Turn: American Life in the Reagan-Bush Era, 1980–1992* (New York: Oxford University Press, 2006).

63. Herbert S. Parmet, *George Bush: The Life of a Lone Star Yankee* (New York: Scribner, 1997).

64. Kevin Phillips, *American Dynasty: Aristocracy, Fortune, and the Politics of Deceit in the House of Bush* (New York: Viking, 2004), 279.

65. See, for example, Megan Barnard, ed., *Collecting the Imagination: The First Fifty Years of the Ransom Center* (Austin: University of Texas Press, 2007); Ty Cashion, *Sam Houston State University: An Institutional Memory, 1879–2004* (Huntsville: Texas Review Press, 2004); Light T. Cummins, *Austin College: A Sesquicentennial History, 1849–1999* (Austin: Eakin Press, 1999); Richard A. Holland, *The Texas Book: Profiles, History, and Reminiscences of the University* (Austin: University of Texas Press, 2006); Chester R. Burns, *Saving Lives, Training Caregivers, Making Discoveries: A Centennial History of the University of Texas Medical Branch at Galveston* (Austin: Texas State Historical Association, 2003); Lewis F. Fisher, *River Walk: The Epic Story of San Antonio's River* (San Antonio: Maverick Publishing, 2007); J'Nell L. Pate, *Livestock Legacy: The Fort Worth Stockyards, 1887–1987* (College Station: Texas A&M University Press, 1988); Clay Reynolds with Marie-Madeleine Schein, *A Hundred Years of Heroes: A History of the Southwestern Exposition and Livestock Show* (Fort Worth: Texas Christian University Press, 1995).

66. Jay C. Henry, *Architecture in Texas: 1895–1945* (Austin: University of Texas Press, 1993).

67. Roberto R. Treviño, *The Church in the Barrio: Mexican American Ethno-*

Catholicism in Houston (Chapel Hill: University of North Carolina Press, 2006); Dwight Watson, *Race and the Houston Police Department, 1930–1990: A Change Did Come* (College Station: Texas A&M University Press, 2005).

68. Martin V. Melosi and Joseph A. Pratt, *Energy Metropolis: An Environmental History of Houston and the Gulf Coast* (Pittsburgh: University of Pittsburgh Press, 2007), 11.

69. Melosi and Pratt, *Energy Metropolis,* 91.

70. See, for example, Michael V. Hazel, *Dallas: A History of "Big D"* (Austin: Texas State Historical Association, 1997); Patricia Evridge Hill, *Dallas: The Making of a Modern City* (Austin: University of Texas Press, 1996); Darwin Payne, *Big D: Triumphs and Troubles of an American Supercity in the 20th Century* (Dallas: Three Forks Press, 1994); Michael Phillips, *White Metropolis: Race, Ethnicity, and Religion in Dallas, 1841–2001* (Austin: University of Texas Press, 2006); William H. Wilson, *Hamilton Park: A Planned Black Community in Dallas* (Baltimore: Johns Hopkins University Press, 1998).

71. Robert B. Fairbanks, *For the City as a Whole: Planning, Politics, and the Public Interest in Dallas, Texas, 1900–1965* (Columbus: Ohio State University Press, 1998), 209.

72. Paul H. Carlson, *Amarillo: The Story of a Western Town* (Lubbock: Texas Tech University Press, 2006); Richard A. Garcia, *Rise of the Mexican American Middle Class: San Antonio, 1929–1941* (College Station: Texas A&M University Press, 1991); Kenneth B. Ragsdale, *Austin, Cleared for Takeoff: Aviators, Businessmen, and the Growth of an American City* (Austin: University of Texas Press, 2004); J'Nell Pate, *North of the River: A Brief History of North Fort Worth* (Fort Worth: Texas Christian University Press, 1994); Rodolfo Rosales, *The Illusion of Inclusion: The Untold Political Story of San Antonio* (Austin: University of Texas Press, 2000); Linda Scarbrough, *Road, River, and Ol' Boy Politics: A Texas County's Path from Farm to Supersuburb* (Austin: Texas State Historical Association, 2005).

73. See, for example, Matthew D. Lassiter and Kevin M. Kruse, "The Bulldozer Revolution: Suburbs and Southern History since World War II," *Journal of Southern History* 75 (August 2009): 691–706.

74. Scarbrough, *Road, River, and Ol' Boy Politics,* 2.

75. See Robert S. Maxwell and Robert D. Baker, *Sawdust Empire: The Texas Lumber Industry, 1830–1940* (College Station: Texas A&M University Press, 1983).

76. Thad Sitton and James H. Conrad, *Nameless Towns: Texas Sawmill Communities, 1880–1942* (Austin: University of Texas Press, 1998), 80.

77. John Jameson, *The Story of Big Bend National Park* (Austin: University of Texas Press, 1996), 146.

About the Contributors

CARLOS KEVIN BLANTON holds a doctorate from Rice University (1999) and is currently an Associate Professor and Assistant Department Head in the Department of History at Texas A&M University where he specializes in the history of Texas and the Southwest and the history of Mexican Americans. His book with Texas A&M University Press, *The Strange Career of Bilingual Education in Texas, 1836–1981* (2004) won the Texas State Historical Association's Tullis Prize in 2005.

WALTER L. BUENGER is a Professor and Head of the Department of History at Texas A&M University. He is the author or editor of many books and articles on Texas and the South, including *The Path to a Modern South: Northeast Texas between Reconstruction and the Great Depression* (University of Texas Press, 2001). He also was the coeditor of *Texas Through Time: Evolving Interpretations* (Texas A&M University Press, 1991), the takeoff point for this particular study.

ARNOLDO DE LEÓN is the C. J. "Red" Davidson Professor of History at Angelo State University, San Angelo, Texas. He is the author of numerous works on Mexican Americans in Texas and coauthor of *The History of Texas* (4th ed.; Harlan Davidson, 2007). He was a contributor to *Texas Through Time* and has long been interested in historiography.

PEKKA HÄMÄLÄINEN is Associate Professor of History at the University of California at Santa Barbara, where he teaches borderlands, Native American, and environmental history. He is the author of *The Comanche Empire* (Yale University Press, 2008), a book that has won numerous awards including the Bancroft Prize.

MICHAEL PHILLIPS is a scholar of Texas race relations and the author of *White Metropolis: Race, Ethnicity, and Religion in Dallas, 1841–2001* and *The House Will Come to Order: How the Texas Speaker Became a Power in State and National Politics* (with Patrick Cox). *White Metropolis* won the Texas Historical Commission's 2007 T. R. Fehrenbach Award. Since 2007, Phillips has taught American history at Collin College.

CONTRIBUTORS

KEITH J. VOLANTO received his Ph.D. in history from Texas A&M University and is currently Professor of History at Collin College where he specializes in U.S. and Texas history. He is the author of *Texas, Cotton, and the New Deal* (Texas A&M University Press, 2005) and a coauthor of *Beyond Myths and Legends: A Narrative History of Texas* (Abigail Press, 2008).

NANCY BECK YOUNG is Professor of History at the University of Houston where she specializes in modern American political history. Her previous scholarship includes biographies of former congressman Wright Patman and former first lady Lou Henry Hoover, and she is now completing a book about the political history of Congress during World War II. She has held residential fellowships at the William P. Clements Center for Southwest Studies at Southern Methodist University and the Woodrow Wilson Center for Scholars in Washington, D.C.

 Index

abortion, 128, 161
Acosta, Teresa Palomo, 154, 157, 194
Acuña, Rodolfo, 165
Adair, Christa V., 145
Adams, John A., Jr., 10, 205, 234–35
Advancing Democracy (Shabazz), 128, 146, 197
African Americans
    Afro-Texan identity, 144–48
    civil rights issues, 95, 128, 135–37, 143–48, 158, 192, 230, 246
    in Civil War/Reconstruction narrative, 12–13, 29, 96, 106, 195–96
    in collective memory context, 166–67
    cultural identity and slavery, 144
    and environmental justice, 257
    evolution of narrative on, 195–96
    Ku Klux Klan, 167, 198
    Mexican American relations, 135–37, 192
    in modern culture, 33
    musicians, 239–40
    political activism of, 88, 148, 196
    as soldiers, 106, 108–9
    stereotyping of, 7–8, 127
    women and gender study, 21, 158–59, 194 *See also* slavery
Agricultural Adjustment Administration (AAA), 92–93, 97, 233–35
Agricultural and Mechanical College of Texas, 127
air conditioning and modernization, 257
Alabama-Coushatta Indians, 72, 77

Alamo, The, 21–22, 110–11, 163, 164–65, 180, 185–86
The Alamo (film), 163
The Alamo Remembered (Matovina), 110
"Albany Plan," 151
Almaráz, Félix D., 184
Alonzo, Armando, 188
Amarillo (Carlson), 203
American Dynasty (Phillips, K.), 254–56
American GI Forum (AGIF), 136
American Populism (McMath), 90
Ames, Jessie Daniel, 128
Anderson, Benedict, 139
Anderson, Gary Clayton, 26–27, 28, 65–67, 71, 73–74, 76, 148–49, 187
Angelo State College, 129
Anglocentric perspective, 1–2, 7, 14, 24–25, 77
    See also Eurocentric perspective
Anglos and Mexicans in the Making of Texas, 1836–1986 (Montejano), 129
anthropological methods, 3, 51, 57, 58, 60, 109–10
    See also archaeological methods
Apache Indians, 54, 60, 66, 72
Arapahoe Politics (Fowler), 61
Araucanians (S. Amer. Indians), 64
archaeological methods, 54, 55, 58, 76, 109–10
    See also anthropological methods
archetypal Texan paradigm, 11–12, 125–26
Architecture in Texas (Henry), 256
Arreola, Daniel, 201

INDEX

art as historic resource, 100
arts and modernization, 237–40
Asian immigrants, 159–60, 199
Association of Southern Women for the Prevention of Lynching, 128
Atkapa Indians, 75
Atlantic World, 34, 201–2, 204
At the Heart of Texas (McCaslin), 208
audience for Texas history writings
    black *v.* brown experience, 143
    and genera convergence possibilities, 36–38
    marketplace, power of, 114
    national arena, expansion to, 3–4, 32–33, 37–38, 52, 78, 139–43
    and New Indian History movement, 56
    and three genres of focus, 30–31
Auerbach, Robert D., 10, 248
Austin, Stephen F., 35–36, 94, 125, 183, 192–93
Avila, Manuel, 136
Axtell, James, 51

Babe (Cayleff), 10–11
Bailey, Anne J., 11–12
Baker, Karle Wilson, 193
Baker, Robert D., 259
ballads as historic resource, 100
Baptists in Texas, 20
Barbara Jordan (Rogers), 88
Bárbaros (Weber), 63–64
Barker, Cullen Montgomery, 96
Barker, Eugene C., 94, 180, 184
Barker, Scott Grant, 238–39
Barnes, Ben, 129
Barr, Alwyn, 195
Barr, Juliana, 23–25, 68–69, 150, 151–52, 153, 187, 194
Barta, Carolyn, 88
Barthelme, Marion, 89
Bateman, Christopher, 162

The Battle for the Black Ballot (Zelden), 241–42
Baum, Dale, 90, 194
Bean, Peter Ellis, 193
Beaumont, Texas, 101
Beeth, Howard, 203
Being Comanche (Foster), 57
berdaches, 159
Bernstein, Patricia, 138
Beschloss, Michael R., 266–67*n* 49
Betty, Gerald, 56–57
Big Bend National Park, 206–7, 260–61
"Big Tex," 125, 165
Bill Clements: Texian to His Toenails (Barta), 88
biographical narrative
    evolution of, 87–88, 93–94, 98–100, 102, 192–93, 193–94
    and gender studies, 151
    of Indians, 108
    of Lyndon B. Johnson, 97–98
    of military figures, 106
    and modernization, 237–38, 244–45, 246–47
    and performing arts, 239
    of women, 236–37
    See also political figures
bisexuality, 161
bison, importance of, 84*n* 30, 150
Black Dixie (Beeth and Wintz), 203
The Black Family in Slavery and Freedom, 1750–1925 (Guttman), 147
Blackland Prairie, 20, 99, 156
"Black Legend," 73, 184
Black Nationalism movement, 144
"blackness" divisions, 147–48
The Black Regulars, 1866–1898 (Dobak and Phillips, T.), 108–9
blacks. *See* African Americans
Black Soldiers in Jim Crow Texas, 1899–1917 (Christian), 109

INDEX

Black Unionism in the Industrial South (Obadele-Stark), 196
blanqueamiento, 141
Blanton, Annie Webb, 193
Blanton, Carlos Kevin, 135–36, 179, 190, 198
"Bloody Sunday," 145
Blum, Elizabeth D., 257
Bob Bullock Texas History Museum, 164–67, 198
Bolton, Herbert Eugene, 63
"Bolton school," 66
"The Bones of Stephen F. Austin" (Cantrell), 125
Border Boss (Quezada), 244–45
borderlands history
    and East Texas, 201
    emergence of, 61–62, 66
    and fluidity of national identity, 142–43
    and South Texas, 201
    Texas' place in, 200
    See also new Texas Indian history
borders, importance of
    in focus of writing, 20, 21, 35
    and Indian relations, 55, 58, 67–68
bossism, 244–45, 259
Boswell, Angela, 21, 193, 194
bottom-up perspective. *See* New Social History perspective
Bourbon era influences, 63, 66
Brager, Bruce L., 11
Brammer, Billy Lee, 200
Branch, Taylor, 145
Brear, Holly Beachley, 21–22
A Breed So Rare (Carleton), 100, 240–41
Brewer, John Mason, 144
Bridge on the River Kwai (film), 107
Britten, Thomas A., 60
Brooks, James F., 51, 68
Brown, Dee, 50
Brown, George R., 242–43

Brown, Herman, 242–43
Brown, John Henry, 127
Brown, Not White (San Miguel), 140–41, 190
Brown & Root, 242–43
Brown v. Board of Education, 128
Buenger, Victoria, 100
Buenger, Walter L., xi–xiv, 1, 98, 100, 101, 179, 182, 185, 207, 222, 224–25
"Buffalo Soldiers," 108
Builders (Castaneda and Pratt), 242–43
Building the Borderlands (Walsh), 201
Building the Death Railway (Marcello), 107
Bullard, Robert, 205
Burma-Thailand Railway, 107
Burton, H. Sophie, 201
Bury My Heart At Wounded Knee (Brown), 50
Bush, George H. W., 254
Bush, George W., 162, 254–56
business history, 99, 102, 103, 227, 242–43
    See also economic history of Texas, recent; oil industry
business leaders, evolution of narrative on, 99, 100, 102
Bynum, Victoria, 160
Bywaters, Jerry, 237–38

Cabeza De Vaca, Álvar Núñez, 188
Caddo Chiefdoms (La Vere), 58, 59
Caddo Indians
    cultural values of, 69
    dispossession of, 72
    equestrianism of, 54
    evolution of narrative on, 58–59
    parallels with Charrúas, 64
    stereotyping of, 6, 75
    trade system of, 54, 66–67
Caddo Indians (Carter), 58
The Caddo Indians (Smith, F.), 58
"The Caddo Nation" (Perttula), 58
The Caddos, the Wichitas, and the United States (Smith, F.), 59

INDEX

Callaway, Isadore Miner, 193
Calloway, Colin G., 51
Calvert, Robert A., xi–xiv, 5–8, 26, 179, 185, 222
campaign (military) narrative, 106–7
Campbell, Randolph B., 25–27, 96, 129, 168, 182
Camp Hearne, 123*n* 48
Canada's North-West Mounted Police, 74
Canales, J. T., 19
Cantrell, Gregg, 35–36, 88, 94, 125, 137, 183–84, 192–93, 195, 229
Capitol Women, 88
Captives and Cousins (Brooks), 68
Carleton, Don E., 100, 240–41
Carlson, Paul H., 106, 203
Caro, Robert, 98, 248–50
Carraro, Francine, 237–38
Carrigan, William D., 22–23, 137–38, 192
Carroll, Mark M., 160–61, 194–95
Carroll, Patrick J., 91–92
Carter, Celia, 58
Cartwright, Gary, 200
Cashion, Ty, 206, 243–44
Castañeda, Carlos Eduardo, 136, 184
Castaneda, Christopher J., 99, 103, 242–43
The Cast Iron Forest (Francaviglia), 205
Catholicism, 20, 153, 157, 203
cattle industry, 103, 104–5, 167
Cayleff, Susan E., 10–11
Centennial of Texas, 184
Central Texas
    cotton culture in, 100, 156
    demographic diversity of, 133
    "marginal whites" in, 205
    racial violence in, 138, 192
    regional and cultural identity of, 20, 22
    in Texas political history, 90
    urbanization of, 205
Changing National Identities at the Frontier (Reséndez), 35, 64–65, 142, 188–89
Charrúas (S. Amer. Indians), 64
Chauncey, George, 161
Cherokee Indians, 61
The Cheyenne Nation (Moore), 61
Chicanas, 88, 154, 157
Chicanas in Charge (Gutiérrez, Meléndez, and Noyola eds.), 88, 154
Chicanismo, 141
Chicano movement, 92, 140–41, 157, 190, 253
Childs, William R., 37, 102–3, 227–28
Chile, 63, 64
Chinese Texans, 160
Chipman, Donald E., 62, 188
Christian, Garna L., 109
Christian eschatology, 135
chronological approaches
    to economic history, 99
    in new Texas Indian history, 58, 59, 66, 72, 75–76
    periodization, 223–24, 228, 230
The Church in the Barrio (Treviño), 153, 203
citizenship, ideology of, 17, 19, 135, 189–90
Civilian Conservation Corps, 97
civil rights
    African American, 95, 128, 135–37, 143–48, 158, 192, 230, 246
    evolution of narrative on, 93, 95, 143, 196–97, 241–42, 249, 253
    and frontier ethic, 8, 28
    Mexican American, 92, 93, 108, 118*n* 16, 190
    women and, 127, 155, 158, 236–37
Civil War, 11, 13–14, 94, 106–7, 111
    See also Reconstruction era
Claiming Citizenship (Quiroz), 118*n* 16, 190

INDEX

Claiming Rights and Righting Wrongs in Texas (Zamora), 34, 37, 117n 9
class issues
    among Mexican Americans, 16–17, 18–19, 95, 139–40, 241
    and black racial identity, 147–48
    class-based politics, 245–46
    farming hierarchy, 147–48
    and whiteness paradigm, 20–21, 100–101, 132
Clear Fork region, 206
Clements, Bill, 88
Cline, Isaac Monroe, 204
Coacoochee's Bones (Miller, S.), 61
Coahuiltecan Indians, 6, 69, 75
Cole, Stephanie, 160
collective memory
    and African American history, 165
    and disconnect with historic fact, 162–63
    and Indian history, 148–53, 164–65
    and myth exemplar (Bob Bullock museum), 164–67
    overview, 137
    and postmodernism, 126–27
    of race and gender historiography, 125–26
    and racial violence, 21–23, 137–38, 166–67, 192
    and Tejano national identity, 139–43
    See also myths
colonialism, focus on, 25, 51–52, 63, 69–71, 188
    See also Indian–Euro-American relations
Colonial Natchitoches (Burton, S. and Smith, F.), 201
Colorado County, 21, 193
Colorado River, 10, 205, 234–35
Columbian Exposition, Chicago 1892, 155
Columbus Quincentenary, 50, 62
The Comanche Barrier to South Plains Settlement (Richardson), 57, 73, 187
The Comanche Empire (Hämäläinen), 34–35, 69–71, 149–50
Comanche Indians
    cultural values and power relations, 65, 69–71
    dispossession of, 72
    ethnogenesis of, 66–68, 149–51
    evolution of narrative on, 56–58, 149–50
    influence of, 24–25, 28, 34–35, 37–38, 59–61
    parallels to Araucanians, 64
    Quanah Parker biography, 108
    stereotyping of, 6, 75
Comanche Political History (Kavanagh), 57–58
Comanches (Fehrenbach), 56
The Comanches (Hoebel and Wallace), 57
Comanche Society (Betty), 56–57
commemorative approach, 1, 112
common folk, representations of
    evolution of narrative on, 97, 99
    lack of, 5, 7, 13
    See also soldiers, common
community identity
    and modernization, 231
    in new Indian history, 57
    in new social history, 6
    in revisionist writing, 15
    in Spanish colonial era, 188
    See also regionalism
compadrazgo, 154
computers, xiv
Confederate army. *See* Civil War
Connally, John, 129
The Conquest of Texas (Anderson, G.), 26–27, 28, 71, 73–74, 148–49
The Conquest of the Karankawas and the Tonkawas (Himmel), 55

INDEX

Conrad, James H., 259–60
consensus approach, 1–2, 7, 17, 27–28, 94–95
conservativism and identity of place, 258–59
contextual approach to postrevisionist history, 86–87, 93–94
Contrary Neighbors (La Vere), 61
convergence of three genre, 34–38
Corpus Christi, Texas, 203–4
correspondence as historic resource, 89, 93, 107, 109, 110, 136–37
Cotham, Edward T., Jr., 106–7
cotton industry, 20, 92–93, 103–4, 107, 156–57, 232–34
Coushatta Indians, 72
cowboy image, 125, 162–63
Cox, Karen L., 132, 181
Cox, Patrick, 225, 232
coyotes, 16
Craft, Juanita, 158
Crager, Kelly E., 107
Creating the New Woman (McArthur), 21, 91, 154–56, 194
Crisp, James, R., 111, 185
The Cristal Experiment (Navarro), 93
Crockett, Davy, 111
cross-culture themes, 23–24, 55
    See also Indian–Euro-American relations; whiteness paradigm
Cross Timbers forest, 205
Crystal City, Texas, 93
cultural constructionism
    characterization of, 2–4, 18–19, 182
    evolution of, 1988–1991, 5–8
    evolution of, 1988–2009, 18–25
    genera convergence possibilities, 34–38
    profile of 1988–2009 writings, 9–10
    venue and audience for, evolution of, 29–34

Cunningham, Minnie Fisher, 155, 193, 236
Cycles of Conquest (Spicer), 65–66
Czech immigrants, 20, 198

Dallas, Texas
    "Big Tex," 125, 165
    Chinese in, 160
    civil rights movements in, 158
    and identity of place, 257–58
    Jewish immigrants in, 134–35, 157
    John Thomas Gay and Lesbian Community Center, 161
    racial divisiveness in, 136, 137, 191
    scholarly neglect of, 128, 145, 148
    urban histories of, 202
The Dallas Myth (Graff), 137
Dallek, Robert, 98, 250–51
Damming the Colorado (Adams), 10, 205, 234–35
Davidson, Chandler, 91, 130, 245–46
Davis, Edgar B., 102
Davis, Edmund J., 90
Davis, Ronald L., 182
Davis, Stephen, 200
Deception and Abuse at the Fed (Auerbach), 10
Decker, Stefanie, 158
Defense of a Legend (Groneman), 111
Dehahuit (Caddo chief), 59
de la Teja, Jesús F., 15–16, 25–26, 28–29, 188
Delay, Brian, 70
De León, Arnoldo, 6–8, 26, 129, 141–42, 187–88, 189, 191, 202–3
Democratic Party, 130, 246, 249, 253
demographics
    of Texas historians, 162
    of Texas population, xv, 33, 253
Desegregating Texas Schools (Ladino), 146
desegregation. See segregation
De Vaca, Álvar Núñez Cabeza, 188
De Zavala, Adina, 184

278

INDEX

diaries as historic resource, 107, 109, 110
Dimmick, Gregg, 109–10
disaster histories, 204–5
discrimination. *See* racial discrimination
disease
    health care narrative, 205–6
    and Indians, 51, 67, 164
    and women's activism, 155
dispossession of Indians, 55, 59–60, 71–74, 76, 78
Dobak, William A., 108–9
Dobbs, Ricky Floyd, 162–63, 230, 246–47, 251
Dobie, J. Frank, 180, 184
Downs, Fane, 193
drama-centered *v.* theory-driven approach, 56–57
Dulaney, W. Marvin, 148
Dumping in Dixie (Bullard), 205
Dunning school of interpretation, 96
DuVal, Kathleen, 68
dynasty, political, 254–56

East Texas, 201, 230–31, 259–60
East Texas Historical Journal, 147
eclectic approaches, 86, 101, 109
economic history of Texas, recent
    approaches, 99–102
    background, 98
    and frontier military, 113
    and modernization, 224–25, 227–28
    new interpretive trends, 104–5
    themes in, 102–4, 195
Edgar B. Davis and Sequences in Business Capitalism (Froh), 102
Edmund Pettus Bridge march, 145
education of historians in Texas, 127, 129, 162
Edwards, Laura, 182
Eisenhower, Dwight, 130, 247
elections, study of, 90
electricity and modernization, 234–35

elite-centric perspective, 1–2, 11–12, 86
El Llano Estacado, 207
El Llano Estacado (Morris), 207
Elman, Colin, 132
Elman, Miriam Fendius, 132
El Paso, Texas, 205
An Empire for Slavery (Campbell), 26, 129
Energy Metropolis (Melosi and Pratt eds.), 204–5, 256–57
Enstam, Elizabeth York, 154, 202
entrepreneurial biography, 99, 102
environmental histories, 205, 234–35, 257
equestrianism among Indians, 54, 60, 64
eschatology, 135
"ethnic cleansing" *v.* genocide, 148–49
ethnic issues. *See* Jewish immigrants; race narrative
Ethnicity in the Sunbelt (De León), 141–42, 202–3
"ethno-Catholicism," 153
ethnogenesis, 64–66, 67–68, 149–51
eugenics, 161
Eurocentric perspective
    Anglocentric, 1–2, 7, 14, 24–25, 77
    and collective memory of myth, 164
    of traditionalist and revisionist writings, 6–7, 15, 26, 28–29
    See also Indian–Euro-American relations
European immigrants, 132–33, 134, 135, 197–99
Everett, Dianna, 61

Fairbanks, Robert M., 257–58
Fair Employment Practice Committee, 117*n* 9
family cultures, 147, 156, 157, 193
Farmers' Alliance, 90
farming, 99, 103, 121–22*n* 37, 230–31, 233–34
Fehrenbach, T. R., 7–8, 56, 73, 126, 127

279

INDEX

Felix Longoria's Wake (Carroll, P.), 91–92
female consciousness *v.* feminist consciousness, 155
Ferguson, Miriam "Ma," 128, 159, 193
Fertile Ground, Narrow Choices (Sharpless), 121–22n 37, 156–57, 193
Filisola, Vicente, 109
fine arts and modernization, 237–38
The First Texas Navy (Powers), 111–12
The First Texas News Barons (Cox, P.), 225
The First Waco Horror (Bernstein), 138
fishing/shrimping, 104
Flawed Giant (Dallek), 250–51
floods, 205, 234–35
Flores, Richard R., 21–22, 110, 185
fluidity of national identity, 142–43
Focault, Michel, 131, 139
Foley, Neil, 20–21, 100–101, 133–34, 136, 191, 241
Foner, Eric, 13
Foo: A Japanese-American Prisoner of the Rising Sun (Fujita), 107
football, high school, 243–44
forest narrative, 205
Forgotten Gateway (exhibit), 198
Fort Davis, 113
For the City as a Whole (Fairbanks), 257–58
Fort Worth, Texas, 100, 143, 202, 238–39
Foster, Morris W., 57
Fowler, Loretta, 61
Francaviglia, Richard V., 111, 205
Franciscan missions. *See* missions, Spanish
Frear, Yvonne Davis, 197, 230
"Freedom Summer," 145
Freeman, Elizabeth, 138
French-Indian relations, 153
Froh, Riley, 102
From Can See to Can't (Sitton and Utley, D.), 99
From Dominance to Disappearance (Smith, F.), 15, 71–72, 73

From Out of the Shadows (Ruiz), 143, 153–54
From Sail to Steam (Francaviglia), 111
From Texas to the East (Castaneda and Pratt), 99, 103, 242–43
The Frontier Army in the Settlement of the West (Tate), 112–13
Frontier Crossroads (Wooster), 113
"frontier ethic," 8, 28
frontiers as contact zones, 63–64
  See also borderlands history
Fujita, Frank, 107

Gallay, Alan, 51
Galveston, Texas, 153, 194, 198, 199, 204
García, Hector P., 88, 136
García, Ignacio M., 95, 253
Garcia, Richard A., 16–17, 18, 19, 139–40
Garner, John Nance, 235
Garrison, George P., 180
Garvey, Marcus, 148
Garza-Falcón, Leticia, 194
Gay and Lesbian Archives of Texas (Houston), 161
gay identity, 161, 195
Gay New York (Chauncey), 161
gender narrative
  and African American women, 158–59
  evolution of, 21, 25, 128–29, 194–95
  and Indians in Texas, 24–25, 68–69, 151–53, 194
  and Mexican American women, 153–57
  sexuality and identity, 159–60, 160–61, 194–95
  See also women in historic narrative
generational approach, 141–42, 189–90, 229, 230
genocide *v.* "ethnic cleansing," 148–49

INDEX

genres of truth in Texas history, 33–34, 34–38
  See also cultural constructionism; revisionism, persistent; traditionalism, updated
geography/"place" historiography, 256–61
geopolitical strategies of Indians, 57–58, 59, 67–68
  See also ethnogenesis
George Bush (Parmet), 254
German immigrants, 20, 21, 198–99
Germans of Texas (Struve), 198
Giant Country (Graham), 200
Giant under the Hill (Linsley, Rienstra, and Stiles), 100
globalization of Texas history, 18, 74, 86, 103–4, 201–2, 221–23
  See also modernization of Texas history
Going through the Storm (Stuckey), 144
golden age of Texas focus, 1–2, 98, 146
Goldstone, Dwonna, 197
Gone to Texas (Campbell), 25–27
Gonzalez, Henry B., 248
González, Jovita, 184
Good Neighbor Policy, 117*n* 9
governors, 33, 88, 90, 128, 159, 246–47
graduate schools and history genre, 34
Graff, Harvey J., 137
Graham, Don, 163, 200
Grass-Roots Reconstruction in Texas, 1865–1880 (Campbell), 96
Graybill, Andrew, 71, 74
Great Depression, 92–93, 96–97, 260
Great Lakes region, Indians in, 51
Great Plains, 206
Groneman, Bill, 111
Gulf Coast, 203–5, 256–57
Gutiérrez, José Angel, 154
Guttman, Herbert G., 147

Hagan, William T., 108
Halbwach, Maurice, 137
Haley, James L., 94, 228–29
Hall, Jacquelyn Dowd, 129
Hall, Thomas D., 65–66
Hämäläinen, Pekka, 34–35, 50, 69–71, 149–50, 151, 187
Hamilton, Andrew Jackson, 90
Hamilton, Donny L., 76
Hardin, Stephen L., 109
Hardwick, Susan Wiley, 204
Harris, Charles H., 14, 18, 19, 27
Hasinais Indians, 67–68
Hearne, Azeline, 194
Hell under the Rising Sun (Crager), 107
hemispheric history, 64
Hemmingway, Ernest, 200
Henry, Jay C., 256
Her Act and Deed (Boswell), 21, 193, 194
hero myth, 21–22, 23, 35–36, 106
Herskovits, Melville, 144
Hickerson, Nancy Parrott, 54, 76
Higgins, Pattillo, 99, 101
high school football, 243–44
Hill, Patricia, 157
Hill Country, 235, 251
Himmel, Kelly F., 55
Hinton, Diana Davids, 226
historical consciousness. *See* collective memory
historical imagination *v.* myth, 199–208
historical memory. *See* memory, role of
historical societies, 206
History and Legends of the Alamo and Other Missions in and around San Antonio (De Zavala), 184
The History of Texas (Calvert and De León), 6–8, 26, 29
The History of Texas, from 1685 to 1892 (Brown, J.), 127
Hoebel, E. Adamson, 57
home economics, 155

281

INDEX

Homesteads Ungovernable (Carroll, M.), 160–61, 194–95
Hood's Texas Brigade, 11
horses, adoption by Indians, 54, 60, 64, 150
Houston, Sam, 90, 94
Houston, Texas
    black civil rights in, 145–46
    environmental issues, 204–5
    and identity of place, 256–57
    M. D. Anderson Cancer Center, 205–6
    and segregation in schools, 144–45, 253
    Tejano religion in, 153
    urban histories of, 202–3
Hoxie, Frederick E., 61
Hughes, Sarah T., 88
Hunt County, 230–31
hurricanes, 204
Hyman, Harold, 198

Iber, Jorge, 190–91
identity struggles
    gay identity, 161, 195
    Mexican Americans, 16–17, 18–19, 139–40, 188–89
    racial identity construction, 132–35, 135–37, 141–43, 241
    See also gender narrative; myths; race narrative; state identity in narrative
imagination and public memory. *See* myths
immigration/immigrants, xv
    Asian, 159–60, 199
    European, 132–33, 134, 135, 197–99
    German, 20, 21, 198–99
    Jewish, 134–35, 157, 199
    stereotyping of, 17
    See also Mexican Americans
In a Narrow Grave (McMurtry), 200

Indian Agent (Jackson J.), 193
Indian–Euro-American relations
    borderlands studies, rise of, 61–62
    collective memory perspective, 148–51, 164–65
    cultural values and power relations, 68–71
    Eurocentric viewpoint of, 62–64, 64–65
    Indian dominance in, 15, 23–24, 28, 71–72, 73
    indigenous viewpoint, 65–68
    Spanish-Indian relations, 6–7, 23–24, 60, 62–65, 152–53, 194
Indians
    and cultural traditions, 58, 59
    and disease, 51, 67, 164
    dominance in relations with Spanish, 15, 23–24, 28, 71–72, 73
    evolution of narrative on, 29, 34–35
    marginalization of, 2, 5–7, 16, 26–27
    smaller tribes, focus on, 76
    stereotyping of, 6–7, 28–29, 52, 127, 187
    traditional historic division of, 53
    as victims, 15, 27
    See also new Texas Indian history; *individual tribes*
The Indians of Texas (Newcomb), 75
The Indian Southwest (Anderson, G.), 64–65, 66–67, 148
indigenous adaptability, 55, 57–59, 60, 64–65, 70
indigenous agency, focus on, 51, 65–71, 75–77, 78
Inherit the Alamo (Brear), 21–22
Inperial Texas (Meinig), 186
In Struggle against Jim Crow (Pitre), 88, 158
Integrating the 40 Acres (Goldstone), 197

interdisciplinary approaches to post-revisionist history, 86, 100–101, 109–10
Internet, xiv
interviews as historic resource, 89, 99, 107, 110, 156, 161, 244
Intimate Modernism (Barker and Myers), 238–39
intra-Texas focus of writing, 30
Inventing Texas (McLemore), 183
Irish immigrants, 133, 198
Iroquois Confederation, 151
irredentist movement, 201
Isaac's Storm (Cline), 204

Jackson, Dolla, 166
Jackson, Jack, 193, 209n 2
Jameson, John, 206–7, 260–61
Jennings, Francis, 51
Jerry Bywaters (Carraro), 237–38
Jewish immigrants, 134–35, 157, 199
John, Elizabeth A. H., 71
John B. Armstrong: Texas Ranger and Pioneer Ranchman (Parsons), 12
Johnson, Benjamin Heber, 18, 201
Johnson, Lady Bird, 206–7
Johnson, Lyndon B., 97–98, 205, 230, 235, 248–52
John Thomas Gay and Lesbian Community Center (Dallas), 161
Jones, C. Allan, 103
Jones, Jacqueline, 202
Jordan, Barbara, 88
Jordan, Jonathan W., 111–12
Jordan, Terry, 187
Journal of Southern History, 182
Jumano Indians, 54, 66, 75
The Jumanos (Hickerson), 54
Juneteenth, 229–30

Kadohadachos (Caddos), 58, 59
Kamphoefner, Walter, 198

Kaplowitz, Craig A., 92
Karankawa Indians
    cultural values of, 69
    dispossession of, 55, 72
    in new Texas Indian history, 55
    in revisionist writings, 6
    and sexual identity, 159
    sterotyping of, 75
The Karankawa Indians of Texas (Ricklis), 55
Kavanagh, Thomas W., 57–58
Kellar, William Henry, 95, 144–45, 146
Kelton, Steve, 99
Kempner family, 198
Kennedy, John F., 95
Kenneth and John B. Rayner and the Limits of Southern Dissent (Cantrell), 88
Key, V. O., Jr., 91, 245–46
Kickapoo Traditional Tribe of Texas, 77
kidnapping, 69
King, Larry, 181, 200
King, Will, 138
kinship among Indians, role of, 24–25, 56–57, 68–69
Kiowa Indians, 54, 60, 72, 75, 108
Kirby Lumber Company, 260
Knight without Armor (Almaráz), 184
Ku Klux Klan, 167, 198

labor issues
    African American activism, 196
    class identity and "whiteness," 100, 133–34
    in economic history, 98, 99
    evolution of narrative on activism, 117n 9, 129
    and globalization, 202
    women activists, 91, 152, 157
    women workers, 105, 156–57
Lack, Paul D., 94, 183, 186
Ladino, Robyn Duff, 146
La Forte, Robert S., 107

INDEX

language
    barriers to, 24, 190, 198
    in postmodern narrative, 131, 132
    and stereotyping, 75
La Plata (S. America), 63–64
"la raza," 141
La Raza Unida, 253
Las Tejanas (Acosta and Winegarten), 154
"Latin American" appellation, 140
Latinas, 156–57
    See also Chicanas
La Vere, David, 58, 59, 61, 75–77, 187
law enforcement and modernization, 237
Lawrence v. Texas, 195
LBJ: Architect of American Ambition (Woods), 251–52
League of United Latin American Citizens (LULAC)
    and cultural identity, 17, 19, 108, 140, 142, 190
    and nationalization of Texas history, 92, 143
    and whiteness, 136–37
Lee, James Ward, 112
"Lee Peacock Feud," 96
legendary past themes, 11–12
Leonard, Marvin, 100
lesbian identity, 157, 161, 195
letters as historic resource, 89, 93, 107, 109, 110, 136–37
A Line in the Sand (Roberts and Olson), 110
Linsley, Judith Walker, 100
Lipan Apache Indians, 60, 72
The Lipan Apaches (Britten), 60
Llano Estacado, 207
"*lo mexicano*," 142
Lonesome Dove (McMurtry), 200
Lone Star: A History of Texas and the Texans (Fehrenbach), 7–8, 73, 127
Lone Star Lawmen (Utley, R.), 237

Lone Star Navy (Jordan), 111–12
Lone Star Pasts (Cantrell and Turner eds.), 137, 183–84, 229
Lone Star Rising (Dallek), 250–51
Lone Star Stalag (Waters et al.), 123n 48
Longoria, Felix, 91–92
Los Comanches (Noyes), 56
"Lost Batallion," 104
Lost Cause stigma, 96, 125, 183, 207
Lowe, Richard G., 13–14, 109
Lower Colorado River Authority, 10, 97, 205, 234–35
LULAC (League of United Latin American Citizens)
    and cultural identity, 17, 19, 108, 140, 142, 190
    and nationalization of Texas history, 92, 143
    and whiteness, 136–37
LULAC, Mexican Americans, and National Policy (Kaplowitz), 92
lumber industry, 259–60
lynchings, 22, 23, 26, 134, 137–38, 167, 192
Lynching to Belong (Nevels), 134
Lyndon Johnson and His Times (Dallek), 98, 250–51

Make Haste Slowly (Kellar), 95, 144–45, 146
Making Cancer History (Olson), 205–6
The Making of a Lynching Culture (Carrigan), 22–23, 137–38, 192
male-centric perspective, 2–3, 8, 27–28, 125–26
Mao Zedong, 126
Marcello, Ronald E., 107
Maret, Elizabeth, 105
marginalization of minorities, 2, 5–7, 16, 26–27, 125–26, 127, 183, 186
"marginal whites," 134
Maril, Robert Lee, 104

markets for Texas history books, 4, 31–32, 114–15
Marks, Paula, 25–26, 28–29
Marten, James, 94
Martínez, Anita N., 154
masculinity and identity, 159–60, 194–95
Massey, Sara, 105
Master of the Senate (Caro), 249
Matovina, Timothy, 110
McArthur, Judith N., 21, 91, 152, 154–56, 194, 236–37
McCaslin, Richard B., 30, 208
McCollough, Martha, 67–68
McFarland, Fanny, 165
McLemore, Laura, 183
McMath, Robert C., 90
McMurtry, Larry, 200
M. D. Anderson Cancer Center, 205–6
Means of Ascent (Caro), 249
media and modernization, 225, 232
Medrano, Pancho, 136
Meinig, D. W., 186
Meléndez, Michael, 154
Melosi, Martin, 204–5, 256–57
memoirs as historic resource, 107
memorials and public memory, 137
memory, role of, 109, 110, 229–30
    See also collective memory
Mercado, Bianca, 174
Merell, James H., 51
Merritt, Jane T., 68
Mescalero Indians, 60
Mexican Americans
    and black civil rights, 135–37, 192
    Chicano movement, 92, 140–41, 157, 190, 253
    civil rights of, 92, 93, 108, 118*n* 16, 190
    identity struggles of, 16–17, 18–19, 139–40, 188–89
    political activism of, 95, 120*n* 30, 184, 190, 244
    and racial identity construction, 135–37, 141–43, 241
    and segregation, 140, 190, 252–53
    women and gender study, 153–57
    See also League of United Latin American Citizens (LULAC); Tejanos
Mexican Americans and Sports (Iber and Regaldo), 190–91
Mexican-American War, influence of, 11–12, 70–71
The Mexican Frontier (Weber), 64
"Mexicanist" identity, 120*n* 30, 189
"*Mexicano*" identity, 139
Mexican period
    evolution of narrative on, 188–89
    immigration failure, 70
    Indian–Euro-American relations in, 64–65
    Mexican perspective on Texas Revolution, 109–10, 111
Mexican Revolution, influence of, 11–12, 14, 18–19, 141–42
middle class of Mexican Americans, 16–17, 95, 139–40, 241
The Middle Ground (White, R.), 65
military history of Texas, recent
    approaches, 106–10
    background, 105–6
    and frontier economy, 113
    new interpretive trends, 112–13
    themes, 110–12
Miller, Char, 202, 203
Miller, Susan, 61
"The Mind That Burns in Each Body" (Hall, J.), 129
mining industry, 105
Minnie Fisher Cunningham (McArthur and Smith, H.), 236–37
minorities, marginalization of, 2, 5–7, 16, 26–27, 125–26, 127, 183, 186
missions, Spanish, 15–16, 55, 60, 69

INDEX

Mississippian culture, 76
Mississippi valley region, Indians in, 51
modernization of Texas history
    1930s historiography, 231–40
    1940s through 1960s historiography, 240–42
    advent of, 224–31
    conclusions and future outlook, 261–62
    criticism of, 230–31
    definition and overview, 221–23
    and "place" historiography, 256–61
    post 1970 historiography, 252–56
    post WWII era historiography, 242–52 (*See also* nationalization of Texas history)
Moneyhon, Carl H., 13
Montejano, David, 129, 187–88
Moore, John H., 61
morality themes, 10, 32, 182
Mormons, 161
Morris, John Miller, 207
Mounties, Canadian, 74
movies and public memory, 163
Murdock, Steve, 186
music and modernization, 239–40
mutualistas, 189
Myers, Jane, 238–39
Mythic Galveston (Hardwick), 204
myths
    Alamo, 21–22, 110–11, 163, 164–65, 180, 185–86
    construction of, 183
    deconstruction of, 181–86
    "frontier ethic," 8, 28
    hero myth, 21–22, 23, 35–36, 106
    v. historical imagination, 199–208
    and historiography, overview, xi–20
    "plantation myth," 146, 180
    of Reconstruction era, 12–13, 166–67
    refutations of, 184–85, 199–208
    and state identity, 125–28, 162–63, 179–81
    Texas creation, 73, 180
    of Texas fighters, 111
    of Texas Rangers, 12, 14, 73
    Western mythos, 206

Nacogdoches, 201
Nameless Towns (Conrad and Sitton), 259–60
narrative and postrevisionism, 89
National Association for the Advancement of Colored People (NAACP), 22, 88, 138, 145, 146, 241–42
nationalization of Texas history, 3–4, 32–33, 37–38, 52, 78, 139–43
    See also modernization of Texas history
National Park Service, 260–61
"National Science Foundation Survey of Earned Doctorates," 162
National Youth Administration, 97
Native Americans. *See* Indians
The Native Americans of the Texas Edwards Plateau (Wade), 61
Navarro, Armando, 93
navy, Texas, 111–12
Nelson, Willie, 185
Nevels, Cynthia Skove, 134
Newcomb, W. W., Jr., 75
The New Deal and the States (Patterson), 97
New Deal programs, 96–97, 205, 232–35, 234–35, 238
New Indian History movement, 50–53, 77–79
New Left politics, 163
New Military History, 106, 107
A New Order of Things (Saunt), 61
news barons, 225
New Social History perspective
    characterization of, 6–7

286

INDEX

current and future status of, 130–31
emergence of, 2, 126, 129
and gender narrative, 151
and New Indian History, 51
and New Left, 163
and New Military History, 106–7
in revisionist writings, 85
See also postrevisionism
New Spain. *See* Spanish culture
newspapers and modernization, 225
The New Texas History Movies (Jackson, J.), 209n 2
new Texas Indian history
    comparison of 1960s era work to modern, 75–77
    dispossession and Anglo-American takeover, 71–74
    impact and future outlook, 77–79
    Indian-Indian relations, 66–68
    New Indian History movement, 50–53, 77–79
    and New Military History, 108
    tribal histories, traditional *v.* modern, 53–61
    See also Indian–Euro-American relations
1941: Texas Goes to War (Lee ed.), 112
nineteenth century, bias toward, 1–2, 98, 146, 229
Northeast Texas narrative, 101–2, 103, 115, 207, 224–25
North-West Territories, Canada, 74
Norwegian immigrants, 198
Not Room Enough (Stewart and De León), 189
Noyes, Stanley, 56
Noyola, Sonia Adriana, 154

Obadele-Stark, Ernest, 196
Offshore Pioneers (Castaneda, Pratt, and Priest), 242

oil industry
    and identity of place, 256–57
    and modernization, 225–27, 240–41, 242–43
    profiles, 99, 100, 101, 102
    regulation of, 227–28
Oil in Texas (Hinton and Olien), 226
Oleander Odyssey (Hyman), 198
Olien, Roger M., 226
Oliphant, Dave, 239–40
Olson, James S., 110, 205–6
On the Border (Miller, C.), 203
oral history as historic resource, 89, 99, 107, 110, 156, 161, 244
oral tradition as historic resource, 100, 108, 156
The Ordeal of the Longhouse (Richter), 61
O'Rear, Mary Jo, 203–4
"othering" (racial), 55, 56

Pan American College, 129
Panhandle Eastern Corporation, 243
Parading through History (Hoxie), 61
Parisi, Philip, 238–39
parks, 206–7, 235–36
Parks for Texas (Steely), 235–36
Parmet, Herbert S., 254
parochialism of Texas history, 221–23
Parsons, Chuck, 12
Parten, J. R., 100, 240–41
Parting the Waters (Branch), 145
The Path to a Modern South (Buenger), 101, 207, 224–25
Patman, Wright, 102, 230–31, 248
Patterson, James T., 97
Pattillo Higgins and the Search for Texas Oil (McDaniel), 99
Peace Came in the Form of a Woman (Barr, J.), 23–25, 68–69, 151–52, 194
Pecos Bill (Carlson), 106
Perales, Monica, 205

INDEX

performing arts and modernization, 239–40
periodizing Texas history, 223–24, 228, 230
Perttula, Timothy K., 58, 76
petrochemical industry. *See* oil industry
Phil Johnson Historical Archives and Library, 161
Phillips, Kevin, 254–56
Phillips, Michael, 125, 128, 134–35, 191, 202
Phillips, Thomas D., 108–9
Pigskin Pulpit (Cashion), 243–44
Pitre, Merline, 88, 158
"place" historiography, 256–61
"plantation myth," 146, 180
Policing the Great Plains (Graybill), 71, 74
policy analysis approach, 92–93, 232–37
polio, 206
The Polio Years in Texas (Wooten), 206
political consensus focus, 94–95
political dynasty, 254–56
political figures
    as exemplars, 27–28, 87–88
    governors, 33, 88, 90, 128, 159, 246–47
    Johnson, Lyndon B., 97–98, 205, 230, 235, 248–52
    national-level leaders, 162, 247–52, 254–56
    state-level leaders, 246–47
political history of Texas, recent
    biographical approach, 87–88
    framework expansion approach, 92
    and identity of place, 258–59
    and modernization, 232–35, 236–37
    narrative approach, 88
    new interpretive trends in, 95–98
    nonquantitative interdisciplinary approach, 91–92
    quantitative analysis approach, 89–90
    reform movement study approach, 90–91
    synthesis approach, 92–93
    themes for, 93–95
political socialization theory, 158–59
Políticas, 88
polygamy, 161
popular literature and mythic ideology, 200
Populist movement, 89, 90
postmodernism
    and civil rights coverage, 145
    deficiencies of, 131–32
    emergence of, 131
    and public memory, 126–27
    See also collective memory
Post Office Murals initiative, 97
postrevisionism
    appellations for, 2–3
    conclusions and future outlook, 113–15
    overview and methodologies, 85–87
    See also cultural constructionism; political history of Texas, recent
Powers, John, 111–12
pragmatic federalism, 227–28
Pratt, Joseph A., 99, 103, 204–5, 242–43, 256–57
preservationist approach, 1
presidents, Texan, 162, 254–56
    See also Johnson, Lyndon B.
presidios. *See* missions, Spanish
press, choice of. *See* publication of Texas history books
Priest, Tyler, 242
prisoner of war narrative, 107
Progressive movement
    in myth context, 183
    and Tejanos, 18–19
    and women, 154–56, 194

INDEX

psychobiography, 98
publication of Texas history books, 30–31, 31–32, 36
public health issues, 155, 205–6
public memory. *See* collective memory
Pueblo Indians, 54, 76

Quanah Parker (Hagan), 108
quantifiable evidence *v.* myth and anecdote, 6
quantitative analysis in postrevisionism, 89–90
Quest for Equality (Foley), 136
Quezada, J. Gilberto, 244–45
quinceañera, 153
Quiroz, Anthony, 118*n* 16, 190

Rabe, Elizabeth R., 147
Race and Class in Texas Politics (Davidson), 91, 130, 245–46
race narrative
    evolution of, overview, 125–29, 130
    and modernization, 241–42
    racial identity construction and whiteness, 132–35
    See also immigration/immigrants
"race suicide," 161
racial discrimination
    among Texas soldiers, 109
    and dispossession of Indians, 73
    oppression as rite of passage, 134
    in traditionalist writings, 7–8
    and white collective memory, 22–23, 137–38, 166–67, 192
    See also segregation; whiteness paradigm
racial identity construction, 132–35, 135–37, 141–43, 241
racial politics history, 244–46
radio and modernization, 232
railroad industry, 37, 101–2, 103–4
Ramírez, José A., 18, 190

Ramsdell, Charles W., 29, 180, 185
ranching, 12, 99, 100, 103, 105
Randolph, Frankie Carter, 88
Rangers, Texas, 12, 14–15, 19, 73–74, 201, 237
Rayburn, Sam, 235
Rayner, John B. and Kenneth, 88, 195
Reaping a Greater Harvest (Reid), 196
Reconstruction era
    in collective memory context, 23, 166–67, 195–96
    evolution of narrative on, 12–13, 14, 29–30, 94, 95–96
Reconstruction in Texas (Ramsdell), 29
Red Power movement, 50
Refugio mission, 55
Regaldo, Samuel, 190–91
regionalism
    East Texas, 201, 230–31, 259–60
    economic, 103–4
    Llano Estacado, 207
    and news media, 225
    older images of place, 206–7
    overview, 206
    "place" historiography, 256–61
    Southern *v.* Western state identity, 125–26, 143, 145, 207
    urban histories, 202–4
    West Texas, 105, 106, 206
    See also borderlands history; South Texas
Reid, Debra, 196, 197
religion
    Catholicism, 20, 153, 157, 203
    and ethnicity, 20, 90
    Jewish immigrants, 134–35, 157, 199
    missions, Spanish, 15–16, 55, 60, 69
    Mormons, 161
    and Tejano racial identity, 153, 203
Remembering the Alamo (Flores), 21–22, 110, 185

289

INDEX

Renderbrook Ranch, 99
reproductive politics, 161
Republican Party, 91, 130, 246, 258–59
Reséndez, Andrés, 35, 42, 64–65, 188–89
reservation system in Texas, 59, 71, 72
revisionism, persistent
    characterization of, 1988–1991, 5–8
    characterization of overview, 2, 182
    evolution of in 1988–2009 writings, 9–10, 13–18
    genera convergence possibilities, 34–38
    venue and audience for, evolution of, 29–34
Revolution! (film), 166
Revolution in Texas (Johnson), 18, 201
Rhinehart, Marilyn D., 105
Richards, Ann, 159
Richardson, Rupert Norval, 57, 73, 187
Richter, Daniel K., 61
Ricklis, Robert A., 55
ricos, 16–17
Rienstra, Ellen Walker, 100
"ring shout," 144
The Rise of Southern Women's Progressive Culture, 1893–1918 (McArthur), 152
Rise of the Mexican American Middle Class (Garcia, R.), 16–17, 18, 19, 139–40
Road, River, and Ol' Boy Politics (Scarbrough), 259
Roberts, Randy, 110
Robinson, Charles M., III, 108
Roediger, David R., 132–33, 191
Roe v. Wade, 128
Rogers, Mary Beth, 88
Roosevelt, F. D., 96–97
Ross, Nellie Tayloe, 128
Rozek, Barbara, 187
Ruiz, Vicki, L., 143, 153–54

Runnels, Hardin, 90
rural "place" identity, 259–60
rural socialism, 231
Russell, Charles, 198

Sabine Pass (Cotham), 106–7
Sadler, Louis R., 14, 18, 19, 27
Salisbury, Neal, 51
San Antonio, Texas, 15–16, 16–17, 139–40, 203
    See also Alamo, The
San Antonio de Béxar (de la Teja), 15–16, 188
Sánchez, George I, 135
San Jacinto, Battle of, 111, 163, 165, 167
    See also Texas Revolution
San Miguel, Guadalupe, Jr., 140–41, 190, 253
Santa Anna, 94, 97, 110, 166
Satanta (Kiowa chief), 108
Saunt, Claudio, 61
Sawdust Empire (Baker, R.), 259
Scarbrough, Linda, 259
schools, segregation in, 95, 127–28, 144–45
Schutze, Jim, 145
Scofield, Cyrus, 135
Scott, Joan Wallach, 160
Sea of Mud (Dimmick), 109–10
Seeking Inalienable Rights (Reid), 197
segregation
    and African American cultural identity, 144–45, 147–48, 196–97
    and black-brown relations, 138
    in colleges, 129
    and modernization, 241–42, 252–53
    in San Antonio, 139–40
    in schools, 95, 127–28, 144–45
    See also civil rights; racial discrimination
Seguín, Juan, 163, 165, 166
Selma, Alabama, 145
Serbia, 149

INDEX

sexuality, 159–60, 160–61, 194–95
Shabazz, Amilcar, 128, 146, 197
Shafter, William R., 106
Sharpless, Rebecca, 121–22n 37, 156–57, 193
The Shattering of Texas Unionism (Baum), 90
shelf life of truth in history, 5
"The Shelf Life of Truth In Texas" (Buenger and Calvert), 5
Shivers, Allan, 246–47
Shrake, Edwin "Bud," 200
shrimping/fishing, 104
Silbey, Joel, 89
Sitton, Thad, 99, 259–60
"Slave Children in Texas" (Rabe), 147
Slave Culture (Stuckey), 144
slavery
    and annexation, 89
    and black-brown relations, 136
    and black cultural identity, 26, 144, 146–47
    and black women's roles, 158, 160
    evolution of narrative on, 195–96
    and Indians, 51, 68, 79
    lynchings, 22, 23, 26, 134, 137–38, 167, 192
    "plantation myth," 146, 180
    and Texas Revolution, 165
    and white collective memory, 23
Sleuthing the Alamo (Crisp), 111, 185
Smallwood, James M., 96
Smith, F. Todd, 15, 58, 59, 71–72, 73, 187, 201
Smith, Harold L., 236–37
Smith, Lonnie, 241–42
Smith, Thomas T., 113
Smith v. Allwright, 241–42
Social Change in the Southwest (Hall, T.), 65–66
social networking of women, 21, 155–56

soldiers, common
    evolution of narrative on, 13–14, 106, 107, 109, 115
    Tejano, 190
    Texans in Civil War, 11, 111
songs as historic resource, 100
SoRelle, James, 147
South American frontiers, 63–64
Southern Mercury, 89
Southern Politics in State and Nation (Key), 245–46
Southern v. Western state identity, 125–26, 143, 145, 207
South Texas
    Indians of, 6
    Mexican Americans in, 92–93, 133, 189, 244–45
    in Mexican period, 18–19
    and regionalism, 206
space program, 167
Spanish culture
    colonial era narrative, 188
    elites in modern San Antonio, 139–40
    focus on influence of, 28–29
    Indian relations, 6–7, 23–24, 60, 62–65, 152–53, 194
    missions, 15–16, 55, 60, 69
    in Texas/Mexico narrative, 15–16
    See also Indian–Euro-American relations
The Spanish Frontier in North America (Weber), 62–63, 188
Spanish Texas (Chipman), 62, 188
Spicer, Edward H., 65–66
Spindletop oil discovery, 101
sport history, 190–91, 232, 243–44
state identity in narrative
    evolution of, 207–8
    and historic myth, 179
    national identity, 139–43
    non-Texan's perspective, 181–82

INDEX

state identity in narrative *(cont.)*
    Southern *v.* Western identity, 26, 125–26
    state identity, 125–28
    See also myths; regionalism
statistical analysis in postrevisionism, 90
Steely, James Wright, 235–36
Steinbeck, John, 179
Stephen F. Austin: Empresario of Texas (Cantrell), 35–36, 94, 192–93
Stephens, Hugh, 204
Stevenson, Adlai, 130
Stevenson, Coke, 249
Stewart, Kenneth, 189
Stiles, Jo Ann, 100
Storm over Texas (Silbey), 89
Storm over the Bay (O'Rear), 203–4
Storms Brewed in Other Men's World (John), 71
The Story of Big Bend National Park (Jameson), 206–7, 260–61
The Strange Career of Bilingual Education in Texas, 1836–1981 (Blanton, C.), 190, 198
Struve, Walter, 198
Stuckey, Sterling, 144
"A Study of History, Memory, and Collective Memory in Texas" (Cantrell and Turner), 137
suburbia, 258–59
suffragist movement, 155, 236–37
Sweatt v. Painter, 128
synthesis of history, xii, 7, 25–29, 86, 92, 228–29

Tate, Michael L., 112–13
Taylor, Alan, 51–52
technology and modernization, xiv, 89–90
Tejanas, 153–54, 194
Tejano Empire (Tijerina, A.), 100
Tejano Legacy (Alonzo), 188

Tejano Progressive movement, 18–19
Tejanos
    in collective memory context, 165–66
    in contextual postrevisionism, 86–87
    in economic narrative, 100
    evolution of narrative on, 2, 9, 12, 16–17, 18–19, 127, 188–91
    in political narrative, 88, 91–92
    and South Texas culture, 201, 244–45
    stereotyping of, 127
    Tejanas, 153–54, 194
    See also Mexican Americans
Tejano South Texas (Arreola), 201
television and modernization, 232
Telles, Raymond, 88
Tenayuca, Emma, 157
Texan Jazz (Oliphant), 239–40
"Texan mystique," 8
Texans in the Confederate Cavalry (Bailey), 11–12
Texas, Cotton, and the New Deal (Volanto), 92–93, 232–35
The Texas 36th Division (Brager), 11
Texas after the Civil War (Moneyhon), 13
Texas Agricultural Extension Service, Negro Division, 196
Texas A&M University, 127
Texas A&M University Press, 30–32
The Texas Cherokees (Everett), 61
Texas City, Texas, 204
The Texas City Disaster, 1947 (Stephens), 204
Texas Communist Party, 157
Texas creation myth, 73, 180
Texas: Crossroads of North America (de la Teja, Marks, and Tyler), 25, 28–29
Texas Divided (Marten), 94
Texas Eastern Corporation, 99, 243
Texas Folklore Society, 144

INDEX

Texas: From Spindletop through World War II, 228–29
A Texas Frontier (Cashion), Ty, 206
Texas History Movies (Ward), 209n 2
The Texas Indians (La Vere), 75–77
Texas Literary Outlaws (Davis, S.), 200
Texas-Louisiana border, 71
    Caddo strategy on, 58
    East Texas, 201, 230–31, 259–60
    Hasinais strategy on, 67–68
    Karankawas as buffer on, 55
Texas National Guard's 36th Division, 107
Texas Pacific Coal and Oil Company, 105
Texas Post Office Murals (Parisi), 238–39
Texas Railroad Commission, 227–28
The Texas Railroad Commission (Childs), 37, 102–3, 227–28
Texas Rangers, 12, 14–15, 19, 73–74, 201, 237
The Texas Rangers and the Mexican Revolution (Harris and Sadler), 14, 18, 19, 27
Texas Revolution
    Alamo, The, 21–22, 110–11, 163, 164–65, 180, 185–86
    in collective memory context, 165–67
    Mexican perspective of, 109–10, 111, 188–89
    mythic history of, 11–12, 93–94, 185–86
    navy, importance of, 111–12
The Texas Revolutionary Experience (Lack), 94, 186
Texas Roots (Jones, C.), 103
Texas "singularity," 8, 11–12
Texas Southern University, 146
Texas State Fair, 125
Texas State Historical Association, 30, 206, 208
Texas Through Time: Evolving Interpretations (Buenger and Calvert eds.), xi–xiv, 179, 180, 193, 195, 222

Texas Women on the Cattle Trails (Massey ed.), 105
Texian Iliad (Hardin), 109
thematic approach, 59, 223–24
theory approach, 4, 23, 29–30, 56–57, 223–24
"theory of marginality," 158–59
They Called Them Greasers (De León), 129
Thompson, Ernest, 103
Thompson, Robert S., 257
Three Nations, One Place (McCollough), 67–68
three truths of Texas history, overview, 1–4 *See also* genres of truth in Texas history
Thurber, Texas, 105
Tigua Indians, 77
Tijerina, Andrés, 100, 191
Tijerina, Felix, 88
timber industry, 259–60
Tonkawa Indians, 60
    cultural values of, 69
    dispossession of, 55, 72
    downfall of, 55
    equestrianism of, 54
top-down perspective, 10, 27–28, 88, 98
    See also traditionalism, updated
To the Line of Fire! (Ramírez), 18, 190
Tower, John, 246
trade systems of Indians, 54, 57–59, 64, 67, 70
traditionalism, updated
    characterization of, 1988–1991, 7–8
    characterization of, overview, 1–2, 182, 186
    evolution of 1988–2009, 10–12, 32–33
    genera convergence possibilities, 35–38
    persistence of in modern writings, 5

INDEX

traditionalism, updated *(cont.)*
    profile of 1988–2009 writings, 9–10
    venue and audience for, evolution of, 29–34
transgender identity, 161
transnational approach, 2, 34, 52, 201
Treviño, Roberto R., 153, 203
truth in history, shelf life of, 5
    See also genres of truth in Texas history
Turner, Elizabeth Hayes, 137, 154, 183–84, 194, 204, 229
Tyler, Ron, 25–26, 28–29

Undaunted (Russell), 198
unions, labor, 105, 157, 196
United Negro Improvement Association, 148
United We Win (García, I.), 253
University of Houston, 129
University of Texas at Austin, 127, 164
University of Texas Press, 30–32
urban ethos *v.* regional ethos, 258
urban histories
    and architecture, 256
    Fort Worth, Texas, 100, 143, 202, 238–39
    overview, 202
    San Antonio, 15–16, 16–17, 139–40, 203
    See also Dallas, Texas; Houston, Texas
urbanization of Texas, 226, 259
Urrea, José, 109
Uruguay, 63–64
The U.S. Army and the Texas Frontier Economy (Smith, T.), 113
Usner, Daniel H., Jr., 51
Utley, Dan, 99
Utley, Robert M., 237

vigilantism, 22, 138
    See also lynchings
violence, culture of
    among Comanches, 69–70
    and Anglo takeover of Texas, 73
    and modernization, 225
    and Tejanos in Texas, 18–19
    of Texas Rangers, 12, 19, 73, 74, 201
    and white collective memory, 22–23, 137–38, 166–67, 192
Viva Kennedy (García, I.), 95
Volanto, Keith J., 85, 92–93, 232–35

Waco, Texas, 22
Wade, Maria F., 61
Walker's Texas Division, C.S.A (Lowe), 13–14, 109
Wallace, Ernest, 57
Wallerstein, Immanuel, 91
Walsh, Casey, 201
Ward, George, 209n 2
War of a Thousand Deserts (Delay), 70
Washington, Jesse, 22, 138
water power, 234–35
Waters, Katherine, 40n 15
Waters, Michael, 123n 48
A Way of Work and a Way of Life (Rhinehart), 105
Webb, Walter Prescott, 12, 180, 206, 207, 227
Weber, David J., 62–64, 66, 188
Weiner, Hollace Ava, 151, 199
Weisbrot, Robert, 145
Western mythos, 206
Western *v.* Southern state identity, 125–26, 143, 145, 207
West Texas, 105, 106, 206
"What Happened to the Civil Rights Movement in Dallas, Texas?" (Dulaney), 148
Whiggish narrative, 168

INDEX

White, Hattie, 145–46
White, Lulu B., 88, 145, 158
White, Richard, 51, 65, 68
white collective memory and violence, culture of, 22–23, 137–38, 166–67, 192
White Metropolis (Phillips, M.), 128, 134–35, 136, 191, 202
whiteness paradigm
    and black-brown relations, 136–37, 192
    and class structure, 20–21, 100–101, 132
    criticisms of, 135–36
    evolution of, 191–92
    and racial identity construction, 132–35
whites, poor, 134
The White Scourge (Foley), 100–101, 133–34, 135, 136, 191, 241
"white trash," 134
Wichita Indians, 6, 28, 59, 66–67, 72, 75
The Wichita Indians (Smith, F.), 59
Wilkison, Kyle G., 103–4, 230–31
Williamson County, 205, 259
Winegarten, Ruthe, 151, 154, 157, 194
Wintz, Cary, 203
Wirtz, Alvin, 205
"With Their Hearts in Their Hands" (Mercado), 174
Women, Culture, and Community (Turner), 194, 204
Women and the Creation of Urban Life (Enstam), 202
women in historic narrative
    as activists, 88, 91, 152, 158, 236–37
    in cattle industry, 105
    Chicanas, 88, 154, 157
    and civil rights, 127, 155, 158, 236–37
    evolution of, 10–12, 193–94
    farming, role in, 121–22n 37
    in Indian–Spanish relationship, 24, 152–53
    neglect of, 7–8, 127, 152
    in postrevisionism, 88, 89, 104–5
    in Progressive movement, 154–56, 194
    and social networking, 21, 154, 156–57
    Tejanas, 153–54, 194
    See also gender narrative
"Women in the Civil Rights Movement" (Decker), 158
Women's Christian Temperance Union (WCTU), 155
Woods, Randall, 251–52
Woodward, C. Vann, 5
Wooster, Robert, 113
Wooten, Heather Green, 206
Works Progress Administration, 144
The World of the Mexican Worker in Texas (Zamora), 17, 120n 30, 189, 198
world systems approach, 55, 65, 67, 91–92
World War I, 108, 189, 198
World War II, 11, 107, 112, 117n 9, 226–27, 240–42
World Wide Web, xiv
Wright Patman (Young), 221

Yarborough, Ralph, 248
The Years of Lyndon Johnson (Caro), 98
Yellow Dogs and Republicans (Dobbs, R.), 246–47
Yeomen, Sharecroppers and Socialists (Wilkison), 103–4, 230–31
Young, Nancy Beck, 221, 230–31

Zamora, Emilio, 17, 34, 37, 117n 9, 120n 30, 189, 198
Zedong, Mao, 126
Zelden, Charles L., 241–42